A. Stewart (Alexander Stewart) Walsh

Mary: the queen of the house of David and the mother of Jesus

the story of her life

A. Stewart (Alexander Stewart) Walsh

Mary: the queen of the house of David and the mother of Jesus
the story of her life

ISBN/EAN: 9783742858917

Manufactured in Europe, USA, Canada, Australia, Japa

Cover: Foto ©Lupo / pixelio.de

Manufactured and distributed by brebook publishing software (www.brebook.com)

A. Stewart (Alexander Stewart) Walsh

Mary: the queen of the house of David and the mother of Jesus

MARY:

THE

QUEEN OF THE HOUSE OF DAVID

AND

MOTHER OF JESUS.

THE STORY OF HER LIFE.

GABRIEL.—"Hail, thou that art highly favored, the Lord is with thee: Blessed art thou among women."
MARY.—"All generations shall call me blessed."

BY
REV. A. STEWART WALSH, D. D.

WITH AN INTRODUCTION BY
REV. T. DE WITT TALMAGE, D. D.

ILLUSTRATED.

PUBLISHED EXCLUSIVELY BY
A. S. GRAY & CO.
SUCCESSORS TO
CENTRAL PUBLISHING HOUSE AND KEYSTONE PUBLISHING CO.

PITTSBURGH, PA.

1889.

TO WOMANKIND THROUGHOUT THE WORLD

THIS

STORY OF A LIFE

MOST

BEAUTIFUL, BENEFICENT, AND INSPIRING

Is Dedicated

BY THE AUTHOR.

INTRODUCTION TO

THE QUEEN OF THE HOUSE OF DAVID.

By Rev. T. De Witt Talmage, D.D.

HAVE been asked to open the front door of this book. But I must not keep you standing too long on the threshold. The picture-gallery, the banqueting hall and the throne-room are inside. All the fascinations of romance are, by the able author, thrown around the facts of Mary's life. Much-abused tradition is also called in for splendid service. The pen that the author wields is experienced, graceful, captivating, and multipotent. As perhaps no other book that was ever written, this one will show us woman as standing at the head of the world. It demonstrates in the life of Mary what woman was and what woman may be. Woman's position in the world is higher than man's; and although she has often been denied the right of suffrage, she always does vote and always will vote—by her influence; and her chief desire ought to be that she should have grace rightly to rule in the dominion which she has already won.

She has no equal as a comforter of the sick.

What land, what street, what house has not felt the smitings of disease? Tens of thousands of sick beds! What shall we do with them? Shall man, with his rough hand, and heavy foot, and impatient bearing, minister? No; he cannot soothe the pain. He can not quiet the nerves. He knows not where to set the light. His hand is not steady enough to pour out the drops. He is not wakeful enough to be watcher. You have known men who have despised women, but the moment disease fell upon them, they did not send for their friends at the bank or their wordly associates. Their first cry was, "Take me to my wife." The dissipated young man at the college scoffs at the idea of being under home influence; but at the first blast of typhoid fever on his cheek he says, "Where is mother?" I think one of the most pathetic passages in all the Bible is the description of the lad who went out to the harvest fields of Shunem and got sunstruck; throwing his hands on his temples, and crying out, "Oh, my head! my head!" and they said, "Carry him to his mother.' And the record is "He sat on her knees till noon and then died."

In the war men cast the cannon, men fashioned the muskets, men cried to the hosts "Forward, march!" men hurled their battalions on the sharp edges of the enemy, crying "Charge! charge!" but woman scraped the lint, woman administered the cordials, woman watched by the dying couch, woman wrote the last message to the home circle, woman wept at the solitary burial, attended by herself and four men with a spade. Men did their work with shot and shell, and carbine and howitzer; women did their work with socks and slippers, and bandages, and warm drinks, and scripture texts, and gentle soothings of the hot temples, and stories of that land where they never have any pain. Men knelt down over the wounded and said, "On which side did you fight?" Women knelt down over the wounded and said, "Where are you hurt? What nice thing can I make for you to eat? What makes you cry?" To-night, while we men are soundly asleep in our beds, there will be a light in yonder loft; there will be groaning down that dark alley; there will be cries of distress in that cellar. Men will sleep and women will watch.

No one as well as a woman can handle the poor. There are hundreds and thousands of them in all our cities. There is a kind of work that men cannot do for the destitute. Man sometimes gives his charity in a rough way, and it falls like the fruit of a tree in the East, which fruit comes down so heavily that it breaks the skull of the man who is trying to gather it. But woman glides so softly into the house of want, and finds out all the sorrows of the place, and puts so quietly the donation on the table, that all the family come out on the front steps as she departs, expecting that from under her shawl she will thrust out two wings and go right up to Heaven, from whence she seems to have come down. O, Christian young woman, if you would make yourself happy and win the blessings of Christ, go out among the poor! A loaf of bread or a bundle of socks may make a homely load to carry, but the angels of God will come out to watch, and the Lord Almighty will give His messenger hosts a charge, saying, "Look after that woman, canopy her with your wings, and shelter her from all harm." And while you are seated in the house of destitution and suffering, the little ones around the room will whisper, "Who is she? is she not beautiful?" and if you will listen right sharply, you will hear dripping through the leaky roof, and rolling over the broken stairs, the angel chant that shook Bethlehem: "Glory to God in the highest, and on earth peace and good will to man." Can you tell why a Christian woman, going down among the haunts of iniquity on a Christian errand, seldom meets with any indignity?

I stood in the chapel of Helen Chalmers, the daughter of the celebrated Dr. Chalmers, in the most abandoned part of the city of Edinburg; and I said to her, as I looked around upon the fearful surroundings of that place, "Do you come here nights to hold a service?" "Oh, yes," she said; "I take my lantern and I go through all these haunts of sin, the darkest and the worst; and I ask all the men and women to come to the chapel, and then I sing for them, and I pray for them, and I talk to them." I said, "Can it be possible that you never meet with an insult while performing this Christian errand?" "Never," she said; "never." That young woman, who has her father by her side, walking down the street, and an armed policeman at each corner is not so well defended as that Christian woman who goes forth on Gospel work into the haunts of iniquity carrying the Bible and bread.

Some one said, "I dislike very much to see that Christian woman teaching these bad boys in the mission school. I am afraid to have her instruct them." "So," said another man, "I am afraid too." Said the first, "I am afraid they will use vile language before they leave the place." "Ah," said the other man, "I am not afraid of that; what I am afraid of is, that if any of those boys should use a bad word in her presence, the other boys would tear him to pieces—killing him on the spot."

Woman is especially endowed to soothe disaster. She is called the weaker vessel, but all profane as well as sacred history attests that when the crisis comes she is better prepared than man to meet the emergency. How often have you seen a woman who seemed to be a disciple of frivolity and indolence, who, under one stroke of calamity, changed to be a heroine. There was a crisis in your affairs, you struggled bravely and long, but after a while there came a day when you said, "Here I shall have to stop;" and you called in your partners, and you called in the most prominent men in your employ, and you said, "We have got to stop." You left the store suddenly; you could hardly make up your mind to pass through the street and over on the ferry-boat; you felt everybody would be looking at you and blaming you and denouncing you. You hastened home; you told your wife all about the affair. What did she say? Did she play the butterfly; did she talk about the silks and the ribbons and the fashions? No; she came up to the emergency; she quailed not under the stroke. She helped you to begin to plan right away. She offered to go out of the comfortable house into a smaller one, and wear the old cloak another winter. She was one who understood your affairs without blaming you. You looked upon what you thought was a thin, weak woman's arm holding you up; but while you looked at that arm there came into the feeble muscles of it the strength of the eternal God. No chiding. No fretting. No telling you about the beautiful house of her father, from which you brought her, ten, twenty, or thirty years ago. You said, "Well, this is the happiest day of my life. I am glad I have got from under my burden. My wife don't care—I don't care." At the moment you were utterly exhausted, God sent a Deborah to meet the host of the Amalekites and scatter them like chaff over the plain. There are scores and hundreds of households to-day where as much bravery and courage are demanded of woman as was exhibited by Grace Darling or Marie Antoinette or Joan of Arc.

Woman is further endowed to bring us into the Kingdom of Heaven. It is easier for a woman to be a Christian than for a man. Why? You say she is weaker. No. Her heart is more responsive to the pleadings of divine love. The fact that she can more easily become a Christian, I prove by the statement that three-fourths of the members of the churches in all Christendom are women. So God appoints them to be the chief agencies for bringing this world back to God. The greatest sermons are not preached on celebrated platforms; they are preached with an audience of two or three and in private home-life. A patient, loving, Christian demeanor in the presence of transgression, in the presence of hardness, in the presence of obduracy and crime, is an argument from the throne of the Lord Almighty; and blessed is that woman who can wield such an argument. A sailor came slipping down the ratlin one night as though something had happened, and the sailors cried, "What's the matter?" He said, "My mother's prayers haunt me like a ghost."

In what a realm is every mother the queen. The eagles of heaven can not fly across that dominion. Horses, panting and with lathered flanks, are not swift enough to run to the outpost of that realm, and death itself will only be the annexation of heavenly principalities. When you want your grandest idea of a queen you do not think of Catherine of Russia, or of Anne of England, or Maria Theresa of Germany: but when you want to get your grandest idea of a queen you think of the plain woman who sat opposite your father at the table or walked with him, arm in arm, down life's pathway; sometimes to the Thanksgiving banquet, sometimes to the grave, but always together; soothing your petty griefs, correcting your childish waywardness, joining in your infantile sports, listening to your evening prayer, toiling for you with needle or at the spinning wheel, and on cold nights wrapping you up snug and warm; and then, at last, on that day when she lay in the back room dying, and you saw her take those thin hands with which she had toiled for you so long, and put them together in a dying prayer that commended you to the God whom she had taught you to trust— oh, she was the queen! The chariots of God came down to fetch her, and as she went in, all heaven rose up. You can not think of her now without a rush of tenderness that stirs the deep foundations of your soul, and you feel as much a child again as when you cried on her lap; and if you could bring her back to life again to speak, just once more, your name as tenderly as she used to speak it, you would be willing to throw yourself on the ground and kiss the sod that covers her, crying, "Mother! mother!" Ah, she was the queen!

Home influences are the mightiest of all influences upon the soul. There are men who have maintained their integrity, not because they were any better naturally than some other people, but because there were home influences praying for them all the time. They got a good start. They were launched on the world with the benedictions of a Christian mother. They may track Siberian snows, they may plunge into African jungles, they may fly to the earth's end, they can not go so far and so fast but the prayer will keep up with them. Oh, what a multitude of women in heaven. Mary, Christ's mother, in heaven. Elizabeth Fry in heaven. Charlotte Elizabeth in heaven. The mother of Augustine in heaven. The Countess of Huntingdon is in heaven—who sold her splendid jewels to build chapels—in heaven; while a great many others who have never been heard of on earth, or known but little of, have gone into the rest and peace of heaven. What a rest. What a change it was from the small room with no fire and one window, the glass broken out, and the aching side and worn out eyes, to the "house of many mansions." Heaven for aching heads. Heaven for broken hearts. Heaven for anguish-bitten frames.

No more sitting up until midnight for the coming of staggering steps. No more rough blows on the temples. No more sharp, keen, bitter curses.

Some of you will have no rest in this world; it will be toil and struggle all the way up. You will have to stand at your door fighting back the wolf with your own hand red with carnage. But God has a crown for you. He is now making it, and whenever you weep a tear, He sets another gem in that crown; whenever you have a pang of body or soul, He puts another gem in that crown, until after a while in all the tiara there will be no room for another splendor; and God will say to his angel, "The crown is done; let her up that she may wear it." And as the Lord of righteousness puts the crown upon your brow, angel will cry to angel, "Who is she?" and Christ will say, "I will tell you who she is; she is the one that came up out of great tribulation and had her robe washed and made white in the blood of the Lamb." And then God will spread a banquet, and He will invite all the principalities of heaven to sit at the feast, and the tables will blush with the best clusters from the vineyards of God and crimson with the twelve manner of fruits from the tree of life, and water from the fountains of the rock will flash from the golden tankards; and the old harpers of heaven will sit there, making music with their harps, and Christ will point you out amid the celebrities of heaven, saying, "She suffered with me on earth, now we are going to be glorified together." And the banquetters, no longer able to hold their peace, will break forth with congratulation. "Hail! hail!" And there will be a handwriting on the wall;

not such as struck the Persian noblemen with horror, but with fire-tipped fingers writing in blazing capitals of light and love and victory: "God has wiped away all tears from all faces."

And now I leave you in the hands of Dr. Walsh, the author of this book. He will show you Mary, the model of all womanly, wifely, motherly excellence— the Madonna hanging in the Louvre of admiration for all Christendom, and for many millions in the higher Vatican of their worship.

T. DE WITT TALMAGE.

CONTENTS.

CHAPTER I.—THE QUEEN'S PORTRAIT.

"A form beloved comes again"—Inspired painters in a voyage of discovery—Tributes to Mary, honoring all womankind—Guido's wish—Madonnas of many climes. Raphael's "Transfigured Woman"—Savonarola's bonfire—St. Luke's picture of the Virgin—The Vandal spirit. . . . . Page 29

CHAPTER II.—THE PILGRIM, CRUSADER AND VIRGIN.

Life a pilgrimage—Pilgrims of many faiths—A struggle for holy places between the Pilgrim-Crusaders and Moslem—The harem and the home—The rise of Chivalry—The Knights and "Our Lady"—The results of the Crusades. . . . . Page 36

CHAPTER III.—ARMAGEDDON! "THE KEY AND SICKLE."

"The wandering hermit wakes the storms of war"—Acre and Esdraelon, the "Armageddon" or "Mountain of the Gospel" of the Scriptures—The battle-field of nations—The City of Jeanne d'Arc. The jewel in the sickle-haft—Prince Edward, the Crusade leader—Sultan Kha-tel—The sacking of Acre—Actors introduced. . Page 48

CHAPTER IV.—SIR CHARLEROY; THE SOLDIER OF FORTUNE AND KNIGHT OF SAINT MARY.

The flight from Acre to Nazareth—The born-leader—Life estimates with Death holding the scales—A prince honors, a bishop blesses, and a mother loves—An epitome of paradoxes. . . . . Page 53

CHAPTER V.—NAZARETH.

Nazareth, the place of Mary's nativity—The choice of a leader—The coward king—The Virgin's Fount—English songsters—The Knights' mountain Litany—Longings for home and mother—Nain and Endor's lessons. . . . . Page 61

CHAPTER VI.—THE FUGITIVES.

A night bivouac amid sacred scenes—The "Knight of the Holy-Sepulcher" who fled on "a white charger with black wings"—The funeral at dawn—Mary's palm-bearing angel-guard—The twelve knights separate into two parties—Will-makings and farewells—By Endor to oblivion. . . . . Page 74

CHAPTER VII.—ICHABOD.

Sir Charleroy's band approach Shunem, the City of Elijah—The surprise—Sir Charleroy the captive of Azrael the Mameluke—The Mohammedan heaven depicted—"A hair, the bridge over hell"—The odoriferous houris—A gorgeous charnel-house blasted—The prodigal becomes the herald of purity—The Knight of Saint Mary and the Jewish Spy—Adversity makes the Knight and the Jew friends—The Knight instructing Ichabod—"'Till Shiloh comes"—"The true, refined and final Judaism"—"The east and the west embracing; truth leading."—An honest doubt is a real prayer. . . . . . Page 82

CHAPTER VIII.—FROM JERICHO TO JORDON.

The radiant proselyte—Climbing to glory—The ghostly forms hovering over submerged Sodom—Jordon's sweetening—Siddim-angels among the willows and oleanders by the Dead Sea—Summonsed to fight for the Crescent or go to the slave mart—Nourahmal "The light of the harem" becomes the disciple and friend of Ichabod—A debate concerning women—A rarity and a wonder—"I told her women had souls; she laughed like a monkey"—The flight from Jericho by night—The lightning—God's torch—"Canst thou dance rocks into camels?"—A mummy's flight, and the burial of a live man—"Unclean"—The solemn passage of Jordan. . . . . Page 93

CHAPTER IX.—THE FEAST OF THE ROSE.

A breakfast of lentils and barley in the wilderness—The gloom of the Knight and the joy of the Jew—Sermons on fate and songs in flowers—The poetry of Ichabod—Celibacy a reward at Rome—Kneph "The father of his mother"—The heathen and the Christian "Feast of the Rose"—The summary of the events in Mary's life and in the life of Jesus—The Egyptian Rosary—Neb-ta the maiden sister—The egg and the cross, ancient signs of immortality—The Copt priest—The insights of the Egyptians symbolized by the Sphinx. . . Page 113

CHAPTER X.—AFTER EVE, ESTHER OR MARY?

By Jabbock, in the native place of Ichabod—Israelitish maidens keeping the feast of Esther—Religious love, filial love and lover's love—The poetic Jew's rhapsody concerning affection—God's voice in the Garden—The ideal women of the Old Testament and of the New—The Jew's cry for mother—Vacillating Sir Charleroy—"Echo's Magic"—Jewish customs. . . . Page 135

CHAPTER XI.—THE FEAST OF PURIM.

A night-scene by Jabbock—Harrimai the priest, and his daughter Rizpah—The religious ceremonial and the revel—Sir Charleroy and Rizpah as "Ahasuerus and Esther"—The Knight's secret discovered—Conquest of a woman's heart through pity—"Of what metals Jewish maidens are." . . . . Page 152

CHAPTER XII.—ASTARTE OR MARY?

The Knight of Saint Mary enslaved by a Hebrew beauty—The journey toward Bozrah—The Mameluke attack—The hand to hand fight—Sir Charleroy wounded and Ichabod slain—Rizpah's heroism in peril—Espousal in the face of death—A wonderful vision. . . Page 170

CHAPTER XIII.—FROM RAMOTH GILEAD TO DAMASCUS.

Teacher and pupil become patient and nurse—Perilous relations—Delights, assurances, fears and clouds—Harrimai's discovery and his malediction—Love's debate and decision — Elopement by night—the Knight and the Jewess wedded at Damascus. . . . . . Page 182

CHAPTER XIV.—THE THEATER OF THE GIANTS.

The death of Harrimai—A honey-moon in the " Eye of the East"—To Bashan with the Mecca chaplet-seekers—Nature, art and desolation—Lejah's black lava-sea—The frenzies of Gerash's passion-flower—Reaction after exaltation—" A camel voyage in-sea"—Rizpah's challenge —Jealous of Sir Charleroy's love for Mary—" Illusion " —The church of Saint George at Edrei—Recrimination —Ridicule costly to pride—Neither Christian, Jew nor Pagan—A woman with unsettled faith—A babe poisoned by its mother's passion—The lamp and the palm-trees —The Knight's appeals—Omens—A beacon needed—Fleeing the Lejah—To Bozrah. . . . . Page 195

CHAPTER XV.—THE REVELS OF MEN AND THE RITES OF THEIR GODDESSES.

Kunawat at the City of Job—The Shrine of Astarte—The Cyclopean image—Questioning the Soul, Time and God—Hugeness, greatness; littleness, caricature—The naked worshipers of the golden calf—Sins exposed—Purity's vision—Phallic mysteries—Khem—Female deities—Dualism—Immortality by progeny and by regeneration—The fire-worshiper's mystic number eight, and the Jewish covenant number seven. . Page 212

CHAPTER XVI.—A BATTLE OF GIANTS AT BOZRAH.

Houses forty centuries old—The old stone-house of an ancient giant becomes the home of the knight and his wife—How circumstances change people—Recriminations and reconciliation—" The gall taken from animals offered to Juno, goddess of marriage "—Rizpah's temper that seemed brilliant before wedlock, afterward seems to

Sir Charleroy very like that of a virago—The charming nonsense of those for the first time parents—Shall she be named Davidah, Angela, Marah or Mary?—The Christian and Jewish faith battle about the cradle—The separation of husband and wife, in anger—The sick child and the desolated, deserted wife—Rizpah longs for a mother, such as Mary of Bethlehem. . Page 224

CHAPTER XVII.—RIZPAH THE ANCIENT MOTHER OF SORROWS.

After many years, Rizpah dwells in Bozrah with her three children—Rizpah of Bozrah fascinated by Rizpah of Gibeah — Miriamne the daughter of Rizpah — The daughter appalled by her mother's mysterious hallucinations—The wonders of mother-love—The story of the ancient, Jewish "Mother of Sorrows"—The omen of the bat and the parable of the stars. . . Page 245

CHAPTER XVIII.—THE QUEEN PROCLAIMED IN THE GIANT CITY.

The old and the young Jews—The old Christian priest and his Jewess proselyte—Attacked by Mamelukes—The 'Old Clock Man"—The Balsam Band—Miriamne, the Jewess proselyte, questions concerning the queen of the old priest's heart—The miraculous picture of Mary at Damascus—Silver hands and feet—Crown jewels. . . . . Page 264

CHAPTER XIX.—THE STORY OF MARY'S CHILDHOOD.
Page 282

CHAPTER XX.—THE WEDDING—THE BIRTH AND THE FLIGHT.

The birth of Jesus and the flight to Egypt—Miriamne reads to her mother a Christian account of Mary's espousal—Rizpah curious but doubtful. . Page 293

CHAPTER XXI.—THE QUEEN AND HER FAMILY IN EGYPT.

Father Adolphus and Miriamne converse of the Holy Family's sojourn in Egypt—Heliopolis and the Temple of the Sun—Fire-worshipers—At Memphis, the snrine of Apis the sacred bull—The red heifer of Israel—The Holy Family rescued in Egypt by a robber who afterward died on the cross next to the Savior—The legend of a gipsy's prophecy concerning Jesus—Zingarella won by the Virgin. . . . . Page 312

CHAPTER XXII.—THE SHADOW OF THE CROSS.

Rizpah dreading heresy yet charmed by the story of the "Girl Wife"—" Behold my mother and brethren"—Christ's message to his widowed mother—The "Church of the Terror"—Rizpah's vision of "Glad Tidings." Rizpah of Bozrah allured from Rizpah of Gibeah—A hot-chase after an old love—The sword that pierced Mary—The shadow of the cross horrifies Rizpah—The faith of the Nazarene denounced—Miriamne driven from home by her mother. . . . . . . Page 322

CHAPTER XXIII.—THE MISERERE AND THE EASTER ANTHEM.

Miriamne alone at night in the giant city—A refuge at the Christian priest's—The midnight Miserere—Penitents—Easter at Bozrah—Finding the mother-love in God's heart. . . . . Page 337

CHAPTER XXIV.—A HEROINE'S PILGRIMAGE.

The convert's yearnings—"Go and tell"—When parents oppose each other which shall the child follow?—A child of the kingdom in a new family circle—Jesus, Mary and the elect—Miriamne's two great ambitions—Living apart may be as sinful as actual divorcement—Father Adolphus encourages and Rizpah opposes Miriamne—Rizpah recounts to Miriamne the story of her love for Sir Charleroy, his madness and her own futile visit to London in the effort to win him back—The curse of heredity—"I'll disown thee with tears in my voice and kisses in my heart." . . . . . Page 351

CHAPTER XXV.—CONSOLATRIX AFFLICTORUM.

Miriamne's welcome by the London Palestineans—The daughter meets her father in a mad-house—Disappointment—The flight—The search—The White Madonna of the Asylum Park—Love the remedy of minds perturbed by hate—Pallas-Athene the virgin of the heathen—Miriamne's letter to her mother and its grim answer. . . . . Page 367

CHAPTER XXVI.—THE WEDDING AT CANA.

Sir Charleroy giving signs of recovery under Miriamne's ministries—A remarkable service in the chapel of the Palestineans—The knight interested in the story of Cana—The address of Cornelius, on "Home" and "Marriage"—"Is this London or Bozrah?"—Sir Charleroy's sudden relapse—Miriamne's adroit ministries—Memories that awaken hopes—The clouds again lifting—Mary's life motto. . . . . . . Page 381

CHAPTER XXVII.—THE STAR OF THE SEA.

Sir Charleroy, partially restored, with Miriamne and Cornelius journeying toward Syria—Passing Cyprus—Olympus—A storm rising on the Mediterranean—Cornelius presses his love suit on Miriamne—Miriamne pledges love, but pleads her mission as a barrier to marriage—Conflicts below, tempests aloft—A dream ; Venus's court and Mary's triumph—Sir Charleroy in frenzy defying the billows—An hour of peril—The "Lightning Song" of the sailors—The twin stars—"Mary, Star of the Sea".—The victims of fabricated consciences—Parting. . . . . Page 397

CHAPTER XXVIII.—THE QUEEN IN THE VALLEY OF SORROWS.

Father and daughter at Acre—The mysterious Hospitaler—From Acre to Joppa—"The myths are as full of women as the women are full of myths"—The wars of men about women—At Jerusalem—The wonderful words of the Knight-Hospitaler, turned preacher—The *Via Dolorosa*—The Valley of Jehosaphat—The mountain outlook—"Soldiers Speed the Cross"—Mary, the sun of women, rising in moral grandeur above the women of the grove-shrines—The panorama of the ages, passing before Mary's mind. . . . . Page 419

CHAPTER XXIX.—TWO DEAD HEARTS UNITING TWO
   LIVING ONES.

From Jerusalem to Bozrah—The tomb of Ichabod—Sir
Charleroy argues against meeting Rizpah—Miriamne's
strong argument in behalf of the lasting obligations of
marriage—A husband reaching the climax of revenges
—Joseph by kindness kept Mary in sweet mood and so
blessed the unborn Christ—"Miriamne, I am a bundle
of contradictions!"—The news-rider—A plague at Bozrah
--De Griffin's twins nigh death—Miriamne meets her
mother—Reconciliation—A strange funeral; only two
women as mourners and pall-bearers. . . Page 437

CHAPTER XXX.—THE "KNIGHT OF SAINT MARY" AND
   RIZPAH AT THE GRAVE OF THEIR SONS.

Father Adolphus and Sir Charleroy—A ruined temple and
a ruined man—"A woman, a woman leading in religion!"—
Jesus and Magdalena—The twelve appearings of the
lingering Christ—The Savior's love-letter from heaven to
His mother—Lucifer's attempt at suicide—The kiss
befouled by treason—The meeting of Sir Charleroy and
Rizpah—"The tomb of giant-love grown to mad-hate."
                                              Page 453

CHAPTER XXXI.—THE ROSE, QUEEN OF HEARTS IN
   BOZRAH.

A scene of domestic happiness—Love the vassal of the will
—Neb-ta in the "Judgment Hall of Truth"—The lambs
that are offered by sectarian hates—The Arcana of
glorious wedded love—Rizpah transformed—Miriamne's
public profession of Christ—Cornelius Woelfkin again
appeals for union in wedlock—An inner and an outer
Miriamne—The coronation of love—The solemn espousal.
                                              Page 467

CHAPTER XXXII.—THE QUEEN AND THE GRAIL-SEEKERS.

"The gold of my heart to the man that piloted me to happiness"—Miriamne yearns for a world in sin—Has the
Church or God failed?—A revolutionary reformer—The
story of the grail quest—The quest of a heavenly cure

for human ills—The triumphant Adam and Eve—The queenly women of patriarchal times—The mother of the Savior as the wife of a carpenter—What kept her young heart from breaking—Miriamne's farewell to Bozrah.
Page 484

CHAPTER XXXIII.—THE HOSPITALER'S ORATION.

The secret meeting of the Knights at the house of Phebe—Swords bent sickle-like and spears crossed—After war, social victories—Sunrise at midnight—Each career determined by the life that gives life—The girdle of Venus—Next after God, Mary chiefly instrumental in giving the world a Savior. . . . . Page 498

CHAPTER XXXIV.—MEMORIALS AT BOZRAH.

The death of Dorothea—The priest of the wayside—The wedding of Cornelius and Miriamne—A pilgrimage to the tombs of Adolphus, Charieroy and Rizpah. Backlook, and outlooks. . . . . Page 510

CHAPTER XXXV.—THE SISTERS OF BETHANY.

The Missioners at Bethany—The site of the Home of Jesus—Miriamne's ideal society—The miracle age—A home, not a throne, the place of Ascension—Will Jesus so return?—The angel bivouac. . . . . Page 522

CHAPTER XXXVI.—THE QUEEN OF THE HOUSE OF DAVID.

The Knight's Pentecost—In the upper room of Joseph of Arimathæa—Mary's title and realm—Luke, the word-painter—The smoke side and the fire side of Pentecost.
Page 529

CHAPTER XXXVII.—THE CORONATION OF THE QUEEN.

The Hospitaler deemed a prophet at Bethany. The legitimacy of Jesus as the "son of David" assured through His mother—"The reign of blood"—First born—Pagan Rome made sponsor for Mary's son—Doomsday books and royal charters. . . . . Page 538

CHAPTER XXXVIII.—THE "LIGHT OF THE HAREM" IN THE "TEMPLE OF ALLEGORY."

The old church at Bethany—A dedication—The wonders of symbolism—Idolatry and Mariolatry. . . Page 548

CHAPTER XXXIX.—CROWN JEWELS.

The Hospitaler warns the Missioners of the Sheik of Jerusalem's designs—The son of Azrael—Immunity purchased—The wedding of Beulah, Nourahmal's grand-daughter to a Jewish convert—The wedding address—Juno-Moneta—Crown jewels of maidens and mothers—Mary sounding the depths of woman's miseries—A malediction for lust—"Knights of the White Cross"—The lost woman dreaming of how it seems to have a mother's arms infolding her—The Virgin's potent example. . . . . . . Page 568

CHAPTER XL.—THE QUEEN'S VISION OF THE AGE OF GOLD AND FIRE.

Noural.mal wed to the Druse camel-driver—the Druse converted—The Hospitaler's message—Ezekiel prophecies fulfilled at Olivet—The "Mother's pillow"—Gabriel, the "Angel of Mothers and of Victories." . . Page 581

CHAPTER XLI.—A CHIME AND A DIRGE AT CHRISTMAS-TIME.

"Motherhood priced"—"Thou shalt be saved in child-bearing—Sylvan gods of Rome—"The Miriamites,"—"In Rama, weeping and great mourning"—Joachim's bleating lamb slain—Woman's supreme hour—Maternity's crucifixion—"The Cæsarian Section"—The ebbing-tide and the stranded wreck, at midnight. . . . Page 595

CHAPTER XLII.—THE MOTHER OF SORROWS TRIUMPHANT AT LAST.

The funeral of Miriamne—The Hospitaler tells the traditions of Mary's death and assumption—What the Druse convert said to his camel—"The beatings of mighty wings"—The tomb of Miriamne in Gethsemane. Page 611

CHAPTER XLIII.—A COFFIN FULL OF FLOWERS, AND A GIRDLE WITH WINGS.

Cornelius and his son at Bethany—Changed scenes—Under the lights and shadows of Chemosh—A widower's grief—Azrael's putative son razes to the ground Miriamne's home and temple—The legend of Mary's coffin and girdle—The last of the new grail-knights—A sad and dramatic tableau. 618

LIST OF ILLUSTRATIONS.

I.
MARY AND THE INFANT JESUS, - - Frontispiece
(The original painted by GOODALL.)

II.
PAGE
THE BIRTH OF MARY - - - - - - 60
(The original painted by MURILLO.)

III.
RIZPAH DEFENDING THE DEAD BODIES OF HER
RELATIONS, - - - - - - - 250
(The original painted by BECKER.)

IV.
THE EDUCATION OF MARY, - - - - - 282
(The original painted by CARL MULLER.)

V.
THE MARRIAGE OF MARY AND JOSEPH, - - 294
(The original painted by RAPHAEL.)

VI.
THE SHADOW OF THE CROSS, - - - - - 332
(The original painted by MORRIS.)

VII.
JESUS AT THE AGE OF TWELVE WITH MARY AND
JOSEPH ON THEIR WAY TO JERUSALEM - - 350
(The original painted by MENGELBURG.)

VIII.
THE YOUTH JESUS YIELDING TO THE WISHES OF
HIS MOTHER, - - - - - - - 366
(The original painted by W. HOLMAN HUNT.)

IX.
THE WEDDING AT CANA, - - - - - 380
(The original painted by PAUL VERONESE.)

X.
MARY AND ST. JOHN, - - - - - - 433
(The original painted by PLOCKHORST.)

THE QUEEN OF THE HOUSE OF DAVID

CHAPTER I.

THE QUEEN'S PORTRAIT.

> " And breaking as from distant gloom,
>   A face comes painted on the air;
> A presence walks the haunted room,
>   Or sits within the vacant chair.
> And every object that I feel
>   Seems charged by some enchanter's wand,
> And keen the dizzy senses thrill,
>   As with the touch of spirit hand.
> A form beloved comes again,
>   A voice beside me seems to start,
> While eager fancies fill the brain,
>   And eager passions hold the heart."

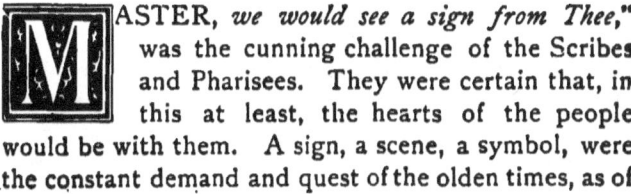ASTER, *we would see a sign from Thee,*" was the cunning challenge of the Scribes and Pharisees. They were certain that, in this at least, the hearts of the people would be with them. A sign, a scene, a symbol, were the constant demand and quest of the olden times, as of all times. Even Jehovah led forth to victory and trust, as necessity was upon Him in leading human followers,

"with an *outstretched arm,* and with *signs* and with *wonders.*" The Jews, seemingly so doubtful and so querulous, after all articulated the longings of the universal humanity. The longing stimulated the effort to gratify it, and forthwith the artist became the teacher of the people. Presentments of Mary, as she might have been, and as she was imagined to have been by those most devout, were multiplied. Piety sought to express its regard for her by making her more real to faith through the instrumentality of the speaking canvas, but beyond this there was the desire to embody certain charms and virtues of character dear to all pure and devout ones. These were expressed by pictured faces, ideally perfect. They called each such "Mary"; and if there had never been a real Mary, still these handiworks would have had no small value. Who can say that those consecrated artists were in no degree moved by the Spirit which guided David when "he opened dark sayings on the harp," and rapturously extolled that other Beloved of God, the Church? Music and painting—twin sisters— equal in merit, and both from Him who displays form, color and harmony as among the chief rewards and glories of His upper kingdom. These also meet a want in human nature as God created it. The artists did not beget this desire for presentments through form and color of the woman deemed most blessed; the desire rather begot the artists. Stately theology has never ceased truly to proclaim from the day Christ cried "*It is finished!*" that "*in Him all fullness dwells;*" but no theology, has been able to silence the cry of woman's heart in woman and woman's nature in man which pleads through the long years, "*Show us the mother and it sufficeth us.*" It has happened sometimes that gross minds have strayed from the ideal or spiritual imports of Mary's life and fallen into idolizing her effigies. That was their fault, and must not be taken as full proof that nothing but evil came from the portrayings of our queen. The facts are conclusively otherwise. The painters that made glorious ideals shine forth from the canvas unconsciously painted the shadows largely out of the conditions of all women. Before this second advent of the Virgin, the paganish idea that women were the "weaker sex," the inferiors of men, at best only useful, handsome animals, prevailed. The renaissance of Mary, as the ideal woman, was an event seeded with the germs of revolutionary impulses socially. Like sunrise it began in the East, at first dimly manifest, then it became effulgent and quickly coursed westward along the pathways of Christianity's conquests. Like sweet, grateful light then there came to the hearts of men the braver true persuasion, that the woman who not only bore the Christ but won His reverent love must have been morally beautiful and great. In the track of this persuasion, and as its sequence, there came the conviction that the sex, of which Mary was one, had within it possibilities beyond what its sturdier companions had dreamed. After this it came about that the painters, often the interpreters of human feelings, began to represent all goodness under the form of a Madonna. Not knowing the contour of Mary's face they began gathering here and there, from the women they knew, features of beauty. They combined these in one harmonious presentment. They set out to represent the ideal woman, but had to go to women to find her parts. It became a tribute to womankind to do this. It was like a voyage of discovery, and the artist voyagers depicted not only the best things in womankind, but by putting these things together illustrated what woman could be and should be at her best.

It was thus that Guido produced a picture of the Madonna which enravished all that beheld it. Once he had said, "I wish I'd the wings of an angel to behold the beatified spirits, which I might have copied." After, here and there, he picked out fragments of color and form on earth; then put them into one ideal composition. It was a heart-expanding work; the work of a prophet, since it told of what might be in woman wholly at her best. Then he said, "the beautiful and pure idea must be in the head" of the artist. It was a deep saying. Given the ideal, and the worker will need only proper ambition to present a grand composition, whether on canvas or in the patternings of the inner life. The presentments of the Virgin rose in fineness when priests turned from their exegesis to kneel and paint for men. The great Saint Augustine, held in high honor by Christians of every name, redeemed from a youth of darkest sinning, revered as his guiding star two lovely women, Monica, his mother, and Mary, the mother of Jesus. He argues, in stalwart polemics, that through the acknowledgment of Mary's pre-eminence all womankind was elevated. Her presentment, so as to be fully comprehended, was in the beginning a blessing to every soul in being an inspiration to purer, sweeter living. So far as such presentment now conserves the same results the work is worthy and profitable. In all times the representations of the Virgin, whether by the historian or the master of the studio, varied; but the piety they awakened always seemed to be of one type, and that lofty. Thus we have "the stern, awful quietude of the old Mosaics, the hard lifelessness of the degenerate Greeks, the pensive sentiment of the Siena, the stately elegance of the Florentine Madonnas, the intellectual Milanese, with their large foreheads and thoughtful eyes, the tender, refined mysticism of the Umbrian, the sumptuous loveliness of the Venetian; the quaint, characteristic simplicity of the early German, so stamped with their nationality that I never looked round me in a room full of German girls without thinking of Albert Durer's Virgins; the intense, life-like feeling of the Spanish, the prosaic, portrait-like nature of the Flemish schools, and so on." Each time and place produced its own ideal, but all tried to express the one thought uppermost; pious regard for the Queen and model. All seemed to feel that in this devotion there was somehow comfort and exaltation—and there generally were both.

The writer of the foregoing quotation, a woman of widest culture and admirable good sense, attested the need that many feel by her own rapturous description of the Madonna of Raphael in the Dresden Gallery. "I have seen my own ideal once where Raphael—inspired, if ever painter was inspired—projected on the space before him that wonderful creation." "There she stands, the transfigured woman; at once completely human and completely divine; an abstraction of power, purity and love; poised on the empurpled air, and requiring no other support; with melancholy, loving mouth, her slightly dilated sibylline eyes looking out quite through the universe to the end and consummation of all things; sad, as if she beheld afar off the visionary sword that was to reach her heart through HIM, now resting as enthroned on that heart; yet already exalted through the homage of the redeemed generations who were to salute her as blessed. Is it so indeed? Is she so divine? or does not rather the imagination lend a grace that is not there? I have stood before it and confessed that there is more in that form and face than I have ever yet conceived. The *Madonna di San Sisto* is an abstract of *all* the attributes of Mary."

The foregoing representation marked a step forward in things spiritual. Before Raphael, painters numberless, under the influence of the luxurious and vicious Medici, had filled the churches of Florence with painted presentments of the Virgin, characterized by an alluring beauty which seemed next door to blasphemy. Then came that Luther of his times, Savonarola. He thundered for purity, simplicity and reform; aiming his blows at the depraving, sensuous conceptions of the grosser artists. He made a bonfire in the Piazza of Florence, there consuming these false madonnas. He was, for this, persecuted to death by the Borgia family. They could not bear his trumpet call to Florentines, " Your sins make me a prophet; I have been a Jonah warning Nineveh; I shall be a Jeremiah weeping over the ruins; for God will renew His church and that will not take place without blood—" Art heard his voice, the painters became disgusted with their meaner handiwork, the rude, the obscene, the mischievous was obliterated; finer, more spiritual and loftier concepts of the Virgin appeared as proof of a reformation of morals. And Raphael, later on, seeing these productions, felt the influence that begot them, and then produced that masterpiece. Tradition says Saint Luke painted a picture of the Virgin from life. The picture, reputed to have been so painted, was found by the Turks in Constantinople when that city fell into their conquering hands. They despoiled it of its princely jewel-decorations, then tramped it contemptuously beneath their feet. The latter act was typical, and the Turk still lives to trample in contempt on honest efforts to portray with amplitude and finished details this splendid character, whose outlines alone are presented by the Gospels. But though the Vandal spirit survives, there survives also the strong yearning for the representation of that woman beyond compare, and some will still revel amid the ideals of painters, and some will be gladdened still more by truth's complete presentment which words alone can make.

CHAPTER II.

THE PILGRIM, CRUSADER AND VIRGIN.

" There is a fire—
    And motion of the soul which will not dwell,
    In its own narrow being, but aspire
    Beyond the fitting medium of desire;
    And but once kindled, quenchless ever more,
    Preys upon high adventure, nor can tire
    Of aught but rest."
                        —" *Childe Harold.*"

THERE is something very fascinating about the contemplation of life as a continuous pilgrimage, and the fascination grows on one as the conviction of the truth of the conception is deepened by study of it. The course of our race has been a series of processions from continent to continent, from age to age, from barbarism to refinement, from darkness toward light. Whether measuring the little arcs of individuals from birth to dust, or following along the mighty marches of our universe with all its grouping hosts of whirling constellations, we have before us ever this constant truth; man moves willingly or unwillingly onward, as a pilgrim amid pilgrims. "Move on" is the constant mandate and necessity of being. Man's course is mapped; onward from the swaddling clothes to the shroud, from

life to dust; then onward again; while all the mighty planet fleets of which the earth-ship is but one, move along their courses, over trackless oceans, toward destinations, all unknown, yet concededly in a grand as well as in an inexorable pilgrimage. Partly because the motions of his earth-ship makes him restless, partly because he is a being that hopes and so comes to try to find by distant quests hope's fruitions, and more largely because he is of a religious nature, which impels him to seek things beyond himself, the man becomes a pilgrim. He that is content as and where he is, always, is regarded as a fool playing with the toys of a child, by wise men; by religionists, lack of holy restlessness is ever adjudged to be a sign of depravity. Hence almost all religions, whether false or true, have given birth to the pilgrim spirit. The zeal to express and to utilize this spirit has been often pitiful to behold. Multitudes, failing to grasp the fact that life itself is a pilgrimage, have invented other pilgrimages and gone aside to useless, needless miseries. But all the time they attested human nature seeking something beyond itself, better than its present. So the tribes that lived in the lowlands nourished traditions of descent from gods or ancestors who abode on the mountains, and they inaugurated pilgrimages to seek inspiration or a golden age "on high places, far away." The chosen people of God thus constantly were allured from the worship of the Everywhere and One Jehovah by the enthusiasm of the heathen devotees who flocked to the mountain fanes. Turn which way one will in the night of the ages and the spectacle of the pilgrim is before him.

Ancient Hinduism, followed by that of to-day, witnessed, witnesses annually, pilgrims counted by hundreds of thousands to the temple of murderous Juggernaut, the Ganga Sagor, or isle of Sacred Ganges. The Buddhists journey to Adam's Peak in Ceylon, and the Lamaists of Thibet travel adoringly to their Lha-Isa; the Japanese have their pilgrim shrines amid perilous approaches at Istje, while the Chinese, who claim to be sons of the mountains, clamber with naked knees the rugged sides of Kicou-hou-chan. The pilgrimages of the Jews occupy many chapters of Holy Writ, for all their ancient worthies " *not having received the promises, but seeing them afar off * * confessed that they were pilgrims and strangers."* Christ confronted the pilgrim spirit perverted in the person of the woman of Samaria, at the eastern foot of Gerezim. She and her people rested their hopes in pilgrimages to their supposed to be sacred places, but the Saviour declared to her by Jacob's well, truths, both grand and revolutionary, in these words: "The hour * * now is when the true worshiper shall worship the Father in spirit * * * not in this mountain nor in Jerusalem." " Go call thy husband and come hither. Whosoever drinketh the water I shall give shall never thirst." There were volumes in the golden sentences and they plainly said no need to travel far to find the Everywhere God Who ever comes where men are to satisfy their every thirst. "Go call thy husband." Go to thy home and find the water of life through doing God's will; it is better to be a missionary than a pilgrim unless the pilgrim be also missioner. But the truths of that hour have found tardy acceptance among many. The children of

Jacob are pilgrims throughout the earth, and the disciples of Christ, since His departure, have gone pilgriming often, as did their fathers before them. Constantine, the Roman emperor, and his mother, Helena, by example and precept, urged Christendom to re-embark in such pious journeys, and at the end of the first thousand years of its existence, Christianity had hosts of disciples actuated by the same old passion that sent religionists everywhere to seek shrines, fanes and blessings. Then the belief began to be held everywhere among Christians that the milennial period was at hand. Multitudes abandoned friends, sold or gave away their possessions, and hastened toward the Holy Land, where they believed Jesus Christ was to appear to judge the world. Here two pilgrim tides, utterly opposed to each other, met; the Christian and the Mohammedan. The followers of the False Prophet, like other men, were imbued with the pilgrim spirit. Some of these thought perfection could be attained only within the precincts of Babylon or Bagdad, and others sincerely believed that they could find peculiar nearness to heaven about the stone-walled Kaaba of Mecca. It was held to be not only a privilege but a duty, incumbent upon all, to take these religious journeys; hence men and women, young and old, undertook them. Even the decrepit were under the obligation, and they must either undertake the work, though failure by death were certain, or hire a proxy to go in their behalf. So was rolled up stupendously the numbers of pilgrim graves which have marked this earth of ours. The Christian pilgrims for a time thronged **toward Palestine,** first as a small stream, then **as** a torrent. Europe at large was aroused, and all impulses converged toward the Holy Sepulcher. The soldiers of the Cross soon added swords to their equipments; the flashing of spears outshone the altar lights, and almost before they realized it the priests and pious pilgrims were transformed to mailed knights. There was a root to the impulse, and that the universally felt need of ideals, patterns, personages of heroic mold in all goodness, to show men how to live. The pilgrims turned their eyes to the worthies of the past, and soon came to believe that they could best imbibe their spirit amid their tombs and former abodes. Like most religionists they grew to believe God their especial friend, and they therefore soon came to feel that, against all odds, He would help them to victory. Then they easily grew to believe that death in their crusades would merit the martyr's crown. Their courage was unbounded, for many went out with a passion to die in the cause they had embraced. The following crusades were marked by conflicts between Moslem and Christian, filled with fanatical and merciless fury, though both the opposing hosts claimed to be doing all they did in God's name and under his especial direction. "*Deus vult,*" "God wills it," was the war-cry of a mighty army, each of which bore on his banner and on his breast the sign of the Cross, the emblem eternally exalted by the Prince of Peace, who willingly died that others might live; but these soldiers were bent on slaying those they could not convert. They were in a transitional state, passing from being pilgrims to being missionaries, but the course was a bloody one. They promoted their self-complacency by persuading themselves that it was a heaven-offending wrong to continue to suffer heretics to occupy the places made sacred by the Saviour when in the world. Then multitudes of Christian priests taught that the pious needed free course to visit the holy places of the East, that they might upbuild their faith and their grasp of theological abstractions by beholding objects associated with the tenets they had adopted. The Moslems had no interest in these proceedings beyond a desire to thwart them. The Christians, to be sure, had the moral disadvantage of being invaders, but then censure of them is mitigated by the fact that Syria was stolen property to the Turk. The latter held it by the stern title deed of the sword. The reader of this summary will be chiefly advantaged by remembering that this conflict was one of the mightiest efforts in the direction of missionary work ever attempted by man, and that being attempted by force it failed utterly. Now the Crusaders were believers in Christ and devoted to Mary. These facts awaken questions as to how, since the spirits of these twain are finally to conquer all hearts, their champions were so defeated? The Crusaders desired to promote the glory of the Man of men and the woman of women, but sought it by aims only weakly worthy, and means often atrocious. It never matters to Christ's kingdom who possesses His grave if He only possesses all hearts. The Crusaders, beginning with a warm sentiment of respect for the Virgin, suffered their sentimentality to run mad, and mad sentiment is ripe for folly and defilement. An opal, they say, will change its color when its wearer is sick; so a man wearing a priceless virtue on the sleeve of his creed, will find its luster bedimmed when evil sickens his heart. The Crusaders had grand banners, mottoes, war-cries and ideals, but they did not know how to honestly and truly apply them. Their efforts and results well serve to emphasize the truth that moral advances are made with grander forces than those of the sword; that in the end the heroes and heroines of the world's regeneration will appear potent and regnant solely in the sweetness, truth and exaltation of personal character. Crusader and Moslem, at heart, were each desirous of making the world better, but they each, in fact for a time made it fearfully worse. Probably the followers of the Cross and the followers of the Crescent would have been glad to have bestowed all kindness each on the other, if only the one would have accepted the creed of the other. But the humanity and charity of each were as to the other eclipsed utterly by a zeal for theories. There was need to both that there arise a harmonizing ideal. It would seem as if Providence suffered these opposing pilgrims to peel each other until each in sheer disgust was driven to seek some better way. An able historian affirms that the Crusades did not "change the fate of a single dynasty, nor the boundaries and relative strength of a nation "—but they did leave a history, the contemplation of which affords rare thought-food. The conflict ended in the utter route and flight of the Christians. The tragedy ended at Acre, but there were left some things that took shape in mens' thinking, and the world was made thereby better. The populations and properties of Christain Europe had been squandered to a startling degree in these religious wars, and it was fit-

The Pilgrim, Crusader and Virgin. 43

ting that there be some return to compensate. The result of all others, that grew out of the Crusades, and was indeed also a leading cause of their vigor, was the rising of the spirit of chivalry. The dawn of chivalry first begat brave fighting, but in time the chivalrous discovered a theater for their activity amid the amenities of peace. Chivalry was a rebound from the rugged, barbarous belief of the semi-civilized, whose trust was in brute force and whose constant *dictum* was, "Might makes right." Men became impressed with a spirit of tenderness, and, little by little the duty and beauty of the strong's helping the weak dawned upon humanity. To be chivalrous, by the unwritten laws of custom, became the obligation of every man who sought popular respect. Chivalry was in the creed of the noble and brave, and men delighted to become the companions of lone pilgrims, patrons of beggars, protectors of children and defenders of women. Toward the gentler sex, the spirit of chivalry finely expressed itself by not only defending helpless females amid physical perils, but by according to woman kind distinguished courtesy, refined politeness, and all those proper respects that so appropriately garnish and ornament the social intercourse of the sexes in properly cultivated societies. Before the advent of this chivalric time, women had been deemed as generally every way inferior to men; chiefly desirable as ministers to the necessities or appetites of their lords; useful as mothers, but worthy of very little respect, confidence or lasting admiration. The dawn of this new and fine gallantry was a step toward woman's disinthrallment. Chivalry tried to express itself in the Crusades; defeated, its ardor still burned, and Europe felt its beneficent glow long after the conflict for Syrian sepulchers had ceased. And here it is of the utmost importance that the reader forget not the key fact, that before the advent of the attractive spirit of chivalry, men's minds in Christian communities were profoundly penetrated and wondrously incited by a deep and new regard for the *Queenly woman Mary, the mother of Jesus!* She had been almost rediscovered. By a common consent, Christian pulpits had begun sounding her praises, as the ideal woman; a woman worthy of the veneration and emulation of all. The various religious communities vied with each other in doing her honor. The Cistercians declared her purity by wearing white, the Servi wore black to commemorate her touching sorrows, and other bodies elected as their distinguishing badges, various garbs or signs solely to proclaim their allegiance to their ideal woman. A popular moral coronation of Mary resulted. The Crusaders outran all others in their adulation of, and committal to, the wondrous woman. They were the first to call her "Our Lady." She was THE Lady of the hearts of all. These chivalrous soldiers to her spoke their pious vows, from her besought holy favors, and in her name, with sacred oaths, committed their all to effort to wrest all Palestine from the enemies of Mary's Son.* Now these millions of men were not mad, nor in pursuit of a phantom. It was all very real to them. They desired to express a long pent-up natural feeling, and they found an object all satisfactory in Mary. The Crusaders returned finally and for good from battling with Moslem; they returned

* Jamison.

thoroughly, disastrously defeated; but with their love for Mary all aglow. When they first called her "Our Lady," there may have been an admixture of irreverence and dilettante in the thought of many; they were purged of these in the hurricane of battle and in the terrors of that inhospitable land of their pilgrimages. Amid trials, far away from his home, often in severe want, frequently confronting slavery and death, the Christian knight while adding "*Ave Marie*" to his "*Patre Nostre*," learned to think of the Madonna as his mother. Missing the latter keenly, worshiping the other unfeignedly, woman took a high throne in his esteem. Sword conquest began to seem to the war-wearied soldier very insignificant as compared to a ministry of comfort, peace and good will. The defeated Crusaders returned to scatter through all Europe a new gospel of humanity. They exalted the Queen of David's line and forgot to recount the fortunes of war in the East in expounding the dawning beauties of the woman that entranced them and the queenship this ideal had gained over their minds. So they prepared multitudes of the sterner sex for a lasting belief in the worthfulness of true womanhood at its best. The Christian world was ripe for such a revival, when the priests began to thunder "On to Jerusalem!" but men needed not so much war as conversion; not so much relics and tombs as loving principles exemplified. It is wonderful how conversion womanizes some men. That is a triumph of the spiritual over the sensual, the beautiful over the gross. It will make a man of brutal, selfish fiber, in time, as tender as a mother toward her child and as self-denying as a maid toward her lover. The Crusaders started out to rescue the tomb of the dead Saviour from unbelievers and failed, but they returned to herald the rennaissance of Mary, the disenslaving of woman; to call the state, the home and individuals to all the refinements which the exaltation of such an ideal of necessity offered. Toward this advening the rising spirit of chivalry was bending the finest hearts when the clarions of war, sounded from altar and baptistry, summoned all to raise the red banner against the Moslem. Right here it is worthy of notice that God's providence presented other, though allied, principles in the conflict against the Orientals. Two pilgrim hosts, thinking to choose their own ways, were wisely led to better goals than they knew. The Turk presented the throng of the harem as his family; the Christian was committed to the union of only two in holy wedlock. One party presented a banner with a Cross, forever the emblem of self-sacrifice; the other the Crescent, emblem of youthfulness increasing, a hint ever of the hope of endless lust, whether borne of the master of a harem or by the heathen follower of the ancient moonhorned Astarte. The last at Acre, by the Syrian border of the Mediterranean Sea, the Saracen hugged victory and the Cross-bearers were utterly routed. So reads human history, but in truth the defeat was only apparent and local. The followers of the Crescent, holding the creed of lust and making pleasure of sense their end came surely toward their destruction when successes encouraged them in their courses; the followers of the Cross, on the other hand, had within some germs of truth, life-giving in themselves and too beautiful to be suffered to die from the earth. Trial and defeat watered these germs and the knightly hosts returned to Europe by thousands to proclaim finer doctrines than those by which the priest had incited them to war. The returning soldiers were transformed from pilgrims to missionaries, from being taught to teaching, from restorers of Palestine's graves to restorers of European society. Of the "Teutonic Knights of Saint Mary," a fine and representative order, an impartial historian writes: "They defended Christianity against the barbarians of Eastern Europe." "After many bloody encounters introduced German manners, language and morals." Of the Knighthood, as a whole, says another, "the institution that could breed such characters as these, obviously rendered an enduring service to humanity. Its spirit lives on, offering examples which the young still welcome in their joyous, dreamy days. The ideal still remains, purified by time, freed from its frailties, and aids in fashioning modern sentiment to the conception and admiration of the Christian gentleman."

CHAPTER III.

ARMAGEDDON, THE KEY AND SICKLE.

> "From the moist regions of the western star,
> The wandering hermits wake the storm of war;
> Their limbs all iron, their souls all flame;
> A countless host the Red Cross warriors came."
> —REGINALD HEBER.

S a traveler climbs the mountain to see the sunrise, so he that would overlook the past or present must needs clamber to some lofty point of vision in a significant era or historic location. There are two plains in Syria; one lying along the Mediterranean, the other jutting out from the base of the former toward Jordan; the two together, in shape very like a sickle, have witnessed events wonderfully instructive and determinate to the student of the philosophy of time's course. These two plains are known respectively as Esdraelon and Acre. The sea and the mountains give these plains their sickle shape, and the geographical outlines are constantly suggestively before the mind as one remembers these plateaus not only as the highways but the battle-fields of the ancient nations. For while, as one says, " the face of nature smiles "—" no spot on earth more fertile," he also says "no field on earth was so

fattened by the blood of the slain." There the Philistines, the Ptolemys, Antiochus, the Maccabees, Herod, Baldwin, King of Jerusalem, Salah-ed-din, Cœur-de-Lion, Melek-Seruf and Napoleon, each in turn, put their ambitions and their beliefs to the stern arbitrament of swords. There the kingdom of the House of David struggled for life; there the splendid dream of the Crusaders ended as a nightmare.

As a jewel in the haft of the sickle, at the northerly end of the plain by the sea, sits the city of Acre. This city compels the attention of the preacher and student of history and gives theme to him who blends symbol into song. Acre gave its name to its adjacent country round about, and though both city and plain witnessed many a change of master in the past, those changing masters, to gratify their whims or strengthen their policies from time to time, giving the places various names. The Knights of Saint John made it their elect city, honoring it as Saint Jean de Acre, the martyr maid of France. From the city itself one may look out over the sea-highway of nations; from the drear and lofty mountains of its surrounding country one may look over many memorable places. Acre was often called the "Key of Palestine" by the soldier strategists and by the chroniclers of events. To their testimony is added that of the inspired writers and prophets who made it their key and mountain of outlook frequently.

These plains, dotted all about by sacred places, memorable for two great victories; Barak over the Canaanites and Gideon over the Midianites; and two great disasters, the death of Saul and the death of Josiah, became to the Jews the symbol of the conflict of right and wrong. Prophetically, and in the serene hope that righteousness at last would prevail, the plain was called Armageddon, "the Mountain of the Gospel." We hear the rapt Zechariah thus descanting: "The Lord also shall save the glory of the house of David and the house of David shall be as God." "And it shall come to pass in that day, that I will seek to destroy all the nations that come against Jerusalem. And I will pour upon the house of David, and upon the inhabitants of Jerusalem, the spirit of grace and of supplications; and they shall look upon me whom they have pierced, and they shall mourn for him, as one mourneth for his only son, and shall be in bitterness for him, as one that is in bitterness for his first-born."

The prophet looked forth to the Pentecostal day of salvation and the assured victories of David's great successor. Following this ancient seer, John the beloved, in the Visions of the Apocalypse repeats, these oracles. During the wars of the Crusaders, Acre was sometimes in their possession and sometimes held by their Turkish foes. In the year 1191 Richard the Lion Heart wrested it from the infidel leader Salah-ed-din. The Christians held it firmly until 1291, the time when the last wave of the Crusader advance ebbed, in bloody defeat, from the shores of the Holy Land. For two hundred years the believer of the West and the Moslem grappled with each other in deadly conflict; war's fortunes often changing, but the awful price in human misery and human blood was inexorably exacted at every stage of the conflict. Acre was the focus toward which the eddying tides ever and anon moved; therefore it saw not only the end but the worst of the Crusades.

Our story begins A. D. 1291 at Acre, the Key of Palestine, in Armageddon, "the mountain of the Gospel." The situation may be briefly depicted: Acre was filled with a mixed and un-homogeneous population. There were the ubiquitous Galilean traders, without politics; shrewd to the last degree in traffic and courtly as a Parisian; there some secret, sullen, silent enemies of the Christian invaders, awaiting the coming end; there hundreds of those camp-following nondescript "good lord and good devil" characters, and there the remnants of the Crusader armies. The latter were not only diminished as to numbers but greatly degraded in moral tone. Their warfare had been belittled to a defense and a retreat. The adventurers were uppermost; courts-martial, intrigues and fanfaronade were their occupation daily. Prince Edward, the Christian leader, had made a sworn treaty with the Moslems long before this time; but his pious followers had quickly, wickedly violated it. Thereupon the Sultan, Kha-tel, had made an irrevocable treaty with himself, sealed with the most awful oath he could register, that he would never tire until he had exterminated the last of the Western invaders now circumscribed and besieged in Acre. With 200,000 dusky followers the Sultan besieged the last stronghold of the Crusaders. The hearts of the defenders sank within them, and scores sought safety in homeward flight, loading down every vessel bound for Europe. Among the first fugitives was the chief leader, Hugh de Lusignan, who wore the phantom title, "King of Jerusalem." He preferred the safety of distant Cyprus to the doubtful regality which was overshadowed with nearing death. Only 12,000 were left to represent the Crusade cause which once mustered millions. May 18, 1291, the devoted city was stormed by the Turks; an entrance was effected and a murderous carnage, heaping the streets with the dead, and redding the foam of the moaning sea, followed. But there was no easy victory to the Moslem, for the steady, vigorous, brilliant, desperate fighting of the knights, laying low piles of their foes for every one of themselves that fell, compelled the respect of the Sultan's host. The Turks attempted to gain a surrender by offering bribes; these failing, terms were offered. The latter, which included permission for the Crusade remnant to depart the country in peace, were accepted. But the Sultan, taught, if he needed the lesson, by the perfidy of Prince Edward's Christian truce-breakers, quickly broke his promise of safe conduct. Though the retreating band was in no way party to the wrong he sought to avenge, they were mercilessly ambuscaded. There followed another struggle to the death, a handful against a host and but few succeeded in cutting their way through the cordon of death. History has often recounted the preceding events up to the point; from this point it is proposed to lead the reader along the career of a fragment tossed out of the foregoing whirlpool of disaster.

CHAPTER IV.

SIR CHARLEROY; THE SOLDIER OF FORTUNE AND KNIGHT OF SAINT MARY.

" 'Tis quickly seen,
Whate'er he be, 'twas not what he had been;
That brow in furrowed lines had fixed at last,
And spoke of passion but of passion past."

* * * * * *

" Chained to excess, the slave of each extreme,
How woke he from the wildness of his dream?
Alas! he told not, but he did awake,
To curse the withered heart that would not break."
—"*Lara.*"

HE course of the knights fleeing from Acre was turned toward Nazareth. There being but one way open to them, they took that way quickly and with one accord. The fugitives from Acre represented various knightly orders, but they were disorganized, without any definite destination and without an authorized leader. Among them was Sir Charleroy de Griffin, a knight famed for valor, a central and commanding personage; one that would have attracted attention in almost any assembly of men. As he went, so went the rest of the fleeing Christians, and when he reined in his panting steed,

after a time, at the top of a fir-crested knoll not far from Nazareth, the knights following him did likewise. Then they drew around him in a semi-circle, without command, and simultaneously, as if to solicit his direction. They had followed the course he took because he took it, and now with one accord they halted because he had done so. There is to some a subtle influence that makes them leaders of men; so the disorganized Crusaders, by an unvoiced but fully expressed concession, admitted the leadership of this dashing horseman. Some may designate this a triumph of personal magnetism, but be that as it may, it was a fact that Sir Charleroy was chief. Sir Charleroy, just at the time of the foregoing incident, presented an admirable study for the philosopher or painter. From his saddle he was able to overlook leagues of bright landscape, but he could not claim the protection of a foot of it; for the first time in his life he yearned for home, now a spreading sea, and a wall of death shut it out from him apparently for ever; by circumstances absolute sovereign almost of the men about him, but doubt and danger were confounding all his ability to give commands. He fell into a train of thought, leaving his comrades to converse with their pawing steeds and to questionings within themselves as to the future. Sir Charleroy had reached an eminence in life, one of those points of out-look where a man's past meets him and demands review, that it may explain the present. He believed that he had reached very nearly the end of his career, and in that belief he began to weigh it for what it was worth. In imagination he saw one writing the story of his life.

Sir Charleroy, the refugee, began faithfully to review Sir Charleroy, the wayward youth, pleasure-seeker and reckless man. The former dictated mentally to the imaginary scribe: " Write, Charleroy de Griffin was the son of a stalwart French Baron, used to duels and trained to war. The boy inherited from his father a splendid physique, of which he was unduly proud, and a restless disposition that he never sincerely asked God to control. By the death of the baron, his son, an infant, was left to the sole tutelage of his English mother. The latter was of high birth, by nature a noble woman, and in every way worthy of a better son than the one whom he had turned out to be. She had idolized her brawny spouse in his lifetime, and when she had recovered from the shock his death caused, her yearning heart, little by little, turned from the idol in the tomb to the child he had left her. Ere long she lived again in the rapture of a love all absorbing, all bestowing, all ruling. She lavished her affection on the youth, not because he was particularly lovable, for he was not, but because he was the only one left her to love, and she was so constituted that she must love; the necessity of loving to her made it easy.

"Then there were many things in the features and form of her son that reminded her of the man who, in brighter days, had won entirely her maiden heart and her young wife love. The child was wont to wonder why his mother embraced him as she did sometimes, with a wondering, startled, wild, passionate embrace; but when he got older he discerned the meaning of these outbreaks. He knew that the mother-heart was having a vision of past wifehood, memory's grace-given solace of widowhood. Besides this the embraces were her appealings or warnings to death; her heart suddenly seizing as if to shelter and save her last and only idol; for the thought would sometimes come with shadows deep enough, that perhaps the boy might also die. Such love would have been a prized wealth and blessing to some; but in this case, on the one hand, it unfitted this mother for the proper disciplining of this son, and this son though, sometimes, when his conceit permitted it, realizing that the love was given, not won, began to expect it as his due or despise it for its lavishness. In due time he entered the period expressively designated, 'The monster age.' This is the time when expanding young life has outgrown the tenderness of infancy and failed of putting on manly and womanly graces; a time when there is a mighty ambition to put on the characteristics of adult life and a mighty lack of ability gracefully to wear them. At this period, perhaps, the majority of youths of both sexes, are interesting chiefly for what they have been, or what it is hoped they will be. They feel, conscious of their growing powers, great self-conceit, and with their growth comes an expansion of their capacities and wants. The plenitude of their wantings makes them avaricious, hence parsimonious toward others of every thing, especially of gratitude. Reverence for elders, respect for fathers, holy regard for mothers, tenderness toward women, chief charms of youth, are buried in the tomb of other virtues by great, selfish, ugly demons of desire. The monster age came to Charleroy in its full virulence, but his mother discerned little of his monstrosity; what she did discern, all unasked, she condoned. She

believed all things, hoped all things good of him,
although seldom comforted by an expression or act of
gratitude on his part. She was to be pitied; but it
may be said that the lad was to be pitied almost as
much as herself. It was the old story over; she unconsciously went about destroying her own happiness and
though she would have willingly died if need be in his
behalf, she harmed him beyond estimate by her indul-
gent loving. Then the youth was surrounded by those
who sought the favor of the baroness by constantly
sounding in her ears, and in the ears of the boy, praises
of the dead baron. They told of his daring, they des-
canted upon his adventures, his powers, his wisdom.
He was the widow's idol, and the incense was grateful
to her, but the worst of it was that they befooled the
lad by continually assuring him that he was the image
of his father, and surely destined to equal, if not surpass, his sire in deeds of valor. A dangerous burden is
wealth; whether it come as great name or great intellect, great physical strength or as much gold, it is a
fateful load which few can gracefully support. The
youth had wealth in all the foregoing directions; if he
had had a mother whose love loved wisely enough to
save, if it need be by pain, he might have been saved;
but her love infatuated her. The youth's folly brought
him frequently into shameful entanglements; but she
extricated him each time. Nobody ever heard of her
even rebuking him; as to chastising him, that were a
thing abhorrent to her thoughts. His face always
bespoke his pardon in advance with her. She would
have smitten her husband's corpse, as it lay in its
coffin, as soon as she would have smitten the one

whose features constantly reminded her of him her heart had held most dear. Then she hoped, with a mother's large-hearted faith, that each escapade would be the last. But as the youth grew older his acts were bolder. Again and again, without notice and with heartless inconsiderateness, he left his home to pursue some adventure, and again and again, mother's love followed him, ever to find him at last in some sore plight, and then quickly to forgive him. By the time Charleroy had reached his majority, the family fortune had been severely tried and depleted in paying the penalty of his follies. He himself had become an old young man, with too many gray hairs and too much experience for one of his years.

"At that time, a few enthusiasts having determined to make one last effort to secure the Holy Sepulcher, Charleroy de Griffin ardently enlisted in the pre-doomed enterprise, allured largely by its very desperateness. The crusade spirit was then a fitful dying flame throughout Europe. England and France were left practically alone to furnish the men and the money for the last crusade. Prince Edward of France was its leader, and De Griffin, having in his veins the blood of both of the supporting nations, a French name, a splendid physique, together with a fearless, dashing temperament, was enthusiastically hailed to the enlistment and pushed forward to leadership. '*Sir* Charleroy de Griffin!' smilingly called out Prince Edward, the day of review, before the one set for departure. The young man's comrades, many of whom had been his associates in former days of wassail, hearing the Prince's word, shouted out with one accord, 'Knighted!

The prince has knighted de Griffin! Hurrah for Sir Charleroy!' The day following Sir Charleroy bowed his head, as he stood on the quay ready to embark, to receive the benediction of a bishop. As the sacrist laid his hands on the young man's head, the latter, throwing back his cloak, reverently touched the cross he had attached to his bosom with his jeweled sword-hilt. The young knight for a little while was very complacent; for he was enjoying a sentimental emotion of virtue, arising from sophistries with which his mind toyed. Some way he felt he had become a soldier of the holy Christ, and somehow it seemed to him he was making atonement for past follies by now placing himself side by side with the pious and noble. Though in reality only bent on seeking excitement, adventure, change, he looked forward to the rewards of conscience belonging alone to the penitent, and to a possible public canonizing as one going forth to die for God. A little piety paralleling one's own desires is often made to do great service in silencing the clamors from within. His proud, tearful mother was by his side. Passionately she kissed his cross, then his brow, then his eyes and then his lips; leaving on the brow the glistening, dewy jewels that told the story of the heart which bade him stay, yet go. The young knight was for once in his life very serious, but tearless. After all this, in rapid steps, followed the disaster at Acre; the desperate struggle outside the city; the flight toward Nazareth. Sir Charleroy finally stands between the sea and the city, a mother's idol ready to be broken; at twenty-five, near the apparent apex and end of a life, having had great opportunities, now, with all lost, he stands there an epitome of paradoxes. He had made life a pursuit of pleasure only to find the pursuit ending in misery; he had enlisted to serve the Prince of Peace, but that service he had undertaken with the sword; he had championed, as he said, the cause of Christ, the all-conquering, but he meets utter defeat. He had taken for his patron saint Mary, after years of libertinism. He elected Mary, he said, because his mother was so like her. But Sir Charleroy's mother demoralized her son by over-indulgence, while Mary, though informed by Gabriel that her offspring was divine, followed her child as a true mother, with the divinely appointed authority of a mother, serenely, constantly directing his career up to the feast of Jerusalem, where he began to reveal his divine commission. Even then, motherhood affirmed its rights in the very presence of God manifest, in the question: '*Son, why hast thou dealt thus?*' Nor was the right challenged, for '*he went down and was subject to*' father and mother!" At this point Sir Charleroy ceased mentally tracing his own career, and lifting his eyes looked intently toward Nazareth. "Ah," he said, but so that none could hear his words, "my mother loved as many another, in part selfishly, for the joy of abandoned love, and I squander that patrimony like a spendthrift, to my harm. Mary's love for her son was like his for the world, a constant self-abnegation. That love survives as an inspiration to the world. By these contrasts I explain my failure in life, and the present is the natural sequence of the past."

By Murillo.

CHAPTER V.

NAZARETH.

"This is indeed the blessed Mary's land,
Virgin and Mother of our dear Redeemer!
All hearts are touched and softened by her name;
Alike the bandit with the bloody hand,
The priest, the prince, the scholar and the peasant,
The man of deeds, the visionary dreamer,
Pay homage to her as one ever present."
—LONGFELLOW—"*Golden Legend.*"

I walked along the top of the hills overlooking Nazareth. A glorious scene opened on the view. The air was perfectly serene and clear. I remained for some hours lost in contemplation of the wide prospect and the events connected with the scene. One of the most beautiful and sublime prospects on earth,"
ROBINSON'S *Biblical Researches.*

HE avenging Turks easily persuaded themselves that they could serve God better by participating in the sacking of fallen Acre than by pursuing the conquered, fleeing Christian knights; so they let the latter escape inland, while they themselves returned to the pillage. Ere long, by stealth, good fortune and Providential leading, the fugitives arrived unmolested at the top of a hill, overlooking the little city of Nazareth, forever memorable as having been once the earthly abiding place of Jesus and Mary. On the way

thither scarcely a sentence had been spoken, for each felt that murmuring would be harmful, mirth inopportune. They chose their course indifferently, all following Sir Charleroy de Griffin because he rode bravely and onward. The fugitives paused, partly sequestered by the shrubbed hillock, forgetting for a time all else in admiration of the outspreading panorama in view. Heaven and earth were smiling at each other; thousands of leagues of sky were filled with the raptured songs of larks, while as echo and challenge of the songs from above, the thrush and robin of the grass knoll and thicket responded. From the plains of El Battaf on the north to Esdraelon on the south Nature, God's flower queen, had decked the earth everywhere with blossoms of pinks, tulips and marigolds.

"Those dusky cowards," spoke Sir Charleroy, "though numbering ten to one, will not seek us here; they'll wait an opportunity to ambuscade us."

We've broken our knight's pledge, never to flee more than the distance of four French acres from a foe, and yet methinks we've made them respect our swords; that's something to say, though we've not made them respect our creed." It was a Knight of the Golden Cross that spoke.

Sir Charleroy continued, while his eyes turned toward the city: "I thirst for the waters of a fount in Nazareth as did David once for one in Bethlehem."

"For all of our getting at it, Nazareth's water might as well be in Ethiopia," spoke a Hospitaler.

"I've a yearning that comes near to sending me on a charge into the city."

"That would be a hot pursuit of death surely."

"A fair one, then, since death has been long pursuing us." After a moment's pause Sir Charleroy continued:

"Ah, death! None can escape, none overtake him; see we are his prisoners now, yet he tantalizes us by a show of immunity. As a sarcophagus is let down by suspending ropes in tedious stages, with jogglings and pauses, into the grave, so passes each through perils and sickenings from life to death. No, no, an undue fear of death intoxicates us until phantasmagoria possess the brain. We call these hopes; they are delusive! But will any of you follow for a charge down to the Virgin's fountain? We can not more than die; that we must soon, in any event. I think I could die more complacently, having cooled my thirst where she was wont to cool hers."

"Ugh," exclaimed the Templar, with a shudder of disgust, "the fountain flows out through an old stone coffin! By my plume! while drinking there I'd be fancying that the ghost of the one robbed of his last house were leering at me and reveling in the thought that I'd soon be poor and thirstless as he. Verily the flavor of a drink depends much on the goblet!"

"We may have plenty of miserable fancies, if we only court such; for me, Templar, I prefer to comfort myself by cheerier thoughts; while I drank there, I'd think of the coolings of death's streams; of her, that at this fountain slaked her body's thirst and from the chalice of death drank serenely at last. My sword, the gift of my king, after having shed torrents of blood, hangs uselessly at my side. It seems cruel as powerless; ay, 'tis hateful! My mother gave me, on my departure, better gifts by far; tears, kisses, undying love, and the charge to call on Mary if ever evil befell me. The latter I know not how to do; but still my weak faith, methinks, would be helped to cry 'Mother' to God, if I could only stand where that mother stood who won the first love of the infant Jesus, the last anxious thoughts of the God man."

"Sir Charleroy is unusually pious to-night; but alas, though I've been taught to say our church's *Litany*, calling on 'the Virgin most faithful,' 'Virgin most merciful,' 'Help of the Christian,' 'Lady of Victories,' I can not use those phrases here. Where's the help, the mercy, the victory now? The *Litany*, belongs to England!"

"We are in our present plight because we have won heaven's neglect through having more vices than graces, probably."

"Whatever the cause, the mocking disappointment is apparent. It is nigh thirteen hundred years since the Holy son and His mother began proclaiming and exemplifying the White Kingdom here. Now in all this land of theirs, we thirteen, fateful number, alone are left of those who openly own His cause. Yea, and the city where He grew in favor, these nature-blessed plains whose flowers gave Him picture sermons, are all filled with burrowing monsters eternally at war with Him and His."

"Faith will rest until assured that the Promiser is dead, and that can never be, Sir Knight."

"My faith staggers at the sights of Nazareth. Chief, look yonder."

The knights all now called Sir Charleroy chief, when addressing him.

"At what?"

"The ruins!"

"Ah, all that's left of our Crusader church. They say it was built on the very spot where Mary fell fainting, when she saw the Nazarenes in wrath dragging her son away to cast him down from the precipice to death. But He escaped, though the church since built did not!"

"True; therefore it seems to me that the hand on time's dial turns backward. This city is filled with creatures having hearts as hard as the limestone walls of the cave-like houses they fittingly inhabit. If Christ and His Mother were again on earth as before, mercy's ministers, the present inhabitants of Nazareth would surpass His ancient persecutors in the zeal with which they would drag not only Him but His mother to the cliffs."

"Over the door of yon ruined church, some hand of faith carved the word 'Victory!' The word is there yet, and though the hand that carved it is dead, the faith which prompted it hath victory assured it."

"'Victory,' in ruins! A meaningless boast, as it seems to me, Sir Charleroy. Such victory as ours; shadowy and very distant!"

At that moment one of the Templars, who had been secretly praying behind a cactus hedge, drew near and the Hospitaler addressed him:

"Brother, any token?"

"Praise Jehovah! yes, of peace."

"How came it?"

"In my communings, God brought to my mind how the wondrous Deborah, not far from here, pushed the pusillanimous Barak from his refuge among the pistacas and oaks, from waverings to courage and to glorious victory over God's foes."

"A happy thought; 'the stars on their course fought against Sisera!'"

"Barak was called the 'thunderbolt,' but Deborah was the 'lightning,' The lightning gave force to the bolt and God to the lightning."

Sir Charleroy, catching the last sentence, joined in the debate:

"Gentlemen, there is another lesson on the brow of that history; it is, that women, having more trust, cleave closer to God in peril than do men. Men are in a panic when their devices fail; women have fewer devices to fail, hence are less easily confounded. For that reason God sent out our race in pairs."

"Hermon's breast holds the last ray of the setting sun," remarked the Golden Cross.

"And the Transfiguration of Christ is recalled! I think some angel of God is holding the sunlight there for our instruction, now," exclaimed the chief.

"Our instruction?" queried the Templar. "I do not discern its meaning; campaigning I fear has dulled my brain."

"The Son of Mary, on yon mount, met Elijah, representative of the prophets, Moses, representative of the law; both called from the deathless land to proclaim the fulfillment of all prophecy and law through His coming passion.

"And still I question how this applies to us?"

"A Knight of the *Red Cross* should easily discern that suffering unto death for truth's sake is the way, all prophecy declares that a reign of law transforming things to spiritual splendor shall at last come to earth."

"Ah, Sir Charleroy, the interpretation is entrancing, but why did the glory need to fade into night, and to be followed by Gethsemane and Calvary?"

"Life is but a series of temporary glimpses of the glory that shall be revealed. Night and cloud come and go, yet the sun never dies."

"But, Sir Charleroy, was it not hard that the loving Immanuel should be forced to bide these pangs though ever pursuing true righteousness?"

"Yea, Templar, but the glory of the Transfiguration came to all that group while Jesus prayed; as the angel hastened to minister when Gethsemane was darkest. These things teach that heaven watches its own, with succor according to want; great light at hand to baffle great darkness and royal answers for anxious prayers!"

"You mean, Sir Charleroy, that we few, surrounded by a sea of enemies, in an inhospitable land, far from home, should despise each despairing thought?"

"Good Templar, I am certain of this, anyway: Suffering for the right has full reward, for after passion as Christ's, so to His followers there comes the ascension."

"Amen," fervently ejaculated several surrounding knights, and Sir Charleroy felt the glow that he felt that time the English bishop blessed him.

As they thus communed, the sun had quietly sunk down into the far-off Mediterranean, flooding the west with light like molten gold. Doubtless one thought came to each at the sight; for all smiled sadly when one remarked: " The *West* is very beautiful to-night !" They thought with deep yearnings of home. But the darkness quickly drew over the scene and the song or the baleful nightingales began to start forth here and there from thickets which, in the darkness, appeared like plumes of mourning on acres of black velvet. One knight, for a while entranced by the grim, gloomy spectacle, shuddered ; then looked up as if to say: "When will the moon rise? the darkness is oppressive!" Another tried to cheer his comrades by crying: " England's songsters know us and come to sing us into hopefulness !"

"Men, to rest; you'll need it." It was Sir Charleroy who spoke. Responsibility made him motherly.

"Let us revel awhile in memories of better days," replied the Templar.

"But listen; do you not hear afar off something like the moaning of the winds before a storm?"

"What of it? A storm could add little to our misery."

" The sound you hear is the cry of jackal and wolf; our omens. Forget now all unnerving thoughts of home and steel yourselves to meet hard fortune. For a while rest. Rest is now our wisdom; night, our mother; for a time in safety she will swaddle us within her black garments. And then——"

" Even so, good Sir Charleroy, and I'm thinking this is her last visit to us. She has come, I guess, to lead us to the portals of eternal day."

"When I say good-night to you, comrades, it will be

with the expectation of next saying good-morning where the wicked cease from troubling," solemnly said the Golden Cross.

"But," interrupted the Hospitaler, "while the pulse beats we have a mortgage on time and a duty to plan to live."

"Bravely said; now tell us how to plan," exclaimed several knights.

"Merge all our orders into one, for the present; elect a leader, and——" The Hospitaler paused, for he could not guess the needs or course of the future. But the knights quickly acquiesced in the unity of action proposed.

"Who shall lead?" was the next question.

"I nominate," shouted the Hospitaler, "the one whom we all believe must be under the especial care of the good angels of these places sacred to all revering mother Mary."

The knights, with one voice, responded, "Sir Charleroy de Griffin, Teutonic Knight of the Order of St. Mary!"

The little band dared their danger for a moment by a spontaneous cheer.

"We have no priest to anoint the chief of the Refugees, but with God to witness, let each who would ratify the choice place hilt to shield, as an oath of service and defense."

Every hilt rang against Sir Charleroy's shield, as the Hospitaler ceased speaking.

"Comrades," said Sir Charleroy, "I thank you for your confidence in this hour when the issue is life or death Let us seek the God of battles." The knights formed a hollow square about their leader, and all kneeled upon the earth.

Their wondering steeds seemed to catch the spirit of their riders, and, drawing near, drooped their heads. For a few moments there was awing silence, and then in deep measured tones the Hospitaler began chanting, "*Kyrie Eleison*" (Lord have mercy). The companions responded, "*Christi Eleison.*" Then, amid those scenes of sacred history, the kneeling soldiers, together, and without command, with only the stars for altar-lights, solemnly chanted a portion of the sublime Litany of their church. Galilee never before, nor since, heard a more sincere orison: "Pour forth, we beseech Thee, oh, Lord, Thy grace into our hearts, that we to whom the incarnation of Christ, Thy Son, was made known by the message of an angel, may by His passion and His cross be brought to the glory of His resurrection, through the same Christ, our Lord. Amen."

As they arose, a Templar spoke: "Companions, if it so please you, put a seal, the seal of the Red Cross Knights, upon our act." So saying, the knight crossed his feet, then spread out his arms horizontally; similitude of the crucifixion. All reverently imitated the action, meanwhile, their swords being in hand with blades crossing, forming a fence of steel.

"Comrades," spoke Sir Charleroy, with emotion, "I accept the trust, and vow by Him that gave the single-handed Elijah on yonder far-off wrinkled Carmel, sign by fire, that confounded Baal and its regal hosts, to lead you to liberty and home or to glorious graves."

"*In hoc signo vinces*, living or dead," was the chorused response. Just then the rising moon flooded their interlaced swords with light, and, as they glittered, the knights took it for an omen that there was a blessing in the union of their swords.

"Sir Charleroy, I proclaim thee king of Jerusalem; what say you, comrades?" exclaimed a hitherto silent Knight of St. John. Once more every knight's sword touched the leader's shield.

"Nobly proclaimed!" remarked the Templar. "When De Lusignan deserted us, ceasing to be kingly, he ceased to be king."

"Have charity, men," interrupted their chief; "it takes a world of courage to fall with a falling cause when a way of escape is open."

"Oh, we'll have charity; the same that Tancred had for that brave preacher and craven soldier, Hermit Peter; the latter ran from peril and Tancred raced him back. We can not reach Lusignan to whip him to duty, but we can vote him dethroned and dead. All cowards are dead to the brave."

"But, companions, I must decline the presumptuous title and phantom throne. Jerusalem shall have, to us, but one king; the Son of Mary. For the future, to you, let me be simply Sir Charleroy. Now let us be moving."

"Whither?" anxiously inquired several knights in a breath.

"Over the valley to the cactus hedges against the limestone cliffs before us, where runs along the great highway from Damascus to Egypt. We shall not need the route to either point, probably; but those hills are full of caves for the living and tombs for the dead." All obeyed.

"Why so thoughtful?" said the Hospitaler to the Knight of the Golden Cross, who marched along with his cloak partly shielding his face.

"I'm living in the past," he sententiously answered.

"The past? Ah, to make up by a back journey for an expected briefing of thy future?"

"No, raillery here, Hospitaler. I was just wishing that since we are so near Endor, Saul's witch would call up some saintly Samuel to tell us where we shall be this time to-morrow."

"Oh, Golden Cross, know we can best bear the good or evil of the future by seeing it only as it comes; for me, I prefer to think of another place, near us, but having a more helpful incident for the memory of such as we."

"Dost thou mean Nain?"

"The same. There a dead only son was raised from the bier to comfort a widowed mother."

"Well said, Hospitaler," responded Sir Charleroy, "and let us not forget that it was a mother's tearful prayers that won the working of the miracle."

"Alas, knight," sighed the Templar, "we have no mothers to so petition for us here, if we be quenched ere long."

"Some of us have living mothers who never cease to pray for us, nor will until their breath ceases. In this land, where God appeared through motherhood, I have a strong confidence that our mothers' prayers, re-enforced by our appealing but unvoiced needs, will move the motherhood of God, if such I may call His tenderest lovings. I'll trust to-night my mother's prayers, reaching from England to Heaven and from thence to here, further than all the sympathy forgetful Europe will vouchsafe us. A nation cheered us to battle, and yet it will never seek for the fragments defeat has left; but the man never lived, no matter what his ill deserts, whom true mother love and eternal God love ever forgot." After this long address, Sir Charleroy again felt the glow within and the approvings that he felt on the quay when the bishop's hands were on his head.

CHAPTER VI.

THE FUGITIVES.

'Tis not in mortals to command success;
But we'll do better, Sempronius; we'll deserve it.
—*Cato.*

HE fugitives slept, some in the obliviousness of complete fatigue and others restlessly, their minds perturbed by dreams of their impending perils. Dawn summoned all to renewed activity, but its coming was not greeted joyfully by the knights.

"Sir Charleroy," mournfully spoke a Hospitaler to the former, as they met at the outskirts of the camping place, "our comrade, the Knight of the Holy Sepulcher, made good his escape from this woeful country during the early morning, before dawn, as our comrades were sleeping!"

"Why, impossible!" questioningly responded the chief.

"Alas, 'twas rather impossible for him not to go!"

"I'm in no humor for such petty jesting! See, his steed is there yet," and Sir Charleroy turned on his heel impatiently as he spoke.

"Pardon, companion, he that departed was borne away by the white charger with black wings!"

"Dead?"

"Mortals say 'dead' of such, but it were better to say he is free."

"*Peace to his soul*," fervently spoke Sir Charleroy.

"Ah, knight, thou canst not imagine the peacefulness of his going!"

"But why were we not summoned? We might have consoled him at least; perhaps we might have healed. What was his malady?"

' A poisoned arrow wounded him in the retreat from Acre. He did not realize his peril until the agonies of the end were wracking his body. Then he said, 'Too late; it's useless to attempt resistance of the inevitable.'"

"Now this is pitiful—a humiliation of us all. Heavens, Hospitaler! there's not a knight among us who would not have periled his life in effort in the dying man's behalf."

"But he cautioned me against disturbing any one on his account. 'Poor men,' he said, 'they'll need all the rest they can get for the struggles of the day to come.' Only once did he seem to yearn for a remedy, and that time he spoke mostly as one dreaming. I remember his every word—'I wish I could bathe these hot and bleeding wounds in the all-healing nards said to exude exhaustlessly from the image of the Virgin Most Merciful at Damascus.' I roused him, then, with an appeal for permission to summon thee, but he forbade me."

"Thou shouldst have overridden all protests of his! By my tokens! I'd have emulated faithful Elenora, who sucked the poison from the dagger stab given her spouse, our knightly Prince Edward, by the would-be assassin at Acre."

"I could not resist him; his face shone in the moonlight with heavenly brightness; mine was covered with tears. Oh, chief, the dying man spoke like an angel. Once he said: 'It is sweet to go out here, nigh where the resurrection angel, Gabriel, gave Mary the glad tidings that her humanity was to join with the Good Father to bring forth One capable of sounding each human sorrow here and hereafter. He overcomes the dread last enemy of all our race!' I watched as he fixed his dying gaze upon the golden cross he wore; his last words still fill and inflame my soul: 'Brother, good-night—say this to each for me. I feel great darkness creeping in to possess this broken, weary body. It comes to stay, but my soul moves forth out of its dungeon. I see gates most lofty, all glorious, and oh, so near! They open to an eternal day.' Then he breathed his last, murmuring tenderly: 'I'm going; good-night; good-morning!'" The Hospitaler ended his recital with a great sob, then burying his face in his cloak, was silent.

Presently the knights formed a hollow square about an old tomb in the hillside. The Hospitaler supported tenderly the head of the dead comrade in his lap. On the naked breast of the corpse lay the many-pointed golden cross of the Knights of the Sepulcher, while round the body was wrapped a Templar's banner, with its significant emblem, two riders on one horse; symbol of friendship and necessity.

"Let the one who received the dying prayer of our brave companion speak," said Sir Charleroy. The knights all knelt, and the Hospitaler still reverently supporting the head of the dead, spoke. " Knight of Christ, sleep; the clamors of war shall no more disturb thee. The dead at least are just and merciful. Israelite, Mohammedan and Christian may lie together in these vales, reconciled at last. They that would not share a loaf to save life to one another, in death share quietly all they have, their beds. The ashes of the long sleepers have no contentions; here are no crowdings of each other; no misunderstandings; no alarms. Sleep, soldier, thy worthy warfare finished; thy cause appealed to the Judge of All! Sleep and leave us to battle on 'mid perils and pain. Sleep thy body, while thy soul fathoms the mysteries to us inscrutable. Rest now, and leave us here a little longer to wonder why it is that human creatures must needs inhumanly oppose and slay each other for the enthroning of Truth, the friend, the quest of all! Sleep, and leave us to wonder why death and conflict are the openers of the gates of life and peace." Some of those kneeling wept, but they were too much depressed to speak. Quietly they laid the body within its resting place; quietly they sealed up the tomb's entrance. Then they mounted their steeds at their chief's command.

"There are but twelve of us left; a lucky number. Perhaps the breaking of the fateful spell believed to follow the number thirteen, was death's beneficence!" It was the Templar who so spoke.

"It is said, Templar," responded Charleroy, "that our Mary, in her girlhood, was escorted ever by an invisible heavenly guard, a thousand strong. In the guard there were twelve palm-bearing angels of rare splendor, commissioned to reveal charity."

"A worthy companionship, chief!"

"I'm inclined to pray heaven to send again to these parts the beautiful twelve, to assure us good fortune and victory."

"Surely the prayers of us all join thine, Sir Charleroy; but methinks we have forgotten how to pray aright, or heaven has forgotten to answer us. We have been praying and fighting for months only to find at last that our prayers and our battlings are alike vain. I fear there are no palm-bearing angels at hand."

The horsemen slowly wended their way back to tne hill-top, overlooking Nazareth, on which they first paused the night before. Again they halted to admire the prospect, as well as to look for a route or safe retreat. Nazareth was astir. The little band on the hill could hear the morning trumpeters calling the Moslem to worship.

"Gentlemen," said the leader of the band on the hill, "it is wisdom to divide into two parties, and make for the sea by different routes. At Cæsarea we may find some vessels with which to leave these to us fateful shores. If we meet the foe anywhere, the odds against us now are so great that death or enslavement must be the result. Perhaps if there be two parties one may escape." The knights paused about their leader a few moments in affectionate debate; all opposing at first the plan that was to scatter them, but all, finally, convinced that it was the highest wisdom to go on their ways apart. Lots were cast by the eleven, De Griffin not participating. Four were grouped in one party and seven in the other by the result.

"I'll join the weaker party, remembering the five wounds of Jesus," said Sir Charleroy, reining his steed to the smaller company. A moment after he continued: "Now, good souls, away with grief; part we must; here and now. May God go tenderly with the seven, a covenant number. Now make your wills; then a brief farewell; then use the spur."

"Wills?" said a Templar, and they all smiled in a sickly way at the word. "We knights, boasting our poverty, our holding of all we have in community, know nothing of will-making."

"True, the pelf we each have is small enough; a few keep-sakes, our arms and such like; but our love is something. Let's will that, and if we've aught to say before we die, we'd better say it now. There is work ahead, and plenty of it. There will be no time for *ante-mortem* statement when we meet the cimeters of the Crescent." So spoke Sir Charleroy. He continued, "My slayer will take good care of my jewels." He commenced writing upon a bit of parchment, using for rest the pommel of his saddle. In a few moments he paused.

"Wilt thou read thine, that we may know how to make ours, chief?" inquired one near him.

"A message to my mother; that's all."

"Enough; that's sacred."

"Yes—but—no. Misery has knit us into one family. I feel to confide." So saying, he read his writing, omitting only the portion that recited their recent vicissitudes:—

"And now, beloved mother, we turn from Nazareth toward the sea with only a forlorn hope of reaching it. I long to meet thee, but the longing must, I fear, content itself in reaching out my heart's best love across the distant ocean toward thyself. It is all I can give in return for the mysterious consciousness that thine is a constant presence. My memory teems with records of my life-long ingratitude toward thyself, that gave me birth and all a loving heart could bestow, and now I'm tasting bitterest remorse for all those selfish days of mine. I wish I could recall their acts. Take these words as my request for pardon. I shall bind this little parchment scrap in my belt in a vague hope that some way, some time, it may reach thee. If it do, remember it is sent to bear to thee, beloved mother, the assurance that thy once wayward boy remembers now, as he has for months, as the brightest, best, most exalting and blessed things of all his life, thy loving words, thy patient trust in him and all thy pious exhortations. I thank God now for all my trials and perils. They have brought me to full prizing of thy goodness and near to the religion thou dost profess."

The reader paused, and the companion knights at once began begging him to inscribe messages for them each, he being the only one in all the company having the priestly gift of the pen. Most of them said, "To my mother" or "To my sister, write:" but one blushed as he said, "I've no mother nor sister." His comrades rallied him at once: "Name her, the other only woman!"

"A heart as brave as thine, knight," said the Hospitaler to the blushing youth, "has a queen on its throne, somewhere."

The youth blushed more and drew away a little.

"Only a lover," said the Templar. "Lovers, absent, assuage their pinings by new mating! They forget; mothers never do. Write for us, Sir Charleroy."

The blush of the youth deepened to anger, evincing his heart's high protest against any hint of doubt being aimed at his queen; but he was self-restraining, silent. "I'll not reveal her by defense even," was his whispered thought.

The writing was finished. "Farewell! Forward."

The chief suited the action to the commands, and soon his steed was dashing swiftly away with its rider, followed by the others of his party. The seven departed toward Nain; perhaps it was an ominous choice, for their route led them toward the cave of incantation, where Endor's witch called up for Saul the shade of Samuel. Most likely the words of the dead prophet to the haunted warrior, "To-morrow thou shalt be with me," would have told the fate of the seven that morning fittingly, for they were never heard from by any of their earthly friends.

CHAPTER VII.

ICHABOD.

> "Oh, that many may know
> The end of this day's business, ere it come;
> But it sufficeth that the day will end,
> And then the end is known."
> —*Julius Cæsar.*

A TEDIOUS ride brought the five knights nigh Shunem, the City of Elijah.

"We'll find no prophet's chamber here for such as we," remarked Sir Charleroy.

"Perhaps," said a comrade, "we may by force or cajoling find a breakfast; a cake or cruse of oil."

"Anyhow," replied the chief, "we must try for a little food. We can neither fight nor flee with gaunt hunger on our flanks. Who knows, after all, but that we may happen on a humane being in these parts."

"Well, good captain, if we should find a Shulamite, black, but comely, she might be as loving to thee as that one of old was to Solomon, although——"

The sentence was broken off by the interrupting command of Sir Charleroy, "Men, quick, to cover; to the lemon-tree grove on the right!"

A glance back revealed a host of armed men behind the knights.

"All saints defend!" cried the Templar, as the little band wheeled toward the refuge.

The tale of the battle to the death that ensued, is quickly told.

Sir Charleroy, though he had fought with reckless bravery, as one hotly pursuing death, alone survived. A bludgeon blow felled him; when he recovered consciousness, he beheld standing by his side a gorgeously bedecked Moslem. The clangor of the conflict was over; the blood in which he weltered, and the vicious eyes that watched him, were all that reminded the knight of what had recently transpired. Presently the latter addressed the one that stood guard:

"Why is the infidel so tardy in finishing his work?"

"Is the Crusader in a hurry to reach night?" sententiously replied the man of gorgeous trappings.

"He would like to stay long enough to execute a murderer—the chief of thy horde."

"My horde? Thou knowest me?"

"Oh, yes Azrael, Angel of Death,' thy minions call thee; but I defy thee as I loathe thee."

The chief's brow darkened; his sword rose in air, and he exclaimed: "Hercules was healed of a serpent bite, ages ago, at Acre; Islamism in the same place recently; I must finish the hydra by cutting off thy hissing head, Christian."

Sir Charleroy steadily met his captor's gaze, eye to eye, and was silent.

The chief paused; then lowering his sword, toyed its point against the cross on the prostrate man's breast.

"Bitter tongue, thou dost worship a death sign; dost thou so love death?"

"Death befriends those who wear that sign in truth; this is my comfort standing now at the rim of earth's last night."

"Thy bright red blood and unwrinkled brow bespeak youth, the power to enjoy life. Youth and such power is ever a prayer for more time; thou liest to thyself and me by professing to seek thy end."

"How wonderful! The 'Angel of Death' is a soul-reader as well as a murderer!" bitterly rejoined Sir Charleroy.

"Well, then, refute me! Here's thy greasy, blood-stained sword; now go, by thine own hands, if thou darest, to judgment."

"Trusting God, I may defy thee; yet not hurry Him!"

"I like the Christian's metal. I might let him live."

"Life would be a mean gift now; a painful departure from the threshold of Paradise, to renew weary pilgrimages."

"I may be merciful."

"I do not believe it."

"Thou shalt."

"When I believe in the tenderness of jackals and tigers, in the sincerity of transparent hypocrisy, I'll praise the mercy of Azrael."

"Our holy Koran reveals a bridge finer than a hair, sharper than a sword, beset with thorns, laid over hell. From that bridge, with an awful plunge, the wicked go eternally down; over it safely, swiftly, the holy pass to happiness. Art ready to try that bridge?"

"Ready for the land of forgetfulness; no swords nor crescents are there."

"No, thou wouldst only reach Orf, the partition of hell, where the half-saints tarry; thy bravery merits that much; but I'll teach thee to reach better realms."

"Turk, Mameluke, 'tis fiendish to prejudge a dying soul; leave judgment to God, and share now all that is within thy power, my body, with thy fit partners, the vultures!"

"A living slave is worth more to me than a dead knight; I've an humor to let thee live."

"Oh, most merciful hypocrite! I did not think thou couldst tell the truth so readily; but let me, I beseech thee, be the dead knight."

"What if I save thy life, teach thee the puissant faith of Islam, give thee leadership, and with it opportunity to win entrance to that highest Paradise, whose gateway is overshadowed by swords of the brave? There thou mayest dwell forever with Allah and the adolescent houris."

"Enough; unless thou dost aim to torture me! I'm a Knight of Saint Mary, and thou full well knowest the measure of my vows; how throughout this land my Order has warred against thy hateful polygamy, thy gilded lusts here, thy Harem heaven hereafter! Ye thrive by luring to your standards men aflame now with the fire that burns such souls at last in black perdition. I tell thee to thy teeth, thou and thine are living devils. But ye war against the wisdom of the world and the law of God; though triumphing now, ye will rot amid your riots and victories."

The chief's face grew black as night for an instant, but recovering himself, he continued, sarcastically at first. then with the zeal of a proselyter:

"Speak low, thou, last dying vestige of a wan faith! Thou mightst make my solemn followers yell with ridiculing laughter! I tell thee of life and of a faith as natural as nature herself. Listen; there is for the brave and faithful a Paradise whose rivers are white as milk as odoriferous as musk. There are sights for the eye, fetes most delicious and music never ceasing to ravish; these lure the brilliantly-robed faithful to the black-eyed daughters of Pleasure. One look at them would reward such as we for a world-life of pain; and the children of the prophet's faith are given the eternities to companion these splendid creatures whose forms created of musk know no infirmity, but survive, always, as adolescent fountains. The heaven of Islamism is eternal youth, eternally luxurious."

"It befits the Angel of Death to gild a deformed hell with bedazzling words. Thou and thine glorify lust, and thy heaven, like thy harem, is but a brothel after all. Now let me blast thy gorgeous charnel-house with the lightning of God's Word: 'Blessed are the pure in heart for they shall see God!'"

Sir Charleroy had raised himself up as he was speaking; now he fell back, exhausted. He again felt the glow in his heart that he felt on the quay when the English bishop blessed him; but it seemed more real now than then, and the approvings of conscience some way came with rebukes that caused tears to flow. He felt something akin to real penitence for a life that had not been always up to the ideal that this debate had caused him to exalt. As he fell back he closed his eyes and turned his face from his captor; the act was a prayer to be helped to shut out of his mind the picture of gilded lust depicted by the false teacher that stood by. For a few moments the wounded man was left to his own thoughts, and then his heart went out toward home crying like a sick or lost child in the night, for "*Mother!*" Once more he returned to that duality of existence which comes when one enters into personal introspections. There seemed to be two Sir Charleroys, one writing the history of the other, and the writer was recording such estimates as these: "As he lay there, nigh death, he drew near to God. He had once been a rover, seeking the wildest pleasures of the European capitals; but meeting passion, presented as the ultimate of life, for all eternity, his soul recoiled from it and he became the herald of purity. Once he had friends, wealth and physical prowess; but he squandered them as a prodigal; when he lay bleeding, powerless in body, amid strangers, a slave, he rose to the majesty of a moral giant." The Sir Charleroy that was thus reviewed was comforted, and he stood off from the picture in imagination to admire it, as one standing before a mirror. Just then he thought of his mother and Mary, his ideal, standing on either side of him, before the same presentment. It might have been a dream; but he believed they smiled through tears, pressed their beating hearts to his and upheld him by their arms with tenderness and strength. His captor left him for a few moments only, undisturbed. At a sign from Azrael, he was soon carried away by a guard; the parley was ended and he that had so bravely spoken doomed to confront that that is to the vigorous mind the worst of happenings, uncertainty. For months the captive mechanically submitted to the fortunes of the

Sheik's caravan; in health improving; in spirit depressed, numbed. The knight had constantly before him three grim certainties, escape impossible; rebellion useless; each day hope darkened by further departure from the sea. The captive's treatment from the Sheik was not unkind. The latter met him by times with a sort of courtly condescension, varied only by an occasional penetrating, questioning glance. They had little conversation, yet the Sheik's looks plainly said: "When thou art subdued, sue for favors; they'll be granted." De Griffin nursed his pride and firmness and prevented all familiarity on Azrael's part. The latter was puzzled sometimes, sometimes angered; but he was too polite to show his feelings. For months the only conversation between the two alert, strong men might be summed up in these words on the Sheik's part: "Slave, freedom and heaven are sweet." "Knight, Allah knows only the followers of the Prophet as friends." On the knight's part a look of scorn or an expression of disgust was the sole reply.

In the Sheik's retinue was another captive, a Jew. He was constantly near the knight; for being more fully trusted than the latter, the Sheik had made the Israelite in part the custodian of the Christian. The knight discerned the relationship very quickly; though both Jew and chief endeavored to conceal it. Sir Charleroy, at the first, treated his companion captive with loathing and resentment, as a spy. After a time, the "sphinx, eyes open, mouth shut," as Azrael described Sir Charleroy, deemed it wise and politic to make the Jew his ally. The resolution once formed, he found many circumstances to aid in bridging the gulf that separated the captive and his guard; the cultured Teutonic leader and the wandering Israelite. They both hated the same man, their captor; both loathed the religion he was covertly aiming to lure them to; both were anxious for freedom. They gave voice to these feelings when together, alone, and ere long sympathy made them friends. The next step was natural and easy; the stronger mind took the leadership of the two, and Sir Charleroy became teacher; his keeper became his pupil and *protégé*.

The twain one day, after this change of relation, walked together conversing, on a hill overlooking Jericho, by which place the Sheik's caravan was encamped.

"Ichabod, thou wearest a fitting name."

"I suppose so, since my mother gave it. But why say so now?"

"Ichabod, 'glory departed,' thou art like thy people —despoiled."

"Oh, Lord! how long?" piously exclaimed the Jew.

"Till Shiloh comes!"

"Verily it is so written," was the Jew's reply.

"But He has come, Israelite!"

"Where?" the startled Jew questioned, drawing back as if he expected his, to him mysterious, companion to throw back his tunic and declare: "*I am he!*"

"In the world and in my heart."

"Ah, Sir Knight, Israel's desolation refutes all that."

"Jew, thine eyes are veiled. I'll teach thee to see Him yet."

The Jew was puzzled.

The twain fell into prolonged converse, and then in that lone place the Crusader waxed eloquent, preaching Christ and Him crucified to one of Abraham's seed.

When the two captives descended to their tents, each was conscious of a new, peculiar joy. One had the joy of having proclaimed exalted truth, faithfully, to the almost persuading of his hearer; the other was moving about in the growing delight and wonder of a new dawning faith.

At frequent intervals Ichabod besought the knight to take him "*to the mountain.*"

Each visit thither was a delight to the new inquirer. On such a journey one day spoke Ichabod: "Christian, I am consumed with anxiety to hear thy words and another anxiety lest they do me harm. I am thinking, thinking, by day, and, what little time my thoughts permit sleep, I'm filled with wondrous dreams! I fear to lose my old faith, and yet it becomes like Dead Sea apples under the light of this new way. So new, so infatuating. None I've met, and I've met many, ever so moved me. Why, knight, I've traversed half the world; sometimes as wealth's favorite, sometimes of necessity in misfortune; I've seen the faiths of Egypt and India in their homes, and walked amid the temples of great Rome, but with abiding contempt for all not Israelitish. Not so this creed of the knight affects me."

"And for good reason; I offer thee the true, new, refined and final Judaism!"

"It seems so, and yet I tremble. I dare not doubt; that's sin; but here's the puzzle that harasses me: What if, in doubting these things I'm now told, I be doubting the very truth, the Jewish faith!"

"Ichabod, thy heart has been a buried seed awaiting the spring. It has come."

"Oh, knight, I'm trusting my dear soul to thee As a dog his master, a maid her lover, so blindly I follow thee. I can not go back; I can not pause nor can I go onward alone. I'm in the misery of a joy too great to be borne, almost, and yet too much my master to be given up. Oh, knight, thou art so wise, so strong! Steady me; hold me up! I can only pray and adjure thee to be sincere with me; only sincere; that's all; as sincere as if thou wert ministering to the ills of a sick man battling death."

The child of Abraham, with a sudden movement, flung his arms with all vehemence about Sir Charleroy. The East and the West embracing, truth leading, love triumphant.

"Poor Ichabod, if thou hads't no soul, thy clingings and yearnings would bind me to thee faithfully. Thou hast tried to give me charge over that that is immortal. A Higher Being has it in loving trust; were it not so, I'd turn in dread from thy confiding!"

"Is mine so bad a soul, master?"

"Indeed, no. Its preciousness to Him that created it, is what would make me dread its partial custody."

"Thou'lt help me, master, now?"

"For three objects I'll willingly die; my mother; our lady, and the soul of one who abandons himself, as thou, to my poor pilotage."

"Then, thou strangely lovest me. Oh, this but more persuades me that thy faith is right; it makes thee so good to a stranger, a slave, a hated Jew!"

But then we are so apart and so unlike each other!

"No, Jew, I want to show that humanity is one. The very creed I'm trying to teach thee and would fain have all thy race, ay, all mankind fully understand, is full of love, joy, peace. These follow it as naturally as the flower the stem, the humming the flying wing made to fly and be musical."

"Oh, my dear light, with thee I'm in joy and wilderment. Thy presence seems to bring me hosts of crowned truths, all seeking to enter my being. I feel like a tired runner ready to faint when thou'rt absent, but when thou talkest the tired runner is plunged into a cooling ocean, whose circling waves, as it were charged with the stimulus of tempered lightnings, glowing with a million rainbows, overwhelm, lift up and rest him. I'm floating thereon now!"

"Thy strange fancies make me wonder, Ichabod."

"Wonder; why my strength dies from over wonder. I was ill for hours yesterday. Light to my sweat-blinded, feverish eyes, all calm and healing, comes when I yield to thy will; but still all my joy is haunted by ghosts which rise in day-mare troops, pointing rebukingly to labyrinths into which I seem to be pushed. I sometimes wonder if I'm seeing real spirits or going mad."

"Dost pray, Jew?"

"I dare not live without praying!"

"Then tell the All Pitiful what thou hast this day told to me. He loves the sincere, down to the deepest hell of doubt, and from it all, at last, will lead tumulted souls safely. An honest doubt is a real prayer, well winged; quickly it reaches heaven, at whose portal it dies to rise again all peace."

CHAPTER VIII.

FROM JERICHO TO JORDAN.

" Through sins of sense, perversities of will,
 Through doubt and pain, through guilt and shame and ill
 Thy pitying Eye is on Thy creature still."

' Wilt Thou not make, eternal Source and Goal,
 In thy long years life's broken circle whole,
 And change to praise the cry of a lost soul?"
—WHITTIER.

EW and Crusader came to love each other after the manner of David and Jonathan, and they were both made stronger and happier men on account of this loving.

"Sir Charleroy, a year gone to day, thou and i climbed to glory."

"Thou hast a prolific imagination or I a poor memory. I have no remembrance of either climbing or glory of a year ago."

"I may well remember the greatest day of my life; the day thou tookst me up yon hill over against Jericho; I saw, as Elisha, in the presence of his great master Elijah, the mountains, that day, full of the chariots and angels of God."

"But, Jew, the chariot separated Elijah and Elisha; we were, in thy 'great day,' made one."

"True, but I got the prophet's insight and power. Oh

now I see Shiloh coming in the redemption of Jew and Gentile."

"Radiant proselyte, give God, not me the glory."

"I'll call thee, knight, Jordan—my Jordan."

"The Jew rambles amid strange conceptions. Why am I like that mighty stream?"

"Its bed and banks, God's cup; they nobly serve, catching the pure waters of mountain springs and heaven's clouds, to bear them, mingled with sweet Galilee, to the black burning lips of Sodom's plains below. I was a dead sea, alive alone to misery; nothing to me but my historic past, and that sin-stained. I'm now refreshed and purified; sometime there'll be life growing about me!"

"The highlands of Galilee gather from heaven, oceans of sweet, pure water, which Jordan, year after year, night and day, hurries down to the Asphalt sea; but still that sea remains lifeless and bitter. Even so, the clean, white truth comes to some, lifelong, yet vainly. I think I'm little like Jordan, but much like that sea."

"And yet, knight, all is not vain that seems so. I learned this once, long ago, in the vale of Siddim, by the sea of Lot. As I entered that place of desolation I thought of Gehenna! The lime cliffs about, all barren and pitiless as the walls of a furnace, shut out the breezes, and intensified the sun's scorching rays. A solemn stillness, unbroken by wind, wave or voice of life, was there; suffocating, plutonic odors ladened the air, and a fog hung over that watery winding sheet of the cities of the plain. I watched that overhanging cloud until my heated brain shaped it into a vast company of shades; the ghostly forms of the overwhelmed denizens of those accursed habitations, now in mute terror and confusion, holding to one another desperately; fearing to go to final judgment. Once I thought they were together trying to look down into the depths, perchance to seek for vestiges of their ancient, earthly habitations. These fancies grew and grew upon me, mad dreamer that I was, until I was nigh to desperate fright; but I found some little angels on the shore who comforted."

"Angels at Sodom?"

"Even so. The first was light and liquid silver; it sang a bar of nature's tireless, varied melody by my footsteps. Ah, the little, fresh spring that burst forth through the rim of the crystalline basin, was an angel to me. Then I found others here and there. At first I was glad, then I began to pity them, and to wish I could change their courses. They all wended their ways to the desolate sea, and their sweet currents were swallowed up in the yawning gulf of death. 'Vainly,' I said at first. Then I saw other angels in the forms of bending willows, and gorgeous oleanders. Just then it all came to me; the springs, though small and few, were not in vain. The oleanders and the willow, whose roots kissed their fresh life, were evidences that the springs had been for good. Aye, more, the flowers rejoiced me in those desolations more than could the rose gardens of the Temple in days of happiness. Yea, knight, thou hast been a rivulet to Ichabod in a day when he wandered as among arid mountains and dead seas."

"Blest child of Abraham, thy faith is great, though

I be but a pitiable guide; yet I'll adopt thy similes. Be thou and I, to each other, Jordan, rivulet and flower by turn; the fresh current gives life to plant and blossom, while plant and blossom both shade and beautify the streams. With both it shall be well, if we well learn to seek deep for the hidden springs of the life that can never die. Already thou hast blessed me very greatly, gathering truths I failed to find. Thou return'st to me multiplied all I bestow."

"Would I could gather for all; for my race, so blinded! Oh, it is a tristful thought that the nearer I get to God, the further I get from them I love next after Him. Even my mother was wont to say to me, when, as a questioning boy, I inquired beyond the traditions of the Rabbis, that she'd disown me to all eternity as a heretic. My belief has made me an outcast to her, and yet the thought of her hating me tears my heart."

"I'll love thy orphaned heart."

"Me? Love me; so far beneath thee and with such pauper power of payment?"

"Thy desolation makes thee rich; having none other to love, thou canst love me the more. Thou know'st this open secret of loving; its selfishness demands all; getting that it gives all. Fear not Ichabod, but that thou'lt find the hunger of thy heart well fed. It is as natural for us to love those we have helped as to hate those we have harmed. Thou know'st how men wonder that the Infinite can love the finite, but they forget, or never realized, that one may love because he has loved. So is it with God. He loves, and that He loves becomes therefore rich and worthful to Him."

The morning after the betrothal, shall we call it, of these two men to each other, long before dawn the knight was wakened by a cautious step on the stone floor of his sleeping place. Sir Charleroy was at once all alert and leaped from the couch, sword in hand, expecting to confront some gipsy thief, for there had been a band of these wanderers hovering near the day before.

"Who's there?" sternly he demanded, advancing, on guard meanwhile.

"Ichabod, Ichabod!" with trembling voice and in a half whisper. It was the Jew.

"I did not mean to fright thee," he hurriedly explained, when he had recovered from his fear of being thrust through, "but I've news; bad news that would not wait!"

"What is the bad? Is it near?"

"Oh, knight, speak low—the news is bad enough and the ill, though not on us, close after us!"

"Thou art excited, my friend; sit down and then unfold the matter. Meanwhile I'll light a faggot.

"In truth, I can't sit, and I've reason to be nervous." Then the man spread out his arms and his fingers as if he would stand all ready to fly; his eyes wide open, staring as he talked.

"Our Sheik leaves Jericho to-morrow; summoned by the sheriff of Mecca. The sheriff is supreme to Moslem. The command is for war toward the east. Blood, blood; when will the world be done shedding blood!"

"Well, my loving alarmist," replied Sir Charleroy, coolly, "that's not very bad news. If the Shiek leaves us, we'll be free; if he takes us, there will be a change and for that I could almost cry 'Blessed be Allah!' I am sickened, crushed, dry-rotted by this hum-drum life; this slavery; dancing abject attendance on a gluttonous master, whose sole object seems to be eating or dallying about the marquees of his harem"

"Oh, Sir Charleroy, the change has dreadful things for us!"

"Why?"

"I heard that the runner bringing the mandate from Mecca brings also command that all prisoners, such as we, must be made to embrace Islamism, enlist to die, if need be, in this so-called holy war, or be sent to the slave mart."

"This is a carnival for the furies! Why, Ichabod, the latter is burial alive; the former death with a dishonored conscience!"

"Sir Charleroy, I prefer the slavery."

"Well, I prefer neither. Is the mandate final?"

"Yes; I've an order to commence packing at sunrise; by noon we will be enlisted or in chains."

"Who gave thee these state secrets, so in detail? Perhaps 'tis only camp-fire gossip recounted for lack of novel ghost stories."

"Ah, 'tis too true. I'd swear my life on it!"

"Rash, credulous; but which now, comrade, I can not tell."

"Master, I had this from one that loves me as I love thee; the young Nourahmal, light of the harem, favorite of the Shiek."

"Well, now it seems to me that this light of the harem is thy favorite rather than the Shiek's."

"She adores me."

"Doubtless! Where a woman unfolds her mind there she brings all else an offering easily possessed. She seals her change of allegiance by scattering the secrets of the dethroned to the enthroned lover. 'Nourahmal'? Is she as charming in form as in name?"

"Hold, now! If thou lov'st me thou will'st not continue thus to wound. I love that girl, but not the way thou meanest!"

"So? Is there an elopement pending!"

"Unworthy gibe! Say no more like it, but answer this: Is it not possible for a man and woman to be knitted together in soul, as I and thou have been, without the shadow of a remembrance that they are animals of different sexes?"

"Possible? Really I do not know. It may be possible, but so very rare that I have failed to hear of any such relationship."

"Then thou shalt hear of it now in Nourahmal and me."

"I'll take both to Paris! Another wonder of the world! But explain further."

"My Nourahmal is a captive; hates the man to whom she must submit as we hate him, and loves me with the new love that you have revealed to me, because I've shown her that I love her that way; so different from any thing she ever knew before."

"Well, there are many women yoked to men for whom they feel no great affection, yet they glorify womanhood by their unfaltering loyalty. Loyalty is woman's glory; the hope of society. If the women be traitors, then, alas!"

"Nourahmal is not a wife! The man that parcels out his heart to a dozen favorites buys but scraps in return. A woman in misery's chains, without the bands of the confiding, utter love of her lord, will talk; she must talk, or go mad. I tell, thee, knight, such gossip is the panacea of suicidal bent. There's many a woman kills herself for lack of a confidant!"

"Thou hast learned much philosophy going around the world. Jew, but perhaps not this bitter truth; the woman who is traitor to one man will be to another. Thou mayst be the next. What if she set us fleeing for the sake of laughing at our forced return?"

"Impossible, knight; she reveres me truly; even as she does God; just as I did Sir Charleroy when he brought me light and rest. I was to her what thou art to me. One day I told her women had souls, as dear to heaven as the souls of men! She laughed at me like a monkey, at first, and reminded me that were I a true desciple of Islam I'd know that only young and beautiful women go to heaven, and they even there have a lowly place. Thou knowest these infidels believe that the large majority of hellians are women."

"Not strange Jew; they treat women as pretty or useful animals, and so degrade, not only themselves, but these very women. A woman so demeaned does not become heavenly, to say the least. But I think, if I were a Turk, I'd keep only argus-eyed eunuchs to guard my harem; in faith, I'd even have the tongues out of those guards."

"There, now, thou dost jest again."

"Well, go on, in seriousness. Tell us the pipings of this seraglio beauty."

"I've won her over completely."

"This is not strange. Poets are always valiant, victorious orators with women. The female heart is emotionally moved up to belief with little logic, if the speaker be fair, or musical, or brave!"

"I was none of these; I told her of the 'Friend of Publicans and Sinners;' that fed her soul. I do not believe there is a woman on earth that can resist that story."

"Oh, well, I'm not going to forget that the first woman outran her mate in evil, nor that she exchanged the All Beautiful for the snaky demon."

"It would be nobler for a knight, truer for all, to judge, if judge they will, by wider circles. Do not remember the sin of one, or a few, to the disparagement of all!"

"Eve, the best made of all, fell; then her weaker sisters are more likely to follow in her way," said the knight.

"She found a sin and fell; thousands of her daughters have fallen by sins that men invented and thrust on them. Thou knowest that most women who go wrong, go in ways they would not without the temptings of the stronger will. The sin that ruins most is that to woman's nature abhorrent, until honeyed over by the tongue of man."

"Dexterous lance, art thou, Jew; but, anyway, some women are born bad."

"No; I'm not able for one so wise as the knight, unless I've the strength of truth. I've heard that our wise men say that if we could trace the ancestry of any one evil, from birth, we would find somewhere, up the line, a father, prëeminent in wickedness. Say, women are weak to resist evil; then, say men are strong to propagate it. Now, which way turns the scale?'

"Oh, I say always, dogmatically, if need be, in man's favor."

"Let me see: Eve's humanity that sinned was out of the finest part of Adam's body, and the serpent which betrayed her was a male."

"I'll parry the thrust by asking why the Holy Writings reveal no female angels? I think there are none."

"I've a wiser reason, knight. It is this: Man has so foully dealt with the angels in the flesh that God's mercy reserves their finer spiritual counterparts for the sole companionships of heaven, which justly appreciates these holy, pure and tender creations. Heaven would not be perfectly beautiful without them and, methinks, can not spare one for a moment!"

"Not even to minister to a needy world?"

"Woman's life is here, generally, all service, all ministry; her return to earth after death would be a work of supererogation. God sends back the male spirits to help restore the world their sex did most to ruin."

Then both the debaters laughed out as heartily as they dared, but there was in the tones of the knight's laughter a part-confession of defeat. After a time Sir Charleroy spoke again: "Thou art calm now, after this diversion, Ichabod; proceed with thy story of danger."

"Well, Nourahmal——"

"Oh, yes, begin again with Nourahmal. Samson was a pretty good man for a giant, but he had a betraying Delilah!"

"True enough; but he had also a noble mother. Remember the better, rather than the worse."

"I remember her peers, Mary and my mother."

"So, then, when sweepingly condemning all the sex, please except the mothers, at least of those who may be thy hearers."

"Good Jew, I'll not wound thee!"

"No pity for me; pity thyself. Such thoughts as thou hast spoken wound thine own soul. We Jews have an order called 'Tumbler Pharisees;' they affect humility, shuffle as they walk and stumble on purpose that they may not seem to walk with confidence. Akin to them we have the 'Bleeding Pharisees;' they walk with shut eyes, lest they should see a woman, and, stumbling against many a post, are soon covered with their own blood, receiving real harm in flying from imaginary dangers."

"'*Maya, Maya,*' Ichabod," laughing aloud, exclaimed Sir Charleroy.

The latter, catching the knight's arm, hoarsely whispered: "Hush! Thou mayst be heard. What dost thou mean by '*Maya*'?"

"Perhaps, Nourahmal! *Maya* was the reputed wife of the supposed god Brahm of the Hindus. It is reported that she was in form like unto fog and her name means 'illusion.' A subtle truth, Jew; even a god, in love, is near a fog bank!"

"Thou dost not know Nourahmal and dost discredit her; that's slander; thou dost know me and ridiculest me; that's—but—I'll not say it."

"I'd not pain my Ichabod."

"Nor discredit Nourahmal?"

"No; but did this angel, or Syren of thine, having shown the peril, present a map to a city of refuge?"

"Ah, poor, helpless girl! she has none for herself, much less for us. She just told me all and wept and kissed me a farewell, praying me to flee. I could think of no question in the delight of hearing her say, she hoped I'd meet her in Heaven, in peace away from Moslem and wars. Only think of her faith! All new; just a little while ago she did not know there was a heaven for women. I felt I could die then in peace. I've taught one woman that she is more than a pretty animal!"

"Then, Jew, to thee, life is worth living?"

"Oh truly! Oh, if this light could only spread over Egypt and all my own Syria!"

"Thy desire is akin to that of Mary's son and noble. Certain it is that we can not spread that light by fighting to sustain the fateful Crescent."

"By the glory of God, I never will."

"Nor I, son of Abraham; so let's decline."

"And go to the slave mart?"

"Oh, no, not while I've a sword, Ichabod."

"Then to flee is the word?"

"The eastern campaigning with the sheik, would be a little longer route to Paradise?"

"Perhaps not; I am assured that we are needed of God by the use He has recently made of us. He will keep us in our flight from bloody persecuting war, and possible apostacy."

"I hate the last word! A knight enchanted of Mary can never become a renegade; not I, at least. I was born October ninth. Tradition says that the holy St.

John Damascene, having had his hand cut off by the Saracens that day, was by Our Lady miraculously made whole, and lived long after to wield a powerful, facile pen in her behalf. I'll trust my head and saber hand, used for her, to her protection."

"And I'll trust Him that led the wandering hosts of Moses; for 'in all their affliction, He was afflicted with them, and the angel of His presence saved them; and He bore them and carried them all the days of old.' Oh, master, I've comfort I can not tell, when I feel orphaned, by thinking of my Maker, not only as a Father, but as a Mother! God is our Mother when we, bereft of mother-love, most feel our need of it. So thou toldst me in the mountains."

"True; but shall we try our escape now?"

"Nay, we had better wait till a little before dawn; the camp patrol is then withdrawn; then we'll embrace freedom."

"The Jew seems very confident."

"Oh, I spent the hour after I met Nourahmal (God keep her), amid the palms for which Jericho is fitly named, and got a token."

"A token?"

"My eyes were touched in the darkness."

"Sweet Nourahmal followed thee?"

"No, but He that opened the eyes of blind Bartimeus near here."

"What didst thou see?"

"Elisha healing the streams about this palm city, type of God healing the floods of bitterest fates; after that I saw Jericho's walls falling at the blasts of

Joshua's trumpets, and remembered that his God then is ours now."

"Didst thou see two poor men fleeing in the dark from peril to peril, pursued by a hundred horsemen, who saber-lashed them; a little further two corpses, one of a Christian the other of a Jew, on which fed fighting jackals?"

"I saw no such horror! I saw two led forth from their captors, as Peter from his dungeon; the angels that blinded the eyes of the monstrous men, who of old sought to defile Lot's house, blinded the eyes of the pursuers of the two; and the angel of Peter gave them guidance and light. But come, the night-guard has retired; between now and the call to morning prayers is our opportunity."

Out of the old stone stable silently knight and Jew glided, threading their way amid splendors they believed to be, but could not see. The ministering spirits were over and around them, their path was through the Kelt, the sublimest waddy of Palestine; but night shrouded the latter; their weak faith dimly discerned the other.

"Can't thou see any way-marks, Jew?"

"I discern but few. Yet, what matter? It is enough that He who leads us sees?"

"The night is getting blacker and blacker; the omen makes my heart shiver as it beats."

As the knight spoke there came a terrific crash of thunder and a succession of blinding lightning flashes. Sir Charleroy clasped the Jew's arm and in startled voice questioned:

"Dost thou not fear these?"

"Why should I? The angel guides swing the torches of the unchangable Father to give us glimpses of our way. All is well; I saw by the lightning flash that we are passing safely the camp lines of our captors."

A few miles were over-past. The storm had abated a little, and the first streaks of dawn, like spears, were rising in the east.

"Would God, good Jew," said the now wearied Sir Charleroy, "that the Prophet of the Moslem, who, near by here, is said once by a stamp of his foot to have brought forth from the rock a camel, were present to dance for us now."

"He is not here, so we must help ourselves, knight."

"Ah, my dear man, canst thou dance rocks into camels?"

"No, but there are houses nigh, and each thou knowst has it's stable-yard in front."

"But there is the thorny nubk tree, surrounding the herds."

"I've faith to try my faith when all I have is faith."

"What for; to steal a camel?"

"Oh, no; I'd not steal a camel but I'd borrow a couple of them. Two; for I'm not one of the knights who exhibit poverty, by riding double, thou dost know."

"Borrow? Well so be it; the black infidels owe us for two years' service. They borrowed us!"

"It's pious to take the beasts; for we pay so honest debts of these heathens and shorten the list of their souls' sins by removing from them, in our escape, the opportunity for our murder."

"If this be sophistry, Ichabod, it is so sweet that it is taken as delightful truth."

"Thou art persuaded?"

"No man can out run me, be he rabbi or priest, in condemning vices, if they be such as I do not care to practice, and I am a profound believer in every creed that's sweet to my desires. Here action treads the heels of persuasion."

* * * * * *

On beasts, borrowed without formality, the fugitives hurried toward Jordan, only there to find a barrier to their progress in the angry torrent swelled by the recent storms. It was clearly futile to attempt a passage, and to tarry, waiting the ebb of the waters, was to bring certain detection. They turned the heads of their borrowed camels toward their master's homes and waited the sunrise, meanwhile moving about to find some means of safety.

"Well, my comrade, I think it will not be long until those Turks will give our souls an Elijah-like ascension except that there will be no chariot. The morning shimmering on his mountain makes me think of this, Ichabod."

"The tracks of our returning camels in the wet earth will guide our pursuers."

"Suppose we climb a tree as Zacchaeus, since we can not have a chariot. By my plume! which I've not seen for a year, I think that would be safety; the Turks never look up except in prayer, and the wolf Azrael seldom prays. But God pity us! there they are coming.

"To the tombs, master! On the left."

"Refuge for jackals?"

"Yes, but also for the miserable, living and dead! Now haste!"

Sir Charleroy obeyed quickly, but recoiled with a groan of disgust as he suddenly pushed against an entombed body. He touched his hilt, as if determined to abandon attempt at flight, and then, overcoming the rash impulse to confront the pursuers, turned about, seized the corpse, and dragging it from its place, hurled it over the river bank into the torrent. He was in the dispoiled nich in an instant. A cry from the pursuers drew him forth. "See, Ichabod, the Turks are running along the river banks watching the mummy bobbing along in the torrent. See, it sinks. Ah, the brutes, how they shout! They think that body alive, and that one poor slave is hounded to death."

"Jehovah Jeireh, now help us; they'll soon be back," cried Ichabod.

"Ah, I forgot; they'll remember there were two of us."

"Calm, Sir Knight, 'By this sign I conquer,' quoting thy words of another. I'll go forth; the only one left; at least so they'll think."

Sir Charleroy turned and looked at the Jew, and was amazed to see him binding in front of himself a board having the ominous words, "Unclean" upon it.

"What; thou, a Jew, and touch that foul thing, worn to festering death by some leper!"

"Better night and a clean soul, though in a body burned by the cursed leprosy, than life in Moslem slavery."

"But what if the disease cleave to thee, and we escape?"

"Sir Knight, thou wilt live to tell others that a once hated Jew was led of thee to truth, and after died a living death, that his benefactors might survive. I think such deeds cause noble lights to glow in human souls."

"God bless and pity thee, Ichabod."

"Ah, he does; even now. I see the scarlet line of Rahab, and it binds the pestilence that walketh by noonday.

The furious pursuers spurred their steeds up toward the tombs, but as they beheld the solitary man, sitting in painful attitude with beggar-like palm extended and wearing the dread sign, they rapidly wheeled their steeds about and galloped away. The Moslem had heard that a Jew would suffer any torture rather than ceremonial pollution; hence judged that the object before them could not be the refugee they sought.

"I wonder not that the demoniac cut himself madly when among the tombs, good Jew. Sure it's like going to glory to get out once more. Methinks freedom is only sweet when taken with fresh air! Well, we are out and the enemy thwarted."

"Methinks, master, that the leper that died here, leaving no legacy but the sign of his death, did some good in unknowingly making me his heir."

"And the corpse I disposed of so unceremoniously left me a house of safety, though small and musty. I've a bitter thought.

"So, Sir Charleroy, tell it me, perhaps I can sweeten it."

"I, the heir for a little time of that soulless clay, am like it."

"Not much being here and alive."

"I rather think like it. See me tossed about by strangers, robbed of my rights, helpless to resist fate's tides, begrudged the room I occupy, and not one who once knew me to weep over my besetments.

"Sir Knight, the miracles of our frequent preservation should make our murmurings dumb."

In the evening Jordan ebbed a little and the two wanderers passed over. Nor did they regret the consequent immersing in its flood. No word was spoken as they passed through the current, for, before they entered, having remembered that at this Bethabara ford man's Savior was baptized, they were each busy with his own meditations. When they stood on the other shore, Sir Charleroy reverently said: "Comrade, I prayed as we passed that we might have the dove of peace henceforth above our souls at least."

"I prayed on my part that God would accept the act as the Christian's typical burial to the world and separation from its sins."

"How like death and birth is that beautiful type. They level all life."

"Are our lives leveled? knight."

"Henceforth; and we are brethern."

"And our King and Savior was baptized here by the herald of His Kingdom, John?"

"Yea; here the new Judaism was formally inaugurated. Tradition says also that Jesus baptized his mother afterward at this ford."

"How filial; how beautiful; how expressive! He

was her God, yet her son, she his mother and disciple; and each by all ties and forms bound together in a fellowship of helpfulness.

"The Jew's an interpreter."

"Sir Charleroy sweetens my trust as Jordan sweetens the bitter waters of Bahr Lut.

CHAPTER IX.

THE FEAST OF THE ROSE.

"They arise now like the stars before me,
Through the long, long night of years;
Some are bright with heavenly radiance,
And others shine out through our tears.
They arise, too, like mystical flowers,
All different and all the same—
As they lie on my heart like a garland
That is wreathed around MARY'S name."

OOD morning and a blessing, comrade." It was the greeting of the Jew to the knight who lay asleep under a palm the day after the flight. The sleeper slowly rising, murmured:

"I'm half vexed at thee, Ichabod; thou hast dissolved a dream filled with sights of home and mother."

"I've brought lentils, barley, and grape-clusters they are better than dreams when the sun is up."

"To those sad when awake, joyful dreams are welcome."

"There are real joys just before us."

"Real joys, just before us? Grim sarcasm; a sorry jest, Jew!"

"No; oh, no. I'm telling thee the smiling, clear

faced truth. We'll be safe at Jabbock's city by sunset!"

"Safe? safe? I'm unused to that word; almost afraid of it. What does it mean in this country?"

"Oh, these cavalrymen! always on the charge; now here, now there. Thy thoughts go by habit, sometimes racing forward, sometimes retreating. A while ago thou wert as full of faith as Gideon, now thou art as timorous as Canaan's spies."

"My habits have grown fat by feeding on piebald experiences."

"Experience is a lying prophet, when it counts without reckoning God."

"I can not see a step ahead. That's certainty to me, though thou callest it doubt. I know not how to hang rainbows upon the ghostly brows of the future when I've no power to lay hand on the ghostly form and have no rainbows."

"He that lifted the burdens of the past from off us holds the changing winds of the future in His fists. One second of life goes ever with only one second of care. I learned this of Sir Charleroy long ago. Now he forgets his own teachings. Shall I call him Reuben, never excelling because unstable as water?"

"Call me slave: Uncertainty's slave! Thou didst waken me from a dream of home, to the shock of remembering again that I was homeless, dead to all that once made life worth living. The gorgeous hopes of thy fertile mind are mocked by stern present facts."

"Odd talk from one just dreaming of his mother; a good woman didst say? then very hopeful; all good women are. Then remember how thou didst lift me to the very gates of heaven yesterday. Thou canst not see a step ahead? Well, then look back; miles; years. Was not our God in thy battles in the thickets; in the mountains; in Jordan? My poor reasoning tells me that He has wrought too much for us to drop us now. He must get His reward in keeping us to the end."

"Some of the past makes me shudder, Ichabod."

"Pick out the best, not the worst. We escaped the very Gehenna at Jericho, following murderers, the storm, slavery; now free, fed, rested, the eastern air washed and sunned to a tonic. I'm drinking lotus balm out of it."

"There it is; the sun's in thy brain, poet-preacher."

"No, I'm only giving thee back some of thine own sermons. I draw from my own heart no monster memories. If I've fought hard battles it sufficeth that I have fought them once. I'll not recall their bloody sweat and tears for the sake of refighting them. No, I'm going back to the sweet, happy hours of babyhood; for I tell thee, knight, there is a world of joy to a man, scorched by stern experience, to forget himself sometimes back to the lullabys and warblings of the days of his innocence."

"I can't do it,"

"I can't help doing it, especially in this place! My whole being feeds on a present scent of home."

"Thou knowest the country hereabouts?"

"My soul laughs in friendly converse with these crocuses, pinks, and asphodels, turning the velvet, grassy plains to palace carpets. I'm saying to myself these blossoms must know me, their bowing heads and offered odors being my reward for nursing their mothers when I was a boy."

"Well, flowers are sincere friends; they never change and are all charitable. That's why they are deemed fit presents to those in prison, or proper offering to be laid on the breast of the dead Magdalene."

"Ah, dead Magdalene; for even the symbol of a broken promise; born to be a queen of love, by perverted love dethroned! Woman, man's ward, by man betrayed; the guide star setting in black night; the savior of human purity befouling all purity! Given the power by which Eve was to crush the serpent's head and using it to breed all serpentine ills. This is Eve turning a volcano upon Eden. Put flowers upon her once passionate, now dead, heart, in awful contrast! Nature at her worst is intensified anguish; at her best an ocean of joy, an universe of light and song. So I learn of nature under man. Listen to nature's perfumed throb now: these thousands of feathered songsters, millions of lesser creatures, whose melody is larger than themselves and more perceptible. Hear the humming, thrumming, buzzing, trumpetings. Oh, this is life as the All-Saving tuned it to utter joy! It widens, deepens, thickens; getting sweeter, louder, happier all the way. A tempest, set to music, knight. I'm caught in it's whirl and join in its praisings. It comes over me as an insight of what nature really is. God cares for it all and made it thus, to throb and exult!" Ichabod paused in transport. "But I sometimes think there's a great waste of these things; there is so much in places where there is no human ear or eye to hear or see."

"Reuben is narrow-viewed just now. Man is not all! God makes happiness because He is so full of goodness He must. Our rabbis call Him 'The Fountain.' There is no waste! He makes these things for His own joy, and, methinks, looks down from the circle of the heavens to say to what is in the desert or wilderness, 'Very good.' Then, beyond this, I've sometimes thought He kept the processions of joy and beauty moving along; coming, going, dying, living, ending and beginning again, as a sort of practice; by action keeping all fresh and new. He causes things of beauty and power to pass through His divine alchemy from one glory to another, as the general causes his squadrons to move through the evolutions of the battle before the conflict. The Father is awaiting man's hour, man's return from sinning; the time for millennial advent; then all delights, as if fresh born, all goods newly harvested, will appear to be multiplied, intensified, transfigured. That will be the beginning of hereafter."

"Oh, Israel, the sun is in thy brain. I forget all logic of contention, charmed out of words, by feasting on thy orisons. Go on, Jew."

"Then I'll say 'twas God, not chance, nor fate, that brought us to wander alone with nature. Read well nature's book that lies open in the lap of the Great Teacher! Only stand close to Him and He will hold the torch, turn the pages and give the sure interpretations of the sweetness that feeds quiet, the picturesqueness which evokes smiles and the stately grandeurs which beget faith."

"Israel, thou climbest the sun-ladder to rhapsody!"

"Whether soaring, climbing, or creeping, I know

not; but this I know, I'm tasting in these wanderings God's kisses. They are in the flowers; my spirit rests on His as my body on the balm of the fresh breezes. Then, animate nature seems so contented and happy! Why, I've been ravished by the songsters; as I've said to myself, they echo the angelic anthem of heaven, peace. Had any such doubt as haunts thee, come to me, since passing Jordan, it would have been sung out of countenance by the winged warblers or dragged from my heart captive in floral fetters by Him that hath two staves, beauty and bands."

"Oh, Ichabod, do not pause. Go on, I pray thee."

"Then thou art glad to hear that nature is not a beautiful widow mourning her dead bridegroom through the ages?"

"I love to listen to thee."

"Listen to a wiser. See those stately heliotropes. They stand above all of their kind with shining faces; great in aspiration, great in devotion. All day they turn toward the sun and when their blossoms fade they leave a hardy seed. The winter may bury it, but it springs forth in vernal days, strong in the life it won by loving the summer sun."

"Ichabod, I'm charmed! Let's abide here always amid these joys of nature."

"What, be hermits?"

"Yes; life's troubles are made by its people; the fewer people the fewer troubles."

"While sharing their troubles may we not lessen them. No man may live to himself; we're wedded to each other."

"Yes, wedded to life. A royal phrase; since I've

been constantly either hating or loving it; fearing to live and then fearing to die. Wedded! ah, ha, ha; the wedded are those who most madly love and then most bitterly hate."

"Say sometimes; then thou'lt be like the stopped horologue, telling the true time once in twenty-four hours, at least."

"Thy poetry runs into caustic quality. What hast thou been lunching on since morn?"

"At least not on Dead Sea apples, fair without, ashes within. My poetry, if I have any, always sings in accord with the company it keeps."

"How many more arrows in thy quiver, hast thou?"

"Only one, and that a question; does my master intend to foreswear marriage himself? He ridicules it."

"I have already done so."

"Well, 'tis well thou didst not live in Rome, for its citizens that dared to live amid the temptations and soul-crampings of voluntary bachelorhood were highly taxed for their disregard of the claims of society and the state."

"Yet even the Romans ever deemed bachelorhood a blessing. In this opinion royal Claudius decreed that the sailors who brought to Rome a ship loaded from the wheat graneries of Egypt in the time of Agabus's famine, should be as a reward permitted to remain unmarried. If I were a Roman and a sailor I'd pray for a famine and a Claudius."

"A world without wives? What a world!"

So saying Ichabod caught up a stick and began marking on the earth.

"How now, Israel; some sorcery?"

"No—yet, may be, yes. I'll picture a world without women."

The Jew outlined the Egyptian deity, "*Kneph*."

"What have we, man or beast?"

"Truly, I think partly both. The knight has described his Elysium and I have here pictured a fit king for it. Behold thy god, sworn celibate. Egypt's adored Kneph. Is this hideous enough?"

"A god! well he's not handsome; a ram's head; four horns; two up, two down; armed as both ram and goat?"

"Both were sacred to him in Egypt; also the horned snake with which Cleopatra put out her life; poor, unfortunate man-wrecked beauty."

"But, Jew, thou dost dawdle! What of this play?"

"Oh, nothing, only Kneph would do well for a sailor, at Rome, under Claudius, in famine time!"

"My poet wanders, but yet stings."

"So? Kneph was a god that boasted, or rather his spokesmen did, that he was the *father of his mother*. What economy! No need to be grateful to or love a mother; no need to wear a wife on the heart. The folly of a dark age by folly darkened in the mad attempt to lift up man without his purer better part."

"How strange, Jew, whenever we touch a new belief, or an old one, new to us, we find peoples following an idea or ideal. There has been a crying through the world ever for a some one for pilgrim man to follow. How passing strange; our century wails the self-same cry; and somehow it always happens that this matter has something to do with woman. See; '*Kneph*' was the monstrous birth of those who thought man superlative, and greatness to be by being all man. How sharply the devotion to the Madonna cuts across this! She was mother of the noblest, and man in the begetting left out. Oh, my head's full of thoughts, but they tumble along toward my lips without system or leader. I talk like a madman, though I think like a Seraph."

"I think, Sir Charleroy, that a healthy son of Adam sneering at all women, publicly, reproaches himself as being one who never knew a true one."

"More javelins! I'd swear, anyhow, that if I'd been Adam, no winged serpent of gaudy colors and honey tongue could have lured me from Paradise, Eve or no Eve!"

"If thou hadst been there thou wouldst have been lonesome with the speechless herds; finding the new woman, would have loved her like the boy who mates just to see how it seems."

"Oh, likely!"

"Then if thy ward or angel attempted to elope with the devil thou wouldst have gone along, too, from curiosity, as lad to a hippodrome, just to see the finish; or as thousands of men since Adam, tied to wayward women, have gone down with them to darkness, preferring hell with their idols to heaven without."

"I suppose so. Oh, how strangely are the fates of men and women interwoven."

"Then thou dost not now elect to live a hermit, without the companionship of the frail, fair and faithful sex which are said to double our joys?"

"Yes and multiply our sorrows!"

"I suspect thou'lt change thy late creed very soon."

"Why so?"

"I expect ere long that we'll meet some living blossoms."

"By my token, that's good news, Ichabod."

"So, then, thou art ready to recant?"

Evening came, and the pilgrims supped on the meager meat they were able to procure in the fields.

"Now poet of the Palm Land mellow my dreams by possessing me of thy meditations. What fixes thy gaze?"

"The monarch of the sky; after a day such as this has been, he seems to me to take his departure with a peculiar sort of triumphal sweep of his trailing splendors."

"Horus exulting over prostrate Set."

"But night, not the green-colored son of Osiris, conquers now, master."

"Night never conquers. It merely lives by sufferance; often routed by the invincible spears of the sun. Darkness creeps forth here because the golden charger in masterful strategy has gone elsewhere to rout other armies of the dark kingdom. Lay this to thy heart, good Jew.''

"I do, as precious ointment to a blister. Enlarge me.'

"There, Jew; see the fleecy clouds over Jordan. How grand!"

"Yea, as I've often seen them; some like alabaster thrones, and others like ships on fire, while others are like silver castles, banded with cornelian and gold, with here and there hyacinthian shields hung on their battlements, all fresh as the stones in heaven's foundations walls! How they career and float along the empurpled ocean of the west! I forget myself even now into their midst. Oh, knight, such pictures, such visions make my soul shout in peals of holy laughter."

"My Israel, the sun which woos the earth into making love to him with flowers never sets in thy brain; thou livest in the poet's constant noon."

"But we both are changing. Even the knight gets mellow. Hardship, the sun and faith are working in us both for good."

"Getting to be? No; thou wert and art poet, painter and singer; all in one. If the world does not hear thee the Seraphim will, by and by."

I've noticed that souls unbent from some long, twisting pain, run, aspire and play. It is mercy's rest, reward."

"God fits some especially to catch passing joys, Ichabod."

"Yea, and it all comes from a serene faith that all is very good as He made it. I'm just opening to the Sun Eternal, at whose right hand are pleasures evermore. I love thy wakening touch, my guide."

"Ah, I'm a bungling player on the harp of thy soul, but I love thy melody. Child of nature, speak more and more to me."

"I can but ill tell all. I'm dumb amid the waves of peace which enhalo, the hopes that thrill, the views of truth that fill my being."

"I believe thee on my soul, Jew. I'd stop now to remember a little, perhaps to sleep, since so I can follow dreams that would craze me to contemplate awake; but if we now sleep, pray God our day-dreams go on and on

I think we are pilgrims following spiritual truths. They'll lead us on high; let's not miss their direction."

"One may sleep, master, when he can not think; for me, now, I'd rather court, awake, my mind's guests, for a time, meanwhile gainsaying the lullabys of cricket and nightingale now floating out from every bush."

"So be it. How shall we proceed to pass the time?"

"Can we set up an Ebenezer? God hitherto hath helped us."

"I have it; we'll to the feast."

"Well, we have what some great kings have not, and so shall find joy in a feast. We have appetite!"

"Thou dost miss my meaning, though thy point is prime. We seldom think to thank the Giver for the power to enjoy as well as for the enjoyable. I knew a French prince, once, who said he'd give his birthright for one good dinner, and he was no Esau, either. He had dinners and dinners, but what were they along with premature decay gnawing at his vitals like a rat, while he himself could eat less than a babe?"

"I see; the knight would have us thankfully commemorate to-day's enjoyment of nature."

"Just so; I think, in loving nature, because we begin to understand her, we will be on our way to all the natural joy of which she is God's interpreter."

"But our feast?"

"The stars are out on the blue; their queen will soon come up from the sea, then I'll induct thee into the feast of the 'Rose.' The rose is the queen of flowers, and flowers the thoughts of God!"

"The feast of the Rose! I've heard it was a licencious, heathen orgy!"

"It was then a shameful misnomer. My Mary found it, transformed it. Out of it, through reverence of her, comes a beautiful observance. See here, Jew."

So saying, the knight took from his bosom a string of precious stones and arranged them, as they glowed under the moonlight, on the ground heart-shaped.

The knight then questioningly observed the Jew.

The latter shook his head and remarked:

"I've seen such often among the Arabs. They have a prayer for each bead to be said the night after the death of one of their number, believing the shade departs not to Hades 'till the prayers are said. Thou dost not practice their enchantments?"

"Bah! Never. My gemmed circle has a deeper, holier significance. Each pendant is to recall to mind some virtue or event in the saintly Mary's life. Then there are guilds called, 'Brothers of the Rosary.' I belong to one such; each member is sworn to pray for all the others wherever scattered. The Turks may have had a praying string, but the Crusaders have appropriated and applied it to nobler uses."

"Tell me more of it, if there be more."

"There are but fifteen in my brotherhood."

"Only fifteen, no room for me?" said the Jew.

"Fifteen; to suggest the fifteen great events in Mary's life; namely, the *Annunciation*; Gabriel announced to Mary that she was to be the Mother of Jesus; the *Visitation;* Mary in the Gospel spirit went quickly to tell her kinswoman of her promised favor; the *Birth of Jesus*, this was the crowning joy; then here is the gem that recalls the *Presentation of Jesus* in the Temple. Thou knowest, Jew, thy fathers often wondered how;

after all, a lamb, an animal, could stand between offended Deity and man. Jesus in the Temple was the fulfillment or explanation of the mystery!"

"Yea, truly, I've seen this. Oh, that all my people could also see it!"

"Then, here is the jewel that reminds us of the '*Scourging at the pillar*' of Him 'by whose stripes we are healed.'"

"Israel reads Isaiah with darkened mind, my loving guide. I've seen this. Oh, that my people could."

"Here is the jewel that recalls the '*Crowning with thorns*' of Him that hath to give, at His right hand, 'pleasures forever more.' He wore that thorny coronet that His redeemed should return with singing, crowned with everlasting joy."

"I've felt it; feel it now. Hallelujah!"

"This one is to commemorate '*Jesus bearing the Cross;*' this one '*His crucifixion*,' and this '*His resurrection.*'"

"The hope of hopes by our Saducees denied!"

"Then we have here another to remind us of our Saviour's '*Ascension*,' with His pregnant promise of a royal return to take at last His children home."

"Come, Lord Jesus, even so, quickly!" cried Ichabod.

"'Wait patiently for Him and He will give thee the desire of thy heart,' oh, heir of faithful Abraham!"

"I weary sometimes, my loved teacher."

"So do we, of our brotherhood; but here is a thought of rest; this bead recalls '*Pentecost*.' We are led of the Spirit, which guides to all truth and comforts by the way."

"But what has all this to do with Mary?"

"Oh, here are two beads; one reminds us of her '*Assumption*' into heaven, the other of her '*Crowning*.'"

"Was she crowned?"

"Yea, in heaven, for the Son of Mary promised to His faithful ones this exaltation; '*I appoint unto you a Kingdom as my Father hath appointed unto me*, ye which have continued with me in my temptation.' Surely, she that followed him from the pains of parturition, as an outcast, to the Cross and the sepulcher, CONTINUED!"

"I would I could have been there to enter the race for such crowning."

"'He hath made us kings and priests unto God; if we suffer we shall also reign with Him,' Jew."

"Hallelujah! would I could shout it to heaven; no, I do; but rather to all Jewry!" exclaimed the Israelite.

"John was only a 'voice crying in the wilderness,' as he thought, but he was heard at the palace and down the ages. Even now I voice his words in this lone place."

"Thou didst not tell me of the meaning of that black and red pendant," said Ichabod, interrupting.

"Oh, *Gethsemane*, Jesus, the intercessor for the world, 'who ever lives to intercede.' The black sign is of that."

"Then I've a Saviour in glory praying for me. Oh, this is balm and water to me! Why do I dare to think of myself as a poor Jew! God pity; no, forgive me! I, repining sometimes and yet defended in glory; honored by royal adoption, elected of God, called to kingship!"

"How we do go up and down; sometimes thou, sometimes I. Now I'm leading, awhile ago 'twas thou. Yea, we are all dependants; but this is healthful meditation, Ichabod, and thy confession rebukes me as well."

"Is this all of the feast?"

"Oh, no. Here are some tokens to remind us of Mary's life; so brief, so useful. See, here, five gems that remind us of the wounds of her son; her wounds as well, for the sword that pierced Him pierced through to her soul also. At each of these emblems we 'Rosary Brothers' repeat the Lord's Prayer. Last of all, reverently clasping this crucifix, we sacredly repeat the Apostle's Creed, the same as I taught thee at Jericho."

"I remember, as I do the water courses, when thirsty."

"What think'st thou of all this formality? Is it like the Arabic mummeries?"

"No, they are mocking devils, are they not?"

"I am not to judge of their sincerity, nor their needs, nor art thou."

"Master, I wish I could be a Rosary Brother. Methinks it would help my ambling faith sometimes, if I could touch a token."

"He above is all tender of baby faiths that can do no better than amble. Remember the words of thy own Hosea: 'I drew them with cords of a man, with bonds of love, I taught Ephriam to go; taking them by the arms; just as a mother teaches her babe to walk,' is it not?"

"Even so. Does the Rosary help some to walk?"

"I believe it does."

"Tell me more about it."

"The Crusaders were the first to call Mary 'The Rose.'

To almost all mankind that flower has ever been the emblem of pure, unselfish love, and when the soldiers of the Cross grew to understand the character of her that gave the world its Saviour, they could think of no title more fitting for that queenly woman."

"I've an Egyptian rosary, knight. See, I wear it on this golden chain, next my heart, for its safety——"

"To ward off witchcraft?"

"Bah! 'Tis a toy in usefulness. I keep it, thinking it may work incantation with the money-lender, and so save me sometime from starvation." Then the Jew laughed aloud at his own wit. It seemed very ridiculous to him to liken his talisman to the real rosary or its saint."

"Wouldst thou let me examine it, Jew?"

The latter handed to the knight a chain and image.

"Egyptian?"

"An image of Neb-ta, sister of Isis, the wife of the Sun God Osiris. It was given me by a Copt priest, whom I saved from drowning in the Nile."

"A Copt?"

"A Copt. He was a professed Christian; but, like some of the ancestral Egyptians, sought to be right by being a little of every thing. He was very superstitious, though he thought himself very broad-minded. He was quite certain that Coptic Christianity was true, though not equally certain that his pagan ancestors were in faith all false. He thought he'd be on the safe side by mixing a little of all creeds with his own, and so he prayed in Christ's name and also Neb-ta's."

"A pretty fool, Jew."

"Yea. He had a story about the goddess, very

pretty when not absurd, running somehow thus: When Osiris was cut to pieces by Set, a type of day slain by night, I think, Neb-ta went round the world with her widowed sister, Isis, to gather up the fragments of her spouse. Isis is the moon above; below, reproduction. She is pictured in Egypt, as all the female deities, with two eggs and a half-circle at the side, to express the latter idea. Isis has in her hand also this sign—a cross supporting an egg, to typify immortality. The old Egyptian priest told me this sympathetic Neb-ta, if I trusted her, would reward me for saving his life, by defending my case in Hades. There is a good deal of mysticism in all this, but I rather prize the gift, since it reminds me that I once saved a man."

"But, Nourahmal? Since thou knew of Mary thou hast saved a woman, Jew."

The Jew was silent. The knight continued:

"These philosophic, inseeing, sign-writing, symbol-making Egyptians were pilgrims, too; a nation of graal-seekers; after an idea, example. I see always the huge Sphinx coming before me when I think of them."

"The Sphinx! Well, that's strange. I'd never think of that, unless I happened upon something very big and very meaningless!"

"No, no; the people that rocked the cradle of religions in their infancy, wrought all their theology into that one mighty symbol, to endure and challenge compare with all that man should find beside."

"I do not see how!"

"The Sphinx faces the East—light!"

"True!"

"It can not reach that light toward which it looks, neither could the Nubians."

"All true."

"It was part man, part beast; but the upper part was man, and this is what we think we know, and all of man?"

"Oh, knight, Phthah, the 'beautiful-faced,' 'secret-opener' of the Nile gods has touched thee."

"The Sphinx was like man's thought; too great for words; at least such words as men can now fit to their lips."

"I see; it's all coming into my mind, master."

"It sat still and was silent, but the world went on; the thought it expressed reached hearts after the men that formed the image had passed away. The truth lives ever, and can not die until it completes its purpose."

"Thou art a magician, who pleases, astonishes, excites, instructs, and at the same time plays with me as if I were a pigmy!"

"It's not I, but the truth. The Sphinx again! Its hugeness, truth expressed, appears mighty when placed by our sides."

"Tell me where I am! Shall I fling Neb-ta away as a bauble, or beg its pardon for hanging so much meaning to a fool's neck?"

"Vehement! The sun is in thy head!"

"But shall I sit and look as a Sphinx, or run mad because I can't?"

"Be calm, and let me tell thee that the dwellers by the mighty Nile plagued themselves with lasting darkness when they banished the people whose leader's face shone from communion with Jehovah. They clung to some half truths, left them by the progeny of Joseph, but the half was dimmed by courted lusts."

"But my people had no Neb-ta, no women divinities to leave in Egypt."

"No, yet Egypt, aiming to exalt the tender, the beautiful, the mother, incarnated certain virtues, and lo, a woman deity! It was an effort to find the 'Rose.' The nation was in a vast, serious pilgrimage through all their dynasties after an idea, a pattern; an opportunity to reach and to express the best things. I tell thee, Jew, the heathen nations sit in darkness; this side and that, along the track of time, holding here and there a torch, waiting through the night whose hours are tolled off at century intervals, for something, Some One. There have passed before them like phantoms, gods and gods; man invented, man evolved; but none of these tarried, none satisfied. Oh, 'the Isles wait for thee,' Jesus, Thou Ideal Man, and also for the true conception of Mary the ideal woman!"

"For two Gods? Is Mary divine?"

"Did I say that? Nay, as the child Jesus was subject to her, so she was subject to the Christ, at last. Christ was the Word, Mary His blessed echo; Christ the Sun, Mary the Moon that reflected that light, showing its beauty in woman's life!"

"But now, what shall I do with my beautiful fright, Neb-ta, Sir Charleroy?"

"Put her away, in mind, amid the galaxies of woman deities; mythical in all but the pitiful sincerity of the adoration of their devotees and in the greatness of the truths they vaguely articulated. See, I'll interpret: Isis going round the world to gather up the fragments of her dismembered husband. Woman's ministry; the restoration of man; wife consecration to an only love. Then there was not only beautiful widowhood, second only to beautiful wifehood, but also the spinster sister. Hail Egypt! Thy Sphinx saw further than our peoples of boasted civilizations. At our best we never rose so near to a just altitude as to attempt the deification of the maiden sister, the omnipresent angel, who mothers other people's children as if they were her own. Egypt worshipped motherhood, perhaps grossly, in adoring the earth's fructifications, but she did not overlook those pious souls who in a glorious self-abnegation play waiting-maids to the real queens of earth, the child-bearers. I'd never tire praising the child-bearers, or all who love them, for they that bring forth a life are greater than the greatest kingly man-slayer on earth. The world is upside down; no religion is wholly false that aids to right it in any degree. Hail, creeds of Egypt, or any other land, that seek to efface from fame's pages the names of life-destroyers that thereon may chiefly shine the names of those who give or save life."

"Oh, oscillating Sir Charleroy, thou art just and courtly now."

"Praise me, then! Mankind would average better by far than it does if all were right half the time."

"Would I could gather all the threads of to-day's blessed communings into a golden band to support over my heart faith's breastplate."

"I can give thee its summary: God, a beauty Creator, out of all things hideous in His good Providence will emerge the fine, tender and loving. Neb-ta, Egypt's ideal, carried the lotus, the flower of unrestrained pleasure, as her scepter; Neb-ta-like the influences that sway most human hearts to-day; but the Rose of the world has blossomed. Mary, the flower of women. They that love and serve, as that warm, red-hearted woman, shall at last reign in eternal bliss within the ruby walls of the New Jerusalem."

"I'm with the knight, to proclaim thy Rose!"

A good profession! It will be well if we remember that woman is as essential to religion as religion to women. As for man he needs the one as the interpreter of the other. Therefore, it was that God sent to earth a flower that could talk."

CHAPTER X.

AFTER EVE, ESTHER OR MARY?

" Still slowly passed the melancholy day,
And still the stranger wist not where to stray:
The world was sad—the Garden was a wild;
And man, the hermit, sighed—till woman smiled."
—MILTON.

HE Israelites, along Jabbock, were all aglow with preparation for celebrating one of their feasts. Sir Charleroy and his comrade journeying along, in the early morning, were apprised of the advent of the festivities by the passing near them of a company of maidens, marching and chanting. The pilgrims drew apart and sequestered themselves behind a clump of nubt trees that they might observe, themselves unobserved, the graceful processsion of singers.

"Well, my poet, didst thou conjure up these fairies, or have we come on the musk-born houri?" Sir Charleroy spoke in an absent-minded manner, perhaps, with an affectation of a lack of very much interest. In fact, long privation of the presence of women had somehow rusted from his bearing, in their vicinage, most of the confident courtier. In a word, he was now bashful in their presence. He spoke with a small witticism to subdue, his own embarrassment. His words were unheard, for the Jew was all engaged in contemplating the passing women.

In truth, the latter made a striking picture; garbed as they were, in holiday attire; all young, oriental in beauty, and fresh in face, form and action. They were rural maidens and that says all. It had been a long time since either Ichabod or Sir Charleroy had met such types of womanhood; all free from affectation; all natural and graceful in motion; a band of women, as sisters, bent to one purpose and that a lofty one, the proper observance of a joyous, pious, religious ceremonial.

Presently Ichabod drew a long breath and rapturously exclaimed: "Praise be to the Patriachs, my people!"

"I'd rather say, Ichabod, praise the Patriarch's daughters, if these be human!"

"Ha, ha! flesh, indeed! Our Hebrew maidens celebrating the Feast of Esther!"

"Are they praying God for Adams, so that each Esther and Vashti may have one all to herself? If so, we are part answers to their prayers."

"Hush such jest! These be holy maidens, now honoring our Esther. Thou knowest about her?"

"Certainly; she was my heroine before Our Lady dethroned in my heart all others. I was wont to wish I'd been about in Haman's time. I'd have aroused that old dotard, Ahasuerus, right quickly. By the sackcloth of Mordecai, if I'd been the king, the hanging would have put the Haman family into mourning long before it did."

"Oh, how like angels! It's years since I saw a woman other than as deflowered by harem life. Heavens, what a spoiler man is at his worst!"

"Dost forget Nourahmal? But no matter; I admire, and wonder that some roving band of Arabs, with less piety, or more force than we, does not swoop down upon these innocents for seraglio prizes. Perhaps these have the liveried angels about, that are said ever to guard saintly purity."

"Doubtless; and besides them, with all the practical providence which belongs to the Jew, thou mayst be sure that the groves, not far away, are full of fathers, brothers, lovers."

"I wish I were a brother to some of them."

"Then thou'dst be a Jew."

"I'd forget that in being a lover to the others."

"Thou wouldst not change thy faith for a woman?"

"Now, I'd swear I would not. If like most men, and in love, I'd swear I would; and then, having gotten my new priestess, in a little while, backslide and drag her with me, or make her heart weep. My comfort in the last estate being my consistency, if not my constancy. What a mad rout it is when religion and love, born twins, cross purposes?"

"That's a very true, yet bitter speech. I'll tell the Hebrew maidens to beware."

"Better tell me to beware, now. It's the beginning that makes the trouble. No beginning, then no after folly."

The procession glided past and the pilgrims followed at a distance.

"We are within an arm of dear old Jabbock," remarked Ichabod, as they came to a river-bank, later.

"Ah, ha! my chartless pilot, does the current whisper its name to thee, in Hebrew? I'd not wonder if it did, since every thing is clannish in this country.—I hope there is no more swimming for us to do."

"Its tumbling waters are full of voices to me, blending with echoes of things of the past; but one who spoke a thousand times more tenderly than ever spoke murmuring waters, told me its name, knight."

"Nourahmal? No! rather some one of those pious beauties we passed not long ago. Oh, roguish Ichabod, I remember thou wert away a long time in the morning after our breakfast of peas and grapes. But, dear Ichabod," continued Sir Charleroy, feigning rebuke, "didst thou so soon forget thy little convert of Jericho? I wonder if thou lifted up thy voice and wept when thou kissed the maid that told thee the river's name? Come, confess, and I'll call thee Isaac."

"Raillery of prime quality, knight; but raillery and ridicule, though keenly pointed, are generally bad arrows for long range."

"Well, no matter. I'm glad thou knowest the place, if thou dost know it. Who told thee the name of this water?"

"One with a voice to me sweeter, kinder than that of any betrothed lover's ever can be."

"Very, very eloquent thou art. Indeed, if we were in Italy, I'd guess 'twas a syren had communed with thee; in France, a Crusader troubadour; in Rhineland, the water sprite, Lurline; but, being in this wondrous country of revelations, apparitions, prophets, angels and the like, I can only as a catechumen, ask thy dulcet informer's name?"

"How oddly thou dost talk when thou talkest as a double man; half sneering infidel; half Christian preacher."

"A truce, Ichabod. That may be a home-thrust well aimed, but it's enough that one of us be bitter. It's sometimes natural to me, but not to thee."

"A bee-sting will redden the high priest's brow."

"Well, I'll not sting thee. Who gave the name of the river?"

"Master, one to me alone of all the world an angel, my mother. I was born near here, and the memories of a youth made happy by one all patient, all loving, rises above and survives all changes."

"My noble friend, forgive my repartee. I'm glad, truly, that we are so lucky as to have this knowledge."

"Lucky? Then all is not fate; there is some chance, if no Providence?"

"Pardon more; the bee-sting is still on thy brow. Ichabod, I can not help my feelings, which sometimes make me think that only God can tread the hidden, narrow line between stern fate and happy accident. They say the Sybil wrote her prophetic decrees upon leaves and flung them recklessly to the inconstant winds. Just so we're in decreed courses, swirled by chance gusts."

"Yet we two are getting on well together."

"So do chance and fate; the pity is to the waif that falls between them."

"I wonder how here, in Holy Land, thou canst think of any control but Providence."

"Wonder? So do I. I'm a bundle of wonderings."

"Listen to Jabbock."

"I do, more attentively than Jabbock to me. What of it?"

"Grander rivers are forgotten; why is it so remembered?"

"We're forgotten, meaner men remembered."

"This river sings through the centuries of history the song of a fugitive of pale heart, who in sheer desperation, long, long ago, seized a fleeting hope and became a prince, having power to prevail with God."

"Ah, Jacob, who worked fourteen years to win a woman. It was, I'm sure, the woman that nerved him to attempt greatness. Such a woman! Had she been like our moderns she would have jilted him, or eloped with him, before the end of one of the fourteen years."

"I'll not tilt with thy sarcasms. It were much better to remember that he, a pigmy, the night in his soul, as that about him, black as Erebus, grappled with the mighty, unknown, unseen apparition to find he was holding Deity. The mysteries of crossing fates and chances are as open nut-bur compared to that of all weakness prevailing with Omnipotence, my good master, I think."

"But ever after that joust, Jacob was a cripple!"

"Oh, but remember, as he halted on his thigh the sun rose over Penuel, 'the place of seeing God,' by interpretation. He was stronger for his laming!"

"A very 'Timor-lame,' this prince of great chances and mean ways."

"Time and trial repaired Jacob's spotted soul."

"There was much room for the mending, I do vow."

"His weightings bespeak some charity. Think; a weak mother, one designing wife, and plenty of wealth!"

"Well, 'tis true, these were enough to have undone St. Anthony, if the devil had only thought to have tried them all at once upon him!"

"Sir Charleroy swings back to his old bitterness toward women; did he never love one?"

"No, not as a lover. I was never tried except by designing coquetries that nauseated finally."

"Perhaps, like most solitary men, thou so revered thyself by habit that there was no room for other person in thy heart."

"I never met one I deemed perfect and available."

"Better to have loved some one far from perfect than none. If thy heart-fount had been once touched it would have set thy imaginations to weaving halos about the one touching. Thou wouldst have enthroned her by a love that would have transformed both. She would have become in time what she was in love's young dream; while thou wouldst have grown by the experience to be twice the man thou hadst been—or art."

"The sun in thy head is settling down into thy heart, Jew."

"Is that so, Charleroy?"

"Yes, but not to harm; heart sunsets ripen heart fruits; that's the reason the autumn suns run low; the low suns ripen. But after all, I'm not so very miserable in heart. I've loved some women; mother and my Mary——"

"Filial love, religious love! somewhat akin and blessing him that feels their mellow, exalting influences;

but, oh, Sir Charleroy, they do not fill completely the heart's temple. There are places there for the expression of ruddy, glorious lover's love. The three make up an all-comprehending trinity, and fill the man as Deity the universe. I see religious love in adoration of God's Fatherhood, mother love in the tender leading of the Spirit, lover's love in the priceless self-surrender of our Saviour. That made the angels sing, and in the being of each of our race there is room, aye need, of the melody which only the experiencing of this passion in full can produce. In love-mating is a wondrous thrill which can be but faintly voiced even by those who have experienced it.

"There are other passions which ebb with time, or, being well fed, wax gross; not so with this one. Inspired by the potencies of life, which lie at the very core of being, it wells up in rills, rivers and torrents of pleasurable sensations. Out from the heart it goes to the remotest members, only to double on its courses and dash again through the beating heart, heating its flame by its doubling and hasting, making the beatings wilder by its hastings, and then hasting more because of the wilder beatings. Of all emotions love is the most tireless. It increases by giving, grows stronger by action and proclaims the secret of its heavenly birth, its immortality, by the way in which it deepens and ripens with every movement of its life. Aye, more, it proclaims itself the power of the resurrection by the way it transforms the lives it possesses. A man may be a lout, ever so crude in fiber, but this musical flame passing through his being, burns up his dross, making him all brave, courteous, tender, poetic, religious! Yea, religious! If it do not utterly redeem a sinner possessed by it, it will take him nearer to salvation than any other power known on earth, except the Spirit of Grace. It is as the opening of the eyes of the blind man, for it opens the doors of a new sense to the realizing of a world as new as delightful. As the thrummings on the harp-strings someway leave a lasting sonorousness and tenderness in the supporting woods about the lyre, so leaves this passion, through the beatings of every wave of it, wealth. Its devotee by it is inducted into exhaustless new realms and possessions, unalterably secured to him, and at the same time beyond all computation. He ever gathers treasures, as a prince from incoming fleets, and is made affluent beyond all counting. He surpasses all in wealth-getting, and yet is infinitely apart from the littleness of avarice. It is to him the advent of charity's full-orbed day. It may be fancy in him, but it's to him very real; the world about, as if having learned his secret, seems to be dressing for the wedding feast, while all things appear to be coming very confidentially to him to whisper the divine mandate, 'marry and multiply.' He is trusted, yet trusts; leads, yet follows. He is proud to display, a little, his conquest, but does so with a sort of alert charming selfishness, which gives notice to the world that he alone is to wear the chosen one upon his heart. He realizes the paradox of giving all and receiving all; the mystery of two lives merged into one by an utter surrender, each to each, which leaves both infinitely richer than the sum of all their ownings could make either if possessed by the one apart from the other. Oh, how almost imperiously each demands that the other shall surrender all and then how great the joy each feels in leading the chosen mate to surprises at the munificence and completeness of the giving up of all by the one who just now demanded all! I do not know the woman's heart, but can readily believe it far surpasses the man's in its consecration, enjoyment and aspiring. I know the man's, but my words are ragged in description. I know that this grand passion makes him wondrously weak and wondrously strong. Sometimes these inner feelings come nigh overwhelming him; sometimes they fall upon his life like the musical ebb-waves on resonant shores. I can not word it all, nor is it strange, since I am speaking of a life of heavenly flights, and best expressed by voiceless signs, embraces. In love's hour the man realizes, as never before, his lordliness and his pride and ambition are fed by a growing conviction that all the world is small beside himself and his; proud as a conqueror of untold wealth, he yields to the tender ties that unrelentingly bind him and crucifies his native roughness that he may be more like, more worthy her he rules and obeys. He is made finer; she stronger. Has she virtues, he appropriates them; at the same time, by the homage implied by his appropriation, makes them to shine more brightly on the brow and heart of his queen. He touches the fires on the altar she has erected within herself to love alone, and the altar-fires blaze until her whole being is illuminated as a temple on fête days. She puts on his best parts, and then he revels in delight as he beholds his virtues refined and so beautifully framed. There are times when, like a mighty anthem, his passion passes over and through him. Then is he nigh to madness, being in the mood to slay himself, or another doing aught to check the rapture of the mighty swellings of the music that pours over every nerve from head to heart, to limb. Then it is he embraces and kisses and embraces again; as an inspired artist of music, exhausting himself to prolong this joy, almost materialized. Indeed, I saw one who said 'this is tangible music. I feel it; taste it; see it! It seems to thicken the air until I rise unwinged, and yet in a flight that seems to me as free and brilliant as that of the golden oriole's. If the enchanted enchanter be pure and true, she leads her captive king, made tender and yet more manly by his captivity, surely upward from tumultous passion's sway to the ambrosial table-lands of higher affection where both may reign tenderly, bravely, hopefully, forever. I tell thee, knight, the finest spectacle on earth is a man in his prime, creation's lord at his best, sincerely, completely in love with a queenly woman. Next after getting God into a man's heart, the greatest blessing is the getting of a woman of genuine parts therein."

"Oh, child of the sunny palm land, thou hast imbibed wondrous eloquence. But thou sayest truly. Now, for the women that are so to queen us men. No woman that I ever knew of could so intoxicate, transform and translate me."

"One like Eve, the gift of God?"

"The first woman, like the first man, was pure without virtue, until tried; then she fell. I think of her chiefly as being a splendid animal, yet, as Adam was not left for man's example, neither was she. I still think Eve passed by in history to be only what she was full proof that love which rises no higher than to give all to and for that which was like the fruit of the tempting tree, good for food and pleasant to the eyes, is not like the love that at last hung on the tree of Calvary. Oh, child of Abraham, I hear the '*voice of God walking in the garden in the cool of the day*,' saying to a world of flitting, false ideals, and those yearning for pilots and patterns, '*Where art thou?*' I don't know, for one, exactly where I am, but I'm going forward and upward someway."

"Sir Charleroy thou dost dazzle me by thy correspondences and insights, if I do thee by my pictures. We are quits."

"But we'll not quit. This pilgrim idleness has value. I never knew what I believed until, thus flung out of life's hurly burly, I had little company but my thoughts. There was method of reason in God's taking His prophets to lone places, to fit them for understanding the rapturing visions with which He filled them."

"'Tis so, true; but what thinks the knight of Esther, the beautiful Queen? She's the idol and ideal in Israel in all times and places."

"Wondrous woman! A girl, petted, ill-trained, from poverty suddenly exalted, surrounded by the skilled intriguants of court, a jealous, exacting, conceited, harem-demoralized old king for a spouse, she was then burdened with the salvation of a nation. I've so pitied her that I've forgotten to admire how well she did in her trying lot."

"Can the world ever have a finer figure or presentment of all that is womanly? I do not challenge thy Mary, but may I not put the two side by side?"

"Israel has two great women in their way. The one, Esther, exemplifying all sweetness and the mild strength of a suddenly developed woman, doing grandly in one emergency when great peril and great love aroused her from only being an entrancing, petted beauty, to be the heroine of an hour. But she was not tried by the searching test of a lifetime. She never meets the needs of mothers seeking an ideal. Rizpah, your other grand woman, was the mother, even the mother of sorrows, of the Old Testament. It takes these two to make an ideal, and yet the pattern is incomplete. God walks yet in the garden where men live, with only these two before them, and ever and anon they hear the unanswerable, '*Where art thou?*'"

"Why, my mentor, master, thou hast touched our Scriptures with the rod that budded; the whole opens to me as if for the first time. Methinks, if I were permitted to lay hands now upon one of our sacred volumes, I'd be fairly overcome by the light that would break out on me from within it."

"'The entrance of the word giveth light,' Ichabod."

"I'm moved, master, along lines I can not turn from, to the one woman of all, Mary. She is thy ideal queen of hearts?"

"I'm a pilgrim and follow her, seeing none better."

"Then thou wouldst be willing to wed such as Mary?"

"Hold! This is sacrilegious! I'll not think of Mary in any such comparison. Leave my patron saint upon her high pedestal. I save her for my soul's health, as every man should save some noble woman, for an inner enshrining, to be all that woman may be at her best, his beloved, his inspirer, and yet touching no spring of his life save such as responds to things of moral grandeur."

"Ah, master, I've not yet been enamored fully of this woman. I feel a stranger to her, but I feel the meaning of the finer things thou hast just spoken. I have the need of which thou dost speak, and my life, like a babe, often now goes out crying, 'Mother, mother.' As we lay, yesterday night, beneath the quiet firmament, I gazed up and asked a sign of God in prayer. It was a baby cry I know, but I saw one star that staid and staid above me. It seemed to be warmed with reddish tintings, and I thought that its glitterings were proof that it was taking part in some anthem of the morning stars. Then I dreamed that my mother was in the star all luminous, holy, happy, looking down in constant guardianship of her outcast boy! Oh, can a child ever be outcast utterly to mother? Can it be that she, who so loved me and so loved God, can hate me now, loving her and loving God as I do? God knows my heart! Will he not tell her all? Her constant mandate to me was, 'keep a loyal heart, an undefiled conscience.' I've tried to do both, but then her soul loathed apostacy. Does she loathe me for leaving Israel's fold? My heart all torn, cries to-day, 'Mother, mother!' I'm sure she can not hate me. To-morrow I hope I shall pray at her grave."

Then the vehement Israelite fell on the ground in an ecstasy, utterly unconscious of his companion, and, kissing the earth as if already he was by that parent's resting place, wildly called, "Mother! my mamma! oh, I'm so lonely, so unhappy! Let me come! God, God, let me go to mother! Mother, I did it as thou midst. I'm no leper. I'm not a heretic! I love thee. I love God. I've kept pure. I've trusted God's care in all my trouble. Mamma, my mamma, let Ichabod embrace thee!" Exhausted and quivering he there lay. The knight was silent. It was holy ground, and the whole thicket about seemed to be glowing with the fire that burns without consuming.

The travelers were encamped again under the sky, and it was now night. A shooting star sped through the constellation of Orion and fell down toward the Dead Sea.

"An omen, Jew."

"Explain, brother knight."

"Life; bright, short, ending in gloom."

"Look at the fixed stars."

"They preach fate."

"Perhaps, but they have the majority. Few fall; I think, too, Someone holds them."

"Thy hopefulness colors thy faith."

"Thy murmurings run toward final madness, knight; the Rabbis, good men, so taught me."

"If one star falls may not all? If Providence hold them, why does one escape?"

"Thou hast heard that the giant Orion having lost his eyes, afterward regained his sight by turning his sockets toward the rising sun; that meteor we saw shot through the constellation Orion. Look up."

"A happy simile and pungent thrust, Jew."

"He that sent the lightnings to show us our way out of dread Jericho, most likely now commissioned some angel to swing a meteor across the sky as a torch or beacon for our guidance. The trail of flame teaches me that God is writing His royal signature on some great message."

"This world is too vast and too thronged with insignificants, such as we, for such especial carings on God's part. There are too many kings, too many shepherds, too many follies for Him to constantly watch any one or two."

"Backward, forward; now good, now bad. What a charging, changing knight! Pray God to get thee right and then fix thee."

Their converse was interrupted by a prolonged trumpet blast, echoing from hill to hill. Sir Charleroy sprang to his feet and clasping his sword hilt, cried eagerly, "We're ambuscaded!"

"No, by the glory of God, 'twas the temple call! How grand it sounds away in this wilderness!"

"No, no, Jew, I've heard that call; this one had six responses."

"Twas echo's magic! Didst thou not notice how the sound spread as it traveled in a sort of sheet of melody? Then it rose and fell from low hill to high. One blast; seven responses. Nature proclaiming against fate and chance; the covenant number."

"I'm not so confident that it's a miracle; what if it were some Mamelukes or Druses, planning one of their pious immolations of heretics with us for the victims?"

"Nay, brother, It's '*Purim*'; that feast is now due, and always begins at early starlight. I know it. Come, I'll put it to the proof."

"Hold; poets are more rash than knights in a

charge, but not so skillful in retreat! Whither wouldst thou?"

"I'll spy out the trumpeters and report."

"Not alone. I'll go, too. This camp will care for itself if they beyond be friends; if enemies, why then, without consulting us, they will care for all we have. But this," said the knight, toying with his sword, "was blessed by a priest to preach to infidels."

CHAPTER XI.

THE FEAST OF PURIM.

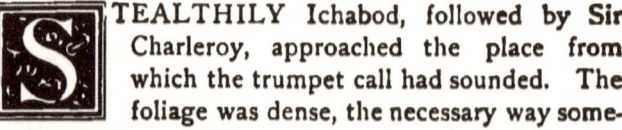TEALTHILY Ichabod, followed by Sir Charleroy, approached the place from which the trumpet call had sounded. The foliage was dense, the necessary way somewhat winding, and these circumstances, together with the fact that it was expedient to move with great caution, made the progress of the explorers very slow. The last ray of day had faded, sung away by the evening bird and insect chorusers, whose concert strains, like the vanishing notes of æolian harps swept by dying breezes, were now blending, without a line to mark the place of transition, into the lull of the night. Nature's lullaby to tired, drowsy life. It was a witching hour in the woods, and the scene that lay just beyond the pilgrims in an opening by Jabbock was an enchantment. The river, reflecting the moon rays and the lights of torches borne by many intermingling feasters, flowed silently along like a stream of mingled silver and fire, while tree and shrub along its sides, as green as green could be, bore as fruits lights of many colors. In the opening, surrounded by beacons, banners and the lamp-bearing trees, the beauty as well as the center of all was a magnificent patriarchal tent, made of costly materials. About the pavilion were mounds of earth, elevated upon high tripods, seven

in all, in symbols of the seven temple candle-sticks. On each mound there blazed a fire fed by resinous faggots, and the lights of the fires falling upon the folds of the tent, caught up here and there by bands of blue and gold, made the whole glisten like jeweled silk.

"Hallelujah," with suppressed joy, exclaimed Ichabod, "the tabernacle of God with men!"

"Hush, rash man, and watch!" rebukingly replied Sir Charleroy.

"Watch? Why, my soul is in my eyes. I'm as one famished for years smelling a feast!"

As they looked on the beautiful scene, they perceived that the front of the pavilion was lifted up and stretched forward as a canopy over an altar, richly decorated with twined olive branches and blood-red blossoms. A little way off, and yet partly encircling the altar, were little walnut trees, each tree having on its branches glistening lamps, half hidden by wreaths of hollyhocks and asters.

The moon sank behind the hills; the night darkened, but the fires and lamps burned still more brightly.

"It's like fairy-land, Jew," after little, spake Sir Charleroy.

"More beautiful, knight. Wait and see."

There was a burst of music, instantly followed by the entrance of youths and old men; some singing, others vigorously playing ugabs, reed-flutes, and tambourines. Somewhere near, though unseen by the watchers, were happy women; they recognized their voices in refrains, choruses, and merry peals of laughter.

"Well, this is not warlike, but what is it, Jew?" queried Sir Charleroy.

"Wait a little."

There came a commanding trumpet blast. Its tones died away in the melody-waves of a score of viols, managed by unperceived musicians. Then silence; presently the huge blue curtain that hung across the tent, just back of the outstretching front canopy, parted, and there emerged an aged man of stately form, wearing an Aaronic mitre and priestly robes; rich as well as ample. He paused before the altar a moment, as if in prayer, and then suddenly the air far and wide quivered with a sound like a cyclone hail. There were also cornet blasts mingling therewith.

"Heavens, Jew, explain!"

"Selah! These the drums and waking clappers; the signal to be given. Now for 'Purim' in earnest."

The groves about seemed to be alive and moving, for from every direction toward the center gathered men and boys, bearing palm branches and torches; these, as they advanced, moved with speeded pace, presently they were in a perfect maze, the music of every kind growing louder and louder, then seeming to die away.

"They're carrying the edicts of Ahasuerus to the Jews to defend themselves, master."

"A fine play, Jew!"

Now the blue curtain parted again, and from the pavilion emerged another stately form, in all except that he lacked priestly robing, the very counterpart of the aged man first at the altar.

"Glory to Shaddah! again I see the holy brothers, Harrimai," cried Ichabod.

The second patriarch motioned silence; all in the assembly bent their heads in breathless attention and the patriarch spoke: "Brethren of Israel, hearken and give God all the glory who this hour permits us, His chosen people, to celebrate in peace, with joy, our glad Purim feast. This day, Jehovah granted me the most wholesome comfort of hearing from a pashaw of our scourge that the last of the armies of the Moslem, beaten by want and internal discord, were melting out of our land like fog banks before the rising sun. He certified to me for a handful of barley (for which he had come to stand in need) that those hated cross-bearing invaders, the knights, were gone, never to return. So God has worked in our behalf as in the days of Esther, setting our enemies to destroying one another and then compassing the slinging out of His holy places, the abominable remnants. So may His thunders, as of old, forever beat on the heads of all who lift themselves against our Israel!"

There was a murmur of applause; first like the buzz of the noonday insects of the groves, then like a careering hurricane. The applause swelled up, drowning all sounds, causing the fires to flicker and flame, making the pavilion's sides sway and wave as if all were feeling the joy present. The musical instruments quickly now caught up the strain of the cheery voices, and all was in a perfect whirl of excitement with one thought, 'praise.' It was free and fluent, because it came from hearts practiced in the ultimate swings from joy to sorrow and then from sorrow to joy. For half an hour nearly, the rhapsody continued, nor did it temperate until sheer exhaustion fell on the revelers.

Presently, after an interval of comparative quiet, there came a flourish of cornets and a roar of the rattling clappers. It was a signal followed by the uplifting of the old priest's hands as if in benediction. All heads were bowed; some of the congregation knelt, and then he spoke in sonorous, yet soothing voice, words of benediction: "Blessed art thou, Oh Lord our God, King of the Universe, who hath wrought all miracles for our fathers and also for us, at this time."

Then the people stood up, and the second patriarch, advancing to the front of the altar, began reading from the holy *Kethubim* of the Jews, the story of the Purim. At each mention of Esther's name the congregation murmured "how beautiful is goodness;" at each mention of Haman's name all in the congregation stamped their feet, also making gurgling noises with their throats, to imitate the false prince's strangling; the whole being made more hideous by the shriek of discordant cornet notes and the springing of rattles.

The foregoing scene suddenly changed; a procession of maidens, in graceful evolutions, emerging from the surrounding groves, presenting a living picture, really entrancing. They were all richly robed in garments of graceful flow, caught round their waists by flowered girdles. Some wore sashes of jassamine, while others were crowned with lillies or asters or violets. Their arms and ankles were clad only with circlets from which pendant bells gave forth music at every motion. Seven of the foremost maidens bore lamps; behind each of these followed one with a harp; behind each harper two with tambourines and cymbals. Seven times this maiden train, with a step in time, half march, half dance, waltzed around the canopied altar. Then were given seven cornet blasts, the procession leaders waving their lamps with each blast, after which there was perfect silence. Now the old

priest moved forward a little toward the procession;
the congregation meanwhile gathering in a semi-circle,
just outside of all, and he addressed the assembly:
"Brethren and children, I would speak to you a little
of the 'Virtuous Woman.' Daughters of Israel, hearts
of homes to be, hopes of the nation looking for a Deliverer and deliverers yet to be born; hear me! Israel
knows no queen of all womanly perfections like unto
Esther, the beautiful. Evermore take her for your
meditation by day and your dreams by night. Then
shall you all realize to yourselves, your fathers, brothers, husbands, all that the holy Proverbs of our *Kethubim* declares of the true woman. Then the priest taking the parchment, solemnly and in mellow tones, read
the last chapter of the book, 'the birth-day chapter,' a
verse prophetic for every day of the longest month, as
the Jews believe."

When the reader ceased, the encampment was dim,
many of the lights having been quenched. Then the
congregation joined in chanting a soft-aired Jewish
hymn.

"The devotions are ended; now for the sports;" so
spoke Ichabod; the first words spoken between him and
the knight during their observation of the last part of
the proceedings before the pavilion. He had scarcely
made the announcement when the second patriarch appeared, dressed in somber black, leading by the hand
a maiden of wondrous beauty, wearing also black, in
heavy trails; on her head a golden crown. As they
appeared the applause as at first burst forth, but now
blended with distinguishable cries of "Hail Esther!"
"Hail Mordecai!"

"It's the play, knight. Watch that pair."

"No fear, Jew, such a wondrous beauty! Had I been Haman and she Esther, I never could have crossed her. Heavens, Jew, it is well said the people of promise produce the most beautiful women of earth. That's why Deity elected one of them, through whom to be incarnate, I think."

"I think I heard the knight say, awhile ago, that the revolution of all religions was to come when men's admiration for women rose far above rapture over outward form. Is it not so?"

"Ah, it's thy remembering and my forgetting that keeps us crossing each other! But no matter; am I looking at an angel or not?"

"That's the priest's only daughter; his idol, ay, the idol of every youth in all these parts of Israel. No nation can be dead while it produces such flowers."

Suddenly the camp blazed with re-illumination, and then began a carnival. Games and dancers were everywhere. Some, evidently men, were dressed as women, and others, evidently women, were garbed as men. For one season, Purim, the command against the interchange of garments between the sexes, was suspended. Each reveler carried a little box. If he asked a favor or a question, the reply was a challenge to try lots. Partners were so chosen, tasks given and predictions made. Laughter was everywhere, and wine was flowing.

"Ichabod, I haven't tasted wine since Acre! Why dost thou not introduce me yonder?"

"Wait; they will all be mellow, soon. They may be, too, for it's a law that a Jew is not deemed drunk at '*Purim*' so long as he can discern between a blessing for Mordacai and a curse for Haman."

"Heavens! how they do imbibe."

"It's natural for doves to twitter after a thunder storm. They remember the past troubles."

"Ay; but I fear they will consume all the beverage before we are with them. We have had plenty of trouble; now take me in to twitter with those doves."

Ichabod started, as if to lead the way, and then drew back and moaned, " no, no; it cannot be. I'm forever anathema here, to them! I could bear their hate, not their contempt. They may call me renegade, but never spaniel nor hypocrite! If I appeared among them they would soon know, if they do not already, that Ichabod is changed. Then they'd sneer and tell me that I tried to play double, or thinking my people's faith not good enough for me, I yet hungered for their feasts. No, no; it must not be! To-morrow, I hope to pray at my mother's grave. I'd choke then if I had to remember I'd done aught that she, living, would have thought mean."

"Now, I'll not persuade thee, Jew, but go alone."

"That's reckless! thou mayst regret it. They may become riotous, being half drunk, and beat thee as a Haman. No, stay away."

"No dissuasion, Jew, but just change garments. It's the fashion to-night." The Jew complied, remarking as he did:

"Will the knight wear this leather thong?"

"Heavens! no, nor the brand on thy neck."

"Christian knights commanded me to wear one, and burned into my flesh the other years ago ; they deemed it necessary to mark all Jews for hatred."

"Dear Ichabod, I never counseled branding any man!"

"I believe it. I have forgotten all bitterness about these marks and have borne them as my cross.

But, Sir Charleroy, don't wear thy cross in their sight!"

"For once, I'll cover it." So saying he hid the emblem.

The comrades parted, and Sir Charleroy quickly found himself by the maiden who personated Esther. He approached unnoticed until he pleasantly said: "Queen of Shushan, a man out there behind a clump of Sharon roses, played me a game of lots. I lost the game, and he has put it on me to come to the Queen to fix the forfeit I shall pay." The maiden turned her head haughtily and examined the speaker from head to foot with repelling gaze. It was her way of freezing off the amorous swains who constantly aimed to pay her court. But when her eyes met those of the self-possessed stranger, she gave a little start. Perhaps she caught sight, by some omen, of her fate; perhaps she felt the magnetism of the strong will which for the first time presented itself. In any event, it was the first time she had ever been alone, face to face, with such as he; a stalwart man, all reverential, yet all self-possessed. They were well matched, and they both felt it, intuitively, instantly.

"Who art thou?"

"A child of God.".

"Of Israel?"

"By faith, most holy of Abraham's seed," responded Sir Charleroy.

"Thy speech bewrayeth thee as lacking our shibboleth."

"I've been a life long wanderer. Thou wouldst not reject one whom involuntary exile had robbed of tokens?"

"But I can not be free with an uncertified stranger. I'm afraid I err in tarrying here 'till now."

"Hospitality is the boast of pious Hebrews who obey Him that 'loveth the stranger in giving him food and raiment.' Thou hast the Great Father's law: 'Love ye therefore the stranger, for ye were strangers in the land of Egypt.' Some have by hospitality unawares entertained angels, thou knowst."

"I'd like to entertain an angel; are they ever so human-like as thou?" she smiled.

"Had I known the Esther of to-night long enough to convince her that my freedom was sincere, I'd say that she was a fine example of the union of the angelic in the human."

The maiden laughed. The insense was agreeable, and the freedom of this feast-time justified her acceptance of this novel, bold flattery. Your proud, daring woman is very vulnerable to such assaults. The world often wonders why such women so often, after all, surrender; but that's because the world does not appreciate the dexterity in such jousts of such skilled men of the world as Sir Charleroy; or how grateful to self-admiring beauties the admiration of superior intellects is.

"Well, will thou give me thy name?"

"Certainly. For to-night, Ahasuerus?"

"A presumptious jest, sir."

"No, for I admire and respect Esther, that's here."

"And then?"

"I plead for help; gain me admittance to the festivities, and escape from inquiry further, as to my identity."

"And afterward, be called by my people brazen by thee, a little fool!"

"Art thou driven from right, the claim of hospitality, by fear of a lie?"

"What if thou wert a Bedouin spy, or a hated cross follower?"

"Thou art a noble hearted maiden."

"Ah, who told thee so?"

"Thy face."

"What is that to thee, if true?" she blushed a little.

"Could'st thou drive from thy bosom a fleeing kid, there seeking refuge from pursuing lions?"

"I do not know 'till tried. Thou art at any rate no kid; there is no lion. If thou desirest refuge, see the path of departure is the one by which thou cam'st hither."

"Well, then, farewell."

The knight made as if he would go, but he knew he would not. The motion gave him excuse for looking sad, and he knew that next to a handsome face a sad one most easily conquers a woman.

"Tarry a moment 'till I think. Can I trust thee?" she was hesitating.

"I've trusted thee, and that's ever the best proof of fidelity." Women like to think they are especially trusted.

"Well——but, see, my father comes; there's no time for argument; let me speak!"

As the aged priest drew near, Esther saluted him, and said, "Father, let me take this Galileean stranger to the youths and their games? He claims our hospitality."

The priest, wont to be on the alert, was disarmed by

the magic word hospitality; then, too, for a long time before, having been wifeless, he had been wont to put his daughter forward, according large confidence to her; hence his reply:

"If thou knowest him, Rizpah."

"I do."

"Welcome, brother, what is thy name?" said Harrimai.

Rizpah, his daughter, quickly made reply, "Ahasuerus, and I've laughed at the *coincidence* until he has been ashamed to repeat it."

"'Tis strange, surely, and not like a Jewish one. I must examine the family rolls to-morrow. Peace be unto thee, son," and the old man turned toward his pavilion. Esther plucked a lily from her crown and handed it to Sir Charleroy saying: "Here, king, a token."

"Of what?"

"Shushan; in our tongue, the name of the flower signifies 'surrender.'"

"They say, Esther, that Judith wore a crown of lilies when she assassinated Holophernes. Is there any danger to me impending?"

"Thou hast a lily. It is said to ward off enchantments, too."

"I am enchanted. I do not want to awaken. In Egypt they call this the lotus, flower of unrestrained pleasure."

"For now then, we'll call it lotus."

"All gods, even Osiris, bless thee, Esther."

So the twain were charmed comrades, till watch fires were dim and the palm shadows were creeping in, like funeral attendants, to carry away the spirit of the dying revel. Here and there was heard anon the voices commending this one and that to pleasant slumbers. The stars were withdrawing behind dawn's feathery curtains, and over all, at intervals, was heard the voice of the chanticleer, triumphantly proclaiming the coming day.

Charleroy and Rizpah were left alone with each other at the end of the last game.

The maiden gave a coy, furtive glance and tardily drew away from the knight. The language of the drawing-room of the day, is as old as the centuries, and that maid of the wilderness used it as finely as a queen, to say without words, "it's time we part; please say so first, nor leave to me, the hostess, the first suggestion of a wish to have thee go——"

Still the knight spake not.

He was delighted and averse to breaking the first pleasure spell of years.

The Jewish maiden, with fine courtesy, renewed the subject: "King, methinks, thou art anxious to exchange the grove for the palace."

"I can never think of weariness when restful Esther is nigh."

"But thy life is precious to thy subjects; care for it, and go with freshness to to-morrow's cares of state.

"Ah, queen, I too keenly realize that with thy departure my kingdom fades to nothingness."

"A truce, my liege."

"Granted, and any thing else, to the half of my kingdom."

Rizpah startled the birds in the shrubbery to premature morning song, with a merry laugh. It was a finishing charge, that laugh, by which she carried her point, for the knight quickly questioned "Why this?"

"I was only thinking how odd thou wouldst appear if thou didst wear away my pepelum. Thy subjects would think their king mad, if he met them veiled as a woman."

"Pardon, queen, I've been so absorbed, I forgot myself—" So saying, he gracefully transferred from his shoulder to hers the shawl she had permitted him for the night to wear. As the maiden adjusted it, something fell out of its folds, glittering to her feet.

"Findings keepings;" she laughed, and stooped to pick up the object. As she arose she turned it slowly toward the setting moon the better to inspect the find.

The knight was alarmed, but it was too late to prevent her examinination now of his Teutonic cross and chain.

At a glance, Rizpah saw it was an emblem, of all others, hated by her people, and with a low, startled cry she made a motion as if to hurl it from her, but she checked herself with a powerful effort; suddenly turning her black, piercing eyes upon her companion she took a step back. She stood there the embodiment of an imperative question.

The knight quietly said: "Be calm, dear maid."

Over her countenance passed a cloud which to the man all too plainly said: "How darst thou use such terms to me?" and then the face hardened again to imperative interrogation.

"Thou trustedst me four hours ago, under the lotus, try now my sincerity by any sterner test.'

Turning her eyes full on his, with a voice without a

quaver, but in deep, measured tones indicative of suppressed emotion, she questioned as she held out toward him his emblem, "What's this?"

"Concealment from thee, having trusted me as thou hast, would be futile not only, but hateful; thou knowst the meaning of the sign."

"Who art thou then?"

"A Christian knight!"

"An enemy of my people everywhere; a spy here!" she exclaimed.

"No, never a spy! a true Christian knight never was such! Our warfare is open and equal. I'm degraded by the defense from such an odious charge!"

"Why debate thy methods; 'tis enough for me to know thou art a foe to me and mine."

"No enemy of thine, but rather the friend of all humanity, woman."

"Bloody friends I've heard!"

"No! Each one of my order is sworn, by awful vow, to protect the traveler, the poor, the weak and woman with our last drop of blood! If we two were all alone here and one of our lives must be forfeited to save the other's, mine would joy to go first."

"Words are cheap, and thou can'st use them finely, knight."

"Thou knowst, maiden, to what that cross alludes."

"The Nazarene Imposter!"

"His followers revere Him?"

"Like madmen, they follow their phantom!"

"Didst ever hear of one wearing that sign, being untrue to it?"

"No, it's their dread black-art."

"Wouldst thou trust me if I swore by it?"

"I might; but I'd fear that devils would flock out of the airy deep to witness thy vowing. Spare me that horror!"

"Maiden, thou'lt craze me by thy distrust and wild words. In God's name tell me what to do!"

"Swear, but wave back the evil spirits, if thou art wont to have them."

"That sign is their lasting terror; but the silent palms and the stars alone shall witness, ay, the God of all, as well. Here, make thou the words as thou wilt. Now, I kiss the cross I love, and am ready. He suited the action to the words. The maiden drew near to him, looking down into his eyes searchingly and seemed assured by their serene frankness."

"Go on, Rizpah, I'll bind my soul with any words coined, and, remember that I believe that perjury would consign me to misery untold here; eternal woe hereafter!"

"I'll trust thy solemn asseverations; they say that a superstition on the right side will make even a Philistine bearable. Repeat, 'I swear never to harm any of Rizpah's kin or clan, except in self-defense."

He complied.

"Again," 'I swear to depart peacefully at once, and no more seek companionship with the people this night met."

He complied, but murmured "cruelty."

"And how?" she questioned.

"Wilt add a little?"

"Add what?"

"Add this 'except by permission of the one ordaining my vow.'"

"It is so fixed."

"I then swear it all."

"Well, now go," and she pointed to the hills.

"I obey, but yet plead delay."

She hesitated and fell from being master to being mastered.

"Why, what benefits delay?"

"Oh, woman, I yearn as only a lonely heart can, to enjoy a little while the fellowship and hospitality of thy people! For years homeless; for months friendless, I've come to feel worthless. This is the first bright hour in my life for many a day. Perhaps, maiden of Israel, thou mightst make life worth living to me."

It was a charge on her sympathy, and he knew it would succeed.

"A Crusader, 'one of the armies of God,' boasting a divine call to conquer and convert the world, so talking?"

"Our armed crusades are ended forever; my occupation's gone."

She had hesitated, now she pitied the man, and woman-like, again surrendered while she protested.

"I do not think there could come great harm from thy staying until sunrise repast."

"Bless thee, the nine sun gods bless thee, Esther."

"Heathen!"

"Well; an Egyptian-Christian-Jew taught me to say this when too cheerful to be solemn, and pious enough not to be frivolous."

"An Egyptian-Hebrew-Christian! He must have been an Arab. That name means the 'mixed.' But go to the men's tents; to-morrow I'll have more wisdom. Peace and grace to thee; good night, Christian-Heathen-Hebrew-Arabic-Egyptian!" She laughingly spoke and the unbending made the knight, bold. He addressed her:

"I'd sleep in perfect peace, if Rizpah would give me a token."

"I? what?" and the maiden drew back, offended. Her innocency remembered no token then, but such solicited by her maiden friends, or given at times to her father, a kiss.

"Place thy hand in mine, Rizpah." She quickly complied, glad she was mistaken, as to her suspicion and blushing within, as she thought how strangely, easily, her mind had had the thought, "Well, now what, knight?"

"Promise me that while I'm permitted to tarry among thy people, I shall have thy heart's friendship; as freely, as loyally bestowed as if I were thy brother."

"Canst trust me, a woman, a girl, almost a stranger?"

"I trust thy woman's heart as Joshua's men of old trusted Rahab, a wreck, but still a woman. Thou art infinitely more noble than she."

"But men think us weak, fitful, garrulous."

"Responsibility makes the weakest of thy sex heroines and pity is the gateway to their hearts. Thou hast my life and my happiness as thy responsibility; dost pity me?"

"Yes: go now. A Gentile hater of my people shall see of what metals Jewish maidens are."

CHAPTER XII.

ASTARTE OR MARY?

> "Who could resist; who in the universe?
> She did breathe ambrosia; so immerse
> My existence in a golden clime,
> She took me like a child of sucking time,
> And cradled me in roses. Thus condemned
> The current of my former life was stemmed:
> I bowed a tranced vassal."
>
> —KEATS.

HE Teutonic Knight of Saint Mary, through all his changing fortunes from the time of his knighthood's vow, preserved his moral integrity, his loyalty to the lofty pattern of life set forth by the Queenly exemplar, Mary, the mother of Jesus. Crusader days had so far improved his life as to make him the outspoken denouncer of all impurity of life. He thought his creed and his committal thereto complete. A change came over him. He that, in the storm of battle, had often cried as his law and his delight "*Deus Vult*," "God wills," now feared to seek to know, much less to do, that will. The intoxications of a new love were upon him; unconsciously he was suffering his queen to be veiled, eclipsed; and he yielded to the tide that swept him toward the Jewish maiden. Sometimes his conscience smote him, but he parleyed with it, called it a fool, or placated it by the assurance that this whole matter could be stopped any time **at**

will. Like many another man, forgetting all else except that he was a refined animal, he passed away from the beacons of Bethlehem to the chambers of Imagery, the gods of Egypt. In chains of roses, though with many fine Christian sentiments on his lips, he went heart first, head first, into an utter committal of all his being to the possession of his enchanter. He expected to regard the laws of the land and society, but nothing more. He was led by his tempting spirit to Ramoth Gilead, now sometimes called Gerara or Gerash. There it was that Rizpah's family took up its abode. With them, and of them, was Sir Charleroy, a welcome guest, his welcome secured by his own personal efforts to please, in part; but more through the *finesse* of Rizpah, who having promised to be a sister, was permitting her mind to wonder what he might become if only her friend were a Hebrew. Such day dreams were sinless, but impolitic if she really meant to keep herself free and painless, when the parting time came. But it so happens that the questions and problems of the heart are thrust ever on life when most responsive, least experienced. The wonder is not that so many decide them ill, but that youth so pressed, so ardent, so callow, as a whole decide so fairly well the master social problem. The life of Harrimai and his following was very Jewish at Gerash. There was an unusual amount of national pride evinced in that locality for the times. Sir Charleroy was interested deeply in the place because of its splendid ruins, he said, but as need not be explained, chiefly on account of its natural beauties amid which Rizpah was peerless. The Israelitish colony revered the place for its ancient part in Jewish history, and because they believed no Moslem invader had ever defiled the place. The knight and the Jewish father and daughter were in frequent companionship. They were becoming very intimate, meanwhile gaining power each to make the other eventually very miserable.

Rizpah was pushing out in a new experience to her. If she were enamored she did not fully know it. She only knew that the knight's companionship was very delightful. If she had any misgivings as to the propriety of her course she silenced them by saying to herself: "Sir Charleroy has sworn to leave us forever when I say he shall. I can end this matter any time." She thought she could, but the shield of her safety was already too heavy for her. She could not have said go, had she tried. Time deepened the perplexity by multiplying the enmeshings of the trio. The knight and Rizpah were much in each other's society. They spoke of this as being a happy circumstance, as youths usually do. "We shall understand each other so well— too well to misunderstand." Some of the Jewish young men were jealous and made some very natural remarks, under the circumstances, though the remarks were rather bitter with jealousy. The older people, some of them, anxious for an alliance by marriage with the rich and powerful Harrimai family, took up the undertone complaints of the young people of their race. Of course, the murmurings were cloaked with declarations that they were all for the sake of righteousness! Harrimai, in heart far from assured, was yet compelled to defend the two secretly loving, in order to defend his daughter's fair fame. The two young people wore the armor of teacher and pupil; the young woman constantly bepraising the knight's wondrous knowledge of the antiquities, etc., of all the out-of-the-way places they visited. So the meshes multiplied, though the caviling was in part silenced. As teacher and pupil they went on, and Harrimai knew, as did Sir Charleroy, that the relationship had its peril, as it existed between a man and woman who could love yet ought not to love. Rizpah did not at first know how easily a woman's heart surrenders to a man to whom she is accustomed to look upward. In fact she drifted in a delight in all pertaining to the knight; her only outlook and watchfulness being toward her father. The way the latter at times keenly, silently observed her and the knight made her uneasy. She knew intuitively that not far away there was impending on her father's part an investigation. She determined to delay, if not prevent it. One day she bounded into her father's presence, aglow with enthusiasm over the wonders unfolded to her by Sir Charleroy during a visit to the ruins of Gerash's temple of the sun. The old man was charmed by her description, and when she declared her intention to pursue her investigations beyond their city he hesitated to forbid.

"And now, father, I'm going to that old city of the Giants, Bozrah."

The father, with an effort at firmness, dissuadingly replied:

"We may all go there, but not now. It is better to bide here quietly, until we learn that the perils of receding war have left assured peace."

"Why, father, I'm not afraid!"

"I know it; so much the more need for me to be; these over-daring daughters need over-careful guardians. Some of us aged ones are suffered to tarry long from paradise, in order that we may see our darlings in the right path thither."

"Give me my swift white dromedary and two attendants and I'll defy the miserables who ambuscade along the way."

Just then, there dashed toward them, over the oleander-fringed road which passed due north along the little river and across the city, a rider on panting steed.

"It's the news runner!" said the patriarch.

"Shall we signal him?" she questioned.

"No, daughter, we will meet him yonder, where the two great streets cross. He will await me."

When the father and daughter arrived, a crowd had already gathered about the horseman. Some pressed him for news, but he looked straight ahead at his horse, now slaking its thirst, and merely snapped out, "News? My beast is thirsty!"

When Harrimai drew near the rider saluted him and at once unfolded his budget: "Father, I'm this day from Bozrah. Its ruins are not ruined. All around there, and from there to here, the herds sleep in the shade, and the carrion birds that have so long been hovering around us for human food have fled back to Egypt and Europe and Hades!"

"Praised be the Father of Israel! I shall live then, as I prayed I might, to see the infidels slung out of our holy places!" So spoke the priest, and as he affectionately embraced some aged Israelites who gathered about him, the horseman responded:

"God reigns and Israel has peace." He put spurs to his horse then, and dashed away across the river to spread to other hamlets the glorious news.

Next morning Rizpah, having carried her point, was ready to depart for Bozrah. She had taken silence on her father's part for consent, and pursued her preparations as if it were so ordered. All things being ready she silenced protest by a good-by kiss.

"But daughter! What escort?"

"Ah," she thought, "victory! I can go if well attended." She continued aloud; "Perhaps Sir Charleroy's Egyptian might attend me, since our servants are busy in the groves." The maiden called to her Ichabod, who had found a home in Harrimai's establishment, his identity hidden under the assumed name Huykos, a name from the Nile land, meaning "Shepherd King." "I'll take it," said Ichabod, one day to Sir Charleroy, "that all unknown I may follow my pilgrim comrade and perhaps honor my new found 'Shepherd King.'"

"One will be a meager escort daughter," interposed Harrimai.

"Oh, fear for me nothing, father. I'll quickly be at Bozrah, where there are Israelites not a few who will be proud to aid thy daughter."

"No, daughter it must not be. I'll call the young men from the vineyard, if thou must go."

"Another victory," her heart whispered; then quickly turning to Sir Charleroy she exclaimed, "My father must not call the workmen from their tasks; what sayst thou? Wilt serve us both by joining my body-guard, Ahasuerus? Come, to please my father?"

The knight had hoped for and expected the summons, so needed no urgency and was instantly preparing for the start.

Harrimai was not pleased by the arrangement, and

yet he was forced to thank the knight for consenting. His native courtliness compelled this much, and Rizpah's genius had precluded all gainsaying on his part. And so they rode away, Rizpah in a delight, which she could not clearly define; Sir Charleroy blinded already by the cry that at last led to giant Samson's blinding, namely: "Get her for me." Ichabod masked under his name, Huykos, followed after, knowing that the knight was captive to the maid and feeling very happy over the circumstance. As he rode, his mind ran forward to the wedding, and he laughed again and again at the witty things he imagined himself saying at that wedding. Suddenly the scene changed from one of careless delight to one filled with the frights of impending peril. At a turn in the road, from behind a wall, there rose up a company of Mamelukes. Rizpah saw them the instant her companion did and exclaimed, as she half turned her camel:

"Let's race back to Gerash!"

But four dusky sentinels were behind them. They were surrounded.

"'Tis fight or flight, the latter futile," whispered the knight. They paused, and Ichabod joined them. Sir Charleroy drawing his sword again spoke: "Comrade it's a desperate chance; a dozen to two; but we have taken such before together!"

"Let the knight say a dozen to three," exclaimed Rizpah, as she drew from the folds of her garments a saber before unseen and touched the edge expert-like with her thumb.

"Oh, brave, pure girl! I don't fear death; I'd court it for thee, but"—Sir Charleroy paused and looked unutterable misery; then instantly recovering and emboldened by the danger that threatened to soon end all, he exclaimed:

"Rizpah, thou rememberest my knight-vow at Purim; thou shalt see how I'll keep it; if I perish, remember I have loved thee as I never loved any other being." The words were very vehement, but probably very true. Rizpah blushed, brushed a tear from her eyes and then, in the frankness that such an hour engenders, replied: "And I thee—" the rest was drowned in the wild shout of the Turks as they close about the three. But they had not counted upon such a reception as those two men and that one woman gave them. Ichabod fought like a roused mastiff, without a thought of fear for himself. He struck vehemently, but a calm settled smile was on his countenance. Sir Charleroy saw it and years after said, recalling the incident. "amidst the greatest perils there's a wondrous peace to one who feels he is striking for God, close to the portals of death and judgment." The knight himself fenced with the rapidity of lightning. Again and again by ones and twos and threes, the enemies charged down upon him, but he fought with the prowess of a crusader, the fire of a lover. Those parts had never before witnessed such splendid swordsmanship. As the attack had been sudden, so was its ending. Two Turks fell beneath Sir Charleroy's weapon in quick succession, and a third fell under his own horse, which was desperately wounded by a sweeping blow from the knight. At the same instant, almost, Ichabod and one of the foemen, whom he was engaging, fell in significant silence, while another struggled to drag Rizpah to his steed that he might make her captive. Sir Charleroy, wounded and faint, dealt the latter miscreant a staggering blow and the maiden, plucking a small dagger from the folds of her garment, finished with a single thrust her captor's earthly career.

Those of the marauders that were able, in fright took flight, wheeling away more quickly than they had come.

"Rizpah, wilt thou go to Ich—Huykos? I can't," softly called out Sir Charleroy.

The maiden flew to the Jew's side, but quickly started back, crying: "Oh, knight, come quickly! He's dead!" Just then, looking back, a sudden horror fell upon her, for she saw Sir Charleroy half reclining against a rock, bleeding and pale. Like lightning she thought: "Both dead; I alone; home miles away; the Turks hovering near."

But the thought of her own peril was only momentary, and after it there came more rapidly than can be written the thought that one dear as her life was dead, dead for her sake. Instantly, on feet that seemed winged, she was at Sir Charleroy's side. All her being merged into one great, instant impulse to save her lover. Over him she bent, and with passionate sorrow tried with her garments to staunch the flow of blood. In the sincereity and frankness that the presence of death ever brings, she arose above all prudishness and impulsively kissed the cold lips of the knight. His eyes opened, and he faintly murmured:

"I'm so happy, dear Rizpah. I know now it is well." A little later he murmured: "Flee now for home. Thou'lt reach it by sun down. Leave me. To tarry is to court a harem prison."

"Hush," impatiently responded she; "see this dagger?" and she held it close to his half-closed eyes.

"My pious father gave it me when I was but a girl. He told me it might some time save me from dishonor. It did so to-day, once. If those black demons return, sure as my name is Rizpah, it will do so again, even though I turn it toward my own heart."

"Better flee, my love."

"Not 'till thou can'st go, too."

"I may die."

"Then, I'll go into the shadow land with thee."

The knight was silent. The pain of his wounds was forgotten in the joy of that lone companionship. But, after all, his mind, perturbed by the shock, the pain, the dangers, was unable to rest. He tried to say to himself the prayer of the dying crusader, but the words were confused. He could not remember many of them; those he remembered, seemed to be unwilling to go heavenward for mercy. Some way in the clearness of judgment as to simple right and wrong that comes to a mind on the confines of death, he found himself condemned. He was haunted by a vision that came to his mind first the day he decided against conviction, at all hazard, to follow the family of Rizpah and Harrimai to Gerash. The vision was that of the false prophet Zedekiah, making himself horns of iron, and with them appearing before the wicked King of Israel, Ahab, to proclaim, not the things of God, but the things the prophet knew would meet the desires of his royal master. The wounded often fall asleep; it's nature's way of recovering from a shock and of chaining pain in forgetfulness. Sir Charleroy knew not whether he was sleeping or not; but the vision passed in painful vividness over his mind. He heard the prophet's voice saying: "Go up to Ramoth

Gilead, and prosper." Then he saw a true prophet of God standing nigh, with sorrowful countenance, and the face was that of the Madonna. The latter moaned in his ear, warningly; "*Who shall persuade, that he may go up and fall at Ramoth Gilead? Then there came forth a spirit and said, I will persuade.*"

The spirit was black-garbed, in a blood-spotted garment, and wore, as Sir Charleroy seemed to see the apparition, a scarlet crescent, and the knight thought of Astarte. He heard in his vision the beatings as of mighty wings, rising to flight, and tried to turn and see who the departing one was. It seemed as if the spirit of Astarte-like countenance transfixed him with a gaze, so he could not turn; but a loneliness and darkness, almost palpable, came over him, and he knew it was the Madonna-faced prophet that had departed. The knight started up as if to rise, but, awakening, found Rizpah's restraining arms about him.

"Stay," she soothingly said. "Thou art feverish, and too weak to rise. Thou'lt be better presently; the blood has ceased flowing."

"Oh," he groaned; "I had such a dream!"

Just then Rizpah beheld coming in the distance, from toward Gerash, a horseman, at rapid pace. Her first thought, "The enemy returns." Her second brought her hand swiftly to her reeking dagger, as she soliloquized: "He's only one, and I'm one; if but a woman."

The rider drew nearer, and she was almost overcome with the revulsion from fear and despair; for the comer was Laconic, the "news runner." He knew the maiden, and wheeling his steed to her side, with his usual brevity, cried out:

"Why, didst thou kill both?"

"Shame on thee; 'twas the Arabs!"

"I thought so. I met two horsemen and two riderless steeds, galloping away down the road. I knew they'd been at some devilment."

"Good runner, in the the name of God, speed thee to Bozrah, or somewhere, for help; and bring it quickly."

"Bring? not so; send. *I* come not 'till my set day!"

"Any thing; but hurry!"

"Hurry! Yes, hurry! I love hurry."

He was away like an arrow, in his course. His steed leaped over one of the dead miscreants and Laconic shouted back: "Carrion dinners! Thank God!"

CHAPTER XIII.

FROM RAMOTH GILEAD TO DAMASCUS

> "Daughters of Eve! your mother did not well:
> *   *   *   *   *   *   *
> The man was not deceived, nor yet could stand:
> He chose to lose for love of her, his throne,—
> With her could die, but could not live alone."
>
> "Daughters of Eve! it was for your dear sake
> The world's first hero died an uncrowned king:
> But God's great pity touched the great mistake
> And made his married love a sacred thing;
> For yet his nobler sons, if aught be true,
> Find the lost Eden in their love of you."
> —JEAN INGELOW.

OR many days Sir Charleroy lay wounded at the house of the Patriarch Harrimai, and she for whom he had periled his life was his constant attendant. He sorely needed her services, and all Gerash, the priest included, conceded the fitness of Rizpah's rendering the aid she was able to render. The maiden was all willing to minister, and as she ministered her interest in the man deepened. When she began to look up to him as her teacher before the battle with Mamelukes, she began a sort of worship; when she saw him fighting to the death in her behalf, her worship became an engrossing adoration. If there had been any thing more required in order to

enlist all the affection of which her being was capable, these opportunities of administering to her suffering lover furnished it. As God loves because He has helped a needy one, so a woman's heart easily flows out toward the object for whom she has performed pious services. On the other hand, Sir Charleroy was more and more enchanted, for there is life and charm beyond all description to the touch of the queen of a man's heart when he is in trouble or pain.

Rizpah, in woman's most queenly garb, the one appointed her at her creation, that of "help-mate," was beautiful indeed, and queenly indeed, to the man whose heart had enthroned her. When alone, they treated each other with the frank, earnest tenderness, fitting as well as natural, to the betrothed. Though they did not admit it even to themselves, they had fully determined to be one, at all peril, in spite of any opposition, reason approving or disapproving. They often said to one another, "Our betrothal taking place at the very gates of death was therefore a very solemn one that nothing on earth can annul." The sentiment was perfect and very agreeable; and with them a beautiful and agreeable sentiment became as controlling as if it were a revelation from heaven. In this, they were perfectly human. They even persuaded themselves of God's favor, thanking Him for what they were pleased to call His Providence, namely the peril and long sickness leading to the betrothal and days of love-life together. They were right in conceding that God's hand was in the battle; but they were impious in interpreting His Providence to be fully in accord with their desires. In this, too, they were very human. But there were shadows about them; for while at times they drifted along on prismatic tides of Lethean delights, there were other times when they remembered that there was to come a day of explanation, with probable following storms. Both were glad and sorry at once, in view of each day's improvement of the knight's physical condition. Convalescent, they both realized, meant a great change in their relationship; perhaps a long separation. Their anxiety was deepened by a change in the demeanor of Rizpah's father. His eyes no longer questioningly followed the young people; but his words, uttered in tones of steely coldness and very deliberately, bespoke discovery, conviction, conclusion and determination. One sentence often addressed to the lovers, was to them like the rumblings of an approaching, gathering storm. "Our friend is improving, and I'm very glad that he will be able soon to go to his own dear people." The lovers discerned a peculiar emphasis on the words "I'm glad" and "his own dear people." The politic priest, having read, as from an open book, the heart-secret of the young people, was awaiting with self-confidence an opportunity to confound them utterly. The crisis came one Sabbath morning, just after the morning meal of the convalescent. Harrimai had paid his usual visit and uttered his steely sentences. This time the words seemed especially cruel to Rizpah, for she was nervous, indeed ill; the prolonged services and anxieties she had experienced of late were telling on her strength. As Harrimai departed, she gave way to a flood of tears. Rizpah was not wont to weep, nor was Sir Charleroy skilled in comforting; but both he and she were lovers, hence it seemed very natural to her frankly to pillow her head on the knight's shoulder, and very natural to him to seek to comfort with a tenderness all new to him. Had one asked Rizpah if she were going back to babyishness, or forward toward heaven, she could not have answered. Had one asked the knight if he were becoming motherly, or turning priest, he could not have answered. He felt very tender, and his work of comforting seemed like an an act of high piety. Both were glad of the tears which brought the joy of comforting and being comforted, then, there and that way. They were passing into a superb mood when quite unexpectedly to them, but quite expectedly to himself, Harrimai suddenly re-entered the apartment. He expected to surprise them and he did so, thoroughly. The scene following was exciting, dramatic and decisive.

Rizpah, with a slight scream, disengaged herself from Sir Charleroy's embrace, and hid her face in her hands. The eyes of the knight and priest met; neither quailed; both remained for a few moments silent; but their fixed gaze said plainly enough, each to each, "We must have a settlement here and now!" Harrimai spoke first, addressing himself to his daughter: "Young woman, this conduct is immodest and disgraceful! In a Hebrew maiden, heaven defying! I'll speak to thee further of this presently. Now, begone, and leave me to deal with this man!" Harrimai made arrogant by his profession and the implicit obedience he had been wont to receive from his followers, expected to fill the young people with dismay by the suddenness of his assault. But Rizpah, though young, was no tongue-tied spring, and Sir Charleroy of Gerash was still Sir Charleroy of Acre.

The words "dishonorable," "immodest," stung the

maiden; sullenly, defiantly almost, she settled back in her seat and leaned toward the knight, as if to say, "I cast my lot with this man." Her eyes plainly, angrily said to the man whom all her life hitherto she had reverently obeyed, 'Now do thy worst." It was impious, passionate, love going headlong from filial duty and religious instruction to the shrine of Astarte. The parent was chagrined at this unexpected repulse, but with his usual adroitness pretending not to notice it, he turned to the knight. "Stranger, this outrage excuses abruptness on my part; who art thou?"

Sir Charleroy arose from his hammock, the excitement and shock of the rencounter finishing his recovery, by rousing all the machineries of his system into normal activities.

"Sir Priest, I've nothing to conceal. I love the truth and this maiden too well to lie—I am a Christian knight."

"I knew it; but thy confession shortens our parley. Now, 'Christian knight,' tell me why thou didst attempt to allure to thyself the affections of a mere girl; a Jewish maiden whom thou canst never hope to wed? Dost thou so pay our hospitality; setting at defiance parental authority and our Jewish laws? Dost thou under the favors of this house intrigue to quench all its light?"

"Thou brandst that girl and me with the epithet 'dishonorable;' and thou a priest! Men of thy holy calling should never slander, especially not their own kin and strangers." The knight was livid, but not with fear.

"Can an Israelite slander Crusaders? these professors of high religion, these followers of an impostor, these enemies of my people, these practicers of intrigues, races, jousts, gluttonies and drunkenness; men whose sole serious business is murderous war? Tell me?"

The knight's face flushed a little, but with complete self-control he replied:

"Some of my comrades have been unworthy men, 'tis true; but some Jews have fallen to every crime and violence. Have all fallen? Thou hast not, perhaps! Shall all be maligned for the few? What says Harrimai?"

"Thou art of those, who come to thrust us out of our land and thrust in here a hated creed!"

"I am of those who live to serve the needy and erring."

"To the proof; I've heard from thy clans only of bloodshed."

"Our order sprung up four hundred years ago, under the stirring appeals of religionists as pious and humane as thou; or any of thy kind since Aaron. We were begotten in a time when grim famine made the well-fed wondrous kind. Those hours that make men universally akin."

"Go on; 'Christian knight,' I'd like a lesson of that sort."

"Then remember Noah's covenant of peace. On our banners often we have our spirit expressed by a dove flying toward a tempest-tossed ark; in the messenger's beak an olive branch; around the whole the bow of promise."

"Well what of all this

"The ark is the world; the rest is plain."

"Oh, a charming theory," sarcastically responded Harrimai.

"I wear it next my heart;" so saying the knight threw aside his cloak and drew from around his body a banner he had hitherto concealed. "See here, '*chastity*,' '*temperance*,' '*courtesy*.' Our mottos in peace or war! Women, children and pilgrims, in a word the needy the world around, are the wards of all true Christian knights!"

"Mottoes! words! Oh, yes, words! But then the Crusaders have used swords! Their words I'll meet with words to their confounding, nor while I live will I forget their cruel weapons." So saying the priest swept out of the sick chamber in manifest rage.

He returned in a moment, and with the self-command of wrath, conscious of power, said: "Thou wouldst make all men *akin!* Thou and thine are dreamers, the world thinks; to-day it laughs to scorn this bootless pursuit of a chimera. Leave us forthwith and in the peace that thou foundst here. When the kinship is reality, thou mayst come to us for further talk; 'till then remember thou art a Christian, I a Jew!"

"Thou art religious! Heavens! what a tender shepherd."

Harrimai was very much angered, but he retorted with self-control; "Oh, yes, and the God of all hath seven garments. In creation, honor and glory; in providence, majesty; as lawgiver, might and whiteness; of spotless light when he appears as a Saviour. He is clad with zeal when he punishes, and with blood red when He revenges. I would be like Him. By the glory of God! thou follower of Nazereth's Impostor, sooner than suffer thy blood to contaminate my family lines, I'd hew thee to pieces as Agag was hewn! Rizpah, thou knowest me; wed him and thou'lt be widowed, though carrying the unborn; though widow-hood broke thy heart. I'd rather a thousand times see thee lying dead by thy true Jewish mother than————." The priest, in a tumult of fanatical passion mingled with the grief of offended pride, lacked for words to express the climax of his feelings; so covering his tearless eyes, as one weeping, he rushed out from those he had assailed. He persuaded himself that he had spoken all for the glory of God; the lovers thought of their solemn betrothal and their love which they were certain was as fine as any earth ever knew, and they felt that they were martyrs. Both sides appealed to God and in a spirit very ungodly, but very human, braced themselves for opposing war.

When the maiden became somewhat calm, Sir Charleroy found words to question:

"Harrimai cannot find heart to blast his idol's hapness! He does not mean all he said?"

"Alas, he does. It's part of the Patriarch's religion to hate such as thou, as he does. He means more, if possible, than he spoke. Our people unveil the bosom and cover the mouth; thine cover the bosom and unveil the mouth. Ye talk, we burn."

"Has pure love like ours no sanctity in his sight?'

"Alas, he can not believe any love pure that is between Gentile and Israelite. He was sneering at ours a few evenings ago, when he remarked as we were looking at the stars, 'Hyperius or Venus of the evening is mistakenly called the star of love. Lucifer of the morning is the true emblem of most young love. It rises in maddening brightness, but fades out of sight very soon.'"

Grim omen! We took Venus for our betrothal star; they say it is so bright at times that it casts a shadow. I feel its shadow now," said the knight, meditating.

"Yes, shadows and shadows!" exclaimed Rizpah, with a flood of tears, and she swayed back and forth as she wept. She was driven by tempests of fear that made her ready to flee, and held by anchors of passionate loving that made her ready to brave all fears; therefore the swaying and weeping. At intervals the two communed and debated concerning the one all-engrossing theme, their future course.

"Rizpah," comfortingly spoke the knight, "when in the greatest peril of our lives, we were drawn, by danger, closer to each other." There was a glance of entreaty in her eyes as if to say, "Go save thy life and let the Jewish maiden die alone;" but the knight drew her to his bosom, and she responded by an embrace of passionate clinging.

"I go from Rizpah only at her command or death's," said the knight solemnly.

The maiden shuddered, and again passionately clung to her lover. He interpreted her action, and again comfortingly spoke:

"Fear not; earth has somewhere a refuge for us until death call us!"

"Somewhere? What, go away?"

"Yes. It is that or separation."

She knew that full well. But to flee from home with the knight, the alternative presented to her mind, startled her. At first thought it seemed a reckless, perilous, unfilial, God-defying act; then it seemed attractive because so daring. A tumult of arguments, questionings, fears and yearnings mingled in her mind. She had never learned to arrange arguments, *pro* and *con*, judicially. What woman whose feelings were aroused ever did that?

He pressed on her flight, enforcing each reason presented with an affectionate embrace; her tongue spoke not, but her embraces replied to each of his. She had a conscience, and it asserted itself until she placated it by a half formed resolution to be very prudent and do nothing rashly. The resolution comforted her at first; then she began to follow it, mentally, to its sequence. She thought of her father praising her piety as her purpose was disclosed. Something within, coming like a voice from her heart, mockingly whispered "Go on." She pursued the meditations, and heard, in imagination, her neighbors praising her as a martyr of love for faith's sake. Again the mocking inner voice said, "Go on." Again her thoughts moved forward until she saw that conscience was driving her to separation from Sir Charleroy; in a word, making her walk in a funeral procession, her own dead heart on the bier. The thought made her shudder and recoil; then the knight's arms encircled her more closely than before. Again and again she took the foregoing mental journey, again and again recoiled, shuddering from the alternative of separation from her lover, and at each recoil felt his grateful embrace. Each time she traversed the mental course the journey toward duty by the privation of love seemed more onerous. Distaste was followed by repugnance; then utter weariness. At last, utterly wretched, her purposes and perceptions fell into hopeless confusion, and she exclaimed "Charleroy, Charleroy, save me!"

The knight was at a loss to divine fully her meaning, yet tenderly he answered:

"Save Rizpah? She knows I'd do that in death's teeth!"

"Oh, Charleroy, 'tis not death, but life, that I fear. How shall I live?"

Quickly he ejaculated:

"With me, forever, and safe!"

The maiden remembering many an admonition she had heard concerning the inconstancy of lovers, yet driven forward by the all-abandoning love of her woman's heart, gave voice to all she felt and feared in one vehement interrogation:

"Oh, Charleroy, if I forsake all for my love of thee shall I ever be discarded by ——?"

The knight interpreted her meaning in advance, and answered by an embrace that was all-assuring. He was rejoiced beyond words, for he knew full well that hesitation and questionings like hers were on the rim of full surrender. Suddenly he became very serious and felt that peculiar glow that came over him the day of his departure from England when the bishop blessed him. He appreciated in a measure the responsibility following such a committal of another's life to himself as Rizpah was making, and he embraced her with an anxious reverence, such as a pietist feels clasping an ideal of his God. It was well for both that the man was thus impressed by the committal of that maiden of her soul and body to his pilotage. Pity the woman who reaches the extremity Rizpah had reached if her conqueror be not white-souled and sincere.

Rizpah, an incarnation of passion, a wreath of lotus flowers on a sea of delight, tossed by the winds, borne by the tides, surrendered all thoughts that might disturb, that she might enjoy what she had embraced as her fate to the full.

Sir Charleroy constantly prayed within himself, "My mother's God help me to deal as purely with my sacred charge as I would with the Virgin Patron of my knightly order, were she here now to seek my knightly services." The prayer was effectual, for the Knight sincerely sought to make it so.

Decisive action followed this interview between the lovers. That very night they fled together from Gerash, and with only one trusty servant; after many vicissitudes they reached Damascus. For a time Rizpah placated her conscience by asserting that she would not consent to the wedding ceremonial until it could have her father's approval, or that of some Jewish Rabbi. Finding it impossible to obtain these, she irresolutely suggested the advisablity of delaying until some change, quite vaguely apprehended, might come. But there were two Rizpah's—one that wanted to be a faithful Jewess, and one that wanted only and constantly a darling idol. Sir Charleroy sided with the latter; it was two to one, and the one surrendered. Ere long a Christian missionary at Damascus sealed the vows. They confided their story to him, as if to ask his advice as to what they had best do, but with the impetuosity of lovers they had decided their course before they asked advice, and did not even ask it until they had pledged their vows before this priest. But it was a balm to conscience to ask advice. And the Sacrist answered them briefly: "Venus and Mercury, fabled deities of love and wisdom. They are much alike in the firmament, and revolve in orbits in accord with the earth's. Methinks it is *wisdom* to *love* in the earth. But, children, Venus sets sooner than Mercury; see to it that you make it your wisdom to love as long as you go round with the world." Then they both said "Amen." For a moment Sir Charleroy heard within him that impressive sound as of the beating of mighty, departing wings. He dragged his attention quickly from the introspection to gaze into the eyes of his bride. He was glad that a Christian priest had prayed for a blessing upon himself and her, but all sophistry aside, the truth remained: **Astarte's was the presiding spirit at that wedding.**

CHAPTER XIV.

THE THEATER OF GIANTS.

> "Once more we look and all is still as night,
> All desolate ! Groves, temples, palaces
> Swept from the sight and nothing visible,
> * * * * Save here and there
> An empty tomb, a fragment like a limb
> Of some dismembered giant."

"Og, the King of Bashan, came out against us to battle at Edrei, and the Lord said unto me, Fear him not: for I will deliver him, and all his people, and his land, into thy hand. And we took * * * * three-score cities of the Kingdom of Og, in Bashan." —Deut. iii.]

"Bashan is the land of sacred romance." "His mission [Paul's, Gal., 1 : 15] to Bashan seems to have been eminently successful. Heathen temples were converted into churches, and new churches built in every town." "In the fourth century nearly the whole of the inhabitants were Christian." "The Christians are now nearly all gone." "Nowhere else is patriarchal life so fully exemplified." "Bashan is literally crowded with towns, the majority of them deserted, but not ruined." "Many are as perfect as if finished only yesterday."—PORTER'S "*Giant Cities.*"

FOR a brief period the delightful seasons, the famed rivers, the stately surrounding mountains, the paradisiacal plains, the antiquities, the pleasure gardens and palaces of the city of Damascus, whose name by interpretation is "change," offered sought-for gratification to the knight and his bride. Harrimai died suddenly after the elopement of his child, the only person on earth whom he truly loved, the only one that had ever successfully defied his mandates. He had purposed disinheriting her for her act, but before he could execute that purpose, death disinherited him. Some said that he died of a broken heart; the physicians said he was taken off by a fit; Sir Charieroy said he died because his proud will was crossed. Rizpah inherited a fortune that helped both her and her husband to forget the old priest's maledictions by enabling them to enjoy all there was to be enjoyed in Damascus, "the eye of the East." They gave up unreservedly to pleasure, and centered the world more and more in themselves. Sir Charleroy did this easily, reasoning that, having had so many pains, he was entitled to compensating pleasures. He heard from England; and the news was to the effect that there had been changes and changes in his native land. Many of those he once knew, including his mother, were dead; and he himself was forgotten as dead. Sententiously, bitterly he summed up his feelings: "They thought me dead, and, my mother and her fortune being gone, did not care to find out whether I was dead or not; therefore let them think as they thought." Rizpah feared the lashings of conscience, and, having given up every thing once dear to enter the life she had, courted forgetfulness of the past, pleasure for the present. The two had within themselves exuberant youth, a wealth of possibilities of happiness; the elements that, like the abundance of the volcano, paints the sky gorgeously when rising heavenward; like it, in the downward course, followed by darkness and disaster. The two, differing in almost every thing but fervor of temperament, were in accord in pursuit of change; they persuaded themselves that they were growing to be like each other, when they were only exalting the one thing, love of excitement, in which they were alike.

Damascus, naturally, in time, became uninteresting and vapid to them both. They wore it out; they wanted new scenes. They heard that a caravan of Mohammedan pilgrims was to pass through their city on the way to Mecca to procure besim balm and holy chaplets, and promptly determined to journey with it; but not to Mecca. The caravan was to pass through Bashan, and the two excitement-seekers desired to visit the latter land of wonders. They readily garbed themselves as Mohammedans, though once they would have loathed such garbing as a defilement. They desired company toward Bashan, and since the time they defied their consciences in order to be wedded to each other, their consciences had been wont to be very submissive in the face of their desires. They explained to themselves the absence of qualms of conscience in the face of a pretense of being Moslems, as the result of a growth toward liberality on their part. The explanation made them comfortably complacent, although the fact was that they had passed far beyond liberalism toward nothingism.

Passing Musmeth and Khubat of the Argob, they tarried after a time at Edrei, just inside the shore line of that mysterious black, lava sea, the Lejah. They were in a country where nature, art and desolation had done their greatest. Following a passing impulse seemed to them to have brought them thither, but one believing in God's constant providence will readily believe that they were led thither as to a school. There were omen and prophecy confronting them. These fervent souls had gone from hymen's altar filled with romancings, under a glow of prismatic auroras, never pausing to perceive that from each wedding time there winds a troop of serious years burdened with many a commonplace duty. Their love had been volcanic, their impulses ecstatic, their aims toward things filled with commotion. The wine in their cup was to leave dregs; after the fire there was to be ashes, and it was fitting that they contemplated a specimen of great desolation and dreariness, the result of great fires and great storms.. So they were within that wonder of the world, three hundred and fifty square miles of awful plain, filled with ruined towns and cities. Heaved up here and there by jutting basalt rocks, the plain seemed filled with black ice-bergs; ridged at intervals the plain suggested an ocean wave-tossed. Therein is many a cave and cranny place, fit abode for the wild beast or robber; fit abode for ghosts, if one seeks to believe there are such. But therein were only a few green spots, oases, to bid the traveler welcome. Ere long the knight and his consort wore out the Lejah, and, in so doing, in part, wore out themselves They had a fullness of the pleasure of the kind which lacks recreation. As it was, they stayed there longer than it was well for them to stay.

Rizpah, the passion flower of Gerash, experiencing the supreme exaction of womanhood now, began to droop. Months spent in pursuit of excitement, the great change in her manner of life, as well as the oppressive desolations of her surroundings, had drawn heavily upon her resources physically. Reaction after exaltation, and nervous discord after nervous tension are natural results, always.

The knight discerned the change of temper, and as an anxious novice went about correcting the matter. He knew little concerning woman, except that love of her intoxicates; delighting in the intoxication he sought to stimulate Rizpah's flagging energies by pushing her onward into the feverish brilliancy that was so delightful to himself. It was an attempt to cure physical impoverishment by the renewal of its causes. She was at times complacent, because incompetent to resist ; passive, because enervated. He was most selfish, though not realizing the fact, when trying to be most tender. In fact, the twain were on the rim of a test period in their married life and being unskilled in its common places, unfitted to stand the test. Sir Charleroy had recourse to the only physician he deemed adequate ; one whom on account of his dress he called "Old Sheepskin." This was a guide, with a motly group of Druses assistants, and an unpronouncible name.

"Come, Rizpah, 'Old Sheepskin Jacket' has put on his red tunic and leathern girdle to carry us a camel voyage in-sea ; if we do not give the man a job he'll fall to stealing again."

Rizpah languidly shook her head.

"But we must patronize the man to keep up what little honesty he has, and he has some. He told me but yesterday he'd rather work than rob—though the pay be less, so is the danger less."

The knight was telling the truth as well as trying to be facetious.

Again Rizpah replied with a weary shake of the

head, her hands rising deprecatingly, then falling into her lap as if almost nerveless.

"But, Rizpah, while we are here we ought to fully explore the changeless cities of this dead, black, lava sea. There are none other like this on earth! 'Tis nature's desperate effort to outrun phantasmagoria."

Rizpah shook her head and waved her hands; this time vehemently, as if to repel a horror.

"What? A fixed no?"

"No more excursions into this counterpart of hades for me."

"Well, so be it to-day, at least," with surrendering tones, the knight replied.

"To-day? All days! Oh, God, remove me from this nightmare?"

So exclaiming, the woman covered her eyes, shuddered and wept hysterically.

Sir Charleroy was almost overcome with sudden amazement. The tears, the terror, the complete change before him, were beyond his comprehension. After a time he again spoke: "Why, this is a sudden freak or frenzy. I thought Rizpah fascinated here!"

"I've had my notice from the dread sprits that infest the place to go! Didst thou note what dark and threatening clouds dipped down like vultures upon me when we were last there?" vehemently Rizpah replied.

"I only saw a threatening of rain that came not. It seldom rains in the Lejah."

"There was rain enough in my poor, shivering, weeping heart!"

"But, I wonder, Rizpah, thou didst not tell me of these feelings before!"

"I could not confide then; I was too jealous!"

"Jealous? What a word! But of whom, me?"

"I can never forget that thy union with me has made thee alien to thy people and in part neglectful of the faith for which thou didst once fight bravely. I can not forget that the Teutonic knight was the devotee of a bepraised Lady Mary. I thought of this that black day, and I felt as if those dry, grim clouds were her frowns. It was thou, my Christian husband, who named the Lejah, 'Tartarus,' and it has been such for some time to me. Its sight has constantly burned me with remorse! That day it seemed to me thy Mary pitied thee and blamed me! I writhed under the thought! I, for a moment, hated her. I felt like climbing some height, and, club in hand with defiant curses, challenging her right to have a finer care of thee than I have. I'd have done it, if thou hadst not been here to laugh at the folly of my frenzy. Ah, husband, if she is or was all that thou dost depict her, she can not love me, and thou must contrast us to my disparagement. I can not forget that thou wert a Christian soldier; sworn to war for her and her son; now thou art wedded to me, a daughter of her and His persecutors!"

"Why, Rizpah, thy changing moods are appalling; thou dost beat the magicians who conjure up the dead, since thou dost create out of nothing the most hideous ghosts to haunt thyself—Maya! Maya!"

"Oh, yes, I know 'Maya,' wife of Brahm, by interpretation 'illusion.' A myth, as a gibe, has a sharp point, effective because so difficult to parry. But, alas, ridicule, though it easily tear to pieces delusion, is powerless to disperse the gloom that sits in a soul as mine."

"I'll not ridicule my Rizpah, but I would bring her light."

"Ah? That is, resurrect the peace thou didst murder?"

"Show me one wound my hand has made and I'l abjectly beg all pardons, attempt any atonement!"

"Dost thou, knight, remember the ruins of the Christian church of Saint George, at Edrei?"

"Certainly."

"And thy conversation there?"

"Yes, that Saint George was England's patron saint, famed for having slain the dragon which imperiled a king's daughter."

"More thou didst say; thou didst expatiate on the princess, saying her name was Alexandra, meaning, 'friend of mankind'; further, thou saidst there was a queenly woman by name, Mary, daughter of the King of Kings, friend beyond all women of humanity, for whom every true knight was willing to be a Saint George."

"True enough; but to what purport now is this reminiscence?"

"Thou saidst Saint George was loyal to the death to his faith, and died a martyr!"

"True again. What of it?"

"Was the Teutonic knight thinking of himself as a martyr because wed to a Jewess? I followed thy thoughts, though they were not all spoken. How naturally that day thou didst tell me of thy visions which thou hadst between Gerash and Bozrah when wounded nigh to death. The English saint, knight, very loyal to creed, rebuked in his dreams, by the beating of mighty wings, the departing of his heart's rose! Oh, why didst thou not tell me this before it was too late! I would have helped thee escape the ingenuous Jewess

Thou didst awaken then with dread bleeding, to find thyself pillowed upon the bosom of a simple-hearted loving girl; I now awaken, wounded indeed, but with none to staunch the wounding! Why, de Griffin, didst thou keep this secret so long? Why unfold it now?"

"I'd be the Saint George of Rizpah and slay her dragon, gloom."

"Poor comfort to offer since the gloom is beyond thy powers! Flout my mood as thou mayst; what use? I vainly denounce it. Thou hast had thy dream; now I'm having mine. I'll not mock thy insights; thou canst not by bantering jeer change mine. My Lejah omens assure me that I'm to have a rain of tears and more; some way thy Mary will be their cause."

"Rizpah errs; the queen I revere was a living epistle of good will; her character the joy and inspiration of all women, especially of those in tribulation. But enough! Rizpah, being a Jew, should abhor the necromancy of omens!"

"Jew! Ah, yes; I was once! But the valiant English knight lured me into his Christian love and my race's hate. I had once the luxurious faith of a pious girl; all feeling, all flowers; too young to reason, but young enough to love the good and beautiful unto salvation. The knight poisoned the blossoms before they ripened by the acids of ridicule! There is a loss beyond repair and a bitter memory, that of a broken promise; under our love-star thou didst swear thou wouldst never lightly treat my believing. Venus has set, Mercury is rising; but wisdom brings a burning glare. The promise that the knight failed to keep was made when I was, he said his idol; now I'm only his wife!"

"Rizpah exchanges the glory of the rose for the bitter gray of the wormwood."

"I'm thy handiwork; now mock the result, if to do so comforts thee."

"My handiwork!"

"Yes, fool!"

"These words are awful."

"I think so and I hate them; though I can not check them. I hate my temper and even myself when in such present moods. De Griffin, pray as thou didst never pray before, that I do not learn to hate thee. I pity thee, because I've some love left."

"Pity?"

"Yes, when I imagine thee wriggling beneath the malignant detestation of which I know I shall soon be capable."

"My wife, in God's dear name, banish these moods! They are impious, unnatural; the crisis of thy being falsely accuses thy heart. Be calm!"

"Calm? 'Be calm!' Very good; calm me, please, if thou canst. Oh, why didst thou make me thus?"

"The God of all peace forgive me if I did, Rizpah'

"Thou wert the elder and shouldst have known?"

"What?"

"That to unsettle a woman's faith, if she be such as I, is to let loose a bundle of blind vagaries and to tumble her, like a drifting wreck, on unknown shores."

"Oh, wife, as thou hopest for heaven and lovest our unborn child, restrain these moods. Thou'lt mark the one to be, with germs of all evil; for such outbursts of mothers re-act with awful effect upon their offspring.

Thou knowest how the old nurse, at Damascus, killed a babe in an instant, merely by giving it her breast after she had yielded to an outbreak of passion. Such tempers hurl poison through all the being!"

"Alas, knight, that all this prudence ever comes just a little too late!"

"What could I have done better?"

"Left the little maid of Harrimai's home free from thy enchantments and to the quiet of her people's state."

"But I loved thee so. That atones for all."

"Thou thoughtst thou lovedst, but 'twas my form which fascinated thee, not my mind nor soul!" Rizpah's face became ashen pale, her eyes had a far-off gaze and were steelly, as she began plaintively to repeat the words, '*There were giants in the earth* * * . *They saw the daughters of men, Adamish, that they were fair and they took them for wives of all they chose, and they bore children and it repented the Lord that He had made man, for He saw that the wickedness was great in the earth.*' Thou wast my giant-lofty. Thou stolest my heart and body. Now for a flood to punish the sin, and my tears are already its first droppings."

"We are wed; shall we not now make the best of it? Even when into this mystic alliance unmated lives converge, they can still with wisdom extract from it at least peace. Go fervently, firmly, back to the faiths of thy girlhood; become again all thou wert, except that thou be ever mine."

"Ah, ha! how little, after all, thou knowest of woman's heart? Thou wouldst command it do and be; and go and come, wouldst thou? Thinkst thou, thou canst make such heart as mine wild with the strange intoxications of unholy fire, filling the brain above it with all the clouds, weird longings, doubtings and misgivings, that fume up from that fire, and then send that heart back without a compass, chart, sail or helm, to find the haven? Send it lashed by remorse part of the time, part of the time half dead to all feeling, and all the time blind, to hunt up lost creeds."

"But God provided an ark; let us ask Him to aid us build one in a home, with happy parents and happy children. Thou readst to me, but yesterday, the Prophets' beautiful description of a lamp burning with oil supplied from two palm trees; one on either side. I'll interpret; the trees are parents, the lamp the light of home, manifest in posterity, reproduction; a prophecy of the resurrection."

"Beautiful mysticism. But the giantesque men rose to play at lust, just beside Sinai of the law."

"Not so I, the Teutonic knight, now the husband. Rizpah; thy desperate misery appeals to all my manhood. I swear to thee I'd turn my heart's blood into the oil to cause our home to glow with the serene light of holy happiness."

"Words, words; how sad, because so beautiful, yet so vain!"

"Oh Rizpah," cried the knight, too anxious to be angry, though the woman's words were stinging, "thy looks startle me! Pray God to rest and hold thy worried soul."

"Pray? I have tried, often of late, to pray, but I do not know how. I fear thou hast stolen even that power from me! Ugh! the last time I prayed, my words seemed like black cormorants rising with loads of carrion; then falling struck dead by the sun, into great black caves, such as abound in our Lejah hell! I heard my words flung back at me in mockery. Pray? I dare not, lest God strike me dead for a hypocrite and a heretic!"

"But my poor, dear wife," soothingly said Sir Charleroy, "He is merciful."

"Oh, yes, to the good and the faithful; I'm neither! I gave Him up for a man, as the Adamish men gave him up for women. I madest thou my God, and now have none other; for He of the heavens is very holy, but very jealous!"

"Rizpah, Rizpah, do not thus give way to these wild imaginations."

"Give way? Alas, all is already given away; soul and body were on an idolatrous altar long ago. I'm buried in the ashes!"

"But Rizpah, trust my love: I'll help thee back to peace and usefulness."

"Bah! the masculine great I——"

"Heavens! woman, is there any love in a heart that so hurls javelins?"

"I don't know! I suppose so, for I pity thee."

"Pity me?"

"Yes; when I think as I do at times, that thy wife is turning into a devil, a very devil! Sir Charleroy de Griffin, knight of St. Mary, dost hear me? A devil, a raging devil, and one that will pity while she assails." The last sentence was almost screamed, then the woman fell on the rug of their apartment and wept convulsively. After a little there was the silence of exhaustion, of chagrin, of shame. Sir Charleroy stood by the prostrate form and with words half commanding said: "Let us ride out a little way." He was trying a new strategy.

"No, no, no! Thou'lt take me to the Lejah, and I shall see that dread omen again."

"What?" As he questioned he raised the woman tenderly from the floor.

"The lava desert, in long rolling waves, black and drear."

"Ah, Rizpah, thou knowest that it was only thy unreined fancy, heated by morbid broodings, that changed the eternally-fixed furrows of the plain, overshadowed by running clouds into threatening billows! God and the sun are above all clouds and behind every anxious heart. Look up; look in, until thy soul finds Him; then the horror of darkness will die away."

"Oh, how thy comfortings hurt me, because I do not believe in thee, nor believe thee! Thou sayst that thou didst abandon thy Christian, perfect queen of women, for me. I know thou must be chagrined at the bad exchange! I can not honor nor trust the faithfulness of one so fickle. No matter for that, but what comes after is worse. Those black sky-drapings were over the Lejah that day because I was there. I know—I know there's a tide of sorrow rolling toward me. I see it as I saw those black, serpent-like, lava waves. But, oh, the suspense! It's awful; let the worst come if only soon!" The knight, sworn to protect helpless women, saw himself disarmed and powerless to aid the one woman of earth for whom he would have died.

Two giants at bay in Giant Land, where another mold of gianthood had died leaving nothing but monuments to attest the greatness of the failure. The two knew only this, that they were very miserable and powerless, by any means accustomed, to extricate themselves.

Sir Charleroy wished and wished, in his soul, that his patron saint and queen of women would appear and tell both what to do. He unconsciously was turning his mind's eye in the right direction. Husband and wife both believed there was a right way, a pattern of right, and an ideal of heaven, but they could not lay hold of them. Giant, crusader and husband, each in turn strove in his day at the same spot, and at the same point failed.

Sir Charleroy, in mind, went out along a strangely beset line of thinking. Sometimes he pitied himself, and that brought the balm of conceit. He remembered it was a fine thing to be a martyr, forgetting that some, rewardless, suffer as sinners. Sometimes he heard those beatings of mighty wings, as if some wondrous holy one were departing. Then he became very penitent and full of the entreatings of prayer. Either mood was brief enough to him not yet converted; a very Peter in vacillations. Whether he would finally follow the beating wings or sit down nigh to the gates of certain insanity, the gates that those who over-much pity themselves are sure to reach, was the issue in his life then. The bugles of war call few to the heroism of the field, but millions are daily called by God's bugle to the better achievements which make for glory amid the duties of common life. That latter bugle was calling him, but he was slow to obey, or understand even.

The events recorded in the foregoing pages roused Sir Charleroy to an anxious effort to do something to change the currents of his wife's thoughts. Necessity quickened his discernment, and though he had had but little experience in dealing with those ill in the body or mind, he quickly concluded that a change of place and a change of pursuit would be beneficial. In truth, his own feelings attested this much. He himself was weary of the pursuit of excitement as a sole and constant occupation.

"Shall we leave the Lejah, Rizpah?" he questioned, a few days after the outbreak before mentioned.

"Yes, I say!—I'm leaving it! See here," and she pointed to her cheeks, once ruddy, now haggard. "Oh, Charleroy, take me away or death will!"

"Enough! We'll go. But where?"

"Any place under heaven; say the word and I'll run out of the place instantly, leaving all here."

"What, our effects!"

"Any thing to get away. I feel like a child approached by some monster terror, hour by hour! For days I've been transfixed by my fear or I would have run away, even alone, before this. Now thy words break the spell! Come, let us go before I'm overcome again!"

"There, now, be calm. No more of this undue nervousness. We'll go, and soon. What says Rizpah to Bozrah, southward of Bashan?"

"Yes, to Bozrah; historic Bozrah!" and the face of the woman brightened as she went on: "It was the fairy land of my youth. I've wanted to go there since I was a wee little thing, scarce able to walk." Then the woman unbent and talked with the rapture of a child:

"Oh; I've wanted to see Bozrah all my life, since the days when my old nurse used to talk me to sleep with stories of Og and his bedstead nine cubits long, and how our little Hebrew, Moses, overcame those Rephaim."

"Thy prophets and psalmists, as well as thy nurses, were wont to go into rapturous descriptions of the lofty oaks, loftier mountains, ragged plains, marvelous pastures and goodly herds of the Hauran and Trachonitis."

Rizpah continued in gleeful strain: "Oh, those herds; if I can't see old Og, I'd like to see the famous bulls of Bashan! Show me something huge, no matter how huge, if alive and not black! I'm becoming infatuated with the strong and the large. If ever I lose my soul it will be by worshiping, pagan-like, something mightier than I can imagine; of body or muscle. Yes, yes, I'll be a thorough pagan since I can not be a Jew nor a Christian! Now, I forewarn thee." So saying she laughed merrily. The knight was rejoiced to hear the musical, natural laughter again, and encouraged the play of her wit, which attested a mind unbending to rest.

"Woman-like, adoring the huge when the grand can not be found. Thank God, the giants are all dead; there are none at Bozrah, at least. I'll not fear the little dirty Arabs, or pigmy Druses as supplanters."

CHAPTER XV.

THE REVELS OF MEN AND RITES OF THEIR GODDESSES.

> "Rude fragments now
> Lie scattered where the shapely column stood.
> Her palaces are dust. In all the streets the sprightly chords
> Are silent. Revelry and dance and show
> Suffer a syncope and solemn pause;
> While God performs upon the trembling stage
> Of His own works His dreadful part, alone."
> —COWPER.

"Then shall ye know that I am the Lord, when their slain shall be among their idols, round about their altars * * * upon every high place * * * under every thick oak."—Ezekiel vi.

ASSING from Edrei toward Bozrah the pilgrim knight and his wife with their convoy reached Kunawat, the Kenath of Scripture, once the dwelling place of Job. Here for a time they abode. The number and variety of castles, temples, theaters and palaces in ruins, were sufficient to engage the attention of the travelers for many days. Rizpah was more cheerful than she was at Edrei, but yet restless to reach Bozrah, on which place her heart was set.

One day standing before an old Roman temple in Kunawat, Rizpah, somewhat interested by its well preserved Corinthian columns, and Sir Charleroy deeply engrossed in contemplation of an huge stone image, the former asks: " Has the knight recognized an old Eng lish or a new Bashan love?" The woman was finding the oft-repeated and prolonged visits to this particular place monotonous. She was annoyed, but modified her rebuke into raillery.

"There is something very fascinating in the Cyclopean face."

"A broken stone fascinate a man? But I see 'tis that of a woman; the brain part gone. Would that the English knight had wed such; then he might have been loyal to creed, and not a martyr!"

ASTARTE.

"Rizpah knows that I could never have loved a brainless face, nor any one akin to this Kunawat goddess."

"Not if she echoed thy 'aye' and 'nay' consistently? Be careful; as many strong men have fallen by having their conceit gratified as there have fallen women through flattery."

"How absurd to hint that I could be so lured."

"But the knight says Astarte fascinates!"

"I said so, meaning that I'm fascinated by the train of thoughts that the image awakens. Think a moment; we, the living of to-day confronting the acme of the thought of the ages long gone. Looking at this, I seem to be seeing over rolling centuries, right into the hearts of humanity that lived thousands of years ago."

"All this might have been taken in at a glance! Having seen it, what use is it?"

"Use? To aid in finding a key to life's problems. I'm filled with questionings; do not yearnings, such as beat through the being of the ancients pulse in those of to-day? Are not humanity's temptations and needs ever the same?"

"Since the ancients did not tarry to compare with us, I, being only a woman, of Gerash, of to-day, can give only the shallow answer, I suppose so."

"Oh, I'm not questioning Rizpah; but the ruins, the air, time, my soul, God!"

"And their reply?"

"Bewildering echoes of each question?"

"And it's all a mystery to Sir Charleroy?"

"I know a little; something, next to nothing."

"Possess curious me of that little, and I'll help thee wonder why so much greatness came to naught."

"That wondering is easily met; they had, as god, one whose head could be broken as this one's was; they that would survive must be sheltered by the Invincible."

Rizpah, meanwhile had drawn close to the huge stone face and placing one hand beneath the mouth, the other on the portion of the head just above the moon crown, her arms stretched well nigh to their limits quizically remarked:

"Those that dined with her must have had pyramids for chairs. What dost thou think they were like?"

"Crusaders?"

"Now, I'm tantalized. Crusaders two or three thousand years ago? How absurd!"

"Oh, certainly they were not known by the name, Crusaders: but they that followed Astarte and such-like deities, whether called Kenaihites, Rephaim, Moslem, Christians, or by other appellation are all soldier-pilgrims, dominated by an ideal. There have been many female deities among the pagans and there is a deal of paganism left in humanity."

"That's because half the race are men. Astarte would be very popular to-day with thy sex, if she were here in living form, a whole woman, instead of a fragment and beautiful also—"

"Thou dost not care to hear more of the female deities?"

"Oh, yes; I'll be fearfully jealous if thou dost keep any thing back. Tell me what madmen the ancients were?" She paused, slapped the face of the image, ejaculating "*Virago!*" then continued, "Why did they make their effigy both hideous and huge? Ugly things should be dwarfed!"

"The ancients, who knew not the grandeur of moral power, gave their deities terribleness in their physical proportions, and a mountain of flesh became their ideal of greatness—men ever try to make their objects of worship greater than themselves, thou knowest. Hast forgotten what Ichabod once told us of the Egyptians?

How they expressed their reverence by piling up pyramids and made that very diminutive which they would caricature? Oh, how our true religion, having at its heart an only, all-beautiful, Almighty God, rises above these human devices!"

"I wonder that it did not, at its first appearing on earth, instantly overthrow all others."

"And it is a still more wonderful thing that those who embraced it, having known, should have sometimes gone back to paganism? Thou dost remember that God's chosen people, after enjoying marvels of His Providence, plunged headlong into idolatry in the very presence of His splendor at Sinai?"

"With shame I remember it. I marvel as well that this record, which evokes the ridicule of the grosser heathen, was made part of our Holy writings."

"God's compensation! The people stripped themselves of their jewels to make the calf; then of their garments to worship it according to the lewd rites of Apis. God since has lashed them naked around the world, as it were, by giving their history to all times. '*Be sure your sin will find you out*,' is a stern truth haunting the conscience of the evil doer; but though exposure is a bitter medicine it is a saving one. God as such applies it."

"I think the devil crazed the people at Sinai."

"Yes, Rizpah, but Human Desire was his name. The revelers made their devil as well as their calf, that day."

"But it is said 'they rose to play.' If so disobedient and heaven-defying how could they have found heart to play?"

"Odious, significant word that one is, here. It was

a '*play*' that engulphed all purity. No wonder they ceased to observe the 'burning mountain!' Only the pure in heart can see God."

"Thank God! that thy people and mine have finally escaped, my husband."

"So far as we have escaped, I thank Him; but, alas, the evangels of Egypt's scarlet heresies still go about, and there are many, everywhere, led away in chains that seem of flowers at first, but are found to be of galling iron at last."

"I did not know this?"

"Oh, these modern perverters disguise their horrible tenets with many refined phrases; yet He that overwhelmed gross Sodom and the jewelless, naked dancers about the golden bull, sees through all their thin drapings and will judge the free lover, corrupt socialist and libertine as He did those ancients. The Assyrian and Egyptian representations of Venus generally appeared holding a serpent; a sort of bitter admission of the curse in the hand of perverted love and the fierce lashings that follow it."

"I fail to connect the ancient with the present heresies, my good teacher."

"I pause to-day here, reminded of their common origin and consequences. God put it into the hearts of His creatures to love women, honor motherhood, and worship Him. Read Sinai's law, and this is all manifest. There came a perversion; the love of woman was degraded, motherhood was denied its honor, and men became God-defying. There was a confusion worse than that of Babel, and the worshiping was transferred, first, to symbolized lust; then degraded. They that adored Venus, knowing how her adoration had depraved themselves, came to believe that she scandalized the heaven they imagined. Then came a time when her earthly rites even scandalized the wiser pagans."

" My husband leads me along strange ways. Is it wise to do so ? "

" I see a grand end; follow me. There is a deep significance in the fact that among the pagans there constantly appeared this adoration of woman on account of her power of motherhood. I take this adoration as proof of a conscious need feeling after a vaguely discerned truth. The yearning is suggested by the paired gods. Assyria had its Beltis, consort of Bel-nimrud ; and there were Alleita of the Arabians, the many-breasted Diana of the Ephesians, the Aphrodite of the Greeks, Ceres and Venus of Rome, this Astarte of the Giants; beyond all, in utter odiousness Khem, the Phallic god of Egypt. Amid all these false ideals, the divine home with its pure love and our immortality by grace's mystery, were overslaughed in human thought. The glaring passions, that were unwilling to believe in other immortality than that that comes through posterity, other heaven than that of sensuous pleasure, fascinated and dominated hearts and souls."

" And worshiping women-gods did this."

" Worshiping beings with the form of women did it! Reverence for true womanhood ever exalts and never degrades. But these ancients adored very gorgons with snakes for hair, and having tearing, brazen claws. They set these gorgons with the Harpies, in their mythologies, at the gates of dark Pluto's palace. Alas, where men are led by ill-flavored women, is ever more Pluto's gateway."

"The up-digging of these ancient soils, knight, give forth foul odors. Did they not dread a just and jealous God?"

"No. It is the constant voice of history that false belief concerning these things of which I have spoken, brings both blindness and degradation. Unbelief comes swiftly in the wake of impurity. The gorgons had but one eye and that had the malign power of turning to stone all upon whom its glance fell. When men deify a fallen woman then look for a cataclysm of evils. Rizpah has seen little of the world, but this in time she'll find true; the man whose cult or faith bends toward the libidinous is on the way to utter atheism. So these old-time free-lovers, like those of to-day, push out of the universe in their belief, the Great, Beautiful, First Cause. The pure in heart see God; the impure can not even pray to Him. The latter must be aided by an Immaculate One. They make a gulf betwixt their souls and heaven, which Great Mercy alone can bridge."

"Ah, knight, I'd dread a return of those gross idolatries, knowing mankind's trend, but that I knew that Shiloh was to come as a Reformer." The knight caught at the words of his wife to lead her toward his own dear belief.

"If He came to Rizpah in the form of a man, unique because of his virgin purity, unlike any other in being all unselfish, and accompanied by a peerless woman, exemplifying all that is best in the gentle sex; between Himself and that woman a love deep to love's last depth, pure as a sunbeam, enduring as eternity itself, would Rizpah welcome Him!"

"That would be a wondrous coming; but I'd welcome Him."

"Does Rizpah believe such an appearing desirable?"

"Oh, on my soul, yes! If he should so come, methinks the rites which have gone on in the secrecy of the groves, under the uncertain light of the moon, would be driven from the earth, and men come to worship God, taking that man for the ideal of manhood, that woman as woman's pattern."

"Dost thou see that stone with eight lines crossing, lying just there by the image of Astarte?"

"I see it and the lines; but what of them?"

"In the far East, the land of the Fire Worshipers, on almost all the handiwork of man that symbol is placed. It is to represent an eight-pointed star, the Assyrian sign of immortality."

"Eight lines crossing to represent immortal life? This is inane!"

"Not quite. I had its explanation from my wandering Jew, Ichabod, learned by much travel in the lore of many peoples. He thus interpreted the symbol as the Assyrians understood it; man, a four-pointed star; his four radiate limbs suggesting that likeness. Thou knowest that the Israelites have been wont to call men stars? The Assyrians, not having the sure word, were led to seek by human philosophy a theory of immortality, and they got no further than twice four, two human beings in union; so eight or a double star, their symbol of marriage, represented the only immortality they were able to find; that that comes from reproduction. At least that was the only reality, the rest being very vaguely believed, and believed only because they thought that the mystery of a new life coming forth, was a hint of a spiritual method analogous to the material. They then fell to worshiping the sun, the great fructifier and light of nature; fire, the essence of passion, became their highest god. It is said that those Magi of the East, that arrived long ago at Bethlehem, were fire worshipers, and that in answer to a cry for light, constantly uttered by their race, they took their journey to Judah, seeking it."

"The world must turn to Israel ever for the truth, Sir Charleroy."

"For some truth; not all; but there is a tradition that the star the wise men followed was a double one, two planets in conjunction. There is a fitness in the legend, for the seekers of light were brought to the cave where lay a mother and babe; the latter God's finest presentment of immortality, the Incarnation; the fruit of the Divine in union with the human. I stand overcome with wonder and reverence when I remember that they of the East had some light from the Jews they held captive ages before. They lost most of what they had, then, longing for its return, God answered their prayer by taking them to the finest of schools, a blessed home circle. Behold all the East looking for light at Bethlehem!"

Rizpah evaded her husband's graceful attempt to impress on her Christian tenets, by replying: "I prefer the Jewish choice number Seven, though I can not give it fine interpretations, as thou to the Eight of the East."

"Rizpah prefers it because it is Jewish, and I prefer Seven because I read therein a covenant; for Seven is the sacred covenant number of God's Word. Let me interpret: There is a Triune God, symbolized by Three; then man, the child of chance, the being tossed hither and thither by the four winds, a complex union himself of body, mind, animal life and immortal spirit. Four is his representative number, or symbol. The Assyrians paired fours; the Jews vaguely discerned a grander path to eternal felicity through the conjunction of God and man, the Three and the Four. From this they derived their covenant number, Seven."

"These are charming explanations, Sir Charleroy; especially so, if sure ones!"

"But the truths are fairer than my poor words. I read that at creation the morning stars—meaning the beings that know no night, the very sons of God—shouted for joy! They saw an immortality having its springs in the being of the Eternal, and were glad. Since then the race has diverged into two lines. The gross and unbelieving, seeking to effect the apotheosis of human lust, have gone their ways reveling under the moonlight, and building their fanes in the groves which fade, while the believing and God-taught have walked in a covenant toward Him, 'Who only hath immortality dwelling in light.' Rizpah, some day that home group at Bethlehem, a father, mother, and child, surrounded by angels, overshadowed by God, will come to be thought the finest ideal of this life. Yea, a picture of Heaven itself!"

The knight's wife fixed her piercing, dark eyes on his, there were expressed in her countenance admiration and fearfulness. She was charmed by his lofty sentiments, yet apprehensive of being led into some dangerous, Christian heresy. Fanaticism always has a terror of heresy, so-called, even though it seemed to be full of white truth. Presently she questioned:

"So Og, great as a mountain of flesh, and Astarte,

goddess of the pleasure that kills, only, of all Kunawat's ancients, have left enduring names?"

"One other name endures, the ages brightening its luster—Job, loyal to the last, in spite of the devil and a virago wife."

"Poor woman! say I of Job's wife. None have told her side of her family troubles. May be Job haunted the grove of the moon-crowned?"

"May be? Never! His splendid orations bespoke a man walking nigh Jehovah. Listen: 'If I beheld the moon walking in brightness, if my heart hath been secretly enticed, or my mouth kissed my hand, let thistles grow instead of wheat.' He said this amid the votaries of the Lust-Queen."

"And Job may be praised, not only as proof that there has been one patient man on earth, but as proof that a good man will stand pure to the last, though the world about acclaim the praise of delightful sins?"

"He stood because entranced by his beautiful ideal. He loved Him whose name is Holiness."

"Heaven comes at last to such."

"Job was God's best friend on earth in his day, and his Heavenly Father gave him as his reward His best earthly gift—a new, pure, happy, fruitful home."

"Are we through now with the fascinating image, knight?"

"Yes, Rizpah, if we take to heart its warnings. May we preserve our integrity, and have a home as our reward finer than that of the Man of Uz; yea, verily, as fine in its tempers and virtues as that of Bethlehem."

So saying, the knight led Rizpah toward their abode.

CHAPTER XVI.

A BATTLE OF GIANTS AT BOZRAH.

"Sleep—the ghostly winds are blowing !
No moon abroad—no star is glowing.
The river is deep and the tide is flowing
To the land where you and I are going !
    We are going afar,
    Beyond moon or star,
To the land where the sinless angels are !

I lost my heart to your heartless sire
('Twas melted away by his looks of fire),
Forgot my God, and my father's ire,
All for the sake of a man's desire ;
    But now we'll go
    Where the waters flow,
And make our bed where none shall know."
—" *The Mother's Last Song.*"—BARRY CORNWALL.

"How shall we order the child, and how shall we do."-
Judges xiii. 12.

IR CHARLEROY and his consort took up their abode in one of the many deserted ancient stone houses of the city of Bozrah. The latter, situated in one of the most fertile plains of earth, once having upward of one hundred thousand inhabitants, several times having risen to metropolitan splendor, ages ago sank into neglect, decay and desolation. But with wonderful persistence that city preserves the records, or relics, of

what it was in better, greater days. The antiquarian to-day finds in and around Bozrah the dwellings, palaces and temples of many and various peoples, some piled in strata-like courses, one above the other, each layer the tombstone of its predecessor; some is fine as they were forty centuries ago. The annalist there has at hand as an open book the achievements of some of the mightiest men of earth, physically. The latter were contemporary with that line of God's moral giants, of which Abraham, Moses and David were representative leaders first, and Christ finally. The strata of Bozrah tell of differing policies, politics, religions; all alike in one thing—the attempt to build upon the buttresses of giant force; but they present in the end the one result—failure; all being equally dead at the last, if not equally herculean at the first. Sheer robustness in the armies of Rome, the Turk, Alexander, and Og wrought out their best about the Bashan cities, and in that theater played the eternally losing game of all such. It seems as if God had chosen that part of all the world to illustrate this great lesson of His providence. The Roman, Mohammedan, Greek, and others like them, there had their brutal and sensuous existence. There the Crusader carried also his banners; but the end of the Rephaim was the forerunner and prophecy of all the other giantesque gatherings that followed after them. Each passing race and dynasty left its monuments and tokens of possession; but of all, those of the first, the giants, are the most enduring, most wonderful. These dateless, huge, rugged, fort-like dwellings, standing just as they did four thousand years ago, except that they are mostly unoccupied, are impressive monuments and reminders of the mighty denizens who once abode within them. There are ruins of temples, palaces, houses of commerce and places of amusement, but chiefly of homes; the latter, significantly, instructively, being the best preserved of all. Sir Charleroy observed this circumstance, and casually remarked to Rizpah, as they bestowed their effects in one of the ancient domiciles:

"If ever I take to building, I'll build abiding places for people, only. Such are the most lasting."

But while he came thus near to a royal truth, he did not make it his own. It passed through his mind and he felt its light, as one might that from the wing of a ministering spirit, while his eyes were holden and his back turned. He immediately left the angelic thought, to go wandering through years of misery, before coming back face to face with it again. Sir Charleroy and Rizpah, a western soldier and a woman of Israel, two giants in their way, began a new career at Bozrah. It was providential. Measuring power by the only available test at hand, namely, what it accomplishes, it was manifest long ago to all that the brawn of the Cyclops was not the master force of the word. Hercules cleansed the earth of mythical, not real evils. Sir Charleroy and Rizpah are fittingly brought to the theater of the giants for the purpose of testing the potency of giantesque sentimentality and stubborn, mighty ardor. To this end, two will do as well as a nation, and a decade will be as conclusive as a score of generations. The husband and wife entered Bozrah gladly, and quickly adapted themselves to their new surroundings. They were both very impressible, and there were many things in their new environments that impressed and stimulated them. Nature's face and locations may be changed by man, but he can not change her heart. She, on the other hand, is invincible in her conquests of both his face and inner being. Climate and environments determine the characters and careers of the majorities. The sleets of the North, in time, will goad the sensuous Turk or Hottentot to high activity, while the Cossack or Esquimaux, under tropical suns soon fall into luxuriousness and laziness. Bozrah began its molding of the knight and his wife. Rizpah and Sir Charleroy were at first attracted to Giant Land by the hugeness of its monuments and ghostly greatness of its record. They received at Bozrah their first impulse to settle and make a home. Probably they were largely influenced by the conviction that, in its way, there was nothing more entrancing or majestic beyond. For the best results to them, the second selection was altogether unfortunate. They had made their home in the midst of battle-fields, and the atmosphere that hung over all things was like that over a defeated army, sullenly submitting. The new comers from the beginning, in their new home, were immersed in ghostly memories, and that atmosphere so like the breath of a bound yet struggling giant. They were affected more than they realized by all these things.

"No more tours, no more worlds, for us to conquer!" exclaimed the knight.

Rizpah, her cheerfulness of mind largely recovered, replied to this remark of Sir Charleroy with a bantering laugh, at the same time pointing upward. Quickly, and with retort cruel as a giant's javelin, he cried:

"Alas, so soon Rizpah seeks my final departure from her!"

The cavalier was no more; it was the brusque and gross within him that spoke. Had he been courtly, even without being Christian, he would have been considerate enough not to have cruelly jested concerning that which lay in his wife's heart as a possible and sad fact. Often the thought of eternal separation from her husband, even from eternal hope, haunted her now. Her husband knew this.

For a moment his answer seemed to stun her; then the affectations of pouting on her mobile face, coming when she pointed upward, changed into lines of anger. A hot flush mounting up to the roots of her hair, hung out the warning signal.

The knight, pretending not to observe the change, twined his arms about his wife and mockingly sighed:

"Poor girl! I can find no wings on thee. I once thought thou hadst such. They must have dropped off."

There was no reply. He then began to retreat, to placate, and to that intent drew her closer and closer to his heart, until, embracing her, his hands clasped; but, for the first time since the event near Gerash, when the Arabs were vanquished, his caress was without response. He tried a thrust thus:

"Well, beloved, since thou dost banish me, bestow a kiss of long farewell."

Quickly, Rizpah flung aside his embracing arms and cried: "Shechemite! I'm no Dinah, won by false professions!"

"*Shechem was more honorable than all the house of his father*," quoted the knight in reply.

"He loved himself, his passions; to these gods he gave up with all devotion, and they immolated him. That was good!"

"Why, Rizpah, thou art pettish."

"'Rizpah!' Thou art adroit in using bitter similes; a brutalizing power, when brutally used! Now, call me 'Jarnsaxa.' Thou toldst me, yesterday, how that mighty male god of the Norse, Thor, while hating her people, to the death, stole Jarnsaxa. Yea, and how many giants fell for women. Perhaps thou didst want me to pity thee. We are in Giant Land now, and thou canst begin to play Colossus!"

The knight was startled, and quickly entreated: "My queen, lets drop the masks; no more of this; forget my sarcasm, and I'll forgive the recriminations. A truce and pardon, in the name of love. What says Esther?"

"'Esther?' Thou calledst me that when cavalier, turning lover. Thou art neither now!" The sentence ended in a petulant sob.

"Oh, stay now. It was playfulness. I—there, now! Canst thou not brook a little playfulness from me?"

"Playfulness? Bah! Ye men play so like lions, forgetting to keep the claws cushioned! But, now thou hadst better be going, saint—the only one here Go, now, right along to heaven. They want thee there. They want thee, not me." Then she choked back another sob, but instantly thereafter, dashing the rising tear from her eyes, she bitterly exclaimed: "At any rate, thou'lt have company!"

"Whom, pray?"

"The begetter and chief of all restless vagabonds!"

"So; I never heard of him. Has he a name, my dear?"

The knight was sarcastic, because he was nettled.

Rizpah's eyes glittered with the fire of offended pride, and she quickly began in measured tone, as if in soliloquy, and alone, to quote Job's record of satan's joining the assembly of the sons of God :

"*There was a day when the sons of God came to present themselves before the Lord, and satan came also. And the Lord said whence camest thou? Then satan said from going to and fro in the earth and from walking up and down in it.*"

"My wife responds to my penitence with bitterness; but even the pagans were wiser. They ever took the gall from the animals offered to Juno, goddess of wedlock."

"Thy wife promised to be thy helpmate and give thee all she had. Now, just forget thy fine paganism, being a Christian long enough to remember that I'm thy helpmate in all things, even in bitterness. I give thee all, even returning thy giving."

"Thou shouldst not make so much of my little misstep."

"Nothing is little with which one must constantly live. Great breaks grow from little fractures. One may stand a blow, but its the constant fretting that roughs the heart-strings to woe unendurable. Thou hast a habit of playfully hurting."

"Well, this has been a day at school; there ought to be a school for husbands! We do not half understand the fine, sensitive creatures that companion us."

"Oh, thou thoughtst thou wert a woman-reader!"

"Were I to see an angel with a body like a harp, eyes like the unsearchable ocean, heart of flame, arms like flowering vines, covered with prismatic wings, I'd be no more puzzled and abashed than I am now by my high-strung, fine-tempered Rizpah."

"Puzzled! abashed! I'd help thee pity thy wounded conceit, but that I know that thou art soon to ascend. Art thou going now!"

"I'am afraid not, since I've so many more sins than graces. When elephants soar with butterfly wings, thou mayst look for my departure. Till then I'll stay here and practice the patience of Job, beset with his rambling devil."

"How elegantly the cavalier uses simile in coining epithets."

"Heavens! Rizpah, thou dost twist my meanings! Why distort, instead of pardoning my blunders, making both of us miserable!"

"Oh, then, thou hast grace enough not to liken me to thy besetting, evil spirit, at least in words?"

"No, no, 'tis refined cruelty to put me on the defense as to that. Believe it or not, Rizpah of Gerash and Rizpah of Bozrah are the same. My heart to its core says so!"

This second quarrel, that should not have been begun, had the merit of ending, as it should, in reconciliation, tears, embraces and a great many excellent pledges. Yet Sir Charleroy did not greatly profit by the experience. He failed to perceive that these first breaks in the rythmic flow of conjugal love are great shocks to a deeply affectionate woman. He knew that men easily recover from rebuffs, and so did not stop to consider that young wife-hood was the highest expression on earth of utter clinging to one sole support He knew his own feelings and took them for the standard. He set himself up as the pattern, quite unconsciously, perhaps; and after the conflict in which he came off conceded victor, he was condescending in his manner. This was unfortunate. Rizpah did not need to be told that her husband was wiser and stronger willed and more self-possessed and more able to endure life's trial than herself. All this she believed, absolutely, when she surrendered her heart to the man at the first. Woman-like, these were the very circumstances that caused her to love him as she did. A woman never loves completely until her love is supplemented by adoration. She must believe the man, who would make full conquest, is one to whom she can look up; one some way her superior. But while a loving woman will give a devotion almost religious, she will be pained amid her delights of committal by a haunting fear that he whom she adores may rise away from her. In the very plenitude of her fullest love-worship she will deny the reverence, sometimes, in a seeming inconsistency, rebuff and even ridicule her idol. It is with her a sort of hysteria, a confession of secret terror, lest she and he grow apart in mind, and so come to part in body. Hence it is a giant cruelty on the part of a husband, sometimes, to enforce, or thrust forward, his size or his lordship. They may be facts, but God has set over against them as their equal that love which clings, stimulates and supplements, without which the finest man is far less than the half of the united twain. Sir Charleroy blundered along in his error; Rizpah tried to be happy and failed. She did not know how to make the best of her surroundings, and Sir Charleroy did not know, because he did not seek religiously to find out how to help her make the best of them. They had some periods of pleasure, but they continually grew briefer and were more frequently interrupted as time went on. She was ill, he suffered himself to think her at times ill-tempered. As a lover, he admired her outbreaks as very brilliant, and flattered her by remarking that she had the metal of an Arabian steed; as a husband, he thought her very disagreeable when pettish or angry. Indeed, though he never said so to her, he did say to himself that at times she was very like a virago. The only steed that came to his mind then was the ass, to which he likened himself when he considered himself the perfection of submissive patience.

A new event radically changed the picture and situation in this troubled home.

The prayer of prayers was heard in Bozrah; the cry of a baby; a bundle of needs and helplessness, with no language but a cry. Processions of silent centuries had passed through those halls since they echoed the hoarse voices of the brawny beings who built them. One could not hear the infant cry without remembering the contrasts. A baby; a puny one at that, and of the gentler sex, besides being of a race pigmy compared to the stalwarts who builded those abodes. Sir Charleroy and his consort had set up their household gods, and for a goodly period had occupied as theirs a Rephaim home.

The little stranger came, though they did not discern it, with power to bless them both. A poetic visitor, happening on this baby's hammock there and then, might have gone in raptures, to some truths, after this fashion: "It will be the golden tie, angel of peace and hope, to the home!" The philosopher, seeing the little bundle of helplessness, might have said: "Here is a giant, the home is immortal through its offspring, the babe requiring so much, richly repays its loving care-takers by inducting them into the soul expansions of unselfish service." But then poets and philosophers often miss the mark, attempting prophesy.

The parents followed the usual course of those for the first time in that relation. Their love for each other, very intense, and by its sensitiveness witnessing after all that it was very selfish, got a new direction. They soon drifted into the charming fooleries of their like. Sometimes they petted the child unceasingly, and one was anon jealous of the other if surpassed in this. They each struggled for a recognition from the innocent, and debated as to whether the first babble of the little one was "mamma" or "papa." Then there were times when they handled baby very reverently, as if it were something from God, or likely to break.

At such times they each, in heart, thanked God and gave the child, at least in part, to Him. Sometimes they called it "Davidah" or "darling," and laughed as they assured each other, to assure themselves, that the baby looked wise as if understanding. Sometimes they played with it as if they were children and it a toy; sometimes they ministered to it with anxious care, while all the time they felt quite sure it was somehow of finer mold and fiber than any babe before on earth. They were just like all for the first time parents, and their raptures were now for good, being centered around the thought expressed by the sweet word home. Of course, the question of naming the child was discussed, and, of course, no name they could think of seemed quite good enough. Some days the child was given a dozen, and some days it had none; for all the time they kept trying to fit it.

In one thing, both parents were Jewish, namely, the desire to give their darling an appellation expressive of what it was or what they hoped it would be. They first agreed on "Angela," but that was discarded as being a sort of advertisement of the quality of their treasure. In the constant selfishness of love they would keep it all secretly, sacredly to themselves, they said. They sought for many days some significant token or name that should be fully expressive of their thought, and yet by the three only be ever fully understood. One day Rizpah, always abrupt, still nursing an old superstition, said: "Call her Marah, a mournful, sweet, expressive title."

"Why, wife, that means 'bitterness.'"

"Bitterness, since I believe that somewhere, somehow, there is bitterness enough in store for her—and me with her"

"I'd prefer 'Mary,' my wife; surely this little angel is to be all like that blessed one."

Then there was more strife, but of a rather patient kind, which ended in a compromise, they calling the child Miriamne, each in mind meaning different from the other; the one Marah, the other Mary. But on the heels of this came soon the graver problem, How should the babe be reared, in Jewish faith or Christian? It was the old, old story of a difficulty seemingly easily adjusted to all, except to those who have actually met it, and in this case, as usual, the two parties fanatically opposed each other. In the name of sweet religion they loyally served the devil for a time. The highest achievement of a creed or faith is the soothing and elevation of a home here, or the exalting of it heaven-ward for hereafter. That is a travesty of piety which wrecks the substance of joy for the shell of a dogma. This stricture is easily written and may pass without dissent, the reader immediately falling into the error denounced. Of course, as usual, these two parents began the discussion of the subject. At intervals they cautiously pressed their arguments, but each unwaveringly moved toward his or her point. They were like advancing armies, firing occasional shots, but surely approaching a mighty issue. They pretended to argue the matter by times, but it was a farce, for each in mind irrevocably had predetermined the conclusion. Time sped on a year or more, then the conflict fully came.

"Rizpah, we were wed by a Christian, let us take the fruit of that compact to Christian baptism."

"The first act was an error; we shall not atone for it by repetitions in kind! The child is mine; I decline."

"And mine, so I request."

"A mother imperils her whole life for her child, and unreservedly gives to it part of herself; justice, humanity, should give the child to the mother, so far as may be."

"But even under thy faith, I, the father, am the head of the house."

"Under my faith the nurture and training of children belong chiefly to the mother, and my faith has been the finest society-builder of the world in the past. Thou hast often recounted to me the deeds of that golden, heroic time of my people, when the great Maccabean family led us and inspired us. Well, then, the mothers had exclusive control of the daughters until they were wed, and so they had grand daughters among the Maccabees."

"Well, we differ in belief; we had better compromise."

"We dare not barter a little soul to do it."

"Well, briefly then, being lord of this home, I command that the grace-giving sacrament be sought for our Mary."

"My faith, to which thou didst first appeal, forbids fathers to command their children to walk through idolatrous fires. Marah shall not."

"Hush; I only want the loved one inducted into the true faith."

"Mine is the older and truer."

"With thee argument is futile; I insist ——"

"If the father is a foreigner, Jewry's rule is that the children are to be called by the mother's name and regarded as of her family. Make such law as thou choosest for thy family but not for mine."

"I'll end this," cried Sir Charleroy, seizing the child, as if to hasten then to seek some priest's ministry.

Rizpah's eyes glittered with sullen purpose. She sprang before him, and hissed:

"Our fathers escaped at all cost from Egypt. I'll not go back, nor Marah."

The knight was surprised, and his looks expressed it as he said:

"Dost thou rave?"

"Oh, no, I was just remembering that a bearded serpent was the Egyptian symbol of deity; something like a man. You Christians would have all husbands gods to their families! No bearded serpent for mine!"

"Heavens, woman! thinkest thou thy scorn and vituperation can stay me?" So saying he pushed, or rather half flung the woman from him. He had no conception of the rage that any thing like a blow evokes in the heart of a woman that could love as once did Rizpah. On his part it was intended as a masterpiece of strategy, in the hope that the woman would swoon, then surrender in the weakness of following hysteria. The act was hateful to him, but he justified it by the end sought, yet missed that end.

Rizpah was a tigress roused, and like many another mother, beast or human, when the fight is once for offspring was endowed with sudden, supernatural strength. She sprang toward the hammock, plucking her dagger meanwhile from its hiding-place.

"Heaven defend us, woman!" cried Sir Charleroy, glancing about for a means of prevention, "thou wouldst not do murder?"

"Oh, no, thou art not fit to die; but hear me; this blade, consecrated to defense from dishonor, saved me once. Dost thou remember? It will do it again, if need be. The giver sleeps, but his stern charge haunts me still. 'Protect at any cost from dishonor!'"

"Wouldst thou shed blood of any here!"

"Sir Charleroy saw me slay the Turk. Had I failed, thou falling, this blade would have found my own heart. Push me onward by thy imperiousness and I will slay the babe and then myself! Methinks, it would be an atonement for which my parent would forgive my breaking of his heart. Ah, then sweet rest; life's tumults over! God would pity the tempest-tossed soul that, through such bitterness, flung itself on Him."

"Dost mean all this, Rizpah?"

"Can I trifle? Ask thyself. Have I ever? My desperate sincerity made me thy wife, but now it impels me to defy all thy attempts to make me thy minion, unthinking echo or slave; or worse, the ruiner of that girl."

"Well, then, woman, since thou or I must yield and I can not, thou wilt not, I execute my before announced purpose to have my lawful authority acknowledged with thee or——"

"Say the rest, find peace away from me——"

"Which?" sternly demanded the knight.

"As thou dost wish, only I'll not give up my child to Christian sacrifice."

"Then we can not live in peace together."

"To which I reply, that God never ordained marriage to bind people to the home when they can only for each other in that home make a very Tartarus!"

The knight was humiliated. He had believed that the woman's heart could not bear the thought of separation, and now to find her willing to give him up, rather than her will, her faith, hurt his pride. But they had made an utter crossing of purposes. He ran out of their stone house, his heart as stony. A little way off he paused, looked back, and said, "For the last time, Rizpah, what dost thou say?"

"Go; once for love I gave up all. Again I do it; I give thee up for the highest of all love, the love of a mother for her child!"

Caressingly Rizpah embraced the infant, and then fell on her knees with her face averted from her husband. He took one glance, and realizing the defeat of his strong will by that kneeling woman, angrily hurried away. The die was cast. He turned his back on Rizpah, swearing that he would never more return.

For a few days Rizpah lived in a crazy dream; now laughing as she thought of her victory; again letting her maiden love re-assert itself; then assuring her heart that all was over and well as it was. But a woman who imagines that reproach or even open violence can utterly extirpate love that once completely possessed her, knows not her own heart. Especially is this true if to that heart, she at times, press, lovingly, a child begotten in that love, and the form bearing the impress of that man for whom sometime she would have willingly died.

* * * * * * *

One night the baby cried piteously, being ill, and Rizpah was feeling very lonely because so anxious for it. She had sometimes, since Sir Charleroy's departure, prattled with the baby calling "papa" and "Charleroy," mother-like, woman-like. Self-condemning, for this was a half confession that she would have the little one think, if it thought at all, that she, the mother, was not to blame for the absence. The baby had caught some names and in its moaning, feverishly cried: "Abbaroy, Abbaroy; I want my Abbaroy." The cry was piercing to the mother's heart and conscience. She even then wished for the husband's return. Indeed, some hot tears fell as she prayed God to send "papa Charleroy back." The tie of marriage, potent beyond all of earth, now drew her away toward the absent one, and she then began to marvel how easily they had separated; how lightly they had regarded the bonds which after all tightly held them. When lives have blended and been tied together by other lives, it is indeed a prophesy of union "until death do us apart."

"Abbaroy, Abbaroy! I want my Abbaroy," still piteously cried the sick child. The night without was raging; the little lamp sent dancing shadows over the black walls of her room and an unutterable loneliness took possession of the woman. One by one thoughts like these arose; "Father dead, mother dead; husband as good as dead; perhaps really so, and my child like to die! What if she should die thus crying for her father! Oh, God spare me this! I'd go mad by her corpse. "Abbaroy, I want my Abbaroy," sobbed the child in her sleep. The mother heard the waving palms without. Her vivid imagination turned them into persons, spirits. They seemed to be her dead ancestors and they caught up the cry of her child rebukingly "Abbaroy, I want my Abbaroy." She swooned now and slept. In the sleep there came a dream. She thought she saw her daughter, grown to womanhood, but pale and sad. She had the hand of her mother and was drawing her toward the sea. Whenever the mother drew back the daughter wailed "Abbaroy, I want my Abbaroy." Presently their feet touched the water edge, she saw a ship, floating at anchor, but with sails spread partly; on its stern was the name, "*England*." The captain stood by the vessel's side, observing her. At last he cried: "Well, how long must we wait for thee?" A wave seemed to dash against her face and she awakened. The heavy window blind of stone had swung open, the rain was beating in on her. She started up and felt for her child, half fearfully lest a corpse should meet her touch. But she found her hands clasping a little form with fast beating heart and burning skin. The light had gone out, but there alone in that desolate home amid the ruins of past ages, the woman bowed in agonizing prayer. The balm of broken hearts was sought and she for a time was clothed and in her right mind. She arose, serenely, in the morning the cry of the sea captain of her dream in her ears, and the firm resolve in her heart to seek her husband even in far-off England; with him to try for the things that make for peace. Then she opened the iron-bound chest that had come to her from her father and took therefrom a roll of the '*Kethrubim*' and read. And it so happened that seeking to refresh her mind as to the story of how the giant Sampson got honey out of the slain lion's carcass, that she might more fully apply the meaning to her own experience, she came to the story of his birth. That story fixed her attention for days. It was like a new revelation to her. And she read and read these words over and over:

"And there was a certain man of Zorah, of the Danites, whose name *was* Manoah.

"And the angel of the LORD appeared unto the woman, and said unto her, Behold now, thou shalt conceive and bear a son.

"Then the woman came and told her husband, saying, A man of God came unto me, and his countenance *was* like an angel of God, and he said unto me, Behold thou shalt bear a son.

"Then Manoah entreated the Lord and said, O my Lord, let the man of God which thou didst send come again unto us, and teach us what we shall do unto the child.

"And God hearkened to the voice of Manoah; and the angel of God came again unto the woman.

"And the woman made haste, and ran, and shewed her husband.

"And Manoah arose, and went after his wife and came to the man.

"And Manoah said, Now let thy words come to pass. How shall we order the child, and *how* shall we do unto him?

"And the angel of the Lord said unto Manoah, Of all that I said unto the woman let her beware.

"So Manoah took a kid with a meat offering, and offered *it* upon a rock unto the Lord: and *the angel* did wondrously; and Manoah and his wife looked on.

"For it came to pass, when the flame went up toward heaven from off the altar, that the angel of the Lord ascended in the flame of the altar: and Manoah and his wife looked on it, and fell on their faces to the ground."

And as Rizpah read, little by little, the truth and beauty of the scene and its words dawned upon her. Thus she meditated: "This is the way God brought forth His giant deliverer, Samson; God appeared to the woman first, but she hasted to tell of the promised blessing to her husband. When she thought of how that angel-led wife led her husband, she remembered her own fanatical bitterness and was condemned. Then she remembered how Manoah and his wife, together, asked how they should order their child and how, as together they bowed before the Spirit, he ascended in glory over them. "Oh," she moaned within herself, "if we had only put aside our differences and, forgetting all else, just so sought together the Divine directings!" It was evening as she meditated, and she said within herself: "If ever I can get nigh Sir Charleroy's heart I'll tell him all this, and before the altar of a new consecration we'll give ourselves and ours to God, just this way." There came a wondrous joy to her heart and the palms that seemed to moan rebukingly without that other night, "Abbaroy, Abbaroy, I want my Abbaroy," this night reminded her some way vaguely of the beating of mighty wings, approaching nearer and nearer. She felt no longer rage, as she thought about the often bepraised Mary of her husband, but on the other hand, wished she knew more about her, were more like her. It was the woman in her, yearning for a mother.

CHAPTER XVII.

RIZPAH, THE ANCIENT "MOTHER OF SORROWS.

"Oh say to mothers, what a holy charge
Is theirs! With what a queenly power, their love
Can rule the fountain of a new-born mind.
Warn them to wake at early dawn and sow
Good seed before the world has sown its tares;
Nor in their toil decline, that angel bands
May put their sickles in and reap for God
And gather in his garner."

EARLY a score of years passed away, each having wrought its changes, and Rizpah de Griffin is dwelling quietly with her three children at Bozrah. She is companionless though not a widow. Care has left its stern impress on her every feature; the roses have gone from her cheeks and the snows that tarry, baffling all springs, are on her head. But time that has worn has also ripened. Rizpah has become a self-possessed, stately matron; her form is erect, her eye as bright as ever. Bozrah has not changed; the city sits in its sullen, fixed gloom, seemingly unconscious of the ravages that time works elsewhere. But there have been changes and changes among the people since first the woman of Gerash arrived there. Many former inhabitants have wandered away; some to be swallowed up by the tides of peoples of other climes; some have gone to judgment. But new comers have taken the places of those

that had departed and speeded the swift enough forgetting of the absent ones. Rizpah was in high honor, for although she lived in seclusion, mixing very little with any of the people about her, all respected her. Hers was a well-ordered house; Druses, Turks and Hebrews joined in affirming this. She ruled her children firmly and they obeyed her implicitly, for they loved her loyally. We meet her now amid active preparation for the observance of the approaching Jewish Sabbath. With her are two boys, twins, born in London, as like each other as could be, and Miriamne. The latter is in the full possession of her roses, and in the enjoyment of that splendor of personal charm seemingly belonging to all the maidens of Abrahamic descent under " the covenant of the stars and the sand." For are not Israel's women not only plenteous and bright and lofty like the stars, and her men numberless, rugged and restless as the surf-washed sands on every shore? Does not this race, in all history, continually attest the persistence and pre-eminence of all good to those who walk under the Divine covenants?

Miriamne not only is seen to possess a gracefulness like unto that of the palm, nature's pattern of beauty in the East, but she has such robustness of form as might be expected in one born of such a Hebrew mother and such a Saxon father. In her temper, poetic, emotional, oriental, like her mother; in feature and mind more like her father; she was a better, more evenly balanced result than either. It often so happens; the child by some natural selection or some mercifulness, inheriting a character, the resultant of the union of two sets of parental forces, yet finer than either apart. The scientific man in such cases will say, herein we behold, in a new being, physical and spiritual forces in action, the latter gaining the advantage; a prophesy without mystery that at last the fittest only shall survive. The theologian, on the other hand, will see Providence electing the best and preparing choice characteristics for superior works to be done.

At a call of the mother, the children gathered about her, and the group was charming; a picture full of expression and contrasts. The matron cast a look of yearning affection upon her offsprings, and the emotion possessed her until the hard face-lines faded into a sweet smile. Just then she would have been a satisfactory model for an artist painting Madonna. "Thank God, children, the emblem of rest and of hope in ages to come is at hand. I have joyed to-day, in full preparation that this next Sabbath may be piously and earnestly celebrated with all the religious exactness of our people." Then, patting the boys on their heads with playful tenderness, she continued: "Run away now up to the synagogue-ruin on the hill. Don't forget your duty in play, lads; be true little Israelites! When ye see the sun go down back of Gilead's mountains, give us warning of the Sabbath's beginning. Now mind, keep your eyes toward Jerusalem."

The lads sped away, and Rizpah following them with her eyes prayed in heart: "God bless them, and though in this place of desolation, make them little Samuels in faith and service." A little after her face glowed with triumphant joy, for there came back to her ears the boys' voices, mingling in sacred song. It was the psalm of the "Captives' Return" that they sang. The declining sun began to throw its last rays through the open windows of the huge stone home, flooding the

black basalt walls and pavement with golden tints
Slowly the mother's eyes wandered from the scene
without to objects within, until they rested on a huge
painting that covered nearly half the opposite wall. One
glance and her whole being seemed transformed. In
an instant her reverential and weary attitude was
changed to one of excited attention. She grew pale,
her body swayed with a waving motion, suggestive of
the panther creeping toward a victim. Then her form
became rigid like one preparing for some great muscular effort, or endeavoring to suppress some inner tempest. Her face, made habitually calm by the schoolings of adversity, became a theater for expression of the
changing emotion within; the mouth-lines putting on
a firmness almost hideous; her eyes glittered like a
serpent's in the act of charming; contrasting with the
forehead that shone like a silver shield. She was as
one under a spell or in a trance; but for a few moments
only. There came a light footfall; then a quick, half
frightened, piteous cry and Miriamne stood beside her.

"Oh, mother, don't! mother, mother; thou dost terrify me!" The young woman stopped half way between
the open door and her parent. Now she was passing
through a great transition. She had seen all that was
happening, often before; had often run away from the
spectacle to hide it from herself. Now she was trying
to nerve herself to penetrate the mystery in the hope
of preventing its painfulnesss. She was at the turning
point, where a girl changes to the woman within the
circle of parental influences.

But so complete was the absorption of the one gazing upon the spectacle upon the wall, at first the cry
was unheeded. In a sort of sudden, trembling despe

ation the young woman quickly bounded between her mother and the picture. Then, as if realizing the unfilial imprudence of the act, but still unwilling to recede from efforts to break the spell that bound her parent, she fell upon her knees before the seeming devotee and burst into tears. The mother started up a little as one awakening from a dream; then said, with perfect control of voice and manner; "Marah, what ails thee? Art ill? Are the Bedouin coming?"

"No, no," replied the other; "the picture; the picture!"

"What is it child?"

"I do not know. I only know that your strange, wild gaze upon its hideous group terrifies me! For years I've learned to feel a mingled disgust and fright in the presence of the woman in that presentment. When I came in, your face looked like hers. You did not seem to be my own tender mother, but an angry virago. Oh, why do you shadow all our Sabbath eves, by this mysterious, cruel staring and moaning before this imagery of death? You've made me to dread the approaching Holy-Day, promise of all delight to our people, as the advent of all pain to us."

"Marah, this is wickedness in thee. Thou shouldst learn to wrap thy soul about with the joys thou knowest, and leave all this that thou dost not understand, most likely terrible to thee chiefly because thou dost not understand it, to go its way."

"I've tried and tried for months to reason thus; but how little comfort to be saying over and over, 'it's all right,' 'its nothing,' to a fear that stops the very beatings of the heart. Oh, that I could fly from this land of desolations. Its loneliness and shadows keep coming and coming around me until I dread, lest they enter my very being and become part of me. I've leaned hitherto alone on my mother's greater strength for rest. If I come to fear her, I'll lose my reason!"

"Marah," said the mother, with enforced calmness, "thou art feverish to-day; thou hast wrought too much. Now retire and say this pillow Psalm; '*He that dwelleth in the secret place of the Most High, abideth under the shadow of the Almighty.*' Thou'lt be peaceful in the morning; as are those ever who abide under the shadow of the King."

But only the more passionately the daughter clung to her mother, and again she renewed her plaint: "Ah, mother, I have'nt strength to take these promises! Oh, forgive me, I can not help it; I feel as if something awful were impending; something coming between us! A curse is on this land. Is it any way over the De-Griffins? Tell me, I beseech you, what is that painted thing? Sometimes I run out of the room when alone, as if those men hanging there were still alive, in death's agony. I've dreamed sometimes that they came down in bodily form charging you and me with murdering them; and when I go out at evening, I imagine that the Ismaelitish woman in the foreground is flitting about my path, while in every thicket I hear the flapping wings of her carrion birds. Oh, mother! let us tear down that sole defilement of our own little, only home, and give it to the pilgrim Rabbi, now in Bozrah, that he may burn it with exorcising rites."

"Then thou thinkest there's witchery hereabouts, Marah," said the mother, severely.

"I? I do not know what I think, beyond this, that

RIZPAH DEFENDING THE DEAD BODIES OF HER RELATIONS.

I'm overcome, terrified, made miserable, and you, under some spell for a time, cease to be my mother."

"My daughter profanes her faith by permitting unreined imaginations to rule her so."

"Oh, tell me all about this hateful thing! Why it so moves you. You said long ago you would when I was able to bear it. I am no longer a child. Mother, you say you read me like an open book, now look into my heart and see that it is bursting with fright and worry! You say you know woman's nature; if so, you know that I can suffer when I understand, but shall go mad in the suspense of constant fear of some threatening ill unseen." Thus speaking and clinging to her mother, with a twining, almost desperate embrace, such as among women implies unerringly that a supreme moment and demand has fallen upon the questioner, she burst forth in tearless sobs. The mother's face was a study and told of a succession of weighty thoughts; parental authority brooked; infringed; new surprised realization that the daughter was no longer a child, but a wise, earnest woman. Then there was a degree of fearfulness springing from deep love. The elder woman perceived the crisis, and knew full well that in such times denials to a woman meant a dead heart, or worse. Then her manner softened, and drawing her child to her bosom with an embrace passionate in fervor, she tenderly, soothingly spoke to her:

"My most dearly beloved Marah! dismiss all thy fears at once and forever. They are needless. Rest, now and always, as thou never canst elsewhere, in all the world, upon this heart of mine. Rest thou in thy present young womanhood, as calmly, as trustingly, as thou didst in baby-hood. That heart guarded thee more tenderly than its own life then, through storms within and without that nearly broke it. In part thou dost know this; remembering what it has been in loyalty to God and thyself, canst thou pain it by one distrusting thought now?"

"Oh, mother, I know, I know; I do not mean to doubt you, and I remember, with a gratitude beyond all my poor power of speech, your toiling, patient, constant, loving care for me and my brothers. I never can forget that you are a Hebrew indeed, proud to emulate the noble mothers of our nation in its olden, golden days; but after all I must think. I think, sometimes, with anguish, that that awful picture may some way come between us!"

"Why, Marah, impossible! thou art my other self; a fairer copy; as I was at thy age." Then Rizpah spoke in unusual, confiding tenderness: "We mothers have our vanities and take a secret pride in wearing our daughters on our hearts as precious jewels. When nature gratifies that pride by giving us daughters in form, features and mind, mirrors or glad reminders of ourselves, as we were in the days of young beauty, romancings and hopes, we hug these in our souls in a way thou canst never realize until thou hast been such a mother. Change? I change toward thee? Ah, girl, not being a mother, thou canst not begin to fathom the ocean-depth, the heaven-height, the eternity-like unchanging endurance of a woman's love, once it has been quickened into the channels of maternal affection. Thou art a woman to all the world, but not so to me. I love thee now as I loved thee when thou wert a babe. To me thou wilt always be a little, lovely, needy creature—an angel touching the fountains of my inmost nature. All earthly friendships change; lover's love, at first fierce, generally dies as the tides of years roll over it; but, mother-love, in all loving, is the exception. Believe this as thou dost believe the tenets of our faith and thou'll find thy troubling thoughts fleeing away like mists of Hermon, before the conquering banners of the morning." There followed a prolonged embrace and a mutual kiss; impassioned, affectionate; an action expressing volumes to one skilled in interpreting the signs, all unvoiced and unwritten, yet, by some constant intuition, known to all womankind as the language of the finest, sincerest loving. That moment these two women passed onward, upward together to a higher, lighter, stronger relationship than they had enjoyed before. They entered the temple where daughter and mother begin the feast of the new revelation; when to the love of parent and child is added that of real companionship. That is a sunny, fruity hour, when a girl is received as a woman by a woman; that woman her mother.

The two sat embracing and happy for a long time; but the old pain suddenly revived—Miriamne's eyes chancing to stray to the picture. She shuddered, then looked pleadingly into her parent's eyes. The mother, quickly interpreting the look, tenderly replied: "Sometime."

"No, oh, no; tell me, mother, all, now! Who, and what are those hanging forms; the horror-frighted, bludgeon-armed woman; the birds of black, hovering over the crosses? Oh! my mother, you trust me; now tell me all or tear that down! You know it's not lawful for us Jews to have any image of things in Hades."

The last words moved the mother more than all else

that Miriamne had hitherto spoken. Heresy, she abominated; and the chief aim of her life had been to make her children true Israelites by precept and example. To her thinking, Israel alone was right; all others were heathen, to whom was reserved perdition. To an apostate, in her belief, there came a final judgment of misery, beggaring all attempt at description. A little while she hesitated, and then came to quick resolve to tell her daughter all. She arose, walked rapidly back and forth over the stone floor of the abode, and, then stopping before the daughter, said: "Thy wish shall be granted. In love of thee, for lo, these many years I've hidden from thee one miserable and dark chapter of our family history. I have drank the bitter waters alone. But too much I love thee to bear the piteous appeal of thy lips, or the look of doubt that sometimes flits in thy questioning eyes. Canst thou bear knowledge that is full of bitterness?"

" Yea, mother," said Miriamne, there is no bitterness in reality like that our imaginations conjure up, when fed by mysteries that hang on pictures of such hideous mien ——"

" Thou dost force me to the explanation, but, daughter blame me not, if, like Saul of old, who fainted at the sight he compelled Endor's witch to reveal, thou art given now some knowledge that kills thy sunshine."

" I'm the daughter of Rizpah and Sir Charleroy. Did they either of them ever fear?"

" Ah! but I have been the very mother of sorrows, ever since thy birth, child. God knows it; and it were best to leave it all to Him alone."

" But, mother, I'd gladly share your sorrows. Sorrow shared is ever lightened by the sharing. Let us bear the corpse between us, and in this lonely life we shall be made more than ever companions, through a common grief."

"So be it then. Thou shalt know all."

And Rizpah, going to a seldom-used iron-bound chest, drew therefrom a parchment roll; handing the same to her daughter, she said: "Read. It's part of Father Harrimai's '*Kethubim.*'" The place opened to the story of the famine in David's time, which endured three years, because of wrongs done to the Gibeonites by the children of Israel. As Miriamne read onward, Rizpah from time to time gave explanations:

"Dost perceive, daughter, that Jehovah, though not revengeful, is a God of recompenses?"

"He was the friend of the Gibeonites though they were not of his chosen people; because they had no other friend, I think," said Miriamne.

"Yes, and He held all Israel responsible for what they were willing to let their blood-thirsty Saul perform. As he had been, so had been the people; they were guilty, and God needed to punish them. How just! Oh! God is sure to press men to a conclusion. Read what David said to the stranger Gibeonites;" Miriamne continued:

"And he said, what ye shall say, *that* will I do for you.

"And they answered the king, the man that consumed us, and that devised against us;

"Let seven men of his sons be delivered unto us, and we will hang them up unto the Lord in Gibeah.

"And the king said, I will give them.

"But the king spared Mephiboseth, the son of Jonathan the son of Saul.

"But the king took the two sons of Rizpah, the daughter of Aiah, whom she bare unto Saul, Armoni and Mephiboseth; and the five sons of Michal the daughter of Saul, whom she brought up for Adriel.

"And he delivered them into the hands of the Gibeonites, and they hanged them in the hill before the Lord: and they fell all seven together, and were put to death in the beginning of barley harvest."

Miramne paused; then addressed her parent:

" Mother, I'd not be an heretic, and yet I can not see the justice of hanging the sons for the father's sins ? "

"Perhaps they were parties to the murder; perhaps publicly, or in heart, defended it. At any rate, from the beginning it has been so. Thou and thy brothers are living here fatherless on account of him that begat you ——"

" Shall I stop reading this bloody story?" quoth Miriamne.

" It pains thee. Thou must go on now, though thou shouldst fall fainting, as Saul at Endor. Read."

The daughter complied, and with quickly revived interest, for she came to the name " Rizpah " the second time, but before she had not noticed it in reading.

" And Rizpah, the daughter of Aiah, took sackcloth and spread it for her upon the rock, from the beginning of harvest until water dropped upon them out of heaven, and suffered neither the birds of the air to rest on them by day, nor the beasts of the field by night.

" And it was told David what Rizpah, the daughter of Aiah, the concubine of Saul, had done.

"And David went and took the bones of Saul and the bones of Jonathan, his son, from the men of

Jabesh-gilead, which had stolen them from the street of Beth-shan.

"And he brought up from thence the bones of Saul and the bones of Jonathan his son; and they gathered the bones of them that were hanged.

"And the bones of Saul and Jonathan his son buried they in the country of Benjamin, in Zelah, in the sepulcher of Kish, his father: and they performed all that the king commanded. And after that God was entreated for the land."

When the last clause was finished, Miriamne cast a glance at the huge painting on the wall.

"I understand in part; that is Rizpah and her crucified children?"

"It is well, daughter. Behold her; this is motherhood of strongest type! Humanity is no where perfect, but of all the erring ones of life, I most believe in those, who, among many perversions of judgment and blemishes of character, have some one or more of lofty virtues. Methinks a soul may be drenched by many sins, and yet, if within its very core it carry sincerely and sacred as its life some noble, dominating passion, like the holy love of parent for a child, that soul will ever have thereby a gate open to the Holy Spirit, a handle for the grasp of saving angels, and, while life lasts, an ever-flying signal lifted toward heaven. Such prayer unspoken is a beseeching, not vainly for the interceding love of Him that weighs the spirits."

"But, mother, you're not such a tigress? Not like that woman?"

"How proud I'd be to be indeed all she was. The exact interpretation of 'Rizpah' is a 'living coal,' but her name interpreted by her life is better called the 'flaming beacon.' We mutually lament the dispersion of our people! Dost thou remember how last Sabbath thou wepst while thou didst read to me the words of the blessed Isaiah foretelling the long-delayed but Divinely-promised regathering of all our tribes?"

"Oh! that the hills of Judea would glow with the beacons of that day!"

"Daughter, God's beacons are chiefly noble spirits, such as Moses of the Exode, Samson, the giant, David, Nehemiah and Cyrus. The world has not yet interpreted Rizpah, the 'burning coal,' the beacon fire. Once I was frail, timorous, wavering, but devotion to that character has transformed me. When the world's mothers look to her pattern, there will be a new order of motherhood; then look for heroic men and an heroic age!"

"But was not Rizpah a Hivite, a descendant of Ham, and so of those forever under God's curse?"

"My child, ancestry is not always the test of worth. The consequences of sin may pass down from sire to son, but never so as to bar the way to hope, nor dam up the stream of ever-pitying mercy of heaven. Rizpah had some true Jewish blood within her heart, and in the long run God's providence doth work to make the better part, of admixed good and ill, dominate. Besides all this, the lovely Ruth, thou dost emulate so well, was foreign to our people. So, too, was Rahab; and our Rabbis tell us she was in the royal line of David, from which at last the Messiah shall arise. Those women, with Rizpah, were beacons to the world! While mankind revere true love, constancy, loyalty and faith, those names will be remembered."

"But, mother, Rizpah was the concubine of Saul,

and as I think of how you oft denounce the harems of our neighboring Bedawin, my very soul blushes at hearing you admire this woman so."

"Ah, daughter, methinks she was more sinned against than sinning. Recall the unequal struggle: Rizpah, a foreigner, of a nation subdued by kingly Saul; he a man, strong of mind, a king, hedged with a sort of divinity that in the minds of the simple ever hedges kings about; making their words and deeds seem always right and just. If women made the laws and customs there never would have been known on earth unclean polygamy, but ever instead thereof the union only, in holy wedlock, of two lives, mutually consecrated, serviceful and constant. Under wrong teaching and tyranny, a woman may do that which purer societies condemn, and yet retain a conscience white and clean before God.

"Within that book of Samuel, which I hold, it is recorded that Ishbosheth, a son of Saul, who for a time reigned in a rebellious confederacy, a horseman's day's journey from here, at Mahanaim, charged Rizpah once with an act of impurity.

"The record makes no mention of Rizpah's reply. Like thousands of women before and since her time, she was defenseless against slander. Men, the stronger, may malign without evidence, and often it doth outweigh, to ears ripe to feast upon the carrion of a scandal, the indignant denial of outraged purity, accompanied even with evidences which make the thought of crime upon the part of the one belied, seemingly an impossibility. But leave all that; I appeal in behalf of my revered Rizpah to her wondrous loyalty as a mother. Tell me not that this sublimely heroic woman, who patiently watched the corpses of her sons and other kin from April, through all the lonely nights and through all those burning days, until October rains wept them to their burial, ever did an act that could let loose upon them living or dead the hounds of scandal! They may have suffered death as malefactors, in God's sight, but still her mother-love clung to them. She who kept those long vigils, lest beast or bird of prey should harm or mar or pollute the bodies precious to her if to no one else, I am assured, beyond all cavil, never did aught that could have stung their brows or embittered their hearts! Such motherly devotion as hers doth fully purify a woman. He who planned society, with its sacred foundations resting so largely on the integrity of its child-bearers, has planted in the bosom of woman this all-possessing love of her offspring, as her safe-guard. It's her wall of fire by day and by night, and verily more restraining to her than any law of man, command of God, or fear of hell!"

"And are loving mothers never unchaste?"

"The Jews hated swine and the monster deities of Chaldeans, because both destroyed their young, and our holy Talmudists declare that Mary of the Christians, not being as pure as the Nazarene's followers affirm, is doomed to bide even in lowest Hades with the bar of hell's gate through her ear. No, I, as a Jewish woman, believe that one of my sex being a mother and impure is neither loving, nor a woman!"

"How I revere the noble sentiments of Rizpah of Bozrah!"

"For all I am, after God, praise that ancient, fervent beacon, Rizpah of Gibeah!"

"I am in part reconciled to her, but yet I wish, in

frightened agony often, that you would renounce this historic Rizpah; lioness-like in her devotion to her offspring, but full of murderous fury toward any that crossed her love. Our holy book must have sweeter, nobler ideals for our inspiration."

"I judge this Hebrew heroine mother by her influence upon me, and that has been for good. The hypocrite or romancer may call the passer-by to prayer and have no more soul in it than the Moslem trumpet. Only those who have some God-like saintliness of character, can win effectually, unceasingly. There is mighty power in the unspoken sermons of such a life. *I cherish* Rizpah, whose touch of moral power, coming where and when I was weak to callowness, girded me with purpose for wavering and thews of steel for rosy softness. I was once like thee, a fragile flower, but the example of that patient woman's heroism, ever before me, has fitted me to meet my awful trials and worthily inhabit this giant-built house. Thou dost remember, Miriamne, at last Passover time they wish, as thou didst read to me of Jacob, that even now a ladder with communicating angels might be set up from earth to heaven?"

"Ah, that would be a feast; angels in burning bushes, or by fountains as in Hagar's time! I often worship in the thicket and pray for heaven's messengers from Paradise to fan the flames of our devotion, as Gabriel did the orisons of Daniel. But I'd be afraid to meet an angel like your Rizpah."

"Not so with me, Marah. Indeed, I often think of Rizpah and Jacob together. Thou rememberest how, not far away, at Mahanaim, Jacob of old met a host of angels? They came to cheer him in an hour of sad depression, the saddest kind indeed; for in that hour he remembered amid his repentings that he was soon to face the brother whom long years before he had wronged. Well, when Rizpah, by the death of Saul, was released from that domineering madman-king, she made her home at Mahanaim, the place near which Jacob counseled with the angels. Methinks she there also communed with the spirits that do excel in strength. She may have been weak before, but in that angel school she outgrew her master. Ay, my child, it is marvelous how a woman rises under the impulses of a noble love, holy companionship and plenty of sorrow. Many a male brute has flattered himself he was crushing into fawning servitude by his imperious, selfish will, his weaker child-burdened mate, only some day to find the victim asserting her individuality with power unearthly. The partridge skulks, terrified amid lowly grasses from the hunter, little by little gathering courage for her pinions, then she suddenly departs to return no more, meanwhile luring the hunter from her treasures."

"That is, an abused wife should run away?"

"Oh, perhaps not; but she may rise above her tyrant."

"I can't but remember the woman's rough strength."

"To me the all-controlling love of Rizpah for her children condones her former errings, her Philistine ancestry, her craggedness. I believe she soars with the angels now, and to Israel she must be a pattern until some more saintly and finer woman arises to take the leadership of woman."

"Will such an one appear, mother?"

God's dial is a circle, with a sweep like eternity

He knows no hurry; yet, though never weary, is never belated. We are not waiting for him, but He is for us. When man is ready to take up his pilgrim march to the highlands of a living, all light, all beautiful, there'll be beacons and beacons from the valleys to the hills."

Just then the lamp by which they had been sitting, for some time having only flickered, was suddenly quenched, and there was a sound of the fluttering of wings in the room. Mariamne screamed and clung to her mother, her thoughts on the vultures of the picture.

"'Twas only a bat, daughter!"

"Oh, this ghostly place!" the young woman cried.

"Ghosts and bats are very harmless; would men were like them!" bitterly spoke Rizpah.

"A bat putting out our light; it's like an omen!"

"Yes, wrongs do put out the light of human joy, but only for a little while; look out to the firmanent, my clinging other self, as I do, for comfort by times. See, the stars are immovable; all bright and in seemingly everlasting calm. Never forget in any long trial, or sudden terror, that when our human-made lights expire we are to turn our eyes toward heaven. In truth, God Himself often quenches our lights to make us look up to His." The mother, approaching the stone casement, and looking out on the sky, continued: "The heavens are full of beacons and lamps. They shall light us to bed as His truth lights those who will to serene, long rest. Good night, my child."

CHAPTER XVIII.

THE QUEEN PROCLAIMED IN THE GIANT CITY.

"Half-hearted, false-hearted! Heed we the warning!
Only the whole can be perfectly true;
Bring the whole offering, all timid thought scorning,
True-hearted only if whole-hearted too."
—HAVERGAL.

NOTHER Passover season was at hand, and the few Israelites in and about Bozrah, not being permitted to celebrate the feast, at Jerusalem were gathering for a "Little Passover" at the Giant City. There was sadness, murmurings and fears in the hearts of the people. Sadness in remembering the decadence of Israel; fears, for there were Mamelukes hovering threateningly in large numbers near the city; murmurings, because faultfindings, the last stage to indifference, flourish when religion is decaying. Faith and doubt waged their eternal battle; and at Bozrah, doubt appealing to present facts, had the easier part against faith, appealing to past providences or unseen hopes. There was clamor for a change, but the leaders of the people were purblind to any new light. They crushed their own secret doubts and continued to enforce what they believed, because they had believed it. They felt a sense of responsibility, and that made them very conservative. Before the sun had reached high-noon Bozrah

was all astir. There were but two principal streets in the city; these ran by the four great points of the compass and crossed at its center. Two companies of Jews of very different make-up, each moving along one of those streets, met, and, in passing, quite accidentally, the two processions formed a cross. One of the companies was made up of priests and serious old men, the true elders of the people. They tried to appear very wise and very pious, and succeeded. They tried as well to cheer and comfort all, and did not succeed very well. The other company was made up of young Israelitish men. They were going eastward; the old men walked northward, away from the sun, now a little more than southeast. By the side of the elders glided a row of shadows of their own making. But they were as unconscious of these as of the shadows their musty traditions flung over the people.

The youths felt like singing, so they sang. The sadness that was so general was not very deep with them. They would have liked to have sung a sort of convivial song; but, that being forbidden, they compromised with their consciences and the situation by singing the one hundred and twenty-second Psalm, with the vigor of a madrigal. They had a surplusage of vitality, and they let it flow out in the pious canticle. Certainly they conserved outward propriety; as to their inward feelings, they themselves hardly knew what they were; hence, it would be unjust, for one without, to pass judgment. The Psalm was appointed to be sung at this feast. They say the returning captives, coming from Babylon, centuries before, sang this song as they ascended to a sight of Jerusalem.

Now, some of the elders had come to think it piety to morbidly nurse their sorrows. They were never happy except when they were miserable. One of these paused and addressed the young singers:

"Children, cease. Your time is too much like a dancer's."

Then all eyes turned toward the leader of the youths, a man with a Saul-like neck, large mouth, wet, thick lips, and burning eyes; all bespeaking a person who is never religious beyond the drawings of religious excitement, for excitement's sake, and never self-restraining, except as checked by fear of a very material hell. Such an one, if he have any regularity in his piety, will have it because somebody opposes, or because, having swallowed, with one lazy gulp, a heavy creed, he thereafter goes about condoning by habit his petty vices, in trying to force others to be better than he himself ever expects to be. Such are never spiritual, and seldom martyrs; but they make good persecutors, and so do a work that compels others, by suffering, to be spiritual, and, may be, good martyrs. This leader made sharp retort, thrusting out his chin to enforce it:

"The Psalm is all right, and, if the old men sang more, they would have less time for moaning. Singing and moaning are much alike, only the former cheers men, the latter, devils!"

"Son," replied the patriarch, "revile not the fathers. We do not condemn thy joy as sin; but yet it now seems inopportune. We are entering captivity, not liberation. Our holy and our beautiful temple is in ruins; our people like hunted quail."

"But, this is feast time," said the youth.

"What a feast! I remember it as it was when the

nation gathered at Jerusalem, to the number of nigh 3,000,000, and offered 250,000 lambs. Ah, now, a handful, in this grim old city surrounded by aliens!"

The elder, so speaking, bowed his head, threw his mantle over his eyes and wept; meanwhile his fellow-elders gathered about him, very reverently, and waved their hands rebuking toward the youths. Just then there drew near a beautiful Jewess, led by an aged man, the latter garbed partly as an Israelite, and partly as one of the Druses. He had a saintly mien, and fixed the attention of the elders; but, the young men, with one accord, youth-like, at once erected, in silent worship, an unseen altar of devotion to the new goddess. The grouping was striking and suggestive. The stranger was silent, and seemed to be intent on passing by so; but the elders felt their responsibility. It is the fate of the religious leader to be expected to explain everything. He must talk to everybody, and about every matter. He cannot, when he will, keep quiet and so get the credit for fullness of wisdom, as do some. He must express an opinion, for silence is deemed a greater sin in such than insincerity or words out of ignorance. The foremost of the elders felt called to act, and so confronting the two new comers, sternly addressed the maiden:

"I perceive that thou art of my people; wherefore comest thou here, and in this companionship? Knowest thou not that women are forbidden to be at the first of the feast?"

The young men were not in accord with the elder: they stood apart, and some whispered to others·

"It is Miriamne de Griffin."

The maiden shrank back a little; but the saintly man with her, advancing a step, replied:

"I am the maiden's guardian to-day, fathers, and responsible for her act. Say on!"

The elder, though knowing full well who the speaker was, and also fully understanding the import of his challenge, pretended to have neither heard nor seen him. He looked past the speaker, who was championing the maiden, and continued:

"Do thy people at home know of these indiscreet acts?"

"Hold, Rabbi! no insinuations." The saintly man's voice was commanding, and compelled silence. He continued: "We go our way, ye yours. Ye can not help yourselves out of your miseries; then presume not to direct us." He checked his rising anger, remembering that he was a religious teacher, and launched out in a wayside sermon. "Ye children of Abraham, hear me, though I came not to counsel. Ye have stopped my progress, now hear God's truth! There are dangers without, but greater ones within; though your eyes, being veiled, ye perceive not these things. I noticed as I was coming this way that the tombs and grave-stones everywhere have been whitened recently. They tell me this was done so as to enable your people plainly to see them and so avoid them. Yet fleeing defilement of the dead, ye live in a grave, all of you. All your prefiguring feasts have ripened into a glowing present that treads out into a full day!"

The old men seemed puzzled and angry; the young men puzzled but glad. They welcomed any sermon if it came with novelty. They reasoned within themselves that the old teachings were dead, and that a new creed could be no worse. If it were novel, it would have at least a temporary freshness.

The speaker proceeded, for the congregation before him, being divided in sentiment, invited him, so far, to proceed.

"Oh, nation, called to be the light of the world, ye bear but phantom torches. Ye move sorrowfully, surrounded by walls of cloud, but just beyond there lies a glorious firmament, aglow with suns of hope and a thousand golden-arched doors made of realized prophecies and promises ripened. Can ye make these ruined habitations of mighty men, now sleeping in the cliffs and valleys about us, again teem with their former life? No, no! yet less readily can ye make your dead, finished, vanishing types take new life. Ye are puzzled and partially angry, but hold in check the hot blood. I'll soon depart; yet before I go, I'll tell ye, all, this for your deepest thinking: Ye can never celebrate again the Passover! God shut ye from your Temple long ago to teach you this; these traveling ceremonials of yours are but mockeries. The last real passover was celebrated when your fathers slew the Nazarene——"

"Let us stone him!" vehemently cried the brawny leader of the youths, and the elders turned their backs, as if to give approval to the violence, but not incur liability by witnessing.

The brawny youth seized a boulder as if to begin; the saintly man did not move, and another youth seized the arm of the youth of brawn.

"Young men, I'll show you an entrancing picture," was the saintly man's calm words. They were instantly intent. "Look, you and your old men make the sign of the cross by your ranks. Look again, by the cross stands this damsel, simple, pure and loving; an ideal woman. Her name, Miriamne, or Mary. Do not delude yourselves into the belief that it will be safe or possible for you to silence truth by murdering me. I'd despise your attempt if I did not pity your thoughtless rage. Do not forget the picture of this hour. The Passover will be fully celebrated when the power of the cross and the presence of purity is universally felt in earth. Only your men attend this your sacrifice. It is well; and when men truly bear the burden of sacrifice, women will be at their feast. Now, then, take heed. Farewell, ancients!"

So saying the saintly man of strange garb suddenly turned away, drawing the Jewess with him. The elders were confounded; they could not find words at the moment for reply; they were stung by the pleased and approving glances that the young men gave the departing couple. The elders would have been pleased to have taken the Jewish maiden from her escort with violence, but the latter was a brawny man. The elders knew the youths would not aid; to attempt it themselves would be likely to be a failure, certainly undignified. They deemed it wise, in any event, to conserve their dignity, and being unable to do anything more terrific, they hissed an orthodox malediction after the departing man and woman. That made the elders feel a little better. The two companies at the crossing of the streets fell to musing and conversing, but in different groups. The old men talked as old men, deploring the present and be-praising the past; the youths deplored the present and be-praised the future; some of them trying to interpret the words of the saintly man. They all wanted to be very orthodox Jews, and yet they all felt that the stranger's words were full of sweetness and good cheer. Some of the youths, like others of their age, had unconsciously sided with the strangers on account of the woman's influence. They admired her, and the side she was on was charmingly invincible.

"*The Arabs are coming!*"

It was a cry starting up from all directions, and passed from lip to lip like the tidings of fire at night. The city was soon in confusion and panic; then mixed crowds surged toward the crossing of the streets like terrified sheep. They needed leaders or shepherds. But the elders so lavish in advice usually, were dumb with fright now. Yet every body looked toward them for direction. Suddenly, the saintly man and the Jewess reappeared; as suddenly transformed to a self-reliant leader, she cried out: "Youths of Israel, to the defense; the enemy come in by the wall toward the Sun Temple's ruins!"

"Perhaps it's the 'Angel of Death,'" cried the thick-necked leader of the youths.

"The All-Father of the covenant forefend!" groaned some of the elders.

"Fathers," cried the Jewess, "pray as you can, but we younger ones must fight as well as pray. Pray the men to go to a charge!"

"A Deborah!" shouted the thick-necked youth, 'Now lead and we'll follow!'

"Shame!" cried the saintly man. "Lead yourselves!"

There was no need of argument; the thick-necked youth waved his hand to the other young men and they all dashed away toward the advance of the enemy; all of the city having a mind to fight, becoming instant volunteers. But the elders, with a piety enforced by prudence concluded to stay at the crossing and pray. Perhaps in their hearts they reasoned that if the enemy were repulsed they might claim the glory of having sustained the fighters, as Aarons and Hurs; if the youths and their followers were overcome, then they, the elders, might claim prescience and say at the end: "We knew it were vain to resist."

Soon there were heard the shouts and clangor of conflict. The fight was on. Miriamne breathlessly carried the news to her mother.

The matron laid her hand on her bosom, not to still a fluttering heart, but affectionately to toy with the handle of her faithful dagger.

"Oh, mother, when will these troublous times end? what shall we do?"

"Daughter, fight! if need be."

"But we are only women!"

"But this is woman's time; remember Sisera!" Rizpah began dressing for departure.

"Oh, mother, wait! Let us send the boys for news into the city. Perhaps the worst has not come, when the mothers must take arms."

Rizpah silently assented. The boys were sent, and in half an hour returned with hot and beaming faces. "The Mamelukes are all slung out of the city! Lots of them killed," both exclaimed, between their pantings.

"How brothers; is it all over?"

"Yes, all over! They're gone! Oh, you ought to have seen how our young men and the Druses raced them," interposed one.

"If it hadn't been for the Druses we'd all been murdered!" cried the other. Then the brothers caught up the narrative in turn.

"And, Miriamne, some of the young soldier-like men, after the fight, went about shouting '*cheers for the the flag of Maccabees and the maid of Bozrah!*' They say the 'maid of Bozrah' means you. What do they intend?"

Miriamne seemed not to hear the question. She was engrossed with her own thoughts and thus was meditating: "It's just as the Old Clock Man said! The Druses by their needed aid prove it; the Jews need a Saviour!"

"Boys," presently questioned Rizpah, "Were many of the heretics killed?"

"Oh, ever so many! Yes, and we want cloths for the wounded," said the questioned lads.

"Now, may the alien dead rot!"

"But we must bring cloths."

"Who says it?"

"The 'Old Clock Man' told every body to help the hurt."

"And who, pray, is this 'Old Clock Man?'"

Rizpah was quickly answered by Miriamne.

"I know him, mother. He's the leader of the Christians here, and a wondrously good old man who heals the sick, feeds the poor, teaches the ignorant and gives the true time of day to every body by the bell of his religious house!"

The mother fixed her eyes penetratingly upon Miriamne for a moment, then frigidly questioned:

"And since thou hast disobeyed me in making the acquaintance of a stranger, thou wilt now explain why thou hast never mentioned to me this 'Old Clock Man' of whom thou dost seem to know so much! Who is he?"

"Why, he's the 'Old Clock Man' who mends poor people's clocks, plays with the children and is doing every body kindness!"

"Some Christian witchery!"

"Oh, mother, he's an angel if ever there was one on earth!"

"Is he a Jew?" almost hissed Rizpah.

"I've forgotten to ask about that; but I'm certain he is, if only Jews are good, for he is a saint of God."

Rizpah's face wore a sneer as she again spoke: "How canst thou tell, Inexperience?"

"By acts. He goes about seeking poor people to clothe and feed, and ne is their physician as well, and will take no pay."

"Some Christian perverter, trying to seduce the unthinking by pretended service. Beware of such, Miriamne!"

"But healing the sick and setting people's clocks right can't do harm! I'm certain of that?"

"How sly; he would set all Jewry to Christian time and faith at the same instant!"

"I love his way, mother; it is so good; more I do not know."

"The old knave!"

"Oh! mother, he is old, but no knave. Ought we not to be reverent to the hoary head in the way of righteousness?"

"Yet an old man may poison women and children. I told thee the story of Agag once, daughter."

"Yes."

"I mean now to tell thee if this man be not a Jew, let him be like Agag, hewn to pieces. Flee him as a leper."

"He don't talk so. He says all mankind are brothers. Only to-day, he cried, to the men in the beginning of the fight, 'save your families as best you may,' kill the wounded Moslem with kindness!" The rapid converse of the two women was interrupted by the impatient cry of the boys for wraps and lint. As they started away, Miriamne darted after them, saying: "I'll go and help those caring for the wounded."

"Wayward" called after her the mother, "remember my commands. Keep away from the old Perverter, and minister to suffering Israelites, only. God can spare the rest! Let them die."

In the midst of the suffering ones, Miriamne soon found herself, and as might be expected; there, too, was the "Old Clock Man." As they met he said, laconically, "It is fitting that woman's tender hands minister thus."

"Thanks," was her reply.

Presently Miriamne questions, with an unaffected diffidence, her companion.

"Will you tell me your name?"

"Call me father, that's enough."

"Ah! but I can not, you are not my father."

"I may be."

"What jest is this! I've a father living?"

"I am father to multitudes, but after the flesh, childless."

"Oh, thy children are dead, then?"

"Nay, some dead and some living; but, living or dead, they are my children."

"This is a wilderment to me. Where is your wife?"

"Everywhere. In early youth, with vows unutterable, I wed my church. She is Humanity's mother, and I the father of all of her children, who will let me serve them."

"And is this the Christian faith?"

"It is mine, anyway."

"I like it. I'm sure it must be safe; being so good, and so you may be my father that way. Are there many fathers like you?"

"Many, and many needed, else sin will make all orphans."

"And you have no wife, no home?"

"A home most beautiful, which, at sunset, I'll enter through a door, once shut, not possible to be opened by my hands, though its fastenings be but grass and daisies."

"You mean death?" As she said it, tears welled in Miriamne's eyes.

"Weep not, my child, death is beautiful, at least to me."

"Oh, good man—father. I do not yet know how to think about you or these things that you say. What made you so different from the people I know?"

"A woman, a lovely woman."

"Your mother?"

"Not as you think."

"Oh, then pardon my curiosity. You had some love?"

"Thou hast said it."

"Why did you not wed her? Did she die?"

"A woman's question? I'll tell thee all some other time. I hear approaching voices."

"Tell me just a little more now; do?"

"Are the wounded all attended properly? Mercy first, stories and sermons after."

"Ah, here come my brothers. I'll inquire;" and away ran Miriamne to a group of youths, singing a roundelay, of which she caught but a few lines;

> "Jew and Gentile, Christian, Turk,
> Equally shall share our work.
> For Adolphus' good
> We'd shed our blood,
> For we have joined the balsam band,
> To cure all troubles in our land.
> We love the man,
> We love the band.
> We love the brothers of our balsam band."

Miriamne comprehended the situation in a moment, and all radiant with smiles, bounded to the side of her aged friend, crying: "Father, oh, you've a bonny family coming; over fifty youths and maidens; some Jews, some Gentiles. They've been comforting the wounded and now have spontaneously formed some sort of friendly guild.

"That's praiseworthy so far," the saintly man replied.

"And don't blush; when I asked the leader what were their purposes and name, a dozen cried out at once; 'We're Father Adolphus's angels of mercy?'"

"They could easily have found a better title, but youth in its frank celerity interprets human need. We all must have a pattern or hero. That's the reason there are pagans; not finding the true God, some invent one Anyway, God blesses the merciful."

"Oh, these angels are splendid; so earnest; so happy; so every thing good! They all wear balsam-twig crowns, and are singing improvised ditties about charity and humanity, and such like."

" Praised be God if they mean them, daughter."

" Mean them? Why they'll make the ancients groan if they go to the crossways with their enthusiastic singing. 'Black-frowns!' if they disturb the Passover solemnities, won't there be trouble?

"And Bozrah will never understand the meaning of the ceremonial, the phantom of which meaning some to-day are pursuing, until it beholds sweet charity sincerely applied, rising with healing and life in its wings to pass over savingly where humanity has pains and death."

The old priest looked away toward Jerusalem, as he spoke—his voice meanwhile becoming very tender, almost tremulous. Had one been able to enter his heart, there would have been seen a memory picture of Calvary. Miriamne was awed for a few moments; the old man was lost in thought; presently she recalled his attention: "Father, the band is just at hand. Shall I introduce you?"

"It is needless; I formed that Band of Charity, though I gave them not the name; most all except the recruits of to-day know me."

The singers went by, saluting the priest as they passed; obeying his signal to them not to tarry.

Miriamne turned to her comrade with quickened confidence, and with her usual impetuosity exclaimed:

"I want to be what you like. Make me a Balsamite!"

"Thou hast a mother who might object."

"Oh, no, no; not if she knew all, as do I."

"Some have called my work witchcraft."

"I don't care, since I know better. Make me a Balsamite, now, please?"

"So be it, child. Put thy hand on thy heart and repeat: '*I promise my Merciful Father always to show heartfelt kindness to all His creatures, especially those in misery, because of His everlasting goodness toward myself.*'"

"I promise that gladly. Is that all?"

"Yes; thy badge, a sprig of the evergreen balm-shrub, shall teach thee the rest."

"Teach me the rest?"

"Puzzled again, child? Well, I'll teach thee, and the shrub shall recall my lessons. As thou dost learn to love nature, as thou wilt when getting back to a more child-like faith, nature will talk to thee all the time. See, this is unfading; so is mercy. When torrid suns make the shrub suffer, it sweats or weeps these healing gums. Trials make all good souls fruitful. Then see, this little shrub gives to the world all it receives, transforming its earthy nourishments, sunshines and showers, into a medicament for sufferers. It is a type of the All-Giver. It has but three flowers, and I read in these the signature of a Triune God. This thou wilt, perhaps, read some time for thyself, when thou hast learned the mystery of the Unspeakable Gift."

"My father, your wisdom is very beautiful."

"Would, my child, that my words ever be to thee as the nuts of this little evergreen emblem, though rough-coated, still filled with liquid of honey sweetness."

The maiden yearned to embrace the priest. Had she done so, her feelings would have been like those of a daughter toward a father, or a devotee toward God. She yearned to express love for father. The fountain of that affection, hitherto unevoked, was full. But she restrained herself, and said, as she clasped the old man's arm: "May I be crowned?"

"Yes, daughter; having served the bleeding as thou didst to-day, thou mayst." The priest twined together some of the balsam bows and placed them upon her brow. "I saw once, at Damascus, a painted presentment of the mother of our Lord, on wood, from which, continuously, there exuded a precious nard, of all healing virtue. So they said, at least; and more than this, I was assured it had power to heal even the wounds of infidels."

"Is this really so?"

"I believe a Christian kindness to an unbeliever a medicine to the soul of the blesser and blest. That's why I'm merciful to Moslem."

"But you court dangers, do you not? I remember your telling me once, that fanatics, or men with a false religion, falsely practiced, were like mad dogs—one could never tell when they might bite the kindest master."

"True, some forgetting the essence of all religion worth the name, Charity, to propagate their theories, easily befool their consciences and murder gratitude. But ingratitude is a Christian and Jewish, as well as a heathen fault. In this all are alike. Still, though a man spoil all the good I try to do him, there's one thing he can not spoil."

"And that is what?"

"The bird of sunny plummage that sings in my heart because of the good I attempt. I met a French pilgrim, a while ago, who spent his time mostly in helping, as he could, to make the Mohammedan children he met, happy. He sang to them, gave them presents, acted as umpire in their sports, and if one got hurt he mothered it—(that's what he called his tender, odd ways). Some called him wrong in his head, but when I knew him I believed that one sane, amid thousands crazed."

"Who and what was he?"

"I asked him, and for reply got only this: 'I'm Melchisedec, a priest of the wayside, seeking to win silver hands, silver feet, and crown jewels.'"

"Well, he would have frightened me, if I'd met him speaking that way and in such moods?"

"Oh, no; he was not frightful; he seemed to attract even the birds, and the ownerless curs ran to him when others spurned them. He once, when sick, told me that he came from Toul, in Lorraine, where was enshrined an image of Madonna with a silver foot. He believed that tradition, which declared that that presentment of Mary gave a sign by taking a step, on a certain time, which warned some of great impending danger, and thereupon the member was changed to the precious metal."

"It's a pretty story."

"At least the lesson is honey-like. No being can strive to help another without finding the All-Shining often in his own soul. So our crowns are made."

CHAPTER XIX.

THE QUEEN'S CHILDHOOD.

"Now raise thy view,
Unto the vision most resembling Christ's."
—DANTE.

"Fear not, Mary, for thou hast found favor with God."
—GABRIEL.

IRIAMNE, all aglow with pleasurable excitement and filled with a curiosity which at times rose to very serious questioning as to her own faith, anxiously sought to compass an early meeting with the "Old Clock Man." She could not content herself to wait a chance opportunity, and so, remembering that it was his custom at evening time to visit, alone, for meditation various old ruins like those of the Reservoir, she determined to seek him there; it being not very far from her home. With beating heart she repaired thither at sunset, the day after the Mameluke attack. Having traversed the Reservoir's side some two or three hundred feet, she was on the point of returning, for the place was very lonely, when a voice startled her.

"Oh, Father Adolphus, how you frighten me! I'm so glad you came!"

"Looking for me, yet frightened at finding me. Glad I came, though I scared you?"

"Well, men and women when frightened are glad of the fellowship of any thing seemingly strong. It's easy for the terrified to believe or trust."

THE EDUCATION OF MARY.

"There's rare philosophy in thy head, little woman."

"So? What were you saying when I startled so?"

"That the silvering of the moon brought out thy person beautifully. So she that sits above the moon, a queen in heaven, would beautify thy soul if thou shouldst elect to put on the character she ever wore."

"I can't do that, knowing so little of her."

"A woman's way of saying, tell me more."

"You would not torment your Mary with such repartee."

"Woman again. Art thou jealous already?"

"Fie."

"Say that again! Once the foil of one of thy sex is penetrated, not having arguments, she can at least say 'fie'! Well, even ducklings hiss when helplessly entangled."

"Adolphus Von Gombard, I'll not call you 'father' again, if you approach me any more in this courtier fashion."

"Again, I say, an old head; but I'd plead privilege."

"At least old enough to discern the sacred line that bounds all proper commerce between the sexes. You plead privilege; I grant you the noblest any woman can give, the privilege of guiding my immortal soul; but I remember to have heard that he who would shepherd such as I, must be to her as a woman. The relationship between us must be as that between the angels of heaven who neither marry nor are given in marriage."

"Some young women receive teachings most willingly from fine-favored and patronizing instructors."

"I know it; but let none patronize me so. I've begun to adore the Sacrist of Bozrah, but if a breath or word passes that makes me think of him chiefly as being a man, then I shall sit in his presence in fright, or flee as I would were I to find the place changed into a lonely night-draped waddy, my only company an image of some leering, giant Bacchus. But this unequal defence is painful."

"Then desist and tell me what I'm to do."

"You have been my ideal man, for heaven's sake rob me not by changing!"

"Right nobly spoken, daughter. Now pardon me, for I was putting thee to a test."

"A test?"

"Yes. It's forbidden, by customs hereabout, for man and woman, as we, alone to converse face to face; perhaps wisely, if one be bad and the other weak. Yet the custom is heathenish—low moral tone engendering mighty suspicions!"

"Did my priest think me a heathen?"

"No, not that; but they say the moon makes lovers and others mad. I was wondering whether I was dealing with a bundle of romancings or an earnest girl?"

Delicately the maiden avoided the query with another:

"You loved Mary; why did you not wed her?"

"Woman again; doomed to make all vistas end in wedlock. With your sex love, beginning to give, gives all readily, and seems to find no rest until there's conjugal union."

"I have not desired to give all that way to those I've loved!"

"It is all or nothing. Ye women love only relatives, and never cease to desire to make all relatives whom ye want to love. Why, girl, my Mary is a saint; she died ages ago, after the flesh; but as a model for all womankind lives forever."

"How was she your Mary, then?"

"She belongs to every noble minded man as his inspirer."

"Mary—you call her Mary. I thought all the holy and the great had uncommon names?"

"In fiction they do; in reality the name is nothing."

"Was she wise and beautiful?"

"One of our most holy teachers, Epiphanius, who lived less than four hundred years after Mary, spent many years at Bethlehem and gathered facts that caused him thus to write. 'She was of middle stature, her face oval, her eyes brilliant and of an olive tint; her eyebrows arched and black, her hair a pale brown, her complexion fair as wheat. She spoke little, but she spoke freely and affably. She was grave, courteous, tranquil. In her deportment was nothing lax or feeble.' Saint Denis, the Areopagite, who is said to have seen this queen of David's house in her lifetime, declared that she was 'a dazzling beauty,' that he 'would have adored her as a goddess had he not known that there was but one God!' Of this much I'm certain, my Bozrah Miriamne, one so serene of character, and so pure, must have reflected her inner, imperishable beauties in her features."

"Father Adolphus, you mention strange names. There are none that sound like those revered by my people. Do you ever hate my race? If you do you must not teach me any doctrine."

"Hate? Why, I love all peoples, and by faith I am made a child of Abraham."

"Then you are a proselyte?"

"Not by any forms. I believe in the God of Abraham and His Messiah. That makes me a perfect Jew."

"This is strange. My mother never unfolded it to me."

"Ah, she has not yet looked into these royal mysteries?"

"But, good father, is your name among our chronologies?"

"Thanks to the God of the Patriarchs, yes; it is with that of Moses, David, Elijah, and all the rest, in the Lamb's Book of Life."

"Where?"

"In Heaven."

"How wonderful; yet I'm afraid to hear more."

"Shall I take thee home?"

"No; tell me more of Mary. You say she made you lonely and a father?"

"I must then begin her history, and show thee how and why she lived?"

"Do you think it will tire me?"

"Fear not! Her story is a poem, a picture, a tragedy; it's one long delight."

"Then tell it to me, I pray you."

So the priest proceeded:

"When the world was very wicked, and therefore very sad, God in His goodness was drawn to send from heaven a light-bearer—some one to tell man his duty and able to win back to the Great Father mankind's straying affections. Thou dost know this much, and hast read in thy sacred Scriptures how God called to the universe, all chaotic and dark, to come forth into beautiful form; how he said to the darkness, '*Let there be light.*' That history bears within it a fine sermon.

It's a picture of God's. Out of sin, darkness, confusion, there emerged a perfect man in a Paradisiacal home, with a perfect, beautiful woman as a help-mate by his side. That was God's ideal of perfection and happiness. It delighted the Father of Joys to make it. This is ever true; behind all clouds in God's Providence is sunshine, and beyond all disorders somewhere at last will walk forth unalloyed pleasure, a Sabbath-like rest, and fullness of harmony."

"Oh, can you make me believe and feel this?"

"Wait patiently."

"I try to do so; but I'm discouraged by the present miseries in my family and in all our nation."

"God mourns over all our sorrows before they or we are born, but His wisdom and power of cure are faultless. Wait. Times are mending, and the moral sphere is dipping into the rim of light's oceans. I think the angels perceive the world now, as thou perceivest the new moon."

"The poetry of the words I can not interpret."

"The moon's a dark globe, with a ribbon of silver across it."

"And things have been worse; now are bettering?"

"Assuredly so. Believe there is a God, and thou'lt rest in hope. Go back a little in history to when Cæsar Augustus, of awful pagan Rome, ruled the world, having won dominion through desolating wars. The most educated Romans then believed in no hereafter, and sought openly, without restraint, the grossest pleasures. The ignorant believed in fabled monstrosities. Rome set the fashions of all the world. The Jews, thy people, God's people, were lower, morally, then, than ever they had been before. They were divided into warring families and sects, holding a few forms and traditions, but having little heart in religion. The rest of mankind was barbarous. Thou hast heard how the Roman Titus overthrew Jerusalem, slaughtering thy people by thousands, defiling their holy Temple and seeming to blot out nearly the whole of thy race. That time of Titus was midnight; since that the day has been slowly advancing. Before that awful culmination of sorrows, the Divine Trinity held august council, and, as say the traditions of my church, determined to bring a holy sunrise to the earth's midnight. The trouble of all creation was that man had fallen. The Divine Council decreed to confound the devil, who broke up the first home and ruined the first pure pair by causing to emerge from another home, another pair. They came, this time mother and Son, to be the moral patterns for the race, the beginning of a new, sin-conquering dispensation. The fathers hand down these sayings: 'The august, regal Triune Council thus decreed: " Let us make a pure creature, dearer to us than all others." They say she was begotten upon the Sabbath, the birth-day of the angels, whose queen she was to be. Then one thousand of the ministering spirits were commissioned to defend her; while Gabriel was sent to announce the glad tidings of the birth of a Saviour's mother, in Hades. Her angels appeared as young men, of majestic mien, of marvelous beauty and pure as crystals. Their garments were like gold, richly colored, and could not be touched any more than could be the light of the sun."

"How charming! But is this all true?" exclaimed the maiden.

Without reply, the priest continued: "They were

crowned with diadems, exhaling celestial perfumes; in their hands they bore interwoven palms; on their arms and breasts were crosses and military devices. They were swift of flight, some of them six-winged, like the angels of Isaiah's vision."

"How dazzling! But is this all true?" Miriamne persisted.

"Well, it's not in thy sacred books nor in mine so written."

"Then you are giving me your imaginings?"

"Oh, no; but after the manner I have spoken, it is recorded in revered traditions of my church, and none can very well disprove the sayings."

"I wonder if such honors made Mary proud?"

"A strange query."

"I'd like to love one such as she, but could not if she were haughty or lofty, like the great of earth."

"It would have made such as thou proud, perhaps; but there was none of the serpent in her whose Offspring was to crush the serpent's head."

"Is there any of the serpent in me?"

"I'm not thy judge."

"Then she was immaculate?"

"Ah, that's a question for the doctors. I'm too simple to know beyond what is written. I'm glad to know that she rejoiced in her son, as a God and a *Saviour!*"—"She was of noble family, though her parents were poor," the priest continued. "Her mother was by name Anna, and worthy of the name, which is by interpretation '*gracious.*' Traditions of her goodness are many, and the good and great have honored her memory. I paid Anna homage, that of a youth respectful of worthy motherhood, at Constantinople, in a church erected in the year 710 to commemorate that saint. Among others, also Justinian, the Emperor, in the year 550, dedicated a sacred place to Mary's mother."

"Then she had her meed of praise, at last?"

"Tradition, though tardy, has been just; but I trust not tradition alone. I easily reason that there must have been much of goodness and womanly beauty in the mother that bore such a woman as Mary. I know that God can bring forth angels from the offscourings, but that is not His way. He works by steps upward. I tell thee, girl, the mother gives her life to her offspring, and in spite of training, almost in spite of regeneration, the characteristics of this parent will reappear in the child. But to my story about Mary's parents, Jehoikim and Anna.

"Blessed be God, Anna and Jehoikim were untainted by the pride of life, and, though living in a time of loose morals, walked lovingly, constantly with each other, through all their days. I talk to thee as to a prudent, but not prudish, young woman. Society is well rotted when divorce is about as common as marriage; it was that way in Anna and Jehoikim's time. Why, even the exacting Pharisees then taught that a man might divorce a wife who had lost her personal beauty, or badly cooked her husband's meat. Jehoikim might have left Anna, for she was childless; that was reason enough for divorcement to the average Jew, then. But their love was beautiful. The man, as was his duty, clung tenderly to his wife; her misfortune making her all the more in need of his tenderness. Dost thou not think so?"

"I suppose so. I don't know."

"Pardon my earnestness; it made me forget thy inexperience!

"Well, God rewarded their constancy, and they became the parents of my Mary. The father had a noble ancestry; but, what is better, within himself a royal heart. He bore by right the priestly office; but that was not much to such a man, in respect to worldly gain. Honest priests in his time were generally poor; the priestly preferments went, most richly laden, to those who dealt corruptly, and truckled to the ruling powers. Mary's father was above sordidness and simony. He had little to give or to leave to his beloved, but he left his child a good name and the remembrance of the blessed. So while God chose the humble to confound the mighty, and serenely exalted those of low estate, He was mindful to choose His elect from the ranks of the morally great. Such are found in all places and times, and when surrounded, as were these pious parents, by the gross, low and selfish, they shine with transcendent splendor. In Tisri, the first month of the Jewish civic year, while the smoke of the holocausts were ascending, to invite heaven's pardon, Mary, who was to bring forth the world's greatest offering for sin, was born at Nazareth. Her career was foreordained, and she was soon walking her course of piety and sorrow. Though inexperienced and tender-hearted, sorrows in heaviest, grimmest forms fell upon her. Her father died when she was, it is said, only nine years of age; not long after, the girl knelt, a mourner, by the bier of her mother; the golden hairs of youth mingling, in the disheveling of utter grief, with the gray, which crowned the queen and guide of her heart, her mother. On the threshhold of her life Mary's parents were called away from her, leaving her no heritage but their precepts and example. They say that Jehoikim's hands were stretched out, as in benediction, when he died, and so remained until his burial, reminding all that his last act was a commendation of his little daughter to Him who carries the lambs in his bosom! The picture of these outstretched hands, and of the girl embracing the aged dead mother, are often in my mind; they never fail to deeply move me Poor orphaned lamb!"

Miriamne brushed away a tear, a sort of self-pitying tear. She ran forward in mind, to the day when she, herself, would be orphaned, without a benediction, or, perhaps, a cheering memory. Then she questioned:

"Did your Mary have other friends?"

"Yea, her Heavenly Father. It is said, also, that she was cared for by the elders of the people, and religiously trained under the very shadows of the Temple. We may readily believe this; for, in her after life, she evinced a self-possession in adversity that witnessed of a thorough religious culture. If there was no other evidence, her splendid poem, the '*Magnificat*,' would convince any seeking proof, that Mary had had surpassing benefits and privileges in the study of God's words, as well as in the best learning of her people, the Jews. But, Miriamne, I'll weary thee; let us turn toward thy home." Presently they stood not far from the old stone house of Rizpah; then Von Gombard drew from under his mantle a roll of writings. "Here, take and read. After its perusal I'll see thee again." So saying, the old priest lifted a hand in blessing, and then moved away toward his abode.

CHAPTER XX.

THE WEDDING, THE BIRTH AND THE FLIGHT.

> " Seraph of heaven ; too gentle to be human,
> Veiled beneath the radiant form of woman.
> Sweet benediction of the eternal curse ;
> Veiled glory of the lampless universe !
> Thou moon beyond the clouds, thou living form ;
> Thou wonder and thou Beauty——
> Thou harmony of nature's art."
>
> —SHELLEY.

"Take that one hour at Bethlehem out of human history, and eighteen centuries of hours are left but partially explained."
—PROF. NEWMAN SMYTH.

"WHAT so engages thee, daughter?" questioned Rizpah, as they sat together at evening in the old stone house.

" I'm reading the story of a lovely orphan girl. I wish I were, in heart, as lovely as she."

" Was she a white citadel, pure and strong?"

" Peerless, indeed; the very queen of women, I think."

" Oh, then thou must be reading of glorious Rizpah ! Now fill me with this matter! I thirst to hear."

Miriamne, though fearful of further exposing her thoughts and study, obeyed, knowing full well that nothing would so stimulate her mother's curiosity as attempted evasion.

" I've been reading of the orphan girl's marriage. Shall I go back, or continue from that period? Her name was Mary, and she was a Jewess; that's the sum of the beginning."

"Go forward," sententiously replied the elder.

Miriamne complied:

"The guardians and relatives of Mary determined that she should early wed some proper person to be her protector, and so, according to Jewish custom, they went about the selection of a husband for her as soon as she had reached her fourteenth year. This selection was deemed a pious and serious duty by all the participants therein; therefore it was made by an appeal to the Lord with lots. Zacharias, the presiding priest, managed the proceeding, as follows: He first inquired God's will in prayer. An angel brought reply, saying: 'Go forth; call together all the widowers among the people, and let each bring his rod.'

"In truth here is refreshment! If all weddings were contrived under the wisdom of older heads, there would be fewer mad marriages." Rizpah swayed back and forth as she spoke. She was remembering, now, the curse of Harrimai that day in Gerash, long years before. She thought him a monster then, but now she was enshrining him in mind by the Angel of the Lots.

"Shall I go on, mother?"

"Go on."

"He to whom the Lord shall show a sign, let him be husband of Mary," read Miriamne.

"Ah, the Lord would not trust the youths to draw! He knows that a man is like to harass the life out of one woman before he learns to care for another rightly. God was good to Mary in hedging her in to a widower. If needs be that she must marry."

Rizpah did not sway back and forth now; she sat erect and laughed bitterly.

THE MARRIAGE OF MARY AND JOSEPH.

Miriamne continued:

"There were many splendid youths who rejoiced to be permitted to bring their wands.'

" Oh, ho! then they were suffered to draw for the girl? But what matter—the Angel of Lots presided! He'd not let the youths succeed!" Again Rizpah laughed, and as mockingly as before.

Miriamne again read:

"After prayer each deposited his almond tree with the aged Temple priest. In the early morning they anxiously sought the verdict. It was found that all the rods were dead, except that of Joseph, the son of Jacob, the son of Mathan; but his blossomed as that which, ages before, confirmed miraculously the priesthood of Aaron's sons. Then there appeared another miracle, for as Joseph reached forth his hand to take his blooming branch, there issued from among its luxurious blossoms, miraculously, a white dove, dazzling as snow. For a moment the dove gracefully suspended itself in the air, turning its eyes from one to another of the competitors; then it alighted on Joseph's head. 'Thou art the person chosen to take the Virgin and keep her for the Lord,' said the priest, solemnly, to Joseph. All the rivals responded 'Amen,' and then the dove flew away toward heaven. Joseph was thirty-three years old, of pleasing countenance, very modest, graceful, and of comely figure, and a widower.

" When all was told to Mary she modestly replied: ' I knew it, for the Lord has been with me.' Zacharias told Mary that Joseph was a true, honest Jew, a carpenter by trade, and trained by a father who fully believed the adage of Rabbins, which said that ' He who would not make his son a robber makes him a mechanic.' ' Besides this,' said the Temple priest, ' thy espoused one is like thyself, of the royal *house of David*. The blood of twenty kings mingle in the veins of you both. God grant that to that house of David there soon be born another, greater than all before, to deliver our holy nation from foreign masters.' Mary made no reply, but as a blush of hopefulness passed over her face, she looked very earnestly toward heaven and seemed to be repeating the prayer of the priest to the All Father. The formal betrothal then took place. Joseph presented his chosen bride a small token of silver, saying. ' If thou consentest to be my bride, accept this.' She took it, smiling affectionately, and then the witnesses signed the usual Jewish compact, which read as follows:

"' I Joseph, said to Mary, daughter of Jehoiakim, become my wife under the law of Moses and Israel. I promise to honor thee; to provide for thy support; thy food and thy clothing ; according to the custom of Hebrew husbands, who honor their wives, as is befitting. I give thee at once thy dowry and promise thee besides nourishment, and clothing, and whatsoever shall be necessary for thee, also conjugal friendship, a thing common to all nations of the world. Mary consents to become the wife of Joseph.' The two signed the document."

"See Miriamne, the Jews were wise; they made the husbands do most of the promising. They knew that the wives would be all wifely without such pledging." And Rizpah again bitterly laughed.

"Shall I proceed ?"

"Yes, oh, proceed; it's a Jewish poem."

"Thereupon Joseph placed a jeweled ring upon Mary's fourth finger, with a smile and a blush, saying, the 'physicians say, my beloved, that a nerve and a vein, reaching the heart together, lay close to the surface of that finger.' And she understood and was happy. A benediction was pronounced, and then the espoused pair were ready to depart to Joseph's house. He was to be the guardian of the maiden from that hour forth. The hereditary servants of the families took up the line of march, bearing flaming torches ; immediately after these followed a procession of women, richly garbed and wearing golden tiaras and pearl bedecked girdles. Behind these attendants of the virgin, followed a goodly company of dexterous musicians and singers, discoursing rapturously the significant canticles of Solomon. As the latter went on from time to time they broke out of the line of march and disported themselves in the eastern stardance, saying as they did so, to one another, ' the morning stars sang at creation ; the dawn of a new home coming by love, is next to creation the most joyous of all events.' So the dancers went on, and as they rejoiced in poetic motions, they thought of the stars which yet tremble as if with the thrilling of that first delight they shouted. Of all, the sweet orphan girl now companioned was the center. She was bedecked with costly jewels, the glad tributes of those that loved her; over her was the significant veil, and, so beneath the wedding canopy, she entered Nazareth to be a wife. Her sky had become very bright, for her's was a heart that took exquisite joy from the honeyed petals of affection's flower. No bride ever more fully entered into that supreme state, the all exalting, entrancing, expanding, thrilling period of new married life. She went forward in the proud consciousness that her weakness had overcome a giant, and that while she lead a royal captive, she was supremely happy in her utter bestowal of her all upon the one only man now became almost next to God in the temple of her soul."

Miriamne paused, and Rizpah wept a little
"Shall I go on or pause, mother?"
"Go on, dear."
"But you weep, are you ill?"
"Oh, no, except in memory. This is sweet sorrow, that beats us back and forth; contrasting dark endings with bright beginnings; heaven high hopings with black disappointments, and happy lives with our own, all interwoven with miseries. I walked once in the sweet illusions of bridal days, but an utter widowhood came before death called. That's the worst bereavement."

"But some marriages are all happiness, are they not?" queried the daughter.

"Some, but not many. That's the rule. Most of them begin well enough, but wedded mates are not as wisely tender as lovers; they too soon entomb all their joys in graves of selfishness and lust. So then the dove flies from the blossom of espousal never to return."

"Perhaps, such as they did not love enough to begin with and so separated?"

"Some who would die for each other before marriage, would die to be quit of each other, after. Hence the brood of suicides, and that blackest crime of all, murder, which often raises its treacherous, cruel head within the marriage chamber."

"How comes this error, trouble, horror?"

"In wedding bodies, without consents or courtings of the souls, if those, who, though mismated, happen to join lives, were only wise, they might yet be happy, growing together. But read more daughter."

"In the fullness of time, the angel Gabriel, known amid the Seraphim as God's champion, the chosen of Jehovah and His messenger of comfort and sympathy from heaven to man, was commissioned to carry the glorious news to earth. He spread his rainbow pinions, and with his own radiance to lighten his course, passed from the confines of the august court of the Divine Presence, the companionship of his fellow archangels, Michael, Raphael, Uriel, to go out across the planet-lightened realms of everlasting space. His course was watched with throbbing interest by the spirits of mercy appointed for ministering to man. Gabriel sped on, with sweeps of power which almost devoured distances, nor paused to bask for a moment in the many-colored lights of the golden and silvery shielded planets or constellations that he passed in his rapid flight. The wheeling suns and rushing worlds, marching and charging along the shoreless oceans of eternal space, had no splendors nor powers with which to challenge his high mission; though theirs was grand, his was grander. He traveled at love's behest, on mercy's work, to carry to this little earth, rolling along, mostly in shadows, the mandate of glory, the news of heaven's great saving device. He bore proclamation in its substance and its realizations forever the manifold wisdom of God; the wonder of all who know to think or reason. And so that voyage passed into the pages of history and the records of eternity as well.

The Wedding, the Birth and the Flight. 299

"Mary, whom Gabriel sought, was engaged in evening prayer as was her wont, with her face toward Jerusalem's Temple."

Miriamne paused; she perceived that she had arrived at a part of the manuscript which Father Adolphus had marked with a red line to remind her it was from his Christian Bible. She feared to read this portion to her mother.

"Read on, daughter, the words are precious; they are as songs in the night to my soul."

Miriamne continued:

"And in the sixth month the angel Gabriel was sent from God unto a city of Galilee, named Nazareth,

"To a virgin espoused to a man whose name was Joseph, of the house of David; and the virgin's name was Mary

"And the angel came in unto her and said, Hail! thou art highly favored, the Lord is with thee: blessed art thou among women.

"And when she saw him, she was troubled at his saying, and cast in her mind what manner of salutation this should be.

"And the angel said unto her, Fear not, Mary: for thou hast found favor with God.

"And, behold, thou shalt conceive in thy womb, and bring forth a son, and shalt call his name JESUS."

Miriamne read the last word "Joshua."

She proceeded:

"He shall be great, and shall be called the Son of the Highest; and the Lord God shall give unto him the throne of his father David.

"And he shall reign over the house of Jacob forever; and of his kingdom there shall be no end.

"Then said Mary unto the angel, How shall this be, seeing I know not a man?

"And the angel answered and said unto her, The Holy Ghost shall come upon thee, and the power of the Highest shall overshadow thee: therefore also that Holy Thing which shall be born of thee shall be called the Son of God."

"Hold! hold!" cried Rizpah. "What is this? the faith of the Nazarene?"

Miriamne was awed. She feared she had proceeded too far; but quickly remembering an explanation of Father Adolphus, replied: "Be content, mother, I read but that that appears in our holy prophets, Isaiah, the poetic and vehement; his words you so much prize have here an echo."

Rizpah gazed at her daughter, with a puzzled, questioning expression for a moment, and then sententiously said, "Read on." She was alert, though severe. Her curiosity was ruling, but her prudence was conserved, at least in her own mind. The daughter was anxious, but could not retreat; she knew she must read further or make a futile effort to explain her reluctance. The two were a study; each afraid of the other; each anxious to aid the other to truth; both on guard, and, while professing to be all love for each other, attempting to move forward to a fuller fellowship by indirection. The outlines of the cross were appearing in that household, and never was there to be complete accord until there it ruled all hearts.

Miriamne continued to read, but confined herself chiefly to notes made by the old priest on the margin of her manuscript.

"Presently Joseph, the affianced husband of Mary, discovered that his beloved was to become a mother. At first the discovery was like a dagger in his heart, for as yet the marriage had not been consummated. It was a crisis of great import and trial to husband and wife. Joseph, though now a plain man and a mechanic, carried in his veins the noblest blood of his race, being descendant of the ancient kings and in the line of Solomon and David. Besides that, he had all the abhorrence of the better Jews for adultery, that their awful law of death as its penalty, implied."

" Did he help the mob to stone her?" cried Rizpah.

Miriamne was startled by her mother's angry earnestness.

" Oh! we'll see."

She continued reading:

" He met his affianced in the evening on her return from Hebron's rosy hills, whither she had gone to visit her kinswoman, the mother of John, by name Elizabeth. The interview of those two noble women had prepared Mary to tell her betrothed all that troubled and rejoiced her. When her espoused met her privately and for the last time, as he intended, he found her sweetly, serenely singing, as was her wont, a Davidic psalm. He was at first astonished, not knowing how she could be so happy under such stigma as seemed to rest upon her. His patrician blood was roused, and for a moment he was ready to denounce her to the Sanhedrim as an adulteress. Then he looked at her, pitifully, questioningly. It could not be, he meditated, that one so young could be so depraved as to sing God praises, being a criminal. She must be insane! He tore himself from her presence, but instantly returned when she called out: ' Joseph, God knows all ; touch not His anointed.'

" 'Woman!' he cried ' explain ! explain ! Thy seeming sin hangs scorpions over my eyes, and turns my heart to ashes. Thy calmness is a wonderment !'

" Then Mary quietly recited to him the wondrous story of Gabriel's visit.

" Joseph was pale, and reverently attentive ; but still the sadness of his countenance betokened his incredulity.

" Mary, self-possessed, confident in her own integrity, continued : ' For three months I have been secluded with my kinswoman, Elizabeth. She knows I saw no man, and thou canst testify of the manner of my living since our espousal; but I got words from God, at Hebron. When I first went into my kinswoman's house."

"Elizabeth was filled with the Holy Ghost:

"And she spake out with a loud voice, and said, Blessed art thou among women, and blessed is the fruit of thy womb.

"And whence *is* this to me, that the mother of my Lord should come to me?

"For, lo, as soon as the voice of thy salutation sounded in mine ears, the babe leaped in my womb for joy.

"And blessed is she that believed: for there shall be a performance of those things which were told her from the Lord."

"No sooner had Elizabeth finished that salutation, than the Spirit of the Most Holy Ghost possessed me and I, thus, without premeditation prophetically said:

"My soul doth magnify the Lord.

"And my spirit hath rejoiced in God my Saviour.

"For he hath regarded the low estate of his handmaiden: for, behold, from henceforth all generations shall call me blessed.

"For He that is mighty hath done to me great things; and holy is His name.

"And His mercy is on them that fear him from generation to generation.

"He hath shewed strength with his arm; He hath scattered the proud in the imagination of their hearts.

"He hath put down the mighty from their seats, and exalted them of low degree.

"He hath filled the hungry with good things; and the rich He hath sent empty away.

" He hath holpen his servant Israel, in remembrance of his mercy.

" As He spake to our fathers, to Abraham, and to his seed forever."*

" I tarried until Elizabeth's son was born. He is to be the herald of mine ! Joseph was amazed. The wisdom and stately character of her *magnificent* description and ascription were unaccountable. But he doubted still her integrity. Yet his wrath was softened into pity a little He hesitated, and then, *being a just man and not willing to make her a public example, was minded to put her away privately.*"

" Ha, ha ;" laughed Rizpah, bitterly ; " I see now, 'tis a beautiful fable thou art reading ! Put her away privately ! a man do that under such circumstances ! Bah ! rather would a real man parade the woman's guilt from the house tops. In truth, to show that he was sinless because he was such a Nemesis of sin ; or to get the pity of light-headed fools, who would gladly take the place of the discarded ! A pretty, baby face can catch unerringly the man who pities himself well, if she will only gush with real or affected pity for him. Pity and flatter a man and he'll be—a Lucifer ! But read it all. This is refreshing ; its so absurdly uncommon !"

The girl continued :

" But while he thought on these things, behold, the angel of the Lord appeared unto him in a dream, saying, Joseph, thou son of David, fear not to take unto thee Mary thy wife : for that which is conceived in her is of the Holy Ghost.

"And she shall bring forth a son, thou shalt call his name JESUS : for he shall save his people from their sins.

" Now all this was done, that it might be fulfilled which was spoken of the Lord by the prophet, saying,

* The Magnificat.

"Behold, a virgin shall be with child, and shall bring forth a son, and they shall call his name Emmanuel, which being interpreted is, God with us.

"Then Joseph being raised from sleep did as the angel of the Lord had bidden him, and took unto him his wife.

Miriamne again read "Joshua" for Jesus, but yet felt assured that her mother was in heart, recognizing the source of the story. Rizpah, by silence, pretended not to know she was listening to parts of the Christian Bible, for she was very curious now. Miriamne was willing the harmless pretense should continue. But they furtively observed each other.

"I see; this is a story based upon some of the Christian's heresies," interrupted Rizpah. "If the stories be so unnatural, I'd never fear their sacred books!"

Miriamne was rejoiced, for her mother was becoming interested, and that was nigh being fully persuaded that their home was not contaminated by the hated Christian's Bible. Miriamne read again:

"Mary now was contented. She had the approval of God and her conscience, and that for which her young heart greatly yearned the approval of the one man of earth whom she loved. It mattered little to her that few others knew her wondrous secret. She knew her position was one of peril, and yet she felt certain God would be with her to the end. The joy of Joseph was full, and the revulsion of feeling from crushing shame, to lofty hope was unutterable. A while before he was ready to die, as he began tearing from his heart its idol, and attempting to consign her to the tomb like that of death, forgetfullness. Now he perceived himself elect of God to defend, vouch for and shelter the woman of women, the highly favored of Deity.

"And it came to pass in those days that there went out a decree from Cæsar Augustus that all the world should be taxed.

"And all went to be taxed, every one into his own city.

"And Joseph also went up from Galilee, out of the city of Nazareth, into Judea, unto the city of David, which is called Bethlehem, (because he was of the house and lineage of David,)

"To be taxed with Mary his espoused wife.

"And so it was, that, while they were there, the days were accomplished.

"And she brought forth her firstborn son, and wrapped him in swaddling clothes, and laid him in a manger; because there was no room for them in the inn."

"How barbarous! They surely could not have been Jews who kept that inn, or a woman in bearing would have had tender welcome. They must have been Christians; they are the people whose women blush when carrying little life, and, as if ashamed, forgetting that God had royally privileged them, hide themselves. Bah, I'm sick of the thought! I've seen Christian husbands ashamed of their pregnant wives;" so soliloquised Rizpah.

"There were no Christians at the time of these events, mother. But shall I read of the company Mary had, to comfort her?"

"Yes, do; I'd like to have been there, just to rail at the inn's folks."

Miriamne continued,

"And there were in the same country shepherds abiding in the field, keeping watch over their flock by night.

"And, lo, the angel of the Lord came upon them, and the glory of the Lord shone round about them; and they were sore afraid.

"And the angel said unto them, Fear not: for, behold, I bring you good tidings of great joy, which shall be to all people."

"It is said that even the cave, where Mary was, was filled with supernal light," remarked Miriamne digressingly.

"I believe it on my word. If angels ever come to earth, it must be surely to hold glad torches about the couches where beings, to be at last perchance like themselves, are coming forth to life," said Rizpah.

"It is thus reported," continued Miriamne:

"Now when Jesus was born in Bethlehem of Judea in the days of Herod the king, behold, there came wise men from the east to Jerusalem,

"Saying, Where is he that is born King of the Jews? for we have seen his star in the east, and are come to worship him."

Miriamne substituted Joshua for Jesus in the reading.

"Joshua, 'Joshua,' what 'Joshua' is that?"

"Joshua means "deliverer;" this one was to be such; for the rest, I've not before read it, mother."

"Read on, again," tritely, Rizpah spoke.

"When Herod the king had heard these things, he was troubled, and all Jerusalem with him.

"And when he had gathered all the chief priests and scribes of the people together, he demanded of them where Christ should be born.

"And they said unto him, In Bethlehem of Judea: for thus it is written by the prophet,

The Wedding, the Birth and the Flight.   307

" And thou Bethlehem, in the land of Juda, art not the least among the princes of Juda: for out of thee shall come a Governor, that shall rule my people Israel.

" Then Herod, when he had privily called the wise men, inquired of them diligently what time the star appeared.

" And he sent them to Bethlehem, and said, Go and search diligently for the young child; and when ye have found him, bring me word again, that I may come and worship him also.

" When they had heard the king, they departed and, lo, the star, which they saw in the east, went before them, till it came and stood over where the young child was.

" When they saw the star, they rejoiced with exceeding great joy.

" And when they were come into the house, they saw the young child with Mary his mother, and fell down, and worshiped him: and when they had opened their treasures, they presented unto him gifts; gold, and frankincense, and myrrh.

" And being warned of God in a dream that they should not return to Herod, they departed into their own country another way."

Miriamne read 'The Annointed' where the text said Christ.

" Miriamne, who could these men have been, Rabbins?"

"I think not, mother; I see upon the margin of my '*megellah*' a note which says, These were light or fire-worshipers of Persia. They, or rather their ancestors had heard, centuries before, from the Jews, then their captives, that there was an expectation, based on wondrous prophecies, that some time, there was to be on earth a man, born of woman, in character like God and in mission the bringer in of the golden age. These Magi were seeking that person, like pious pilgrims."

"Oh, the Messiah. Alas! we all long for His coming!" Then Rizpah fell into a revery from which Miriamne roused her with the question: "Art too weary to hear more?"

"No, no; read, on. These things strangely move and rest me."

Miriamne continued:

"When eight days were fulfilled, they circumcised the Child, calling him Joshua, offering, according to the law, a pair of turtle doves."

"Circumcised? Ah, I'm glad! They were good Jews, though poor ones, since they offered the gifts of the poor, two pigeons," exclaimed Rizpah.

Miriamne read onward:

"There was a man in Jerusalem, whose name was Simeon; and the same man was just and devout, waiting for the consolation of Israel.

"And it was revealed unto him by the Holy Ghost, that he should not see death, before he had seen the Lord's Christ.

"And he came by the Spirit into the Temple; and when the parents brought in the child.

"Then took he him up in his arms, and blessed God and said:

"Lord, now lettest thou thy servant depart in peace, according to thy word:

"For mine eyes have seen thy salvation,

"Which thou hast prepared before the face of all people;

"A light to lighten the Gentiles, and the glory of thy people Israel.

"And Joseph and his mother marveled at these things which were spoken of him.

"And Simeon blessed them, and said unto Mary his mother, Behold this child is set for the fall and rising again of many in Israel; and for a sign which shall be spoken against;

"(Yea, a sword shall pierce through thy own soul also;) that the thoughts of many hearts may be revealed."

"How mysterious and contradictory, and yet how true the old man's word, Miriamne? He blessed the parents amid their pious services toward their offspring, yet predicted a sword thrust for the mother. Ah, the sword for the mother is ever impending! But read further."

Miriamne continued:

"And Anna, a prophetess, who was a widow of about fourscore and four years, which departed not from the temple, but served God with fastings and prayers night and day.

"And she coming in that instant gave thanks likewise unto the Lord, and spoke of him to all them that looked for redemption in Jerusalem."

"What a finished picture, Miriamne," interrupted Rizpah. "See, a young mother committing her child to God; a blessing and a sword of pain revealed; then the finest human sympathy in the form of motherhood chastened by years coming to encourage her. Oh, the years have sadly wrecked a true woman if they have put her beyond saying, from her heart: 'Poor girl, I love thee,' to her younger sister in her hour of maternal trial. But what followed?"

Miriamne replied by again reading:

"The angel of the Lord appeareth to Joseph in a dream, saying, Arise, and take the young child and his mother, and flee into Egypt, and be thou there until I bring thee word: for Herod will seek the young child to destroy him."

"Ha! the jealous old hypocrite! But I remember, Herod murdered his wife. A man brute enough to do that could easily seek the life of an innocent babe. If Apollyon ever be dethroned because of the appearing of one more devilish than himself, the dethroner will be a wife-murderer!" exclaimed Rizpah, almost in a passion.

Miriamne continued:

"Joseph took the young child and his mother by night, and departed into Egypt.

"And was there until the death of Herod."

"So Jewry, our Jewry, gave one of its young mothers a stable for a bed chamber, a manger for her babe; then refused her these by making her an exile. Cruel Israel said go or be childless! Oh, Israel! how Pagan Rome defiled thee!" passionately exclaimed the Jewish matron.

Miriamne paused until the mother questioned:

"Was there a pursuit?"

"A hot one, though a vain one; my manuscript reads as follows:

"Herod had charged the Magi to tell him, on their return from their quest, the abode of the Child born under the star. He pretended to desire to pay it homage, but in heart he was intending to murder it. The Magi, impressed by the goodness and sanctity of mother and Infant, never returned to Herod to betray them."

"Then Herod, when he saw that he was mocked of the wise men, was exceeding wroth, and sent forth and slew all the children that were in Bethlehem, and in all the coasts thereof, from two years old and under, according to the time which he had diligently inquired of the wise men.

"Then was fulfilled that which was spoken by Jeremy, the prophet, saying:

"In Ramah there was a voice heard, lamentation, and weeping, and a great mourning, Rachel weeping for her children, and would not be comforted, because they are not."

"So a dark wave of misery rolled over Bethlehem. Hundreds of women, weeping over their own dead, were led to understand the cruel injustice of the spirit that drove the Virgin and her child into exile, and that, until the end of time, there will be sorrow in the homes of the land that does despite to the virtues and characteristics exemplified, so well, by that mother and that Child."

With these words Miriamne rolled up her parchment, saying: "This is all there is written here."

"All? It is well, for thou art weary child. We'll now retire; to-morrow I must speak with thee about the book. Good-night, now."

"Good-night, mother."

CHAPTER XXI.

THE QUEEN WITH HER FAMILY IN EGYPT.

"It is curious to observe, as the worship of the Virgin mother expanded and gathered to itself the relics of many an ancient faith, how the new and the old elements became amalgamated. . . . The Madonna assumed the characteristics . . . of the types of fertility."—ANNA JAMISON.

"Babe Jesus lay on Mary's lap,
The sun shone in His hair,
And so it was she saw, mayhap,
The crown already there."
—GEORGE MCDONALD.

HE day following Miriamne's readings to her mother, she eagerly sought Father Adolphus that she might receive more of the narrative, delightsome to herself and evidently interesting to her parent.

Finding the priest at dawn in one of his accustomed walks amid the ruins, she scarcely waited for his "Peace, daughter," until she exclaimed, "More! I want more of the story!"

"Hast finished that I gave thee so soon?"

"Yes, and read it all to my mother! Is that not wonderful?"

"Temerity!"

"No; it charms her. She has fallen in love with the child-wife. Oh, what if my mother should come to think and believe as you—then I would!"

"Thou mayst alone; but what part of the story desirest thou?"

"All! Nothing less than all! What became of the Holy Family in Egypt?"

"Now sit down on this shattered column and I'll recount to thee the traditions in order, leaving thee to judge which is true."

"Tell me what you believe and I'll believe it. That's enough!"

"I scarcely am able to do that, not knowing whether to believe or disbelieve some of the things reported. But I remember them, and perceiving that though they are only traditions, they are very beautiful and very natural, I remember them with delight, that is very near to giving them full credence."

"Then, so will I do."

"It may be the wise way, for I've believed that the good angels who, under God, watched over the little outcast family drifting about in strange places, have also watched over the drifting stories of their wanderings, letting the facts profitable for us to know, come safely to us, though they have come without the seal of authenticated history."

"Now, I believe all this, too."

"Well, then, ardent catechumen, listen. For three years the queenly Mary, with her consort and child, tarried in Egypt —"

"How did they subsist?"

"Oh, the God of the outcasts Ishmael and Elijah, who provided water for one and bread for the other of those two, was the One who sent the Holy Family to Egypt with the charge that they 'be there until He brought them word.' Now, thou hast learned that when God sends any on His work He charges Himself with their support."

"Did they find friends in Egypt?'

"Thou wilt learn in time, daughter, that two of that family had, as none on earth before, the secret of making friends. They had the love-enchantment from on high, which has been winning its way ever since over the world. But I'll proceed. There were in Egypt at that time multitudes of Israelites who had sought its refuge from the persecutions practiced toward them nearer home. Doubtless these exiles received Joseph's family kindly. Also, in all the East at that time there were many artizan leagues, banded together to aid their fellow-craftsmen. Joseph being a carpenter, I doubt not, found among these sympathy and help."

"At what place did the family abide?"

"Tradition says they tarried for a considerable period at Heliopolis, the city celebrated the world over for its splendid temple, where centered the Egyptian Sun worship. To me this tradition seems most reasonable, when I remember that the child of that family was pointed out before, by a miraculous star, which led the Fire worshipers of Persia to his cradle. The Fire worshipers of the far East and the Light worshipers of Egypt were much alike in their beliefs. They were all seeking light, and, impelled by the necessity of man's nature for some religion, revealed or man-made, able to do no better, looked up to the sun, the greatest light of which they knew. God's hand was in that meeting of the old and the new. There is a tradition that when the Holy Family arrived at Heliopolis all the idols in the Sun Temple fell on their faces. Be that as it may, the pathos of the poor prayers of the Light worshipers moved the Divine Mercy to send them the Sun of Righteousness, and all the handiwork of Rhameses, at On, lies in great, grim silent ruins, while the faith that had its germ in that little outcast family is overspreading the earth. Alas, poor Egypt!"

"Why poor Egypt?" questioned Miriamne, wonderingly.

"Those living now are so like their ancients who, in fright and helpless doubt, sought to save themselves by placating both good and evil; the light struggles in Egypt to-day, entering slowly and often retiring. Yea, poor Egypt, I pity thee! But I digress. It is said that the Holy Family also tarried for a season at Memphis, on the Nile, the city where chiefly was practiced the worship of *Apis*, the sacred bull. Thou rememberest how Israel was nearly ruined by doing homage to a golden calf at Sinai? That calf-worship was the same as the Apis-worship of Egypt. The Egyptians, in common with all mankind of old, earnestly looked for a manifestation of God in visible form—an incarnation. Their priests practiced on their pitiful yearnings and credulity, and taught them to believe that their greatest god appeared from time to time under the form of a bull, which *Avatars* they, the priests, claimed that they only could discover. The Egyptians, highly esteeming endurance and passionate vigor, readily accepted the animal pre-eminent in these things as the abiding place and expression of their god. The Child Jesus, the token of a better faith, was fittingly brought, therefore, to Egypt's Temple of *Apis*. Thus the *Light and Immortality* confronted that typified grossly at Memphis, and the incarnations that were as false as they were offensive, were brought face to face with the *Incarnation* sung by the angels. The devotees at the fanes of Memphis degraded man by preferring the beast. He that made man a little lower than the angels first, afterward exalted him to sonship by appearing garbed in the likeness of a man. Christ, at Memphis, was to do what Moses did at Sinai."

"I do not comprehend these words!"

"As Moses ground the golden image worshiped by Israel to powder, so Christ came to overthrow and blot out of the world every vestige of the religions or believings that exalts the animal and degrades the spiritual in man. He heralded the age of gold and fire."

"And was *Apis* overthrown by the child?"

"Not immediately; that is not the way of Him who knows no haste; but in His own good time its fall came. Egypt, hoar with deep thinkings on the master problems of life, death, eternity, did much in distant times to color and express the beliefs of all peoples. It became a school of religious as well as the theater of some of their greatest, bloodiest conflicts. Let me recall some of the steps. First, I'll begin with the revival of the true faith under Moses, which was the revival of escape, the only way to preserve God's people from utter defilement. Thou hast read in thy Holy writings how the conflict began between the king and Israel's leader:

And Pharaoh called for Moses and for Aaron, and said, Go ye, sacrifice to your God in the land.

And Moses said, It is not meet so to do ; for we shall sacrifice the abomination of the Egyptians to the Lord our God: lo. shall we sacrifice the abomination of the Egyptians before their eyes, and will they not stone us?

We will go three days journey into the wilderness, and sacrifice to the Lord our God, as he shall command us.

"Why was Moses so anxious to get away so far!"

"I'll show thee; that was then a mystery, now explained. Egypt worshiped a bull devoutly; the Israelites were commanded to sacrifice to God a red heifer. The color, red, was an antetype of the saving blood to be shed on red Calvary. Moses, methinks, desired to get away that he might reveal this sacred mystery, so far as he discerned it, to those to whom it was sent. Follow me now with pious, frank heart. The Israelites antagonized the customs of Egypt sharply by offering before God the finer, weaker animal, and now, girl, as I read of Mary and her child waiting about Memphis, I discern the past and that present meeting. It seems to me that He who thundered to Pharoah '*let my people go*' reappears in the form of the child, the pitying shepherd, seeking the lost sheep amid earth's offscourings. More, as I think of Mary, the beautiful outcast, following the fortunes of her Divine Child down into that dark land, and also remember how His blood finally crimsoned her life, I recall the red heifer offered on Israel's ancient altars. Mary, for the world's sake, through her maternity, was laid on the altar."

"Father Adolphus, you dazzle and yet convince me. How wonderful all this seems!"

"I see the Holy Child in Egypt, the building nation of earth, as the founder of a new order of building. Now follow me, child. After the garden and the wilds, where primitive man abode, there came the Tabernacle and Temple. When man enters into the benign influences of social life, he begins building a house to shelter and seclude his own. When he takes God or a god into his society he builds a temple. If there be growth and culture he decorates his buildings, hideously at first, æsthetically after practice. Presently he becomes a scientific builder and a philosopher. Then to him life is all building. He grasps the thought that he is the architect of himself, of his character, of his future. If his religious life is deepened he expresses all his philosophy, all his aspirations in monuments and temples. Moses and Solomon, in tabernacle and temple, but repeated the deeds of Egypt. But Egypt built under the sun, the patriarchs under the Spirit. Egypt had done its best, reached the end of its resources, having filled the land from the Delta to the cataracts of the Nile with pyramidial monument and august fanes. But building under the sun, in the light of nature only, was building in the dark, at least half the time. Christ, the architect of all that is enduring, confronted the achievements of those ancients as a merciful destroyer. He came to them to turn and overturn that, after the ruins, their mind be turned to a building upon and with the precious living Corner-Stone! Try to remember all this. Christianity is on the eve of a new building age. The crusades are ended. Now for religious palaces! But these in turn will be thrust aside, that all may give themselves to build souls up for eternity!"

"I am dazzled good father, indeed; but oh, I can not remember all these things! I'm like a child in my love for stories, and I can re-tell such to my mother, as I can not these deeper things you utter."

"I forgot, child. But we priests preach by habit everywhere!"

"Tell me more of Mary and Joseph and Jesus. Were the Egyptians kind to them?"

"As kind as the followers of the Pharaohs to the descendants of Joseph! No more. There was no more room in Egypt for Jesus at His coming than there was among His own people. But the God of Moses, ever the living God, though opposed, may never be thwarted nor killed!"

"Oh, now do not tell me these things, too deep for me; just tell me the simple story of the sojourn in that strange land."

"So be it, girl. If I digress, recall me. They say that the Holy Family found in that land a few to accept them kindly. One such was a robber, who, happening upon them, was at first about to do them violence; but he was restrained by the demeanor of the saintly mother, and his heart was all changed toward compassion of the little company. Instead of robbing, he gave them a temporary home in his mountain retreat. It is said that he was the one to whom the child of Mary, long after, while dying on the cross, companion in death with that same robber, gave repentance, with the promise of Paradise."

"How good and natural!"

"Then there's another legend. It is that Mary and her loved ones were met in that strange country by one of the world's pilgrims of pilgrims—a gipsy, who was a sorceress. There's a charming little dialogue, part in prose and part in verse, all about that meeting, which I have here. I'll read it. The sorceress begins chanting:

GIPSY—I come, I come from the land of the sun,
        From the dim, dim past of the far-off dawn;
        The waif of the world, the froth of the sea,
        Of a clan that has been and ever shall be.

MARY—God give thee grace and forgive thee thy sins.

GIPSY—Ye are pilgrims, too; no lodge for to-night,
        Ye are outcasts here in a flight of fright!
        But the mother charms and my heart say come.
        Ye may come; shall come to my gipsy's home.

"'The gipsy, Zingarella, took the babe in her arms, but then suddenly broke forth into a mournful chant, as she held the hand of the infant:

    'Here's a cradle song, and a tear and a moan;
    Here's a crown of thorns and a cross, when grown.
    Here's a vale of blood and a black, black night.
    Here's a flocking world and a rising light.'

"'And then suddenly falling upon her knees, the gipsy asked alms; but this time, as never before, with both palms extended and craving neither silver nor gold, but eternal life. It was granted.'"

"Oh, father Adolphus, I'll never forget this story."

"Forget not, either, its simple lesson; the gospel comes to the very waifs of life, and so there is help for the sinning, wherever found, in the Holy Child; encouragement to all holy longings in the meanest breast of the meanest woman, once within that circle, all radiant with the beautiful virtues of that Saviour's mother."

"Surely, I'll treasure this lesson, which is both balm and heart's ease."

"I must go now, so must thou. I'll send at noon to

the Reservoir, another parchment. Let one of the lads meet the messenger. It will be suitable for reading to thy mother, Rizpah. Be not so soon over-hopeful. We must proceed with her slowly. Those most needing the light will curse it if, coming too suddenly, it chance to dazzle. Israel still goes down all unconsciously to Egypt for gods, and the spectacle of man changing the invisible down, down, continues everywhere. Slowly, we who would be faithful, must raise up His only true presentment. We must allure after us, with all wisdom and tenderness, those we would win, while striving ourselves to rise toward Divine ideals ever beyond and above us. God bless my little missionary."

They parted; and there were tears on Miriamne's face; but not of anguish.

CHAPTER XXII.

THE SHADOW OF THE CROSS.

> " Day followed day, like any childhood passing;
> And silently Mary sat at her wheel
> And watched the boy Messiah as she span;
> And as a human child unto his mother,
> Subject the while, He did her low-voiced bidding—
> Or gently came to lean upon her knee
> And ask her of the thoughts that in him stirred.
>
> " And then, all tearful-hearted, she paused,
> Or with tremulous hand spun on—
> The blessing that her lips instructive gave,
> Asked Him with an instant thought again : "

OTHER, I've another volume of that charming story, full of wonderful things. Shall we peruse them to please our woman's curiosity, to-night?"

"Woman's curiosity?" angrily ejaculated Rizpah.

"They say all women are inquisitive; do they not?"

"They! The fling of the 'lords of earth!' Eaten up with anxiety solely concerning themselves, they plunge into introspections and questionings pertaining to their own worth; the ultimate of their own preciousness, that they call philosophy. Our sex, in self-forgetfulness, ask questions out of sympathy, and with desire to help others; that's 'curiosity!' Faugh, the fling is sickening!"

"My book is both curious and philosophical; it's interesting to both sexes therefore. Shall I read?"

"On thy promise to tell me later whence it came, who its author, thou mayst read it to me."

Miriamne, perceiving that her mother was curious to hear the whole story, though the former placated her conscience by a show of indifference, responded: "I'll begin with the return of the wanderers." So saying, she read:

"'But when Herod was dead, behold, an angel of the Lord appeareth in a dream to Joseph in Egypt, saying, arise, and take the young child and his mother, and go into the land of Israel: for they are dead which sought the young child's life.

"'And he arose, and took the young child and his mother, and came into the land of Israel.

"'Being warned of God in a dream, he turned aside into the parts of Galilee:

"'And he came and dwelt in a city called Nazareth: that it might be fulfilled which was spoken by the prophets. He shall be called a Nazarene.'"

"Nazarene!" Rizpah ejaculated, interrupting the reader. "Does the word not taste like wormwood, girl?"

The maiden replied, adroitly: "We read the pagan inscriptions on the monuments about us without being harmed! Surely we may safely read these nobler peoples' words and deeds." So saying, the maiden continued:

"'Now his parents went to Jerusalem every year at the feast of the passover.

"'And when He was twelve years old, they went up to Jerusalem after the custom of the feast.

"'And when they had fulfilled the days, as they returned, the child Jesus tarried behind in Jerusalem: and Joseph and His mother knew not of it.

"'But they, supposing Him to have been in the company, went a day's journey; and they sought Him among their kinsfolk and acquaintance.

"'And when they found Him not, they turned back again to Jerusalem, seeking Him.

"'And it came to pass that after three days they found Him in the temple, sitting in the midst of the doctors, both hearing them, and asking them questions.

"'And all that heard Him were astonished at His understanding and answers.

"'And when they saw Him, they were amazed: and His mother said unto Him, Son, why hast thou thus dealt with us? Behold, Thy father and I have sought Thee sorrowing.

"'And He said unto them, How is it that ye sought me? Wist ye not that I must be about my Father's business?'"

"That was rude, was it not, daughter? Was not his father's business his mother's? He was young for such philosophy, so like that of tyrant husband."

"He meant God's business!"

"Then his earnestness was just. God first, kin after—mother or husband—say I. Did the mother gain-say him?"

"It is thus recorded," replied the maiden.

"'And they understood not the saying which He spake unto them.

"'And he went down with them, and came to Nazareth, and was subject unto them: but his mother kept all these sayings in her heart.

"'And He increased in wisdom and stature, and in favor with God and man.'"

"Daughter, there was a fine spirit in that house; it was enhaloed by the girl-wife's character! No wonder that the son increased in favor with God and man! He was able to cope with the doctors mentally, yet subjected himself to his mother. I'll certify that he was wonderfully like his mother. The traits of the woman that bore him are prominent in every man of fine measure."

"And are fine daughters, like their fathers," laughingly questioned Miriamne, as she glanced at a reflection of herself in a metalic mirror suspended on the wall before her.

"Ah, that depends on whether they have wholesome fathers." Then, turning her eyes affectionately toward her daughter, Rizpah continued: "Thou hast enough of Hebrew in thee to leaven thee. Yet, let me plant this in thy memory, my lamb, destined most likely some time to lie in anguish on the altar of maternity: Mothers determine beyond all else the fate of the world by determining beyond all else the characters of their offspring. Yea, girl, in the homes of industry, the bugle-calls of the soldier, the moving orations of the holy teacher, there are ever heard echoes of their cradle days." Rizpah paused, drew a long sigh, and again broke forth: "But, alas! men and women walk in pairs. How can the gentler of the two, alone, or opposed by the stronger, succeed? I've seen paired birds battle the sly serpent, creeping toward their birdlings, victoriously; paired weakness triumphant over huge danger; and I've seen the lords of creation dropping serpents upon their own mates and their own nestlings! If one would find a monstrous cruelty, he must needs seek in human homes!" Then the speaker, pausing, bowed herself, and sat swaying from side to side, with her hands over her eyes. Miriamne, accustomed to such action on her mother's part, and knowing it was best when she was in such moods to leave her to herself, withdrew quietly. Yet, Rizpah seemed not alone to herself, for her mind was peopled with ghostly forms from her gloomy past; all painful companions, but still courted by the woman in her periods of morbidness. Presently she slept; the sleep of sorrow, that mercy balm of nature which comes to pained or wounded humanity as the power to grieve or ache is exhausted. The sleeper passed from consciousness of things about her, followed by the forms that had haunted her memory, and was soon among the wonders of dream land. Then came to her the sound of mighty contentions, and it seemed as if opposing forces were in conflict concerning herself. Rizpah, of the ancient, seemed to be trying to drag the dreamer toward seven crosses supporting seven stark forms. The babel of contending voices was silenced by others, exulting, as if in victory. There was a change; the sleeper seemed to be lifted up from caverns unutterably deep, and suffocating, upon a ruby cloud, soft as down to the touch, but irresistible in uplifting. She was borne swiftly, over vast realms of space, toward a golden gate way with tomb-like arch, whose cross-shaped portal swung invitingly open. A river of light spreading to a sea, and vibrating with sense-entrancing melody, flowed outward through the mighty gate-way. On either side of the portals, and moving along the river, were many glorious beings. The latter soared

on wings of mighty sweep, whose motions seemed to
beat in accord with the melody of the flowing light,
while, from within and without the gate-way, there came
the sound of countless voices, all, as it were, mingling
in the triumphant swellings of a grand anthem. The
dreamer discerned in the anthem two words, repeated
over and over, tirelessly: "*Glad Tidings!*" "*Glad
Tidings!*" "*Glad Tidings!*" The golden gate became
rose-tinted; the color deepening to purple and gold
as down the stream of light there floated an island of
gardens, and on the island appeared two human forms;
a youth and a maiden. The anthem "Glad Tidings"
continued; but sweeter, louder, deeper than before.
And the sleeper perceived that on the wings of the
glorious beings there were emblems; red crosses, about
each cross a ring of fire; above the crosses, bejeweled
silver cups; then she knew that the twain on the island
were bride and groom. The scene changed; there was
a consciousness of a flight of time. She looked again,
and on the island she beheld a mother lovingly bending over a babe; over mother and babe tenderly bended
a man, by the pride and the affection he expressed,
attesting himself the husband and father. Rizpah was
enraptured, and in her dream she prayed the scene
might tarry. She was nigh being envious of that
happy mother. But her prayer was denied her, for
soon she was startled by a voice at her side, saying, in
tones of mournful rebuke: "Farewell, forever!"

The dreamer, looking about, beheld in her vision, her
ideal, Rizpah; but the latter was wonderfully changed.
Her eyes were dim and sunken; her form dwarfed,
bowed and age-shriveled. Suddenly the whole vision
faded into thin air, and Rizpah, of Bozrah, awakened.

filled with condemnation. Before she fully realized that she had been dreaming, she cried out:

"Rizpah, oh, Rizpah, tarry a moment!"

Silence was her sole reply. Little by little, as she collected her thoughts, she comprehended that her vision, while sleeping, expressed the facts of her life while waking. The heroine girl-wife of Nazareth, the newer, finer, surer, truer ideal of womanhood, was demolishing in the mind of the woman of Bozrah her former idol, the lioness of Gibeah's hill. She knew this, for she found herself contrasting the two ideals, and in mind lingering by preference and with the greater delight about conceptions of the younger. Then began the struggles of the giants in her conscience; clean truth against hoar prejudices; sweet mercy against bitter revenge; Mary of Bethlehem against Rizpah of Gibeah. The matron of Bozrah, usually hitherto so self-sufficient, was changing. She felt that yearning inevitable in the career of most women for a confidant. She could not sleep; she could not now go down to get inspiration by standing before the grim Rizpah-painting, in the lower room; she was miserable, lonely and restless.

Mechanically, she moved toward her daughter's chamber, some way feeling that even a sleeper would be company to one so lonely as herself. Rizpah, alone, at night, in the grim, giant house, groping her way toward Miriamne's sleeping place, was unconsciously illustrating her soul's quest. She was in heart seeking alone, and in the dark, some one to take the place of her demolished ideal. Had the queen of women been there, in person, Rizpah, then, would have welcomed her. She groped her way to the maiden's couch, feeling that, as she believed, her daughter was pure and good and loving. Could the matron have analyzed her own feelings, she would have found that she was in part led toward Miriamne because the latter some way seemed like, or near to, the girl-wife who was supplanting in the heart of Rizpah of Bozrah, the wild Rizpah of Gibeah. A cloud passing let a flood of silvering moonlight full on the sleeper's couch, and Rizpah, feasting her eyes, murmured: "I wonder if that woman of Bethlehem were not very like this maiden?" As the mother gazed on her offspring she presently began noting features in the sleeper's face that reminded her of the absent father and husband. She recalled him as he appeared under the palms that night at Purim, and as he was that day he lay pale and bleeding in her all-giving arms. The whole past, that was delightful, came trooping up, and with it there came the full light of an old love revived; a renaissance of that she had supposed buried forever. Soon the aged woman, all youthful again within, was mentally in hot chase after the pleasure she had parted from so hastily long years before. She was glad of her thoughts, for they were rejoicing; glad she was alone, for the thoughts seemed sacred. It was no use, had she willed, to resist; so she just gave up to the impulse, and with a half-suppressed cry, passionately twined her arms about the sleeping girl, and covered the face of the latter with burning kisses.

The maiden started up in affright, breaking the spell that swayed her mother, but only in part at first. Rizpah was almost angered by the awakening, which caused the vision her soul was embracing to take swift flight. Her first glance seemed to say to the now awakened girl: "Begone, intruder! Leave me for a time alone with—" but she recovered herself, and was silent. Yet her mind ran on after the vision. She had not been embracing the girl, but the girl's father, in heart. Had he happened there then, he would have been all-forgiven, all-welcome. So wonderful the heart of one capable of deep loving as well as deep hating; so wonderful the nature of such a woman as Rizpah, when her emotions, aroused, spread their throbbing pinions to soar at the behest of revived affection. "Human passion," sneeringly some may say, and truly. But human passion is a gift of grace. When it travels along right lines, it quickens the one enriched by it to the noblest deeds. He whose name is Love came to earth through the Incarnation to show the splendor of human affection, working at its best in the kingdom of its finest displays—the home circle. The fate of Eden made men believe a lie, but Bethlehem refuted that lie for all time. Rizpah turned bitterly from the fiery, disappointing love she had experienced to stamp all loving, except parent love, a mockery. She had nursed her false creed, and suppressed her rebel heart by adoration of the wintry ideal of Gibeah. Now she was touched by a new influence, and it was to her as the touch of spring to winter-prisoned nature. For a few moments daughter and mother contemplated each other; the one as if dreaming, the other full of wilderment. Then the former quietly said: "I've been very nervous to-night. I'm quieter now, and will go to rest. Sweet dreams follow thee, daughter."

The maiden composed herself to sleep, and the elder woman passed out of the room. The latter, in going, perceived on the floor-slab a parchment, and bore it away with her. She said within herself as she did so: "It is best for Miriamne that I know of her reading." But, after all, she was very curious to know all about the new matter, of which she had recently heard a part, on her own account. The writing, that of a masculine hand, ran as follows:

"MIRIAMNE:—As I promised, I have herein recorded, for the help of thy memory, further facts about the Bethlehem Mother, MARY. Keeping constantly in heart the wonderful words of the angel Gabriel, she followed with constancy the wanderings of her Son as He went forth to heal and preach. She heard with pride and joy that a Dove of Peace from heaven overshadowed Him at His baptism in Jordan; but immediately she was plunged into anxiety, for he disappeared from the haunts of men in a prolonged absence. This was during the time of His temptation in the wilderness. He returned to gladden her, but immediately set forth to new trials, labors and dangers. The young Miracle-Worker was denounced and driven from among the people of His youth. Tradition points to the very place where his mother fell fainting, when she saw the people of Nazareth dragging her Son to a precipice by the city, with intent to cast Him down to death. At that place of the mother's overcoming the Empress Helena built the sanctuary called the '*Church of the Terror.*' But that loyal mother never wavered in her allegiance to her Son, but, shortly after these things formally, publicly, bravely, received baptism at His hands in Jordan, at Bethabara. Indeed, this act on her part evinced not only the faith of a disciple, but the zeal of motherhood; her Son's cause seemed to be failing, and she espoused it to strengthen it in its most trying hour. She was willing to dare all things to win for her Beloved a possible gain, however small.

"The gathering storm grew darker about the Carpenter's Son, and the leaders of the people were planning His destruction; but He pursued his work of healing and teaching serenely; His mother constantly hovering near him to encourage Him. She heard that John the Baptist, son of Elizabeth, the herald of her own Child, had been slain because he had been true to God. The harlots of the Court of Herod had procured John's death, because that holy man had rebuked their vices. But even this shocking event did not overawe the mother of the Founder of the New Kingdom. She stood in splendid contrast with the murderers of the prophet. It was purity, almost single-handed, against lust corseleted by the nation; two phalanxes; one of few, the other of many; but, as common in this world, each led by a woman. Mary, like a parent bird fluttering over her nestling, sought by the fowler, hovered around her offspring. She exemplified the finest, fullest utterance of faith, 'Jusus only,' by determining to break up the home in Nazareth, in order that all the family might keep near the beloved One in His journeys. So it happened that when He was near Capernaum, working Himself nigh unto death, they visited Him to persuade Him to rest. Of this it is written:

'*While He yet talked to the people, behold, His mother and His brethren stood without, desiring to speak with Him.*

'*Then one said unto Him, Behold, thy mother and Thy brethren stand without, desiring to speak with Thee.*

'*But He answered and said unto him, Who is my mother? and who are my brethren?*

'*And He stretched forth His hand toward His disciples, and said, Behold my mother and my brethren!*

'*For whosoever shall do the will of my Father which is in heaven, the same is my brother, and sister, and mother.*'

"To all He herein proclaimed the doctrines of His kingdom, self-denial, and though the words seem harsh, they were most kind, for by them He said, as it were, to His disciples: ' Behold these all-sacrificing relatives of mine are twice related to me; by blood and by sufferings.' It was, on Jesus' part, a public adoption of His own family. As He had been publicly adopted from on high when He typically submitted to death in His baptism, so when He beheld His mother, having forsaken all to be with Him, he proclaimed those that had elected to share His sufferings His kin indeed. The sword of His suffering bitterly wounded her when the rabble howled

THE SHADOW OF THE CROSS.
By P. R. Morris.

after the Healer, "*Thou wast born in fornication.*" But He, amid all His engrossments, never forgot to minister to His mother as a courtly, reverent, loving Son. These words of a holy book not only speak of the workings of the providence of God, but assure us that He that uttered them was prompted to comfort His own widowed mother : ' But I tell you of a truth, many widows were in Israel in the days of Elias, when the heaven was shut up three years and six months, when great famine was throughout all the land ;

"' But unto none of them was Elias sent, save unto Sarepta, a city of Sidon, unto a woman that was a widow.'

" And now for the present I close with all holy salutations.

"A. VON G."

Rizpah was so engrossed with the matter of the letter that she scarcely observed the initials at its end. As she turned the letter over there fell into her lap a pictured parchment. It represented a woman, half kneeling and with arms outstretched toward a beautiful child, the latter balancing, and, as it were, taking a first lesson in walking. "That woman's face is some way very like that of my Mariamne's in beauty and thoughtfulness," soliloquized Rizpah. Then observing a tent in the picture, at one side and under the tent, the form of a strong, dignified man, she again scrutinizingly exclaimed, "In truth, that face is Harrimai's! How like my father!" For some time she sat considering the group, and then again spoke to herself: "Ah, I see, these are none other than the girl wife, husband and child of whom Mariamne has been reading ! But what an improper legend at the bottom? '*A sword shall pierce through thine own soul also !*' A sword has no place in that happy group!" And Rizpah still gazed at the charming presentment. Suddenly she started from her seat. "What's this?" she cried as she traced a dark cross made by the shadow of the child's outstretched arms and reaching from his feet to the mother's bending knees. "I have it now; the cross is the sword! Some of the Nazarene heresy, the witchery of the 'Old Clock Man!'" Rizpah flung the picture from her as if it were a serpent. She thought she saw a paramount duty, and without an instant of delay she hastened back to Miriamne, this time in angry mood— Rizpah of Bozrah, the fanatical Nemesis of heresy.

"Here, girl! Whence this book of devils!"

Miriamne, in fright, leaped from her couch, and Rizpah, laying hold of her arm, half dragged the bewildered, trembling girl to the adjacent apartment. "These?" imperiously questioned Rizpah, as she pointed vehemently toward picture and manuscript lying together on the floor.

The maiden, overcome by the suddenness of the stormy outbreak, spoke tremblingly, pleadingly:

"Oh, mother, forgive me if I've done wrong! Father Adolphus, the old —"

"Oh, yes, the old wizzard! he gave them to thee," interrupted the mother. "Enough! 'tis as I expected; the Christian's doctrine of devils!"

Miriamne reached forth, mechanically, to take the denounced objects, but Rizpah at once intercepted her, spurning them with her foot.

"Don't touch the leprosy! To-morrow we'll hire some Druses beggars to burn them!"

"But, mother, they are not ours; we must return at least the painting; it cost great labor!"

"Leave that to me! Now, further and finally for thee, rash girl, I've commands. Listen! Thou art never again to meet or speak to that hoary-headed old wizzard, Von Gombard."

"But, mother—"

"No evasion nor compromise!"

"I can not treat the kind old man that way. He is so good, and all the people, Jews and Gentiles, love him," pleaded Miriamne.

"Enough! and, in brief, meet him or speak to him again, and I'll disown thee! I'd drive thee, daughter of mine though thou art, out of my home to starvation and pray God to send all the plagues written in His book to haunt thee, while thy life remained, rather than tolerate heresy!"

So saying, Rizpah fell upon her knees, as if even then to utter an imprecation.

In terror the daughter ran to her, and shielding her eyes from the parent's anger-distorted countenance, she pitifully cried:

"Mother! Oh, mother! Don't curse me! Save me! save me!"

The elder woman's body swayed and dilated as if she were possessed of some furious demon, checked and muzzled, but struggling to break forth. Evidently the pathos of the daughter's appeal touched some responding chord of mercy, for the mother restrained herself and then suddenly arose and swept out of the bed-chamber. And yet Miriamne was not reassured; she felt the fascination of dread. With trembling her eyes were riveted on the open door; her ears heard the heavy, stately, threatening, departing footsteps, and great misery overwhelmed her. She felt, if she could not express it, that the breakers of a mighty wrath were heaving and tossing in that bosom on which she had hitherto rested when in pain or peril. She knew the meanings of those wavy motions, so like those of the boa retiring for renewed attack She saw them passing up and down the form of Rizpah as the latter went out, her eyes burning, her body dilating. She had observed these things in her parent before, but never as now directed toward herself.

In terror and anguish Miriamne fled out of the old Giant-house. There was relief and a sense of getting more truly under the sheltering wings of God in getting out under the serene canopy of heaven. So, often, the grief-stricken seek solitude, absence from all that has crossed and hurt, separation from all earthly, in a lonely appeal to the Holy and Loving. And so these two women, bound to each other by the strongest human ties, needing, because of their isolation, each other supremely; after all, loving each other with a choice, tried love, willing each to endure any cross, even unto death, for the other's weal, and both anxious to serve God loyally, went apart. They exemplified the cross-purposes and misunderstandings that beset and mar life's pilgrims. They needed sorely, both of them, pilot and beacon; some one to inspire as well as to exemplify all that is best in womanhood. The need was patent, but the remedy but dimly discerned.

CHAPTER XXIII.

THE MISERERE AND THE EASTER ANTHEM.

"Under the shade of His mighty wings,
    One by one
    Are His secrets told,
    One by one.
Lit by the rays of each morning sun,
Shall a new flower its petals unfold,
With its mystery hid in its heart of gold."

"But even unto this day, when Moses is read, the veil is upon their heart. Nevertheless, when it shall turn to the Lord the veil shall be taken away."—11 Cor., 3: 15.

MIDNIGHT and moonlight were in Bozrah, and midnight and moonlight were in Miriamne's heart as she wandered out into the city. She did not see her way further than to know it must be some direction other than toward her home. That place all her life hitherto the dearest spot on earth, was become her dread. As she moved away from it she did not look back. It seemed to her that there was an angry cloud enveloping it; a cloud holding a furious thunderbolt. As she went on, she rapidly passed through a series of painful feelings; those that naturally beset the runaway girl. First she felt very reckless, then, surprised at her recklessness, then very lonely as if every tie that bound her was broken, and then affrighted as she thought of confronting the great, strange, selfish world alone. A woman so young and so inexperienced; a bird with half-fledged wings, thrust out of the parent nest into a storm; altogether a pitiable creature. In the moonlight of her conscience, after a time, she dimly discerned a line of duty. It seemed to her that it were best for her to turn toward the church of Adolphus, and she resolutely turned thither. Before the resolution she had walked aimlessly; now with an aim and with some soul comfort. She did not have power to analyze her feelings; had she had such power she might have discerned the fact that she was turning toward something her reason told her was very good, therefore the soul comfort came as the harbinger of conversion. As yet the moonlight within, like that without, was not strong enough to resolve the shadows in and about her. She knew, and that alone, certainly, that she was miserable, wounded, bruised. So storm-beaten, in a flight from the ancient Rizpah and her counterpart, Rizpah of Bozrah, the maiden naturally turned toward the place where there seemed rest, escape; the haven known to all the troubled and sick of the Giant city. With a great throb of joy she at length drew nigh the Church of Adolphus. All was silent about it; but its up-pointing spire, emblem of eternal, aspiring hope, rest on a rock, stability— in grand contrast with the grim ruins God's revenges had scattered in dire confusion all around, assured her. She remembered then that she had heard some say that they had been blessed beyond all telling, in hours of trouble, by the services of that sanctuary. She perceived that the church, from spire to portal, was flooded with silvering moonlight, while all beyond and

around it was in shadows; then she wearily sank down
by a small porch near the great entrance. As she
sank she moaned a broken prayer: "Oh, God, take
me!" Utterly overcome, she wished for a moment for
death's release; and death's similitude, fainting, sometimes sent in mercy, came over her. How long she
lay unconscious, she knew not. She was suddenly
aroused by the stroke of a muffled bell; she opened
her eyes and beheld forms gliding out of the darkness
into the chapel. For a moment she felt a superstitious
fear that chilled her. She vaguely remembered that
that bell had been wont to toll thus solemnly when
there was a funeral. Simultaneous with the thought
she questioned, Was she herself dead? But she
quickly collected her thoughts and then comprehended
that there was to be a midnight service in the chapel.
She remembered that Father Adolphus was wont to
have such, at intervals. She longed to taste the joys
within of which she had heard, and was at the same
time restrained, lest by entering she should in some
way part from her mother and the faith of her childhood forever. Conscience and desire waged war with
each other, and the girl was too much excited to stand
still or to reason clearly. She, therefore, mechanically
moved through the open doors with the throng, out
of the darkness into the light. Once within the
place the grateful sense of peace and the splendors of
the various appointments, beyond all she had ever
before experienced, engrossed all her thoughts. The
lofty arches, the well wrought pillars, the niches, in
which were here and there saintly paintings, the lights,
disposed so as to produce an impression of seriousness
and rest, the hum of subdued voices, all came to her

as balm. At the east she beheld a silver altar, velvet draped; on either side of it lofty columns with golden plinths and capitals; just back of the altar, in a light that made the face of the presentment more beautiful, she discerned the image of a woman, splendidly robed and jewel-crowned. For a moment she thought she was looking upon one living, for the crowned woman was so beautiful, so much a part of the place, and seemed so inviting. She contrasted her, in mind, with the terrible picture of Rizpah. Just then, with little persuasion, she could have run toward the woman, back of the altar, and plead for sympathy. The feeling was momentary. Little by little the truth dawned upon her, and she thought, " this represents the beautiful Mary of Father Von Gombard." Then the moonlight within the maiden's soul began to change into dawn. She gazed and gazed, and as she was so engaged, her thoughts took wing for heaven and her soul cried within itself as a babe for its mother. She knew not her way, but she knew she needed and yearned for a guide as pure as heaven and as serious as God. Her meditations were interrupted when she perceived the place growing darker about her, the forms of the congregation now becoming like so many moving shadows. All around her bowed their heads as in prayer, and, impressed by the solemnity of the place, she did likewise. There was a long silence. The hush of death was over the place, the only sign of life the stealthy movements of a tall, dark-robed personage, who glided about the chancel. The tower bell tolled again, once, twice, thrice; its muffled tones, as they died away, being prolonged, then caught up and borne onward with organ notes which filled the trembling air with entrancing melody. Then the organ tones softened and died away into subdued minors. "How like the sighings of autumn evening breezes, before a rain," thought Miriamne. The place again was full of melody, the organ being reinforced by lutes and dulcimers, played by unseen hands. But the worshippers were silent; all bowed, aparently, in prayerful expectation. It was all new and exceedingly impressive to the maiden, and she was carried along by the spirit of the hour.

The draped figure passed down from behind the altar-lattice and moved, on tip-toe, from one to another of the worshipers. Miriamne was curious, yet frightened. "What if he came to me?" The question she asked herself made her tremble. If it were the priest, she was sure he would be very kind and yet how would she explain her absence at that hour from home? She was alert to hear the words he spoke to others near her, and when she did, she took courage. They seemed just such as she needed. She knew the voice; it was that of Father Adolphus, in the tenderness and triumph of one filled with unearthly hopes and heavenly sympathy. The cadence of his voice accorded with the plaintive tones of the organ. Miriamne's heart fluttered like a caged bird, back and forth, from yearnings to fears, as the priest drew nearer and nearer to her. She yearned to hear spoken to herself his balm-like benedictions; she feared, lest recognizing her, he should reprove. He seemed about to pass, as if not perceiving her. Now more intensely she yearned and dreaded than before. She could not restrain herself, and so she sobbed aloud like a child in pain. The priest tenderly placed his hand on her head and softly said: "*If we confess our sins He is faithful and just to forgive and to cleanse us from all iniquity.*"

"Oh, Father Adolphus," she sobbed, "is this for me?"

The priest started, but quickly recovered himself, and again spoke in the same tone as before, his voice rising in accord with a triumphant strain of the music: "*He died that we might live!*" Miriamne clasped and passionately kissed his hand.

The place had become darker, little by little; the organ tones meanwhile growing deeper and more solemn, while voices from an unseen choir blended with them. Miriamne, recognizing, from the words of the singers, the penitential Psalms, followed the worship with deepened interest from the fifty-first to the fifty-seventh of the sacred songs. They expressed the pains and tempests of her own soul as they voiced sublimely sin-beseeching pardon. The Christian and Jew were for the moment made akin. The man at the organ was a master of his art, and while handling the keys of his instrument, he also played on the hearts of his hearers. He was aiming to reproduce Calvary, its scenes, emotions and meanings, and he succeeded. The devout assembly, following the motive and movement of the composition, was led mentally to realize the journey from the Judgment Hall to the Crucifixion. There were measured, mournful, dragging tones; Jesus bearing his heavy cross; then followed discord and confused uproar, the voices of a mob. Later on there were dirges and silences, followed, as it were, by blows and ugly cries. The nailed hands, the uplifted cross and the sneers of those who passing wagged their heads, were all revived to the imagination. With these sounds, from the first, there ran along a sustained minor strain, sometimes nearly obliterated, at other times ruling. It was as mournful as the sigh of the autumn winds amid the dying leaves and night rains. In the color and movement of that minor there was feelingly expressed the deep, poignant, undemonstrative sorrow of the mother that followed the thorn-crowned and scourged Son to his martyrdom. Then came a long silence, broken only by the fleeting whispers here and there. The worshipers were in earnest prayer. They were at the cross, as the friends of Jesus, in earnest communings. Again the organ broke in on the silence; there was a rush of air as if some one passed in rapid, terrified flight, followed by a sound like swiftly departing footsteps; the fleeing disciples came to the minds of the worshipers. Then the organ tones deepened to the rumblings of approaching thunders—heralds of a climax of catastrophies, while above the rumblings a solitary, piercing voice, which ended in a thrilling, agonizing cry: "*My God, my God, why hast thou forsaken me!*" Following this came peal upon peal from the organ; louder and louder; discord and confusion; ending in mighty crashings. The rocking earth; the earthquake; the rent vail—all the tragedy of Cavalry—was presented in awful realism to the minds of the kneeling worshipers. Every light had been quenched, the temple within was as dark as a tomb, and not a sound could be heard but moans and penitential weepings. To one any way superstitious and not knowing the intent of the presentment, the whole would have seemed very like the realm of the lost, filled with damned souls, making pitiful last appeals to mercy; but to the worshipers there came a vision of a stark, dead form on a cross, standing out vividly against the darkness of Calvary around that cross the amazed, condemned crucifiers and a few disciples, the latter whispering about the burial. The realism was oppressive and some present cried out, as if by the bier of a loved one, while some fainted away. But the Healer was there. Father Adolphus, with a voice full of tears, with the pathos of Him that went down to preach hope to "the spirits in prison," spoke to the penitents of peace, light and glory through faith. As the old Missioner went from one to another the lights of the chapel, one after another, reappeared. Presently the aged consoler stood by Miriamne: "Hast thou felt the power of the Cross, my child?"

"Oh, Father Adolphus, I do not know; I only know I'm very wretched!"

"'Godly sorrow worketh repentance'; but thou wert as happy as a bird thou thoughtst and saidst a few days ago?"

"I was a bird—a girl then! I'm a woman now. I've lived years in hours."

"Any sudden trouble?"

"Oh, yes, a tempest and tempests."

"Possess me of all, daughter."

"I can not. It's every thing. I seem so useless and nobody loves me!"

"Thou art too young to be morbid and art greatly beloved by ONE."

"Oh, I can not come to Him. I'm under His ban; I do not honor my parents. How can I? One, my father, I never knew. I've seen him through my mother's eyes, and to despise. Now I am afraid of her, and my terror is poisoning the love I once felt for her. Oh, I'm miserable, lost! Father, Father, save me!" And the wretched girl flung her arms passionately about the old priest.

"Ah, girl, I can not; but there is One that can save."

"Save, save me—one so lost?"

"He is a 'Prince and a Saviour.'"

"I do not know Him. He can not love me, and one must love me to save me; I'm so needy and wicked."

"Well said, and He is love. Only believe."

"I don't know how to believe."

"Like a poor, sick babe, all need, thou, amid thy weaknesses, hast power at least to cry."

"Cry? What shall I cry?"

"'Help thou mine unbelief.'"

Slowly, by wisely simple gospel-counsels, the aged teacher lead the penitent girl Christward. As they communed the congregation departed, and an attendant lighted the lamps. Presently the music of the organ again broke forth; but now in cheerful and triumphant strains. Miriamne listened, and as she did, a change came over her countenance. Her dawn was coming.

"Art looking up, daughter?"

"This music is like spring morning melodies, and I'm singing to it, in soul, I think."

"It is the morning song of souls; the angel's greeting to Mary. Observe the words; first the 'Hail Mary' before the wondrous birth; then the serene assurance of the mourning mother at the grave, 'He is not here, He has risen.'"

"Ah, Adolphus, how blessed are you Christians in

a religion all mercy, all songs, all love, and all nearness to God!"

"'Come unto me all ye that labor and are heavy laden.'"

"I would I could hear Him say as much to me ; but I can not go, come, nor do anything else ; not even stay away ; I'm a bit of wind-drifted down!"

"Come all ye heavy laden," measuredly replied the priest.

"Oh, if there were some one to bear me onward blind and weak as I am!"

"He carries the lambs in His bosom!"

"Alas, I feel myself cowering away from His Holiness, when I attempt to approach Him alone!"

"All to Him must go alone, in prayer as in death. He meets with a plenteous mercy the confiding ones who come by sorrows' thorny path, as He will meet the needy in judgment who have only faith's plea. Fear not to go alone ; solitude has its benefits, and He is sole accuser or excuser. The terms of His rebuke are eternal secrets, as are the terms of His forgiveness. They lie alone, between the Blesser and the blessed."

"Is the lovely woman there, your Mary?"

"Yes, child."

"And she was the mother of this Saviour?"

"Yes."

"And was He like her?"

"He is, eternal ; the 'I Am'—not was nor shall be—always."

"Oh, yes; but is He like the woman?"

"In my soul I so believe, to my joy ; for she was godly, therefore, God-like."

"Then I can love Him, trust Him, and I'm sure He'll pity me, at least."

"Amen," piously ejaculated Father Adolphus. Then he said: "Now child, rest; it's too late to go home. My sister, yonder, will care for thee till morning, and then thou must hie to thy home. Thou yet mayst be its peace-maker and blesser."

Easter-tide came. All nature was serene and seemed to recognize the memorial of holy, happy association. Father Adolphus was astir early to ply his industry of mercy for the suffering. "Poor, unhappy land, and unhappy because so blind! Oh, man, man, how thine eyes are holden, while fatlings, birds and flowers rejoice!"

"Ah, unbenumbed by sinning, they, like the cattle in Bethlehem's stable, are first to see the Saviour born of woman. 'Praise ye the Lord, beasts and all cattle, creeping things and flying fowl. They shall not hurt nor destroy in all my holy mountain; for the earth shall be full of the knowledge of the Lord, as the waters cover the sea.'" Thus soliloquized the old priest as he passed toward well-known haunts of misery in the Giant City.

Miriamne was called to a late breakfast by the kindly sister of Adolphus. The aged woman said little, but every act seemed freighted with motherly interest, and was like balm to the heart conscious chiefly of loneliness and wretchedness. The maiden longed to have the elder woman solicit her confidence, but the latter did not respond to the mute, though manifest desire. "It is better so. God's work is best done in an hour like this, when He alone is left to searching and counsel." So thought this aged minister. Experience under Father Adolphus had given her this wisdom.

The coming of evening brought to the little religious house its master all cheerful, yet well wearied by a day of ministering for God.

"Art here yet, daughter?" was his first greeting.

"Yes; where else should I be? I'm friendless, lost, unhappy; even to a vague longing for death; but I'm frightened at that longing, since it seems as if I was as friendless in Heaven as on earth. Oh, it's awful to be a two-fold orphan!"

Just then the church-bell rang forth a merry peal.

Miriamne looked a question, and the old priest continued: "Hark, it's the pæan of peace, declaring that the Day Spring from on high has visited all those in the shadow of death."

"Another service?"

"Yes, the best of all. We cling to the hours of this day and battle night away in joy, thus declaring our hope in the resurrection, the end of all nights. Listen, that's my organ, the one I myself made."

Miriamne listened, and there was wafted to her an Easter anthem; at intervals containing the sentence: "Thou that takest away the sins of the world have mercy."

As they passed into the chapel, the maiden remarked: "There are more women here than there were at the other service?"

"The other celebrated death; the chief pain-maker of woman's life; for they live in love whose ties are constantly sundered by man's last enemy. They are allured by the beautiful things, the joys, the hopes of our Easter service. It proclaims eternal victory over the destroyer."

"How beautiful the woman's form back of the altar, good Father, to-night."

"Our moods within appear to us on objects without. So strangely the Kingdom of Heaven, beginning in the soul, spreads everywhere. It is natural, though to think that the resurrection time brought all joy to the childless mother: to this one as it did and does bring a thousand times to other mothers, like her bereaved."

The Easter service went onward, a succession of joys; the march of a pilgrim army with the goals in view; the triumph of truth, the crowning of life, the final discomfiture of death. Miriamne brightened as the service advanced; then came a fullness of joy; then a reaction and she finally fell into a sleep akin to a trance. It was the resting of the wounded on the way of healing. There was a Divine overpouring and a babe-like sleep of perfect trust; from this the voice of the priest aroused her!

"Miriamne seems to rest."

"Oh, such a dream! I followed the songs to the sky and wished my body had wings. God lifted me up and I slept, dreaming myself into His presence. I thought I was in heaven."

"Thou art near it, child."

"Oh, this wonderful calm! What makes me so happy?"

"Hast thou any token?"

"I do not know: I murmured as the people sang these words: '*I know that my Redeemer liveth*;' as I murmured that, every thing, got brighter, and I felt no more under the yoke and load!"

"He is thy Vindicator. 'Tis well."

Then tears coursed down the old man's face.

And so the girl that fled out of her home, away from the phantom of Rizpah of the ancients, away from her mother; a pilgrim; all wants, all yearnings, in a few brief hours, had found a city of refuge, an everlasting hope and was in soul serenely resting.

JESUS AT THE AGE OF TWELVE WITH MARY AND JOSEPH ON THEIR WAY TO JERUSALEM.

CHAPTER XXIV.

A HEROINE'S PILGRIMAGE.

"There is a vision, in the heart of each,
Of justice, mercy, wisdom, tenderness
To wrong and pain and knowledge of the cure;
And these embodied in a woman's form,
That best transmits them pure as first received."
—ROBERT BROWNING.

"Behold, the handmaid of the Lord: be it unto me according to thy word."—MARY.

IRIAMNE, the day after her conversion, at evening, was sitting in the portal of the church at Bozrah, musing. "Oh, how I thank Father Adolphus for showing me the way to this peace!" The western sky, to the maiden's rapt imagination, seemed very like the gate of Heaven, and in her meditations she exclaimed as if talking to those in glory, yet near to her: "Mother of my Saviour, I need a mother! Thou and I, two women, loved of the same Lord, shall we not evermore be friends?" Then the stars glittered through the fading sun light like night-lamps, set along the parapets of that far off city, and the maiden felt as if heaven's doors were being shut. She was oppressed with a sense of being left alone, and thereupon cried out, "Oh, Jesus, Jesus, do not leave me here in the dark; Oh! thou mother, sainted and happy, may I not be where thou art until morning?" The cry or prayer of

the girl, having in it much of the poet, little of the skilled theologian, was one likely to be censured by those adept in stately forms, and yet it was very natural. Miriamne was but an infant in experience and had yet to learn that after the resurrection came Pentecost; then the Ascension. Steps like these are in the believer's experience; conversion is a rising from the dead to be followed by the assuring work of the Holy Spirit, then Heaven. But the soul quickened from the charnel-house of sin and inducted, not only into a new inner life but into a new fellowship, hungers for more and more. Hence, it is a common thing for the young convert to wish to die, and be away from life's turmoils and defilements at once and with the glorified, immediately, forever. It is as if the disciple would pass at once from the sepulcher directly up the Mount of Ascension. In this spirit Mary Magdalene pressed forward to embrace to her human heart the newly risen Saviour that morning when he tenderly restrained her. There was something for her to be and do before the final rest on the Divine bosom, in unending rapture. "*Touch me not; for I am not yet ascended,*" as if He would say, "I myself, have other work yet, before the eternal gates are lifted up for my triumphal entrance as the King of Glory." "*Go to my brethren, and say unto them, I ascend unto my Father and your Father.*" The master words were, "Go;" "say." The load Jesus put on His followers was the same in kind, though infinitely less, that He took on Himself. Some way it was love burdening with blessing, for He that in dying agony sent the Rose of His heart, Mary, to the home of John instead of at once to Paradise, knew surely that then for her that was best. "To go" and "tell" was best for Magdalene, as to stay and work for a time is best for all:

So Miriamne's prayer, though so worded that it would have been censured by the learned churchmen, was heard in heaven, and He that said: "My peace I leave with you," ministered, all unseen by human eye, to that lamb, bleating alone amid the dark giant castles of Bashan and the darker castles of fears that hover not far from each new-born of His Kingdom. She passed from repining, from morbidly wishing to die and from thoughts solely of her own weal, to the second stage of experience; that stage, where the young convert is influenced with a burning zeal to tell of the blessings found and thereby win others for the Saviour. Miriamne soon felt desire inexpressible to run and tell others of her joy. Then her mind recurred to her father, living somewhere far to the westward, just beneath where she had fancied the gates of heaven were a little while ago. "No, no; I cannot go yet! I must stay here and do something. Oh, I'd be ashamed to go to heaven and leave my father, my mother, my brothers, my people in their misery!" As she thus spoke she pulled her hand quickly down by her side. The motion like to one pulling away from some leading influence. A voice at hand spoke: "Behold, he that keepeth Israel shall neither slumber nor sleep."

Miriamne, with a slight startled exclamation, turned to see whence the voice and with joy beheld Father Adolphus.

"Oh, dear Father, I'm glad you came this way! I want to tell you above all others how happy you made me."

Solemnly and tenderly the old man replied: "'Not

unto us, oh Lord; not unto us, but unto thy name give glory, for thy mercy and for thy truth's sake.'"

"Yes, He has done it; but you helped, good teacher; and I am so happy! Oh, I do not know myself! I feel so changed. I'm growing wiser, happier and stronger every minute."

"If so, then, He that called thee, daughter, had a purpose."

"I know it; see it; feel it. I'm called to help my people; to bring together Sir Charleroy and Rizpah."

"Say 'my parents'; it's more filial."

"Yes, but it's so strange. I call them in my mind now all the time by their names. It seems as if I belonged to another family; that of Jesus, Mary and the Angels."

"A child of the Kingdom, indeed! When thy parents are converted, the family tie will be revived. Thou dost feel the love of heaven; the great eternal family bond, as Christ when he said: "My mother and my brethern are these which hear the word of God and do it."

"But if I hope to bring my parents together I must go first to my father and persuade him. I know my mother will object to the journey. Can I disobey her and still please God?"

"Ask God. I have for thee, and already see thy way. I have already acted in this matter."

"I can not forget the law in that I learn that 'He that setteth lightly by his father or his mother is cursed.' Among our noble ancients, the Maccabees, the disobedient child was even stoned to death."

"But thy salvation puts thee under the Gospel although, under the Law even parents had duties; they were forbidden to make their children walk through the idolatrous fires. What says Jesus to thee?"

"I do not know whether it be His spirit or not, yet all the time I hear a voice within me saying: 'These twain shall be one.'"

"I see thy soul abhors this actual divorcement of thy parents. Oh, how some play hide and seek with their consciences around forms as these do; not comforting but hating each other; not bearing together their common burdens; wide seas between them, yet fancying they have violated no law of God, because they have not asked the law of man to do what it never can, truly, proclaim two, neither having committed the deadly sin, apart."

"This separate living is their constant sin?"

"He that starts wrongly repeats the wrong anew each time that, by act or thought, he approves the wrong first done. Sin's name is truly legion."

"What an awful thing is sin!"

"True, daughter. It blinds its victims here, and its wages hereafter is death."

"That's why I fear to disobey my mother; what if it be sin to do so?"

"The command, my child, is 'children obey your parents—*in the Lord.*"

"What does 'in the Lord' mean?"

"I'll tell thee, my little catechumen; there comes a time to some youths, in pious life, when duty to God compels disobedience of parents; as it came to Jonathan, son of Saul. God is Father and mother to the righteous, and His law must be first. Mary left home and every thing, first and last, to follow Jesus. Her way was the Christian's.

",I thought once I was right in obeying my mother without question. Now I think I may be right in disobeying without question. The old and the new law are at war within me."

"Amid these Bashan hills Paul, the Holy Saint, traveled, led of God from thinking that directly opposite to his former beliefs, the truth. Jesus met him then on the way to Damsacus, in power and in glory; Paul had been for a long time a profound scholar, a Pharisee of thy people. On this journey, enlightened by the spirit, he asked and learned sincerely to ask, the question of questions in this life; '*Lord what wilt thou have me to do?*' I beseech thee to ask it daughter, as thy hourly prayer."

"Did God answer Paul?"

"Yea."

"How?"

"The blessed apostle tells all! 'When it pleased God who separated me from my mother's womb to reveal His son in me, that I might preach among the heathen, immediately I conferred not with flesh and blood, * * but I went into Arabia.' Neither wife, friend, child, nor Ephesian Elders, clinging with tears, could hold him back from duty. Then he preached through this wild country."

"But I'm not Paul, and only a woman."

"'Only a woman!' She out of whom went seven devils, a woman, was the herald of the resurrection, and the church; God's glory in the earth, is likened unto a woman. Oh, when a woman is clothed with the Sun, there is nothing more resplendent, and as for power, naught prevails against her. It seems to me if thou dost emulate her who said to God's messenger:

'*Be it unto me according to thy word*' thou wilt go ere long to thy father; but thou must now return!'"

"Return whither? This spot of all earth alone tolerates me!"

"No, that's changed! Thou art the Child of a King. Go home; ay, rise to tell of the One that hath risen in thy heart."

"Dare I? Must I?" Miriamne soon answered, by action, her own questions.

The young woman started homeward; at first with fearfulness. Then there came to her great calmness and courage, as she thought: " If I was wrong in going, I'm right in returning. My mother scared me from home into God's arms. I can tell her that." The new life had quickened within her the springs of affection. In all her life before she had not been so long apart from her mother. She said to herself, " I'll just spring into her arms, when I meet her!" And she would have, if permitted.

The mother with a face like a stone, emotionless, saw her approach. When the latter stood by the threshold, the parent freezingly said: "Well; what dost thou want here?"

A dozen answers pressed for utterance. Some like those shaped by an angry or reckless girl; some such as might come to a politic woman, having recourse ever to cunning against the odds of power. The first thoughts were not of love, the last not of truth. In an instant Miriamne remembered her new personality. She was the missionary! She dared, being right, face any thing, even her mother's wrath; but in her soul she dared not let bitterness rule. She knew as well that she dared not tell the truth so as to convey a false impression. She might have done so once; but not now. "Lord what wilt thou have me to do?" the golden prayer was on her lips and she had instant grace to say quietly: "I was doing no wrong."

"Was where?"

How brave the girl had become. Her reply was calm and courageous. "I was, for a time praying to God; but safe, for God was with me in the Spirit and good Father Adolphus in the flesh."

"The Old Clock Man!"

"Yea."

"The wizard! I so suspected. Here is more of this bad work;" and Rizpah angrily thrust before Miriamne a scroll. "That fawning, heretic-priest came here and left this with mock piety saying: 'I, being the mother, might read it!' I had no humor to converse with him; but of thee I demand the full meaning. Now, no avoidance, girl; dost thou hear!" Miriamne was not only not abashed, but in her new-found courage took the letter, and without a quaver of the voice read:

"TO THE GRAND MASTER OF THE TEMPLE, LONDON.

"*Faithful Knight and Son of the Church:*

"GREETING—I herewith commend to thee and thy most pious and chivalrous offices, my beloved catechumen, Miriamne de Griffin, of Bozrah. She is the truly noble daughter of an English nobleman, now living somewhere in London. He is, I fear, prodigal toward God, and an exile from his family; perhaps in the distress of bodily ailment most grievous. Prompted by holy desires, this young woman, whom I commend, may come to thy city in the hope of finding her father, for the compassing of his restoration to health, his family and righteousness. Had I the power, I would command the thousand liveried angels, said ever to attend the Holy Virgin, to encompass ever this sweet and pious daughter of Knight de Griffin; but being impotent to direct the angel guard, I serenely commit my daughter in the spirit, to the watch, care and chivalrous regard of thyself and thy companion knights.

"All saints salute thee. My benediction be on thee. *In pace.* "ADOLPHUS VON GOMBARD."

"And *thou* dost think thou couldst go alone, half round the world, find that renegade wanderer, bring him here, make him good, tolerable, and re-unite our family? THOU?" Rizpah stopped, her voice almost at the pitch of a scream; her utterance ending in a groan that died with a hiss.

Miriamne responded calmly: "I can not tell what I may achieve, that is with God; but I know what I must attempt. The path of duty is clear, and I enter it unwaveringly."

"And I, as unwaveringly, forbid."

"I expected this command, and in all love for thee, my mother, shall disobey it."

Rizpah turned pale, her eyes became leaden. She was for an instant like one stunned by a sudden, heavy blow, and disarmed. The little submissive child that she deemed her daughter to be, was suddenly transformed before her; changed in fact to a firm, strong, brave woman. But the elder quickly recovered, and while clearly perceiving that violence would be futile, had recourse to the last arm of the half-defeated, to ridicule.

"Disobedience, oh, I see, this is a part of this superior religion of thine and that old 'Old Clock Man;' this Gombard, ha! ha! It was always so. New religions please by freeing from law! What an old idiot that Solomon of the ancients! He taught 'forsake not the law of thy mother.'"

"Mother, I have two parents and obligations to both. I find our home shattered, and I for most of my life half orphan. I have thereby great and lasting loss. My brothers and you suffer as well. I am led of God, in a desire to seek a remedy for our troubles. I would gladly obey your edicts, but first I must obey my Maker and King."

"Girl, false teachings lure thee to a curse."

"You know mother, you yourself cursed the memory of Herod not long ago, when we wandered amid the ruins at Kauawat and saw the remnants of his image, as angry Christians left it, shattered years ago. That day you said a curse on him that broke up families or made innocents mourn, whether he lived anciently or now."

"Well?"

"I say a curse, bitter, on every act that breaks up or beclouds a home! But not I, it is God that curses!"

Rizpah was speechless and withdrew from the room, motioning silence with a stately, angry wave of her hand. She was defeated in the debate, but not subdued. The next day Rizpah renewed the subject, but this time adopting the tactics of kindness.

"My darling, since yesterday I've been thinking thy good intentions worthy of approval for their spirit of love. I'd approve thy purpose did I not forsee that the great sacrifice on thy part would be fruitless. Thy father and I could never live together! If thou foundst him thou couldst not love him as he is, and, as for reforming him, that were impossible!"

"I must try."

"'Tis useless; a woman as wise, as patient, and as

earnestly seeking that result as thou, gave years of devotion, deep as her life, to that purpose. They failed utterly."

"Was that woman my mother?"

"Yes, listen. In the glorious romances of youth I met Sir Charleroy. I pitied him coming to our house a defeated Crusader, a refugee. Pity gave way to admiration. There were few about me whom I could love; I had no mother. In some way I gave him her part of my heart first, then the rest of it. I admired him for his soldier-like bravery. He was older and vastly wiser than I. All my ambitions seemed to be satisfied in climbing up with his thoughts. He was able to teach me a thousand things I never before heard of. Heart and mind were intoxicated. I unconditionally surrendered all to him, with an almost worshipful devotion. I could not have made a more complete committal if my God had come in human form and sought me for His everlasting companionship. I fled with him from my father's home. In the wild Lejah and this Bozrah we lived for a time together, until he changed from lover to hater! Here my unnatural love was murdered by inches. I can now reason better than then, and yet the past seems like a nightmare. Thy father knew a great deal, intended to be kind but did not comprehend the dangerous responsibility of taking to his care such a passionate, imaginative, impressible creature as I was. He did not realize that there is a period in a woman's life when she may be literally made into another being. In every generation women are walking by thousands through a sort of passion week. I walked in mine, ready to be molded almost into any form; but he tried to have me profess to be a Christian, live like a devotee of Astarte and be as Anata of the Assyrians to her husband, but the echo of himself. I might have done all this, but he tried to hasten me by force, and then all fell to ruins like those amid which we lived. That glorious structure of love which romance built, became the saddest ruin here in those days.

"I was then a young woman, just entering the perilous, exhaustive periods of maternity. I was weak and nervous, and sometimes may have tried his patience, but I thought then that he ought to have borne with me. I am now certain he ought. After he left, I was for a time glad. I had renewed freedom from arguments, rasping and crossing of purposes. Then I felt the martyr's joy. I felt I was left, a girl-wife, with babe in arms, to battle alone, for God's sake, for thy sake. It seemed often that the arching heavens above were smiling upon baby and me; that sustained me. But, daughter, my moral training had been as thorough as has been thine. My idea of the solemnity and life-bindingness of the marriage tie could be no higher than it was. I believed it divine to be forgiving, and finally was impelled to turn from our broken home, to find, if possible, my recreant spouse. Dominated by convictions of duty, and often by a revived, wild, soul-possessing love for Sir Charleroy, I went to far off, strange London, I hunted out Sir Charleroy and was ready to be all things, any thing for his sake. He received me tenderly, only to soon change to cruelty. Your brothers were born there, adding to my load new burdens; but I was without help. He never seemed to study my comfort, pleasure nor needs. In a nation of strangers, with strange ways, I was alone. He knew scores; I knew only that one man. Repulsed by him I drank again and again the depths of misery, having no heart in all the great city to counsel nor love me. Then thy father took delight in vice. I was crucified for months; my only comfort communing in memory with the Sir Charleroy that had been, the tender, loving, brave Palestine knight. In those dark days, I found there was a place where persecuted Israelites secretly met; a sort of cleft-rock synagogue. Thither I went for consolation. I was wedded anew to my religion, because it was mother, father, husband and all to me; when there was none but God left to me. I came to long, daily, for the time to go to that meeting place of a few Hebrews just to pray God for two things. One, the most pitiful of prayers for a mother, that He would care for my children and keep them from being like their father; the other that I might be permitted soon to die! Thy father grew constantly more brutal, taciturn and fitful! At last I had an explanation. I found by unmistakable signs that he was going mad. I saw further that that madness took the shape of a murderous antipathy for me and the children. Under the advice of the rabbi, leader of our people at London, I determined, as the only alternative, to return to our Bozrah home and leave him to the care of his companion knights. In blank, leaden grief I left London. I came to these scenes of desolation with a heart as broken as any that ever survived its pains. I could have died. I returned, my fate fixed, the cup of my retribution for having disobeyed my parent full. Once a queenly, blithesome girl, petted and loved by hundreds, changed to a lone, sad widow and prematurely old. A wife without a husband, a Jew without the recognition of my people.

How utterly isolated! Thou know'st the rest, daughter."

The two women were silent. Miriamne was moved by the revelation to a wondrous pity; but her royal sentence: "*Lord, what wilt thou have me to do?*" seemed to be written on the air just before her uplifted eyes.

Then questioned the elder, "And thou my daughter, a woman, wilt not also leave me? It's a woman's heart that pitifully questions."

"I'll never forsake my mother!"

"And never leave?"

"Except, only as God commissions!"

"Oh, say that thou wilt never leave me in life! I said this in cruel pains for thee, Miriamne. Miriamne, daughter, here by the couch in which thou wert born, I plead." So saying the mother dropped on one knee, flung one arm over the bed by her side, and stretched out the other toward her daughter.

The maiden was profoundly moved, her loving heart seemed to be swelling within her, all her emotional nature ready to exclaim, "I'll tarry," but again her royal sentence: "*Lord, what wilt thou have me to do?*" controlled.

"Loved mother, I am not my own. God has bought me, and in His dear love I go. The story of sorrow I've just heard confirms me in my purpose. I'm called, I know, to work out a new and brighter day for mother and father!"

Rizpah was both pained and chagrined, and burying her face in her *pepulum* moaned, "God, pity me!"

"He does, I know, and sends a daughter to bear thee proof, my mother."

The mother, as if not hearing the latter words, continued, growing vehement: "The necromancy of that Nazarine priest has hastened the workings of heredity's curse! Girl, thy father's distemper is taking root in thy brain; thou too, art going mad! This scheme of peril, foredoomed to failure, is worthy of a bedlamite only. Oh, Jehovah, my shepherd, thou lead'st me now by bitter waters!"

"Mother, you called me at my birth, 'Marah,' 'bitterness.' You know how the people murmured by the bitter springs of Marah, in the wilderness, but God showed Moses a tree that sweetened the water. I've seen that tree and felt its power. It grows on the mount called Calvary, and is immortal."

"Be considerate now, daughter, since I meet thee kindly. To one not believing thy Nazarene doctrine, it is useless to appeal with Christian figures."

"Well, mother, you remember Jeptha? He had a daughter, and she was all influential with him."

"He was the cause of her death, as thy father will be of thine."

"But Jeptha's daughter became a heroine."

"When dost thou depart?" questioned Rizpah.

"Next Lord's day I say my last prayers in Bozrah."

"Farewell. As well now as later. I can not bear a long parting, and after to-day we shall speak no more of this." Miriamne was amazed by the sudden change.

"Do I go in peace?"

"Ah, daughter, what a question? A mother's undiminished love will follow thee even unto death, winging a thousand daily prayers to Israel's Shepherd in thy behalf. Yet, I shall condemn thy going, rebuke thy disobedience, perhaps frown upon thee, and even say, 'I disown thee!' But, though I do all this, there will be tears in my voice and kisses in my heart, for my first-born. All my authority as a mother cries against thy going, and all my mother-heart embraces. I'll not kiss thee as thou departest, but waft hundreds after thee when thou art gone. I'm not Rizpah, devotee of Rizpah now. I'm only a woman, a parent, a voice uttering two decrees; one of the head and one of the heart!"

Miriamne was inexpressibly rejoiced by the words she had heard, as they betokened the breaking down of the strong opposition to her purpose; but she could not trust herself further than to say, as she affectionately embraced her mother, "And I can only cry as did that noble Bethlehem mother to God's messenger: '*Be it unto me according to thy word.*' **He leads, I follow.**"

THE YOUTH JESUS YIELDING TO THE WISHES OF HIS MOTHER.

CHAPTER XXV.

CONSOLATRIX AFFLICTORUM.

> " Furl we the sail and pass with tardy oar
> Through these bright regions, casting many a glance
> Upon the dream like issues and romance
> Of many-colored life that Fortune pours
> Round the Crusaders till, on distant shores,
> Their labors end."
> —WORDSWORTH.

IRIAMNE'S welcome at the "Retreat of the Palestineans," at London, was most cordial. The Grand Master of the returned knights and his wife received her as a daughter; the companion knights vied with each other in efforts to serve the child of their once honored comrade, Sir Charleroy de Griffin. But the maiden never for a moment lost sight of her mission. No sooner had she been bidden to rest than she questioned as to her father's welfare. The Grand Master attempted to assure her that she might recuperate after her journey, but she only the more urged her desire to be taken to her parent at once.

"Worthy Master, dalliance would not be rest, but torture, to me. Being now so near my father, I'm filled with a ruling, all-exciting longing to see him, at once!"

"Be patient, daughter, for a little season; all is done for him that can be. The princely revenues of the knights of Europe are at the behest of each of our veterans, as he hath need."

"Ah! but your wealth can not provide him what I bring—a daughter's love!"

"And yet, daughter, since you press me, I must explain that he is under a cloud which would make thy offering vain at present."

"There is no need, kind commander, to make evasive explanations. I have been forewarned of my father's troubles of mind."

"But he is violent at times, and we are compelled to keep him secluded in the asylum of our brotherhood."

"Good Master, that but the more increases my ardor to hasten a meeting with him. I want to try the cure of love upon him; I've all faith in its efficacy. When may I go?"

The foregoing was a sample of Miriamne's words each day. Her appeals touched all hearts and finally over-persuaded the medical attendants, who, in fact, began to fear lest refusal would unsettle the maiden's mind. She was all vehemence and urgency on this subject.

The meeting was a sorrowful and brief one.

She was not prepared for such a spectacle as her father presented, and her cry, "Take me to him," was changed to one more vehement now:

"Take me away!"

Terror supplemented her utter disappointment. To both feelings there was added a sense of humiliation. She imagined her return to Bozrah, empty-handed; the possible gibes of her mother and others. Her great faith seemed fruitless and her enthusiasm ebbed. Then she began to question within herself whether or not, after all, the new faith she had embraced was not a splendid illusion! She was in "Doubting Castle," with "Giant Despair," and the mighty, impelling question, "What wilt Thou have me to do?" little by little lost its grip on her will. It had seemed to her the voice of God; now it seemed little more than the echo of words heard in a dream. She was moved now by a desire to get away from something, but she could not define the thing. Certainly she desired to escape her disappointment, but not knowing how, she sought to get away from its scene. If she could have run away from herself she would have been glad to have done so. She fled from the asylum, as soon as night came to hide her flight. She had not strength to go far, and the Asylum park of many acres of lawns and groves, afforded her solitude; that that she now chiefly desired. The night the desolate girl thus went forth was a lovely one; a reflection of that other night of sorrow when she fled from the old stone-house home to the chapel of Adolphus at Bozrah. And the memory of that night returned to the girl with some consoling. Again she looked up to the firmament and was calmed by the eternal rest that seemed on all above, and again she yearned to go up further to the only seeming haven of righteousness and peace.

Then came the reaction; the prolonged tension had done its work, and the young woman dropped down on the earth. How long she lay in her blank dream she knew not. If during its continuance she in part recovered consciousness, she had no desire nor strength to rise or throw off her weakness.

Ere long her absence was known at the Grand Master's and an eager search was instituted. Foremost in the quest was the young chaplain of the knights, and his quest brought him first to the object of search.

"Can I aid my lady?" said the chaplain, in kindly tones, standing a little distance away from her, in part through a feeling of delicacy akin to bashfulness, and in part fearing lest by any means he should affright her.

The young woman lay motionless; her eyes closed; her face as the face of the lifeless. Receiving no answer, the man questioned within himself: "Is she dead?" Fear emboldened him, and he essayed active assistance. Delicately, gently, firmly he raised up the prostrate woman. She seemed to realize that some one was assisting her, but she was very passive. Her head, drooping, rested on the young man's shoulder, and she sighed a weary, broken sentence:

"I'm so glad you came, Father Adolphus!"

"Not Father Adolphus, but one rejoiced to serve a friend of his."

The maiden was silent a few moments, as if listening to words coming to her from a distance, through confusions. Memory was struggling to re-enforce semi-consciousness. Then came comprehension; she realized the presence of a stranger, and, with an effort, stood erect. Her eyes turned on the chaplain's face with questionings, having in them mingled surprise, timidity and rebuke. The man interpreted her glance and made quick reply:

"At my lady's services, the Chaplain of the Palestineans. We are all anxious at the Grand Master's concerning yourself."

"Anxious for me!" She found words to say that much, and hearing her own words she recalled her recent thoughts of herself, as one being very miserable and very worthless. She turned her eyes from the young man toward the woodland, in the darkness appearing like a gateway to black oblivion. She yearned to bury herself in the oblivion utterly, and her looks betrayed the thought. The youth gently touched her arm, saying:

"Despair has no place here; the Palestineans vanquish it."

She then looked down toward where she had been lying, both nerves and will weakening. It seemed to her a bed, even on the earth, were inviting, especially so if she could take there a sleep that knew no waking.

The young man had ministered to his fellow-beings long enough to have become a good interpreter of hearts. He discerned the thoughts of the one before him, and offered prompt remedies, words wisely spoken:

"Our faith makes us all hope to see our guest happy ere long."

Then she gave way to a flood of tears. The tears moved the man to exercise his professional function, and forgetting all else he spoke as a comforter to a sorrowing woman. She listened, but, except for her sobs, was silent until he questioned: "Shall I stay to guide back to the 'Refuge,' or return to send help?"

She answered by turning toward him a face pale and blank, lighted alone by eyes all appealing. He interpreted the look and continued: "I'll tarry to aid. Shall we now seek the 'Refuge?'"

Then she exclaimed, "Alas, there seems no refuge for me!"

"The troubles of Miriamne de Griffin enlist all hearts at this place, I assure you."

"And this, your kindness, with your happiness ever before me, but makes to myself my own desolation more manifest! Ah, I'm but a hulk in a dark tide!"

"Lady, say not so, I beseech you. Look, there!" Languidly, mechanically, she turned her eyes in the direction the speaker pointed; then suddenly drew back from sight of a white apparition, standing out boldly from a background of dark shrubbery. Her nerves all unstrung were for the moment victimized by superstitious dreads.

"Only, calm, pure marble; a fear-slayer; not fear-invoker! Look at its pedestal!" assuringly spoke the chaplain. The maiden did as bidden and slowly read, repeating each word aloud: "*Sancta-Maria-Consolatrix-Afflictorum.*"

"By easy interpretation: 'Mother of Jesus, consoler of the sorrowing!'" responded the young man.

"Ah, like all consolations nigh to me, this is only stone and set in deep shadows! It can not come to me!"

"True, yon form is passionless stone; but the truth eternal, which it emblemizes, is living and fervent."

"Life and fervor? Death and sorrow submerge both!"

"There is mother-love in the heart of God; to one so nearly orphan as my friend, it must be comforting to look up believing that in heaven there are fatherhood, motherhood and home! This is the sermon in yon stone."

Then the chaplain gently, reverently drew the sorrow stricken maiden toward the "Refuge" and she followed, unresisting. As they moved along, she essayed to seek further acquaintance with her guide.

"May I know the chaplain's name?"

"Certainly; to those that are intimates, 'Brother' or 'Friend;' for such I've renounced my former self and name."

"But if I should need and wish to send for you? I might. I could not call for 'Brother.'"

"Ah, I'm by right, 'Cornelius Woelfkin;' yet the names are misnomers, since I'm not kin to the wolf, nor am I 'a heart-giving light' as my name implies; at least if I give light it is but dim."

The meeting of the young people, apparently accidental, was in fact an incident in a far-reaching train of Providences. The young woman was in trouble and needing such sympathy as one who was both young and wise could give; the young man was courteous, pure-minded, wise beyond his years, free from the conceits common to young men of capacity, and being a natural philanthropist, naturally sympathetic. The young woman was at the age that yearns for a girl friend, and needs a mother's counsel; the young man had much of his mother in his make-up; enough to fit him to win his way into the confidence and fine esteem of a refined and trusting young woman; but not enough to make him effeminate. Somehow he exactly met the needs of Miriamne's life. He could advise her as sincerely and wisely as a mother and companion her as affectionately as a girl friend. Having neither girl friend nor mother, the young chaplain became both to her.

They were both impressible and inexperienced in the matters that belong to the realms of the heart, in its grander emotions; therefore with a charming simplicity they outlined their intentions and the limitations of their relations. They assured each other, again and again, probably in part to assure themselves, that they were to be very true and very sensible young friends. Their converse often ran along after this manner.

"We understand each other so well!"

"Yes, and are so well adapted to each other!"

"We have had too much experience to spoil this helpful relation between us, by giving away to any sway of the romantic emotions."

"There has seldom been in the world a friendship between a young man and young woman so exalted and wise as ours is."

They agreed that she should call him "brother," and he should call her "sister." At first they said they wished they were indeed akin by ties of blood; though in time they were glad they were not. In this they were like many another pair who have had such a wish, and in their case as in many another like it, the wish was a prediction of its own early demise.

Among the works of art in the park of the Palestineans was a commanding bronze of Pallas-Athene, the goddess believed by her pagan devotees to be the patroness of wisdom, art and science. She was the Virgin of the Romans and the Greeks, their queenly woman, deemed by her wisdom ever superior to Mars, god of war. She was represented bearing both spear and shield; but these as emblems of her moral potencies. In a word, she was the result of the efforts of those ancients to express a perfection that was virgin and matchless, because too fine and exalted to have an equal. Between the "White Madonna" and this Minnerva, Chaplain Woelfkin and the Maid of Bozrah often walked, back and forth, in very complacent conversations. They desired themes, the ideals afforded them; they were in a frame of mind that delighted in Utopianism, and the effigies of the women guided their daydreams. Youth, quickened by dawning, though as yet unperceived, love, naturally begins building a Pantheon filled with fine creations. That is the time of heroworship in general; afterward comes the iconoclastic period when every idol is cast down to make place for the only one that the heart crowns. Cornelius praised sincerely Miriamne, when she said she would be as the Græco-Roman goddess — very wise, very pure, very strong. Day by day, he believed she was becoming like Minerva. Then he thought it very fine for the maiden to emulate the goddess in every thing, even her perpetual virginity. Again, walking near the Madonna and discoursing of her as the ideal of womanhood, as the mother, the minister, the saint, the maiden said she would emulate the latter; the chaplain in his heart prayed that she might.

Once he finely said: "A pure, patient woman is God's appointed and best consoler of the afflicted. Miriamne, be like Mary, and Sir Charleroy will find restoration."

The young woman was encouraged by the words to increase her efforts in her father's behalf. Now she did so not only because prompted by a sense of duty, but because filial love seemed a fine ornament for a maiden. Birds in mating-times put on their finest plumage; men and women do likewise. The chaplain was a humanitarian by profession, and naturally joined the maiden in her efforts for her father's recovery. So their thoughts and their works ran in parallel lines. They had unbounded delight in their companionship and common efforts. This delight they innocently explained to themselves as the natural result and reward of their fine, exalted, frank, wise, brother-like, sister-like friendship. In hours of their supremest satisfaction they generously expressed sorrow for the world at large, because so few in it knew how to attain such bliss as they enjoyed. In a word, they were a very fine and a very innocent pair, a complete contrast with Rizpah and Sir Charleroy at Gerash. The latter took their course under the torrid influences of Astarte of the brawny Giants, the former moved forward charmed and led by those things that were held to be the belongings of the fine women whose statues graced the park of the Palestineans. Miriamne asked wisdom later of her elect counselor, and he advised her to send letters to Bozrah urging her mother to join her in London, in efforts in behalf of their insane kinsman.

The young man very wisely argued: "He is a fragment, flung out of a wrecked home; his perturbed mind is clouded by the wild passions of a misled heart. We must balance his brain by calming his heart. He is filled with hatings, and love alone is hate's cure. If the past losses be recovered, he must be brought back to the place of loss."

Miriamne wrote to her mother, glad to please her counselor by so doing, and yet almost hopeless of gaining any answer that was favorable. The maiden renewed her visit to her father's lodge in the asylum. She was not permitted, nor did she then desire, to see her parent. She shuddered when she remembered the one dreadful meeting of the beginning, and was content to sit outside the door of his cell or keep, day by day, to perform such little services as she could. Sometimes she would call the insane man by his name, or title; sometimes she would call out: "Father, would you like to see Miriamne?" or "Father, your daughter is here." At other times she would sit near his door singing Eastern songs, especially such as she had heard were favorites of her parents in their younger days.

Days passed onward, and there appeared no result beyond the fact that when she was thus engaged the knight became very quiet. At the suggestion of Chaplain Woelfkin, she changed her method, and began in hearing of the knight a recital of the history of Crusader days. In this she was encouraged, for an attendant told her that her father each day, when she began, drew close to his barred door to listen. As she came near the time of the Acre campaign, the knight's face was flushed with interest. Having followed the narrative up to the fall of the city and the flight of Sir Charleroy and his comrades, she paused. Then she was surprised and delighted at once, for the incarcerated man in a voice both calm and natural, ejaculated the words: "Go on!"

Miriamne would have rushed to the prison door had not Cornelius, who stood not far away, motioned her to remain seated and to continue. For a moment she was at a loss how to proceed, but then she bethought herself of an experiment. She described by a kind of a parable the career of her father, as follows:

"And the noble knight, after years of illness, was found by his loving daughter. Under her kindly care he recovered, and at her earnest request he returned to his home in Palestine. There he spent many happy years with his reunited family, consisting of a wife, daughter and twin sons. He is living there now, and all that family agree that theirs is the most happy and loving home on earth."

"It's a lie! a lie!" almost shouted the lunatic. "Sir Charleroy is not there. He went mad; the devil stole his skull and left his brain uncovered to be scratched by a million of bats. That's why he went mad; I know him; he went mad, and is mad yet, and you get away with your lying!"

The daughter fled in terror at the succeeding outburst of wild profanity; but she was still rejoiced, that a chord of memory had been struck. It gave a harsh response, yet it gave a response, and that was much. She continued her efforts as before. The interviews were not fruitless, but they were costing her fearfully. She complained to no one, yet her youthful locks, in a few months streaked with silver, told the story of suffering.

One day there was delivered at the Grand Master's a huge package directed to herself. Miriamne, filled with wonder, called help to open the case. Just under the cover she beheld a letter. She knew the handwriting. It was her mother's. Her heart took a great leap, and as a flash of joy there ran through her mind the thought:

"Mother has sent something to help. Perhaps it's her clothing, and she is coming!"

Tremblingly Miriamne read the epistle. How formal:

"MIRIAMNE DE GRIFFIN :—Thou went'st without my leave. Do not return till sent for. Thou left'st a loving mother for a worthless father, and this is a daughter's reward. Thou dost say Sir Charleroy is mad. I knew it, and think that the curse is descending on thee. But I doubt not the man has cunning in his madness, and has prompted thee to inveigle me into his toils again. Once he had me in England, and there he put me on the rack of his merciless temper and lust! Shame on him for that time! Shame on me if he have opportunity to repeat it! I send thee a comforter. Put it before his eyes, and tell him that the woman of Bozrah is before him. Tell him that she, like Rizpah of old, is true to the death to her sons, and, while waking, never forgets to curse the vultures!"

No love was added. There was no name appended. Miriamne felt like one disowned. She dreaded to examine the contents of the case; but a servant, who began the opening just then, spread it out. As she suspected, after she had read the letter, it was the (to her) hateful picture of ancient Rizpah.

It was evening, and the maiden sought a refuge from her troubles in the park. It was, on her part, another flight from the face of Rizpah of Gibeah; another seeking of solitude from man that she might gain that sense of nearness to the Eternal Father under the calm, silent stars of His canopy. It was like that flight from the old stone house of Bozrah to the chapel of Father Adolphus that she had made long before.

The maiden's course brought her to the "White Madonna," and there she found her counselor and brother, the chaplain. He had heard that Miriamne was desponding that day, and had bent his course hither, confident that the "*Consolatrix Afflictorum*" would prove a tryst. The scenery around Pallas Athene was the finer by far, but to a troubled heart there was the more allurement in the place where the love of heaven was expressed. The Minerva expressed self-sufficiency; the "White Madonna," God's sufficiency. One expressed justice, culture, the perfection of human gifts, regnant and victorious; the other spoke of welcome, healing, mercy, and help for those who were in pitiable needs. The virgin evolved by the philosophers of the Greeks was a concept touching but few of humanity, and fitted to be crowned only in a world of perfections, such as has not yet existed. The "White Madonna" depicted a real character who had a human heart and heavenly traits, and that easily found acceptance in human affections.

The maiden and her counselor sat together for a long time; she speaking of her social miseries, he of God's remedies; she describing the thickness of the night about her; he telling her in beautiful parables that there was a refuge and an asylum, though the night obscured all for a time. As they conversed the rising moon flooded the "White Madonna" with silvering light, and the chaplain rapturously exclaimed:

"See, the moon gets its light from the sun, and gives it to the image. We do not see the sun, but we see its work and glory reflected! So God hands down from heaven to His children, by His angels and ministers, the powers and blessings that they need. Miriamne, we have a Father who forgets none and is munificent to all!"

THE WEDDING AT CANA.

Paul Veronese

LIBRARY
OF THE
UNIVERSITY OF ILLINOIS

CHAPTER XXVI.

THE WEDDING AT CANA.

" I would I were an excellent divine
  That had the Bible at my fingers' ends;
That men might hear out of this mouth of mine
  How God doth make His enemies His friends;
Rather than with a thundering and long prayer
Be led into presumption, or despair."
—BRETON.

"Hear ye Him. Whatever He saith unto you, do it."—MARY.

HAPLAIN WOELFKIN heard of Miriamne's reply from her mother. He was both glad and sorry thereat; sorry the heart he tenderly esteemed should have been so wounded, and glad that the wounding afforded him opportunity to show how gently and wisely he could comfort.

"Your trial came at a fortunate time, sister."

"I can not see how such a rebuke can ever be timely, being unjust and cruel."

"True enough; but if fate must assail, it is well to have its hardships fall on us when we are supported by dawning hopes. There are hopes near for Miriamne."

"Let not my brother's warm heart give me false comfort. I've no sight of hope."

"Say not so; there is a surprise in store for you."

"Now, pray, explain."

"You will be permitted to meet your father at the chapel service to-night."

"Oh, but—!" and Miriamne bowed her head and waved her hand as if to repel some unpleasant spectacle.

"Be not perturbed, sister. Let me explain: You came hither to seek your demented parent, hoping that love would find a way to compass his healing. The purpose and effort were alike noble and wise. You lost heart because the results were slow to appear; but the good seed was sown, and now for the fruit."

"Has my father recovered?"

"He has improved, and to-night we'll sit quietly while we apply the balm of Gilead."

"Now am I in a mystery."

"Miriamne's ministries have touched a responsive chord in Sir Charleroy's heart and fitted him to attend our mind-cure services. Love is the surest remedy for a mind gone down under the ruins of the crushed heart. Sir Charleroy calls his daughter 'Naaman's little maid,' and but yesterday said: 'Ah, she'll take me to healing Jordan yet!'"

"Blessed be God," devoutly exclaimed the maiden, glancing heavenward.

"To which I say 'amen,' assured that great things will come through our '*Birth of Peace.*'"

"And what is that, pray?"

"We are trying to soothe the tumultuous minds of our asylum patients by displaying sweet peace in picture garbs. To-night by the aid of a musical and illustrative service we shall depict, in the chapel, the Birth of Jesus. But I'll not explain further now. Wait until the hour of service, sister."

When the people were gathered, Miriamne, glowing with hope, yet silenced by anxiety, was in the midst of the assembly. The preliminary services moved slowly along with a studied absence of hurry. Miriamne could not give them her attention; she was disappointed because she did not see her father present, and the chaplain himself was not there. Presently the music of the occasion arrested her attention. She followed its movement and found it gaining control of her feelings. There was an organ in soft, quiet tones leading voices that murmured words of trust and rest. She followed the flowing tide of melody again and again, each time further, higher, more contentedly, until one strain, expressive of serene triumph, lifted her to a very third heaven of satisfaction. There it left her almost at a loss to say where the melody ceased and the remembering began.

At that instant, the chaplain passed by her side, robed in white, hurriedly whispering so she alone could hear: ".Your father is behind the screen of Templar banners, quietly listening. Be hopeful and pray. God is good!" The words to her soul were as rain whisperings to spring flowers in a torrid noon.

Advancing to the raised platform, the young man told the story of Bethlehem, ending with a beautiful description of the angel song of "*Peace on earth, good will to men.*" The words of the speaker were quietly spoken, and his address mostly like that of one conversing with a few friends; but the words were very impressive. When all had bowed to receive the benediction, Miriamne, lifting her eyes, beheld her father sitting, with the flag screen thrown aside, full in view, but clad as a knight and without manacle or guard. For a moment he sat thus, then arose and calmly moved out of the chapel toward his lodge. She obeyed a sudden impulse and rose to speed after him, but the restraining hand of the Grand Master was laid on her arm:

"Wait; not yet, daughter."

Renewed hope made it easy for her to comply, and she sat down again filled with gratitude toward God. A series of similar services followed, each bringing new causes for hopefulness to the maiden.

"We are going to Cana to-day, sister," remarked the young chaplain some weeks subsequent to the "Birth of Peace" service.

"To Cana?"

"To Cana, and for a purpose."

"I can not fathom it, brother."

Then the young man explained to his fair hearer the scripture event, and the method devised for presenting it at the chapel, as intended that day.

The patients and their friends were assembled in the chapel again. Sir Charleroy among them, but silent and absorbed with his own thoughts.

"We are going to try a device to gain his attention," whispered the chaplain to Miriamne. Just then the Grand Master, dressed in the full regalia of a knight, ascended the platform and uncovered to view a huge earthen vessel, remarking: "Friends, we want to exhibit this evening a vessel, on its way now to France, but left for a time in our custody by some of our comrade Crusaders, who brought it from Cana in Galilee."

"Knights," "Crusaders," "Cana!" murmured Sir Charleroy, as if in soliloquy. Miriamne observed her father's eyes. They were no longer leaden; they glowed with interest. "You all remember," continued the Grand Master, "how Jesus turned the water into wine at Cana? Tradition informs us that this before us is one of the identical water-pots used that time by our Savior; but I'll leave our chaplain to tell the rest." The youth took his position at the pulpit and began informally to talk, as if in conversation, but he had anxiously, carefully prepared for the occasion.

He first pictured Cana, with its limestone houses, sitting on the side of the highlands, a few miles northeast of Nazareth. "This place," he continued, "is the reminder of two instructive events. I have their history here." Thereupon, Cornelius turned to an illuminated volume and began reading, with passing comments. As he read, Sir Charleroy closely watched the reader; the puzzled look of the listener faded into satisfied attention.

"Jesus was proclaimed the Lamb of God, near Cana, by that vehement, self-starving Baptist John. But in habits and manner of living John and Jesus were utterly dissimilar. There was harmony in the great things, faith and charity in all things."

The mad knight nodded inquiringly.

The student continued:

"Jesus, the organizer of the new kingdom, at Cana, unfolded one part of His policy, for nigh here twain questioned: '*Where dwellest thou?*' Jesus instantly invited them to His own abode. They dwelt with Him a day, and were won to be His loyal disciples, thus attesting the power of Christ in the home. And they got a home religion, for one of these, Andrew, at once sought to win his brother Peter to discipleship. On the eve of Cana's wedding feast Jesus won Philip, saying, '*Follow me,*' and Philip hasted to win Nathaniel, crying, 'Come and see.' To these He spoke of a hereafter home with open doors and a holy family. Each of Jesus's true disciples was impelled to haste and tell salvation's story to his nearest kin. Christianity is a feast beginning in the home circle and spreading to all the earth."

The mad knight, as he listened, cast a glance of inquiry over his shoulder at those near him.

"Sir Charleroy applies the lesson to himself," whispered the Grand Master to Mariamne.

Cornelius went on:

"Cana was the home of Nathaniel. We see this poor man sitting in seclusion under a fig tree. Except his doubts, he was alone. To him Jesus went, and at the door of his own home the Master met him. Because Nathaniel believed, on little evidence, God gave him more, and promised him that he should see heaven open and the angels ascending and descending, as in Jacob's vision. So are those winged messengers passing back and forth forever, to minister to and comfort needy man. One may be lost to the world, to friends, to himself, but never lost to the Good Shepherd, who is like the one in the parable leaving the ninety and nine to follow the lamb that was straying."

Sir Charleroy's head bowed, and Miriamne was glad, for she saw the tears falling thick and fast down his pallid cheeks.

A sign from the attending physicians brought the services quietly to a close. They had seen the emotion of the knight, and desired that the feelings aroused be permitted to quietly ebb.

A few days later, by their advice, the Grand Master summoned the chaplain of the Palestineans to hold another service like the last. "Sir Charleroy was blessed that last day. He evinces interest and natural reasonings. Since the former service he has repeated the story of Cana over and over, together with the substance of thy discourse thereon. Besides that, he never tires of inquiring about the 'ruddy priest of the sweet words,'" said the physician.

"I obey, my Master, it's God's will. What shall be my theme?"

"Oh, Cana continued; De Griffin is constantly inquiring as to when the ruddy priest of the sweet words is to continue the tale of the Cana," said the Grand Master.

"Praise the Day Spring that hath visited us!"

"You echo the thought of all our souls, Cornelius."

And it was so that on the day following the chapel of the "House of Rest" was filled with much the same company that met there the last time.

Miriamne arrived early and eagerly questioned Cornelius as he passed her on his way to his robing-room:

"Oh, brother, hast thou a message of grace and hope for me, to-day?"

"*The entrance of thy word giveth light,*" was his quiet reply; and he passed on, not daring to tarry near the woman that so strangely moved him. He felt very serious, and hence avoided that which might distract his attention.

But Miriamne felt assured, while Cornelius was all faith in the efficacy of the Divine word in working the cure of minds perturbed.

Presently he stood behind his reading-desk and, waiting until the organ tone had died away, commenced by reading these words:

"And the third day there was a marriage in Cana of Galilee; and the mother of Jesus was there:

"And both Jesus was called, and his disciples, to the marriage."

Sir Charleroy had entered the chapel, and was moving toward a lonely seat; his motions were languid; his action listless, except when at intervals he gazed into the empty air and hissed some incoherent words at imaginary people. But the word "Cana" arrested his attention. He looked up, smiled, and then exclaimed: "Oh, the red-faced! That's it; tell us more, more of Cana!"

Cornelius complied. "We have here a story of two lives in the most precious tie on earth, marriage."

Then the chaplain read:

"We see Christ at a Jewish wedding, and the Hebrew marriage was ever an occasion of great joy. Not only so, but the weddings of that people were characterized by very instructive and impressive ceremonies. Let me explain. The day before the wedding both bride and groom fasted, confessed their sins and made ceremonial atonement for the errors of their past lives. They were to be part of each other, and felt that each owed it to the other to be free from burden or taint of the past. Both bride and groom at the wedding wore wreaths of myrtle, the emblem of justice, constantly to typify that virtue as supreme in wedlock."

"Oh, young priest, thou art an angel!"

The voice startled all but Sir Charleroy. He had spoken, yet his face indicated only placidity and interest. Cornelius proceeded:

"The bride, veiled from head to foot to show that her beauty was to be seen only by him to whom she gave herself, decked with a girdle, emblem of strength and subjection, was led in triumph from the home of her father to the home of him who was to possess her. Before she took her departure, kindly hands anointed her with sweet perfumes and gave her priceless jewels; while on her way she was met by all her friends, singing songs and bearing torches to gladden her journey toward her new abode. Thus they that loved the bride did bestir themselves to bestow bounties and make the maiden most choice. There was no detraction, no defiling, no effort to belittle. Were wives aided like brides there would be fewer broken hearts among wedded women."

"Wondrous true, ruddy priest!" It was the mad knight's voice. Cornelius continued:

"The feast of the wedding lasted seven days. To such a gathering Jesus once went. Probably this was the marriage of a kinsman. Thus, immediately after His temptation and His baptism, with His mighty redemptional work all before Him, our Lord deemed it a leading duty to give proper attention to this wedding ceremonial, one of the lesser things that make up so much of life. With man supreme selfishness, or natural littleness, engenders apathy to all except some pre-occupying purpose, but He, in whom all fullness dwells, entered into and embraced around about all life. He was as glorious when meddling with human joys and making the waters of Cana blush to wine, as when grappling with the sorrows of sin and setting Himself up on Calvary the beacon and light of the ages."

Miriamne felt the illumination again that first came to her that Easter-day at Bozrah, while Sir Charleroy's face glowed with intelligence and peace. This was a full, round gospel which Cornelius was proclaiming, and every soul present was fed.

After pausing for an interlude of soothing music he again proceeded with his discoursing as one conversing:

"At Cana, Christ bound as a captive, natural law. How He did so we do not know, but we do know that while destroying no part of nature's system he mysteriously made it serve for human happiness in a way unusual and marvelous. It seems to me that the story of Cana is a fireside story. No matter how miserable a home may be, it may have faith that in welcoming the Divine guest it welcomes assured miraculous joy. Life's waters may blush everywhere to heaven's wine!"

The mad knight murmured: "Oh, ruddy priest! if thou couldst only preach this in Bozrah."

The Grand Master, who was sitting by Miriamne,

pressed her hand and whispered: "Memory is reviving —praise to the Day-Spring!"

Cornelius again read his parchment.

"And when they wanted wine, the mother of Jesus saith unto him, They have no wine.

"Jesus saith unto her, Woman, what have I to do with thee? Mine hour is not yet come."

"So," said the reader, "these folks were likely poor, the supply meager, though no man ever yet had enough of the wine of joy at his wedding until it was blessed by the God of marriage."

Just then Sir Charleroy, standing up, solemnly said: "Young man, I'd have thee tell these people why He said 'Woman, what have I to do with thee?' He, the man, was master, that was it, eh?"

"Oh, motion to Cornelius not to debate," whispered Miriamne to the Grand Master; but Cornelius was already adroitly replying:

"True, knight of Saint Mary, but this Master of ceremonies was Divine. Then He was not talking to his wife. He had not wed this woman, hence was not bound by the law of being her other self. Besides that we must not forget that they had often conversed intimately before the wedding; she with all the tenderness of a woman's heart, which in its love ever naturally outruns all plans, all reasonings, to bestow all it has at once upon the all-beloved. She hurried Christ in the way of giving. This to her credit, if her wisdom is reproved."

The knight settled back in his seat, his face very pale but not anger-marked.

Cornelius continued: "The term 'woman' is often used, as here, in all tenderness. Our rugged language ill translates the original. When a people has not fine moods in its living, its language becomes like sackcloth, unfit to clothe the angel-like thoughts of those who live on more exalted planes. The gross degrade all their companions, whether such be beings or merely words."

The leader again read:

"His mother saith unto the servants, Whatsoever he saith unto you, do it."

"This shows the good, motherly Mary supplementing the Master's work. Doubtless, she had her partisans, some who would have sided with her had she chosen to rebuke her Son. But she desired harmony at the feast and in the home. This was the chief end, and for it she was willing to serve and wait."

"Very true! Our Lady was always right and good." It was the voice of the mad knight.

Cornelius continued:

"These were the finest words Mary ever spoke; they were the key to her whole life; indeed, the spirit of the ideal woman ever more standing nearer to Christ than any other being; at a wedding, the very climax of fullest human love, the gateway to home, the counterpart of heaven, Mary points all to the Christ, exclaiming, '*Hear ye Him!*'"

"Our Lady was always a wise, brave, loving, submissive woman," exclaimed Sir Charleroy.

"It is an old tradition," replied Cornelius, "that this was the wedding of John, the beloved and confidant of Jesus. It is interesting to remember that that blessed disciple, in his Gospel, presents the one whom he loved as a mother but twice—once at this wedding, the other time at the crucifixion; the places of highest joy, and deepest sorrow; a way of saying from the altar to the cross, is woman's course; a parable-like presentment of the doctrine that the wife and mother are to appear at these two points, so opposite, so common to all; the lowest dip, the highest heaven."

The mad knight suddenly interrupted them.

"What did Joseph think of all this?"

Perhaps this odd query was fortunate, for it brought smiles to all. The knight laughed out until his eyes were flowing with tears.

Cornelius, self-possessed, quietly replied: "It is said that Joseph was dead long ere this wedding, and that Mary was exhaling the perfumes of her consecrated widowed life to gladdening in pious ministries the people about her. Widowhood has such purposes."

"Ah, she was the Rose," cried the knight. "If Joseph were not dead, he might well stand back, behind such a wife!"

The chaplain of the Palestineans closed with a well-worded climax, recalling the fact that this event made a lasting impression on the Son of God, as evinced by the wondrous tropes of the Apocalypse, where eternal goodness and eternal joy are pictured under the similitude of a wedding-feast.

The mad knight cried out: "Grand, grand! Oh, ruddy priest, I worship thee!"

The Grand Master signaled the conclusion. The worshipers and patients were slowly retiring, Sir Charleroy moving toward his lodge seemingly wrapped in contemplation of some engrossing problem.

He passed near the picture of "Rizpah Defending Her Relatives," which by some mischance had been left near the chapel door. Instantly the knight's attention was fixed; he became excited, then suddenly turning to an attendant, exclaimed:

"Here, tell me, where am I? Is this London or Bozrah?"

"London, good Teuton."

Again he gazed at the picture, and his transformation was startling. His face was distorted, his body became rigid and swayed as that of the hooded snake making ready to strike a victim. Then bounding to the Grand Master's side he snatched the latter's sword from its hilt, quickly returned to the picture, and before any could prevent him began to hack it to pieces.

One tried to restrain him, but was overpowered, two, then three were flung aside. Presently he was pinioned but not silenced.

"Away! Unhand me!" he shouted. "In the name of the King of Jerusalem, the defenders of the Sepulcher, unhand me! Do you not see? There! they've come to make riot at the feast of Cana! Ruddy priest, come quickly. Help! This fearful gang will all be loose in a moment; they be the ghosts of the giants, and war everlastingly against the peace of homes; against our Mary and her Son's kingdom."

He was breathless for a moment, and all were anxious lest he be permanently unsettled. Some were praying for him, others holding him. Then he broke forth again as before.

"Unhand me, infidels! God wills it! Let me cut to pieces yon horrible thing fresh from hot hell; painted by the gory and beslimed hands of devils! See! it's bewitched, and the woman and the hanging men and the vultures are all alive! They'll be at us! One of those black birds has feasted on my heart for years, and yon woman has nightly beaten my bare brain with her club."

They tried to calm him; his daughter pressed to his side, and flinging her arms about the knight, beseechingly cried: "Father! father! it is I! Miriamne!"

"Miriamne? Ha! ha!" cried the excited man. "More mockery! More witchery! Miriamne is lost, eternally lost! Yon group of demons tore her from me! Oh, God, if thou lovest a soldier of the cross, hear me, and blast with burning, swift and quenchless lightnings, yon monsters, and with them all who separate hearts and wreck homes!"

"Father, so say we all; let us pray together," pleaded the girl.

"Father! Who says 'father' to me?"

"It is I, your daughter, Miriamne!"

Suddenly, Sir Charleroy became calm and curiously observed the maiden. "Art thou Sir Charleroy's daughter? I knew him once in Palestine. He died afterward in London and left me his body. But it's not much use. It's sick most of the time. I carry it about, though, hoping he'll come for it. If thou dost want it thou canst have it."

The daughter humored the fancy, and quickly replied: "I do want it. I love it. I'll help you take care of it. Let me now hug it to my heart."

Then he permitted her to twine about him her arms, and when she kissed him the second time he returned the salutation, and tears ran down his hot cheeks.

"Blessed be the God of peace," fervently ejaculated Cornelius. "The day dawns; after tears, light."

The knight continued after a time, addressing Miriamne:

"Sir Charleroy was my friend; and thou art his daughter? Thou wouldst not deceive me, I know.

Tell me in a few words," he said, meanwhile furtively glancing about, "Who am I?"

Miriamne again humored him, and pressing her lips nigh his ear, in a whisper replied: "Sir Charleroy, Teutonic knight, my father."

The old man held her off a little way, gazed at her a moment, doubtfully, then said: "Thou art large for a baby! Miriamne is a little thing." Then he continued: "But thy eyes, they are Miriamne's; and so honest! I believe them! Then thou art Miriamne and I Sir Charleroy?"

"Truly." And again she kissed her father.

"But thou dost not want me—a wreck, a pauper!"

"I do, and the boys do; all Bozrah wants you, needs you."

"Not thy mother! Oh, no; I murdered her long ago!"

"Not so, dear father."

"I did, indeed. See," and he pointed to the painting, "I've killed her again, to-day."

"That's but a miserable painting, and I hate it as much as you do; but it's harmless, henceforth."

"Are all the devils in it dead; the vultures that ate up my heart?"

"Yes, yes; who cares for them?"

"Then I shall get better."

The mad knight suffered himself to be led away quietly. There was great joy among the Palestineans that night. And so Miriamne carried the spirit of Mary, that presided at Cana's feast, into the misery of that English asylum. She had given her life to ministering for others, had begun in her own home circle, her life motto: "*Hear ye Him*"—"*Whatsoever He saith unto you, do it.*" Now she was rewarded, and began to hope that there would be the renewal of wedding chimes at Bozrah, that the wine of its joy would be renewed and sweetened. She questioned the chaplain for advice. "Tell the Master there is no wine in the old stone house, and '*whatsoever He saith, do it,*'" was the young man's answer.

CHAPTER XXVII.

"THE STAR OF THE SEA."

Rocked in the cradle of the deep,
I lay me down in peace to sleep,
Secure, I rest upon the wave,
For Thou, oh Lord, hast power to save.
I know Thou wilt not slight my call,
For Thou dost mark the sparrow's fall,
And calm and peaceful be my sleep,
Rocked in the cradle of the deep.
And such the faith that still were mine
Tho' stormy winds swept o'er the brine,
Or tho' the tempest's fiery breath
Roused me from sleep to wreck and death;
In ocean's caves still safe with Thee,
Those gems of immortality,
And calm and peaceful be my sleep
Rocked in the cradle of the deep."

IKE the morning dawn on a calm sea, after a night of fierce storm, so came now great peace to Miriamne. The heaviest sorrow of her life was lifting. Her father was recovering; his mind becoming rational; and chief of Miriamne's joys, was the fact that his convalescence was accompanied by the appearance of a deep trusting love for herself. He seemed to lean on his daughter for help; cling to her for hope and aim, by every way, not only to express his sense of dependence on but his deep and abiding gratitude toward the patient, chief

minister, in the mission of his recovery. He seemed for a long time to be haunted by a fear of relapse into some great misery that he but dimly remembered and could not define, beyond a shudder. He dreaded to be alone, and often clung to his daughter with furtive glances of fear, even as a terrified child clings to its mother. One day, months after he had begun to be rational, he addressed Miriamne: "We must soon seek another abiding place, daughter. Our Grand Master has discharged with overflowing payment, every debt of hospitality."

"True, father, and I'm glad; the thought for weeks in my mind, is now in yours. But where shall we go?"

"I think, to France, and immediately."

"France?"

"Yes, there I'll seek out some of the De Griffins. They may be able to mend my shattered fortunes, and if I find none of my kin, I shall not be lacking in anything, for there are many of our Teutonic knights. While they prosper, no want shall harass me or mine."

"Father, I do not want to go to France."

"Why, this is strange?"

"It seems far away, very far, to me."

"Art thou dreaming, my Syrian Oriole?"

"No, awake! And very earnest."

"Why, we could walk thither, were it not for the water."

"But I can not go that way!"

"Well, we can not stay here, so where?"

"Eastward; Bozrah!"

"Wouldst thou ask a spirit, by mercy permitted escape from Tophet to return?"

"Yes, even that, if the spirit had a mission and a safe conduct."

"Thou art nobler, braver than I. I can't trust the land of giants and vultures."

"The giants and vultures we must meet are in human forms, and such are everywhere."

"There are over many for the population, in Syria and beyond it."

"But there have been many changes since you left that country, especially, in our city," persisted the maiden.

"Nothing changes in Palestine or Bozrah, daughter, except wives, and they only one way; from bad to worse."

The young chaplain seconded Miriamne's efforts.

Sir Charleroy was spasmodically the stronger, but Miriamne by patience and persistence prevailed. In time, she won her cause, and the three took sail for the Holy Land, the knight protesting that he would go as far as Acre and no further. The journey was slow but not monotonous, for the English trader on which they journeyed stopped at various ports. Cornelius on his part was enjoying a serene delight that had no shadow except when he remembered that voyaging with Miriamne was to have an end; Miriamne on her part had three-fold pleasure; delight in her companionship with the young missionary, delight in the continued improvement of her father's health, and greater delight still in the glowing hope of the success of her mission of peace to her home-circle. As for Sir Charleroy it suited him well to be sailing. He was ever exhilarated by change; each day brought it. He was in theory a fatalist, and the staunch ship pushing onward day and night to its destination, carrying all along, was an expression of the inexorable. Then the conditions about him rested him, for he was freed from any need of bracing of his will to choose or execute any thing. He went forward because the ship went. That was all and enough. Only once during the voyage did he assert himself or express a desire to change his course. THAT WAS WHEN PASSING CYPRUS.

"Here," he cried, "let me disembark!"

Persuasively, Miriamne protested.

"But I must! I've a mission. I want to curse the memory of the recreant Lusignan, the coward 'King of Jerusalem;' he that clandestinely stole away from Acre on the eve of those last days!"

"But, father, Cyprus is called the 'horned island.' I do not like the name!"

"I've heard it better named, 'the blessed isle.' There the hospitable knights had a refuge for pilgrims, and it still abides."

Just then some of the sailors cried, "Olympus!" They had caught sight of that ancient mountain, the fabled home of the gods.

Miriamne adroitly used the cry to divert her father's mind, saying:

"Let those admire Olympus who will; as for me, I prefer holy, fragrant Lebanon."

She pointed eastward, and they saw the dim outlines of Palestine's famous range. The knight's attention was fixed on Lebanon, and they sailed past Cyprus quietly without further objection on his part.

Miriamne and Cornelius, as the night began to settle down, stood together by the ship's side, feasting on glimpses of the distant shore. There were signs of a coming storm, perceived intuitively by those accustomed to the sea, by the young watchers best discerned in the anxious looks of the seamen.

"The captain says the sky and sea are preparing for a duel. You noticed how the blue changed to dark brown in the water this afternoon? He says that, and the muddy appearance of the sky, betoken a tempest."

"How like polished silver the wings of those gulls glisten as they career!" was the maiden's ecstatic reply.

"The wings are as they always are. They glisten now because they flash against a murky background."

"An omen, Cornelius, for good! I'll call the seabirds hope's carrier-pigeons with messages for us."

"I would we had their wondrous power of outriding all storms. It is said they can sleep on the waves, even during a tempest."

"I've the heart of a sea-gull, to-night."

"And not a dread or pang within?"

"No, no! Oh, come, any power, to hurry us to Acre! I'd give way to the merriment of the becalmed sailors, who whistle for the wind, if I only knew the notes of their call."

"But the old sea-captain is very grave. See how the men at his command are lashing up almost every stitch of our ship's dress."

"Oh, well, I'll be grave, too, to please you; and yet I pray that Old Boreas, and all the Boreadal, come in racing hurricanes, if need be, that we may be sent gallantly into longed-for Acre!"

"A storm at sea is grand in a picture or in imagination; sometimes, though rarely, in experience. To be enjoyed it must be terrible; there's the rub; it may come with overmastering fury."

"Bird of ill omen! Why cry as in requiems? As for me, while you are fearing going down, I'll be thinking of going forward!"

"And be disappointed, certainly, on your part, as I hope I may be mistaken on mine. We may not go down; we shall certainly not go forward!"

"Now, how like a wayward man! Since you can not have your way, cross me by predicting my frustration!"

"Oh, do not lay the blame on me! there are broader shoulders to bear it. Lay the blame on the Taurus and Lebanon ranges!"

"Well, this is an odd saying, surely!"

"Wait awhile, and you will find it very true, as well. We are to meet to-night, most likely, the Levanter or off-shore gale, Paul's Euroclydon, charging down from its mountain castles. Taurus and Lebanon together form a cave of the winds!"

"And you seem glad that they are coming to battle us back?" spake the maiden, rebukingly.

"Yes, if they prolong our companionship. I can not rejoice in a speed that hastens our parting."

The last sentence died on the chaplain's paling lips with a sigh.

The maiden turned her eyes full on the speaker, then slowly, meditatively answered:

"I shall be sorry, too, at our parting!"

"'Sorry!' Ah! that's no word for me, this time; agonized is better!" was the young missioner's quick rejoinder.

The maiden was pained, but she mastered her feelings and pleaded:

"The parting must come some time; do not let

such repinings make it harder for both. It is wiser, when confronting what one does not desire, but can not help, to court the balm of forgetfulness. So do I ever, especially now."

"And like all attempted silencings of the heart, by cold philosophy, mocked at last by failure!"

"My philosophy can not mock me, since it accords with the stern facts which confront us. I'll be as frank now as a sister, Cornelius. Our diverging missions part us. You go to Jerusalem to preach the cross; I, to a narrower field, at Bozrah, to attempt the rekindling of love on one lone altar of wedlock. God orders it thus, and I submit unquestioningly; for it is not for one who can scarcely touch the hem of His garment to challenge His wisdom by a murmur."

"But time, Miriamne, may leave you free, your work being completed in the Giant City?"

"Even so. There is a gulf between us; we may love across it but not pass it, in body, in this life."

"And I can not see the gulf?"

"I am in faith, after all, an Israelite; enlightened to be sure, but not likely to renounce the ancient beliefs. You are a Christian; nor would I wish you otherwise. Now, amid the miseries I've witnessed in my own home, I can not but be admonished against any attempt at fusing, by the fire of adolescent, transitory loving, two lives guided by faiths so constantly in antagonisms."

"The faith of Jesus and Mary, truly lived, never failed to fuse hearts sincerely loving. You may call yourself what you like; in substance of faith we are in accord."

"The chaplain reasons well; better than I can, and

yet he does not convince me! I can only plead that he do not persist, and so make the parting harder. It must be; though my heart break, I must suffer the immolation. I've asked this question in the awful sincerity of a soul as it were at the bar of judgment: '*What wilt Thou have me to do?*' I know the answer. I must seek to bring father and mother together."

"And then?"

"Seek to know if the Messiah has indeed come."

"And then?"

"If I find He has, some way tell His people Israel, as only a Jewess can, of the Light Everlasting."

"And then?"

"Why, that's sufficient to measure the lives of generations; but if I survive beyond that work, I have vaguely passing through my mind the coming of a millennial day when all mankind will be akin; all righteous, all just, and the tears of womankind assuaged."

"I pray for that, but how can we hasten joy by breaking our own hearts?"

"I do not know what lies beyond; how that day of glory is to come, but this I know, the spirit of Chivalry was from God. It had, and has a deep, impressive meaning. In contact with it at the west, I felt all the time as if it were blind, but a Samson still, feeling for the pillars of some mighty wrong. I wonder if I may not be the giant's true guide. Or, better still, may I not be, under God, the giantess to do the very work. Perhaps the world awaits a woman Samson!"

"What Miriamne says is to me all mysticism! Explain."

"I do not know how, beyond this: I'm God's bride by consecration, and He will keep me for His work."

"Can't I share it?" almost piteously, the chaplain asked.

"Truly, yes, wherever you may be, with me or not."

"Oh, Miriamne, your passionate enthusiasm entrances me. You are an inspiration to me. I fear I shall languish aside from you."

"I shall love you more, Cornelius, as you are more grandly, heroically self-sacrificing."

"Any thing to win Miriamne's constant love!"

"I shall love you, Cornelius, in a deep, holy way, only and forever. I'd be ashamed to be thus frank, but that I have a love that is as pure as the heaven of its birth. Be true to your God, to your mission; a little while and then at the City of Light, life's brief dream over, the first, after God, I'll ask for will be the faithful man whom my heart knows."

"Ah, what can I do? I'm all zeal; willing to go, but the glow of your cheeks, the flash of your eyes, even in the midst of such noble converse, drag me away from my resolves. That that stimulates me, unmans me, or reminds me I am a man and a lover."

"You ought to teach me, not I you; but you remember you told me of the belief of some in 'penetrative virginity.' That is the purity of Mary passing somehow into others. Oh, all I am that's good, be in you, and more, even all that she was whom you so revere; I mean the mother of the Christ."

"In my soul I reverently exclaim 'amen,' but then again, how strange the question will not down, 'must we part?'" And so saying he flung his arm about the woman, passionately embracing her. He thought for a moment he had overcome her, but the kiss on her lips not resisted, was the end; for slowly untwining his arms and holding his hands at arm's length, she questioned: "Will you promise me one thing?"

"Surely, yes, name it."

"That you will think of me as a friend, sister, henceforth, and let me go my way without further misery?"

The man struggled with himself for a time; then gazed into her eyes with a most piteously appealing gaze.

She was firm.

"Yes—I promise, but say affianced, to be wed in heaven?"

"God bless you," was her instant response. Their lips met and the debate was ended.

And so for the time they separated, persuading themselves that the whole matter between them had been finally sealed. They had all faith in their pledges mutually given, each to live apart from the other. As yet they had no just conception of the power of a rebel heart constantly uprising. Of course, they both foresaw a measure of wretchedness in the future as a consequence of their decision, but distant pain foreseen by the young, is ever dimmed by hope, and very different from present pain. These twain comforted themselves, at first, by the thought that they were martyrs, and it is always agreeable to feel ourself a martyr, especially when expecting a martyr's reward; at least it is so until the reality of the martyrdom comes.

The sky grew darker, night shut down about the ship, the winds increased, and that sense of awful loneliness, felt on the eve of an impending night storm at sea, came to all hearts but those of the sailors. The latter were too busy to think of aught but their duties. Then their captain had his reckonings, and assured them by his bearing that he felt confident that he could outride this storm as he had often before similar ones. Miriamne, yielding not more to the captain's command, than to the entreaties of Woelfkin, went below to her cabin. She soon courted sleep to help her forget the war of the tempest, praying a prayer most fitting, meanwhile. The prayer was a meditation, like unto this: "He that cares for all will care for helpless me, and come what may; keep me until that last great day." The storm strengthened, and she began to be anxious for her father, and her friend. She had said to herself the latter title should define Cornelius. But her heart forgot its fear a moment in a mysterious, merry peal of laughter; such laughter is very real, but it is never heard by human ears. We know it only in those exalted moments when we try fine introspections; when there seems to be two of us; the one observing and entering into the other. Miriamne heard that laughter when she meditated, "Cornelius is just a friend." Presently she became more anxious for those aloft. Then a troop of imperious inner questions came to her: "Might I not stand by him, if the danger increases? Would it be wrong to show him that I am brave and loving?"

"Will he think me cowardly and stony-hearted?" Resolution was being assailed, and weakened. The questionings increased in number and imperiousness: "What if to-night we are all to perish?" Then she let imagination take the rein. She thought of a scene that might be if she and her beloved were as betrothed, soon to be wed, lovers. In the scene she fancied herself, her lover and her father all together in a last embrace, going down into the yawning waves

"Would my lover try to save me?" For the moment there were two of her again, and it was the one that awhile ago laughed so merrily, that now seemed to be saying: "Would my lover try to save me?" The one self heard the question, and by silence, without sign of rebuke, seemed to give the other self plenary indulgence. Then came a free play of her imagination. She saw herself lying in coral palaces, beneath the moaning waves of the Mediterranean, still clasping her lover and her parent. Then she thought of how her friends would receive the news of her demise. Perhaps some poet would embalm the event in deathless poems, and thousands read of the three that perished side by side. Her mind ran back to London. She imagined a memorial service at the chapel of the Palestineans and the Grand Master there saying: "Miriamne de Griffin was lost at sea; in the path of glorious duty, loyally pursued to the end."

Then she thought of Bozrah and the old stone house, with her mother and her brothers, its sole occupants; the mother in mourning garbs, her spirit subdued, and she often tenderly saying to the fatherless, sisterless boys, "Miriamne was a good girl, a faithful daughter, a noble woman."

But after all, these excursions were unsatisfactory to the young woman. And naturally so. When she thought of lying a corpse, with weed-winding sheets, for years, in the caves of the sea, she was repelled. Thoughts of her memorials, possibly to transpire at London and Bozrah, were not very comforting. She was too young, too free from morbidness, too deeply enamored, to court, assiduously, posthumous honors.

Then came thought of a wreck and rescue, and it

was very welcome. It grew out of the possibility of the youth she loved and she alone, of all on board, being saved. She thought of drifting about for days on a raft! Would she recall her resolutions and his, or would he say to her: "Miriamne, I saved you from the deep; now you are mine entirely and forever!" Would she believe his claim paramount? Would duty's requirements be satisfied? Then she was as two again. One voice said 'yes,' and the other did not concur, neither did it gainsay. She could not pronounce a verdict and there were tears flowing.

The storm grew stronger, but the laboring ship rose and fell on the billows at intervals, and she was lulled to sleep. Her last thoughts, as she passed into dreamland, were that it would have been a useless pain, both endured, if now they were to be lost; the pain of determining, as they had, to live apart. As she so thought she wished almost that they had not resolved as they had. Conscience and desire were in their ceaseless warfare. Then sleeping brought a dream of joy, the blessing that comes often to the heart that is clean. The dream was colored by events preceding.

Cornelius had reminded her the day before, as they were sailing along the coast of Cyprus, that, at Paphos, on that island, there was once a temple to Venus, the fabled goddess of love. That divinity, surrounded by multitudes paying her homage, came before the dreamer's mind in all those ravishing splendors of person that are so attractive to human desires. Around the goddess, and very close to her, were hosts of young men and maidens, their actions as boisterous and ecstatic as those intoxicated. Outside of the throngs of youths were others older; and outside of these were others still; those far away from the goddess, seemingly bowed with years. The company of youths was constantly increased by new arrivals who crowded back those there before them.

But there was a depletion as well as augmenting of the vast, surging congregation; for anon, as if mad, some nearest the deity rushed away, both of the men and the maidens, nor did those fleeing stop until they found violent deaths by leaping from cliffs or into the sea.

Then the ancients, crowded continually back by the new arrivals, one after another, with expressions of disappointment and disgust on their features, seemed to melt away into a surrounding forest of trees that were very black and very like shadows. The dreamer in her dream betook herself to prayer that the God of mercy might change what she saw.

Then she beheld the Paphian goddess in all the splendor of her form, a perfect triumph of nature, just as depicted by bard and painter, looking out contemptuously, pitilessly, toward her former votaries, now aged and pushed aside. There came then a voice as if from above: "*God is love.*"

Immediately on the face of the divinity there was an expression as of terror, and she began sinking. Before the mind of the dreamer, the beautiful creature, and her retinue of nude, bold-faced attendants, with all that appertained to them and their queen went down, ingulfed in a foaming, roaring whirlpool. As they went down lightnings from above shot after them And the dreamer looked aloft to see from whence the voice and the lightning came. As she gazed upward she saw a man of noble form, reverently bowing, as a son might bow in the presence of a mother revered and loved, before a woman of noble mien and beautiful beyond all compare.

But this one's beauty had no similitude to that of the departed deity. As the maiden gazed she discerned that the man was the one her heart called lover, the woman the one she had enshrined as the ideal of her soul, Mary. The twain stood above her, on a plain, apparently of clouds very bright, rising in graceful curve from the earth and stretching away in measureless vistas, filled with flowered parks, silvery rivers and stately mountains. Along the rivers, amid the flowery plains and on the verdant mountains, there were numerous buildings; but these latter were inviting; not palatial, nor stately. They were homes surrounded by family groups. And the dreamer discerned true love triumphant and fruitful. She lingered in this presence, anon longing for a presentment of her self amid the scenes of pleasure, until all was suddenly dissolved by a mighty lurch of the ship that awakened her. She started from her couch and all immediately before the dream came back to her mind.

"We're in a storm on the Mediterranean, and the captain is anxious!" Her nerves were now unstrung; a woman's timorousness was upon her. She could hear confused noises aloft, but no voices. For a moment she questioned: "What if all but myself have been swept away?" Then she thought of herself as drifting about in a ship, sailless, helmless, alone! The thought was suffocating. The noises aloft continued, and she gave strained attention to catch the sound of a voice. There was nothing to be heard but the creaking of timbers, the dashing of waves, the shrieking of winds and vague thumpings, as if parts of the vessel were beating each other to pieces.

"I'll not lie still in this coffin!" she exclaimed, and with a bound she made her way to the deck. As she arrived there she thought she saw dark forms, some crouching as if for shelter, and others as if engaged in a great struggle. Were these demons, or the crew in a struggle for life? She could not say. Then there came a cry from the direction of the forward part of the ship; she thought it was her father's voice, but it was very hoarse and scarcely recognizable.

She listened again to the cry: "Ho, ho; ye Olympian demons! tear up the sea, charge now! Ha, ha; have at us!" The cry thrilled her. Again the wild voice rose above the storm:

"Bury her, my darling, if ye dare! What matter! her white soul has eternal wings!"

She was certain it was her father. She longed to rush to his side, but she doubted whether she could find him in the darkness; then, too, even in the terrors of the moment, her maiden modesty asserted itself. She remembered that she was but partly clad.

Again came that voice, wilder than before: "Ye billows, dare ye smite a knight in the face? I'll meet your challenge, and single-handed, in your midst, fight!"

Miriamne's heart was almost paralyzed by the thought, "The boisterousness has overcome my father. He's contemplating leaping into the sea!"

Just then a vivid flash of lightning made everything visible. It seemed to cut under the clouds, which, rain-charged, were running near the billow crests, and at the same time enswathed the ship from the mast tips to the partially exposed keel, in flame.

The maiden saw by that flash her father standing on the head-rail, one hand clinging to a stay rope, the other with clinched fist, as if menacing the boiling waters that leaped away from the plunging prow. His face was livid, his hair wind-tossed, his eyes glaring. With a scream she bounded toward him; her scream and appearance terrifying the sailors. It was so unexpected and they had forgotten the presence of a woman on board. They only saw a white form, with disheveled hair and with a motion light and swift as a creature on wings, passing from companion-way forward.

But the fright was but momentary. Cornelius, who had been vainly endeavoring to calm the knight, knew the form, and loud enough to be heard by all cried:

"Miriamne de Griffin!"

He was by her side in an instant.

The young woman uttered pleadingly one sentence, but it thrilled all who heard it:

"My father!"

Cornelius exultingly answered:

"Saved! See, the captain holds him and has summoned the watch!" Then he could do no less, forgetting as he did in the present surprise, all old resolves, so he drew the trembling form to his heart as closely as he could. She drew back a little, but he whispered, "Miriamne." What else he might have said was lost, for she fluttered a little, then rested, but on the bosom of her companion.

She was a woman in peril, in fright, storm-drenched, and in love. What otherwise or less could she have done than nestle in the shelter that gave love for love and promised her all else?

"Are you not alarmed, Cornelius?"

"No."

"How strange! You have changed places with me. In the evening you trembled when I left you, and I thought I was very brave. Now I tremble; do you not?"

"I cowered a while ago from the cross you presented me; it seemed to bring a lingering death."

Just then the ship's prow plunged under a mountainous billow. Miriamne clung to her support and fearfully questioned:

"Shall we be overwhelmed?"

"No; I've a token."

"From the captain?"

"Not from the one who guides this ship alone."

A flash of lightning revealed the lover's face to Miriamne. She saw his eyes turned devoutly upward, and she understood his meaning. They had withdrawn to a shelter by the vessel's side meanwhile. Presently the young missioner spoke again;

"Our Heavenly Father keeps vigil, I think, sometimes with especial care over this highway between the outer world and the desolate habitations of His chosen people."

"Hark, the sailors are singing! How strange it is to sing in such perils," spoke the maiden.

"They're as happy now as the wave-walking petrels. The Levant has done its worst; they know this by the coming of the rain, hence they sing their 'Lightning Song.'"

"Lightning song?" queried the maiden.

"Listen! How they explode their vocalized breaths in hissings, whizzings, followed by the prolonged crash made by stamping feet and clapping hands at the end of every stanza. That chorus is meant to imitate those heralds of the thunder, the flashing lightnings."

"But it seems presumptuous to me. The lightning is so dreadful!"

"Not that which comes as 'a funeral torch to Euroclydon,' as the sailors say. Some of them call it 'the winking and blinking of St. Elmo going to sleep.'"

"Oh, Cornelius, the storm is breaking! I see a star; yes two!" rapturously cried the maiden.

"Truly, yes; 'Castor and Pollux,' the 'Twins,' the 'Sailor's Delight!' They say these stars are storm rulers and friends of the mariner. Now hear how they shout their song! They see the stars!"

Above the subsiding wind and waves, rose the words of the singers:

> "Now to our harbor safe going;
> Riding the billows, pushed by the gale:
> The torch of the Twins bright glowing —
> Tipping our mast and gilding each sail."

"And do these stars assure, Cornelius?"

"I saw a star no cloud can ever hide, through the darkest part of the storm."

"A star?"

"Yes, 'Mary, Star of Sea.'"

"I do not comprehend you."

"God's love! He that guided the maiden orphan of Bethlehem through the besetments of her life, amid the tempests of Jewry and Rome, purely, safely, gloriously, to the end; while many of noble birth and having every earthly good went down to ruin, walks ever on the wave where faith voyages."

"And you thought of the Holy Mother in the storm?"

"Yes, this Adriatic is full of angels, that come in thoughts, or before the eyes! You remember Paul, tempest tossed a day and a night on this sea, was found by the Divine Messenger that night when the darkness was thickest?"

"And this 'Star of the Sea?'"

"It tells me mother-love was carried by a dying Savior into the heart of the Triune, Eternal God, and we are His children, and He became Father and Mother to us. You have seen the hen gather her chickens, as human mother shelters with her arm or apron her child in pain or peril?"

"How touching! Think you He felt for us like tenderness in the height of the storm?"

"He sought in His plenteous wisdom mother love to sustain Himself, during the pain and perils of His incarnation, and will ever surely grant a love and care to His own beloved ones in suffering or danger as tender as that He sought and needed for Himself."

"Surely this is a grateful, natural reasoning; but do you believe Mary presides over the sailor especially?"

"It is enough for me to know that the Father through Mary exemplified His motherliness."

"I'll never more call yon bright luminaries Castor and Pollux, but rather Jesus and Mary, the guides and the defenders!" And for a long time they gazed at the double stars, the storm slowly abating. Once the youth, drawing the maiden closely to himself, questioned:

"Can not we call the stars in conjunction, 'Cornelius and Miriamne'?"

They had been watching, in sweet converse, there, a long time; there were faint traces of dawn in the east, and Miriamne had just been thinking, "Palestine receives us with illumination;" then she bethought herself that she and the man with her were going hither to proclaim the Gospel of eternal light. The question of her lover recalled the converse of the day before. That seemed fact, unchanged; all occurring since, dream. She arose, pointed eastward, and firmly said: "There lies our work, our all. May a glorious day enhalo all God's chosen country ere long. Cornelius, yesterday we promised solemnly that we dare not turn from now; especially after our wonderful deliverance!" She glided away to her cabin, leaving the man alone to contemplate the poor comfort of being praised as a martyr, on a cross of self-sacrifice; the pains of which, if not as awful as those of Calvary, were destined to be more prolonged. His face was as if sprinkled with white ashes; it was so pale, so blank. After the tempest they spoke very little with each other. Miriamne waved away any attempt at re-opening the subject, with a motion of the finger to the lips, signaling silence, and a glance all tenderness, but full of pitiful pleadings to be spared. The young man but once or twice essayed the discussion, fearing on the one hand to trust himself to speak, and on the other hand feeling that any effort to change his fate would be hopeless. But he and she were full of inner conflicts. Then their pathways seemed stony, brier-tangled. They had both elected, for Guide and Ideal, Jesus and Mary; they were both going toward the cross in a noble consecration of their lives. But they denied themselves that that sustained Jesus, home love, such as he found at Bethany; conjugal love, such as sustained Mary, the wife and the mother, as well as the disciple. They had as their loftiest ambition the purpose of making the world happier and better, and began by making misery for themselves. They had read that a star led the wise men of the East to Christ in a cradle, the light of the Gospel rising first in a little home circle. They looked at the double stars above them after the storm that night almost until dawn, and then turned away to go, each into the dark like a lone wandering star. Each was in part the victim of a fabricated conscience, and of a mis conception of duty.

CHAPTER XXVIII.

THE QUEEN IN THE VALLEY OF SORROWS.

"They had him away to crucify him."—MARK.
"There followed him a great company of . . . women, who also bewailed him."—LUKE.

* * * * * * * *

GABRIEL: "Hail, highly favored among women blessed!"
MARY: This is my favored lot!
My exaltation to affliction high!
—MILTON.

OR many days Sir Charleroy and Miriamne tarried at Acre, the latter seeking to banish repining on account of him whom she had sent away at the behest of conscience, by ministries for her parent. With alacrity she joined the tours of her knightly father, visiting the scenes where he once battled, listening, from time to time, with unaffected delight, to his recitals. The tides of fanatical conquests had wrought few changes on the face of the city, and the realism of those days of siege, of the stern compacts made in the last hours of the Crusaders, the solemn religious services before the last battle, the death struggle and the disordered retreat, was complete. The excitement of revived memories seemed to lift up the knight from the syncope of ill health. This encouraged the maiden to solicit the reviews and recitals of her father. The night before their departure from Acre, as determined, the knight and his daughter stood together contemplating the sacred pile

which stood in the moonlight and shadows, mostly in shadows. The soldier of fortune, having told its story over and over, was now silent, dreaming of the past.

"*Selamet!*"

They both started, for the voice was like one from the tomb, none but themselves being apparent.

"I'm afraid here; let's be going, father," whispered Miriamne, essaying to withdraw.

Thereupon there glided out of the shadows a stately form who, drawing near to the father and daughter, spoke:

"Fear not, lady! Knight, they can not be foes who court kindred memories and hope of like colors at the same shrine!"

"Thou speakest with Christian allusions the 'peace' word of the Turk."

"I wear the Turkish '*selamet*,' as I do this Turkish harness, a loathed necessity, but without; the peace I pray and feel is the mystic inner peace."

"As a Christian?"

"Yea; nor do I fear confession, since I am speaking to those who abhor the Crescent."

"A pious Jew would as soon adhere to Astarte with her orgies as to bow to the mooned-crown she wore."

"Jews? No, not Jews! Such would not sooner run from the moon-mark than they would from the shadows which fall down about you from yon grand and awful sign."

The speaker pointed to the crossed spire above, as he spoke.

"No more avoidance; we are brethren. I'm Sir Charleroy de Griffin, Teutonic knight."

"And not unknown. The story of thy valor, even

here, lives in the bosoms of true companions. I'm a Knight Hospitaler of Rhodes, yet fameless."

The two men came closely together; there were a few secret tests. The Hospitaler said:

"*In hoc signo vinces!*"

Sir Charleroy crossed his feet, stretched out his arms and murmured something heard only by his comrade. It made the other's eyes lighten with pleasure.

To Miriamne it was a dumb show; but the tokens given and received were useful to pilgrims in those perilous times.

"Whither, Sir Charleroy?"

"To-morrow, toward Joppa."

"So, ho! By interpretation, *The Watch-tower of Joy*. From thence one may see Jerusalem! And then?"

"And then? God knows where! A useless life, like mine, is ever aimless."

"No, no, father!" interrupted the daughter; "not useless. No life that God prolongs is useless."

"True; the girl is right, Teuton. Aspiration will cure thee, since it's the mother of immortality. I go to Joppa also."

"They say, Hospitaler, its sea-side is full wild; its reefs like barking Scylla and Charybdis? I hope it may be so; I'd like a terrible uproar."

"The sea is the emblem of change; from calm to weary moan, to howling terrors and back again."

"But the people? They say Joppa's outside is fine, naturally, though, within, the life of its people is mean, colorless; a charnel-house whose activity is that of grave worms!" And Sir Charleroy shuddered with disgust at his own figure.

"I think the legend of Andromeda, said to have

been chained to Joppa's sea-crags for a season, to be persecuted by a serpent, then freed, prophetic. Joppa may have a future."

"How?"

"Oh, the chained maiden was boasted by her fond mother as more beautiful than Neptune's Nereids, hence the persecution. Crescent faiths have been the persecutors of Joppa and all the other beautiful Andromedas of this land."

"And the chains are riveted?"

"No, not certainly. There was, in the myth, a Perseus of winged feet, having a helmet that made invisible and a sickle from Minerva, goddess of wisdom; he slew the serpent, then wed the victim."

"Now the key, further."

"When wrongs overwhelm all, women suffer most; but time brings their deliverance."

"The myths are as full of women as the women full of myths!" exclaimed Sir Charleroy.

"But Andromeda, the woman, was blameless!"

"Yet it's strange that in all men's fightings, as in their religions, constantly the woman appears," replies Sir Charleroy.

"I'd have thee think, knight, of the legend; it tells how men, in those dark times, tied their faith to the sure conviction that right would triumph, wrong be slain, and the martyrs at last go up among the stars. See how they placed their Andromeda in the constellation now above us. Perseus was a Christian, or rather a Christian was a Perseus."

"Now, thou art merry!"

"No; I mean St. Peter; he was a Perseus. Hearken to the word:

"'Now there was at Joppa a certain disciple named Tabitha: this woman was full of good works and alms-deeds.

"'And it came to pass that she died.

"'The disciples sent unto Peter two men, desiring him that he would not delay to come to them.

"'When he was come, they brought him into the upper chamber: and all the widows stood by him weeping, and showing the coats and garments which she made, while she was with them.

"'But Peter put them all forth, and kneeled down, and prayed; and turning him to the body, said, Tabitha, arise. And she opened her eyes: and when she saw Peter, she sat up.

"'And he gave her his hand, and lifted her up; and when he had called the saints and widows, he presented her alive.

"'And it was known throughout all Joppa; and many believed in the Lord.'"

"Why, Hospitaler, thou hast a memory like an elephant or an emperor and a tongue like a sacrist!"

"Well, the time for swords being past I have taken to books; their leaves are wings. The world will be conquered yet by the words of the Swordless King."

"And thou wouldst liken Tabitha to Andromeda?"

"Wasn't she a real beauty, as her name is interpreted? Beautiful old soul! She robed the poor! Peter bringing her to the truth of the new life smote the dragon at Joppa, as a very Perseus."

"A woman! a woman, again leading the army of salvation!"

"After that Peter slept on the house top of Simon the Tanner, and God gave him the vision of Jew and

Gentile, bond and free, rich and poor; all, as one family coming into the benign rays of the Sun whose wings are full of healing."

"And will that day come, Sir Hospitaler? I'm feeling almost a frenzy of desire for it!"

"Surely as the morning to Acre; but we must hie homeward; good-night; I'll see you at the quay to-morrow."

From Acre, Miriamne and her father, next day, set sail. The companions on the journey from Acre by Joppa arrived at Jerusalem, there to separate soon, for Miriamne, with every ingenious device, urged her father forward. Bozrah was constantly uppermost in her mind.

"We part, Sir Charleroy, to-morrow?" said the Hospitaler.

"If thou dost elect to stay in sad Jerusalem, surely.

"Yes; I'd go mad here from doing nothing but wrestling with my thoughts. In fact, I guess I'd go mad anywhere, if long there. I think, sometimes, that my mind's in a whirlpool, moving not like others; yet, round and round in some consistency, carrying its befooling creeds, hopes, dreams, visions, phantasmagoria in a pretty fair march. I'm sure, more than sure, that if I once stopped moving, my brain would rest like a house after a land-slide, tilted over, while all the things in the whirlpool would drift about in hopeless confusion."

"Thou dost talk like a physician, gone mad with philosophy!"

"No doubt of it; that's all because I've been idling here a month; a week longer and God knows who could set me going again, rightly."

Then the knight laughed merrily; very merrily, in fact, for a man who had trained himself to morbidness. The Hospitaler replied:

"I see nothing for me beyond the Holy City and its historic surrounds. I'm training myself to proclaim God's kingdom and must begin at that pre-eminent, world over-looking point, Jerusalem."

"But there are no schools to fit one there?"

"The most informing and man-expanding on earth; the deathless examples of the worthies; best studied where they lived their mightful living. I go now to Golgotha."

"Golgotha? 'The Place of the Skull?'"

"Even so, sometimes called the Valley of Jehosaphat."

Sir Charleroy rubbed his head as one well puzzled, and was silent.

"Oh, knight, thou hast forgotten the goings forward of Ezekiel's mind, prophetically. It was in Kidron, the Golgotha Valley, that he had the vision of the dry bones. Let me read:

"'Behold, there were very many bones in the open valley; and, lo, they were very dry.

"'And He said unto me, Son of man, can these bones live? And I answered, O Lord GOD, thou knowest.

"'Again He said unto me, Prophesy;

"'Thus saith the Lord God unto these bones; Behold, I will cause breath to enter into you, and ye shall live:

"'As I prophesied, there was a noise, and behold a shaking, and the bones came together, bone to his bone.

"'The sinews and the flesh came up upon them, and the skin covered them.

"'Then said he unto me, say to the wind, Thus saith the Lord God; come from the four winds, O breath, and breathe upon these slain, that they may live.

"'So I prophesied as he commanded me, and the breath came into them, and they lived, and stood up upon their feet, an exceeding great army.'"

"And now, soldier, turned exegete, tell me what thou dost make of the strange phantasm?"

"That God will work in this world a marvelous transformation; those living-dead, all around us and beyond, to the ends of the earth, shall stand in new life. The scene is laid to be in this Kidron valley, to bring all minds to the 'Light of the World,' who passed in painful triumph along it, even unto Calvary."

"But this may not be so, yet it so seems?"

"Hearken again to the prophet's happy ending:

"'Moreover I will make a covenant of peace with them; it shall be an everlasting covenant with them: and I will place them, and multiply them, and will set my sanctuary in the midst of them for evermore.

"'My tabernacle also shall be with them: yea, I will be their God, and they shall be my people.'

"All this," continued the Hospitaler, "is what is to come, is coming. The dawn of this day began when Jesus passed over Kidron!"

"And yet, Rhodes, I'm doubtful. Do not the correspondences remote, mislead thee?"

"If a crusade leader sent a summons like this wouldst thou respond, trusting? 'Blow ye the trumpet in Zion, and sound an alarm in my holy mountain: let all the inhabitants of the land tremble: for the day of the LORD cometh, for *it is* nigh at hand?'"

"The Hospitaler knows I would."

"Well; God by His Prophet-Herald, Joel, so alarms the nations. And more, we have a broader summons," and the preacher soldier read again:

"'Multitudes, multitudes in the valley of decision: for the day of the Lord is near in the valley of decision.

"'Let the heathen be wakened, and come up to the valley of Jehosaphat: for there will I sit to judge all the heathen round about.

"'Put ye in the sickle, for the harvest is ripe.

"'The sun and the moon shall be darkened, and the stars shall withdraw their shining.

"'The Lord also shall roar out of Zion, and utter His voice from Jerusalem; and the heavens and the earth shall shake: but the Lord *will be* the hope of His people, and the strength of the children of Israel.

"'So shall ye know that I *am* the Lord your God dwelling in Zion, my holy mountain.

"'Beat your plowshares into swords, and your pruninghooks into spears: let the weak say, I *am* strong.'"

Then the Hospitaler closed his eyes, turned his face upward as in prayer, and began speaking like unto one in a rapture or trance:

"When souls would measure themselves for judgment, they must stand by the scenes wrought out by Him that died for men; just hereabouts, when the last judgment comes, the multitudes of earth, tried by the measure of the God-man, will be brought face to face with God's standard of moral grandeur, sublimely once displayed here. Before its splendor the stars, the finest of men, shall wax dim; human philosophy, the sun of the world, go out, and human religion, ever the child of human desire, shall fade as the setting, waning moon, that emblem of the concupiscent. Then Charity, that never fails, shall come to her throne, the last implement of war be beaten into services of love, while the weak, no more dominated by giant brutality, shall rise to the pre-eminence of moral strength. Adam and Eve, the fallen pair, passed through the valley of sorrow and sin, downward; Christ and Madonna, the new ideals, passed through the valley of sorrow and salvation, upward."

"Oh, Rhodes, the whirl of my brain is as if touched by the swellings of an anthem. I'll come right yet, if thou dost enravish me so!" cried Sir Charleroy.

And Miriamne's face shone as if the sun were on it, but it was not. She was looking away, in soul, to the future. The Hospitaler continued:

"Truly, all heads, as well as hearts, are righted here, where the touch of the Cross makes the dry bones live. Here get I my schooling; this place of the Cross, where the depths of sin, the heights of love, are manifest; from which radiates all holiest tenets, to which and from which flow the streams of Scriptural truth. If only we could get all men to stand sincerely on this lofty hill of vision, overlooking all times to come, all histories past, all mysteries would be explained, all prophecies become clear, and there never would be need on earth again for wars of faith or the burning of heretics. Pilate spake welcome words to the ages when he cried: '*Miles, expedi Crucem*'—'Soldiers, speed the Cross.' Its speed is light's speed."

As they conversed, the three had slowly journeyed along the *Via Dolorosa*—the road to the Cross.

"Here," said the Hospitaler, "it is reported that

Jesus yearningly looking back to the weeping women that followed him Cross-ward, cried: '*Daughters of Jerusalem, weep not for me, but weep for yourselves and children.*'"

"The woman again in religion!" exclaimed Sir Charleroy.

"Immanuel spoke to the world, then. When truth goes to crucifixion, women and children—the weaker—may well weep. It's the Giant's hour. So children and women ever have been the chief followers of Jesus. No wonder that children brought palms of peace to Him and shouted His praises, while women annointed Him with tears. They knew, by an holy intuition, that somehow He was the King of Love, the defender of weakness."

"I begin to think, Sir Knight Hospitaler, that the sun of this country has wrapped its gold about thy brain."

"Oh, father, don't prevent; these words of his are balm to my soul," quoth Miriamne.

"Speak on, for the girl's sake, knight. Speak on; I'll be silent."

The Hospitaler continued:

"Daughter, thou dost follow the story as those holy women followed Jesus, afar off; but with tenderness. As they found later unutterable nearness, so shalt thou; God willing."

"The woman in religion! It's so. I, a man; this Miriamne, a woman, a girl, my daughter. I'm like a pupil to her, yet I professed this cross-faith more than a score of years before she was born. I'd need a millennium to overtake her, in glory, if we both died now. I'm like poor old David, who fled from his rebellious son, Absalom, over the hills that skirt Kidron. I'm dethroned."

"Remember, rather, that He who glorified Kidron was 'obedient unto death.' Mother and son, together all loving, all loyal in that dread hour, here attested that in David's kingdom, at the last, at its best, there will be no trampling on the family ties, Sir Charleroy."

"Wonderful! I never thought of this before, after this manner. But still, the woman leads the world in religion!"

"*The* woman! Yes, but only when she takes her place, as did Mary, as a follower of Jesus to Calvary."

"But how, now, about Astarte, Diana, Baaltis?"

"They had their day; rude, gross phantoms; conceived in the hot souls of low and lecherous men; but I told thee, here we might overlook the world. In this valley Athaliah, daughter of cruel Jezebel, Queen of Ahab, and, like her mother, an Astarte-socialist, worshiped the lewd ideal, Baaltis. Death, in shocking form, took off that heathen queen of Israel. God's revenge, this was.

"And now, I remember that the queen mother of Asa, here, in Kidron, set up the worship of Ashera with its Phallic mysteries; but Asa, the youth, pure of mind and led of God, not only tore down, root and branch the groves and woven booths of licentiousness, but dethroned the woman who had set them up. Just here, in finest contrasts, I remember the Virgin Mary the pure mother, the ideal woman, who, in this valley of decision, rose for all time the exemplification of truest womanhood—a wife, a mother. Mary has broken forever the idols of Baaltis. While Mary's memory lasts, part of the enduring, sacred history, toward which all

Christian eyes turn, Astarte can never rise under any name or form for long toleration. She is forever broken, and her creed of lust fated to reprobation.

"Wherever this gospel story, eternal and eternally new, is told, there will come to the minds of the hearers a vision of those associated in the last dread hours of the Divine Martyr, in a fellowship of sympathy and sorrow. Among these will stand pre-eminent the women. Simon, the Cyrenian, compelled by the soldiers, aided the trembling sorrow-burdened Christ to bear the cross. And it is easy to believe that the wife of that Simon, who appears later, for a moment, in the praiseful salutations of Paul, as the parent of Christian sons, she reverently called by the great apostle mother, was among the women that were most sorrowful and nearest the dying Saviour. Then there were Mary, the mother of James, Salome, Mary Magdalene, and possibly Claudia the wife of Pilate—that brave woman who advocated Christ's cause before the proud, implacable Sanhedrim, the howling mob and Imperial Rome's representatives. What fitting mourners in that touching, yet august funeral march!

"Women are fully capable by nature, through their finest, tenderest chords, ever responsive in woe, to express the whole of grief, however deep! The sex which loves most, loves longest, mourns most easily as well as most sincerely, and has made sorrow sacred by the lavish bestowals of it, whene'er its founts were touched.

"There is an holy, perfumed anointing in their tears. This crucifixion-time was woman's hour supremely. Mary with *magnificent* self-possession, heart-broken, yet strong in faith; weeping in eye and soul, but intruding no wild howlings amid those who wept for custom's sake; tearful, yet retiring in her grief, here passes before our minds at once the most fascinating, winsome, yet pity-begetting woman known to man."

"Father," cried Miriamne, restraining but little her own tears: "Are you listening?"

"Yes, yes; oh, yes. The glory of Eden's noon has fallen on the tongue and brain of Rhodes, and yet I cannot gainsay him; nor would I try to dispel his wise and honored sayings. I can only wonder and wonder how it is that woman rises at the very front when any grand advance is made."

"Good Rhodes, go on," spoke Miriamne.

"I'm easily persuaded, for there is something of a savory sweetness to this grief—welcome mother of true penitence, that comes over souls, who, in imagination, follow the steps to the cross. I've heard that Mary followed her son from the Judgment Hall to Calvary. He moved at slow pace, and well He might; worn by months of toil for needy humanity; by watchings, teachings and the like; until now ready to drop down under the thorn-crown, the scourging and the cross. But the blessed Virgin, still a woman, still a mother, faltered by the way. Sometimes she hid her eyes from the scourging, sometimes she was pushed aside by those who knew her not, or those who knowing hated her because of her goodness. Tradition tells us she fainted several times overcome by the terrors of that sad journey through the valley. She had small strength to witness the climax of brutality when cruel hands drove the awful nails into that One she loved! The history of that dread hour has often wrung tears from stout hearts; and he who under-

B. Plockhorst.

MARY AND ST. JOHN.

LIBRARY
OF THE
UNIVERSITY OF ILLINOIS

stands in any degree a mother's heart, easily believes that she was absent when the mob raised the victim on His cross. But, mother-like, nothing could keep her from the final parting, which death brought to her and her son.

"Sorrow sharpens the language of love to a deep expressiveness; when the end was approaching, Mary and John stood side by side and near to the One, who, to them, was dearer than all. I have heard, and I believe that a sign from the Christ had hurried John away, just before His death, to bring mother to the heart that was yearning not more to give than to receive, the comforts that both needed, the assurance of undying affection. The man on the cross, stripped of all earthly except His flesh, even robbed of the tunic that Mary had made, and for which the men of war gambled, as war has often gambled for the patrimony of the King of Men, had little or nothing of earth to give, other than His rights in the hearts of mother and John.

These were His farewell keepsakes to each. It needs no strained imagination to fathom His heart, for He opened it all in His dying cry, 'My God, my God, why hast Thou forsaken me?' This was not as the cry of a victor, but that of a broken heart; not as a strong man, but typical humanity, alone, facing death as a child. The language He used then was not that usually His, it was the language of His childhood. In every syllable of that cry, one may read, I fear that God, even God, has forsaken me; but mother, my own loved mother! mother, mother, oh, my dying, human heart, leans as a babe on thy bosom!'"

"Here, here!" cried Sir Charleroy. "Quick! Take this cross of a Teutonic Knight of St. Mary; bury it when I'm gone by her grave in Gethsemane! I have praised myself as her champion, and son, and devotee. Heavens! I'm abashed by thy splendid revelation! I never have even dreamed of her glorious worth!"

"Father, my father, be calm, be calm—calm for my sake; you fright me when you so give way. Remember, we're at the place where a wrong past ends at the right beginning."

"Thou art my good angel, Miriamne; but, oh, it's twice sad! I've been a madman half my life and a player in a farce the other half!"

"Be calm, Sir Knight, and look into the wonders of this place. Christ's coming to earth to pardon its errings, right its wrongs, and hang unfading victory crowns on all futures. Listen: There was night when that King died, and the dead arose and went about the city, attesting the eternal fact that He was Ruler of all worlds. And it was the Feast of the New Moon at Jerusalem; the Feast of Venus at Rome; of Khem in Egypt; but the crescent was hidden."

"I see, I see, Rhodes; Mary and Mary's son were to come forth; all others eclipsed!"

"It is attested by history that there was black darkness about the Sun Temple at Heliopolis as Christ was bidding His mother and earth Death's good-night. The Egyptian city of Osiris, by miracle, witnessed of the great event at Calvary. Some there were prompted to say: 'Either the world is coming to an end, or the god of nature suffers.'"

"And Mary, wise and erudite, Rhodes? Tell us more of her."

"'It is finished!' cried her son, and she passed from the grief of those who agonize amid somber, monster pangs impending, into that quiet, subdued, ripening sadness that comes over those who have learned to say: '*Thy will be done.*' At Cana's feast her Beloved told her: '*Mine hour has not yet come.*' Now, she knew the meaning of the mystic words, and saw His hour, with all its mighty imports, at last marked in full; all the prophecies gathered as into a full-orbed sun; the cross rose like a dial, mountains high, the shadows on it telling eternity's time! Mary, the singer of the '*Magnificat*,' her imagination fired, her vision inspired, as she stood by that interpreting, ghastly symbol, could see the course of the sacred past emerging into meaning. Eve leading; the wealth of her bloom no longer sacrificed to primeval, Astarte-like intoxications; the wings of the real tree of life above her; the serpent crushed beneath her heel. Then, following, Noah, the man of the ark, symbol of sheltering covenants between God and man, covenants ever circled by bows of hope, ever surmounted by dove-like peace. After these Abraham, with his typical lamb, followed by a countless multitude of priests, laying down at the cross, as they passed, their temple-pattern, the symbols of its service realized and ellipsed! After these, Moses, the law-giver, with face serene at law's fulfillment, in company with flaming prophets innumerable, all rejoicing in visions realized. Behind all followed Captivity and Hades, Christ's grandest trophies, forever in chains! Teutonic Knight of St. Mary, thy queen saw all these, and as they passed there rose to her view the White Kingdom of David. Now, stand here where she stood; surrender mind and heart to the Spirit and Word, then thou shalt behold the radiant procession, the coming glory!"

The Hospitaler ceased. Then softly, meanwhile waving his hand as if entreating, Sir Charleroy spoke:

"Rhodes, wait a little; don't say any more now. I want to watch that procession. It seems to me I see it. Oh, wonderful, all wonderful!"

"He shall be called Wonderful."

There was a long, long pause, broken gently by Miriamne, who, after a while, said:

"We'd better return to the city; the day is very hot, and I'm—" She could say no more.

Silently Sir Charleroy complied; silently all three journeyed to their abodes. The Hospitaler was content with his effort to proclaim the truths of Calvary, and Miriamne was glad to leave her father to the full benefit of his sacred, all-engrossing thoughts. Miriamne, in heart, was enraptured by her thoughts of the mother of Jesus.

CHAPTER XXIX.

TWO DEAD HEARTS UNITING TWO LIVING ONES

"Let us alone regret, . . .
   . . . Sorrow humanizes our race.
Tears are the showers that fertilize the world;
And memory of things precious keepeth warm
The heart that once did hold them.
They are poor that have lost nothing; they are far more poor
Who, losing, have forgotten; they most poor
Of all who lose and wish they might forget."
                          —JEAN INGELOW.

NDER Miriamne's adroit and patient guidance Sir Charleroy and his attendants made goodly progress until they reached ancient Jabbock, bordering Giant Bashan; but at that point the knight made a stubborn stand, persisting that he would proceed no further Bozrahward.

"I smell Mohammedanism coming to me from the East, and, having had enough of the Saracens in my day, I'll tarry away from their haunts——

"I must go, beloved, to the tomb of my dear defender, Ichabod. I must go to Gerash to do the pious offices of a mourner."

The maiden brought forward every reason her ingenuity could invent opposed to the proposed deflection in course. She enlisted the Druses guides, whom she had employed to accompany them hitherto, to aid her in raising objections, and they magnified the obstacles in the way to Gerash with commendable loyalty to their employer, the maiden, if not with strict regard to truth. They all encamped, and the debate was the sole occupation for hours.

"Now, Miriamne, hitherto my good spirit, thou wouldst lure me to perdition! I've been in the Lejah. I'm certain that black lava-sea is hell's mouth, and Bozrah's its porch!"

"So be it; but if we go carrying the heavenly consciousness of doing our Father's will, we may carry heaven to those gates."

"It's not my duty to go thither. I passed through that purgatory once. Its horrors blasted my life! To return thither would be presumption."

"But you have forgotten the sunrise coming to you. Each day, for months, as you have journeyed eastward, you have gained in health of body and mind."

"Dost thou mean that God blesses those who plunge headlong to destruction, as the possessed swine that ran violently into the sea?"

"Can not my father let faith silence the disquietings of his wild fancies? The memory of a past pain, though a persistent, is often a false teacher."

"Oh, I do remember. Some memories seem to scorch the very substance of my brain! I pray when such come that God give me eternal forgetfulness. I'd rather be an idiot than have the power of coherent thinking filled with such reminiscences!"

"Ah, if we all, always, had the wisdom, while gazing into our dark, deep pools, to gaze until we saw at their bottoms the image of the sky above!"

Two Dead Hearts Uniting Two Living Ones. 439

"Well said, daughter! Bozrah is a dark pool! I saw there only an image of the sky, and that very far away!"

The day of the foregoing they were wandering along the flowery banks and over the forest-covered hills that undulated away from Jabbock's ravine. As they moved along the maiden plucked a hyacinth blossom and affectionately fastened it on her father's bosom; just where he was wont to wear, when in England, his knight's cross.

"Rizpah once placed a lotus there; it made me drunk; a votary of pleasure, mad; but Miriamne, her daughter, places there the flower of serene, deathless affection! Sweet, thou art my good angel, the flower says to Gerash!"

"Why, father! I do not understand!"

"Apollo unwittingly caused the death of a beautiful youth, the friend of his heart, whose name was Hyacinthus. So says tradition, and it's so charming, I more than half believe it! Apollo, in loyal love, made a flower grow from the grave of his friend. This is it! See; here's the color of the dead youth's blood. This blossom is the flower of deathless friendship and I love it."

"A touching story, I'll remember it; but it seems to me the flower says, 'Bozrah,' my father."

"Take this leaf, girl; here."

"And what of this?"

"There, on that leaf, behold those signs, 'Ai' 'Ai'."

"I think some markings are there like what you say, though never 'till now did I so trace them."

"That's the Greek cry of woe. The perfumes of these flowers, in every field of Gerash, remind me of my duty. I must go to the tomb of the man that died in my defense."

"A pious sentiment; but duty to the living can not be pushed aside by such a call. You have other and living friends?"

"Yes, thou art my friend, lover, angel; but I'll keep thee with me, my lamb."

"Rizpah and your sons!"

"Rizpah my friend? that would be amusing, if it were not such a grim sarcasm. Oh, what a miserable race she led me!"

"Misery, like joy, in wedded life, is won or lost by the deed of two; not one. I shall not acquit my mother; but were not there two to blame?"

"Two? no; only one. I could not be peaceful with a panther."

"Be not too severe, and think a little; did not you, after all, do much to make your wedded wife what she was at her worst?"

"What, I? Thou dost not think that?"

"Yes; I know the story of your espousal; your flight from Gerash, and then your after conflicts. You knew before you determined against all opposing, in the face of reasons most grave, and without any thought of your adaptation to each other, to wed, that your tempers, tastes, and trainings were in almost every thing apart."

"Well, we loved each other sincerely; our marriage vows were honestly taken."

"Marriage; that settled it forever! Did you as honestly keep as you took the vows, for better or worse?"

"Now that were impossible. Did you ever see your

mother in rage, her muscles rising in a sort of serpentine wavings from her feet upward? Ugh! I hear her sibilant, hissing words of scorn, now. They'll haunt me forever. She was a lotus in love, and a boa in wrath."

"I may have seen her so, but out on the love that lets such visions displace memories of the best things; a daughter, nurtured by her, can not; a husband sworn on hymen's altar, dare not forget."

"I tried to set her right, Miriamne."

"Not always with kindness unfailing. I've seen the scourge-marks on her heart. I've heard her moan as a wounded dove; no, more piteously, as a deserted wife and mother. You tried to set her right by forcing her to your faith, that, too, when the girl-wife was weak and exhausted by early maternity. You have been wont ever to pity profoundly the holy mother who recoiled fainting from the spectacle of her son scourged to crucifixion. That pity is a fine feeling; but since Mary's day is passed, it is finer to evince a manly tenderness for living women moving toward their Calvary. How you waste your emotions on the dead! Mary Hyacinthus, Ichabod, have all, Rizpah nothing."

"See here, daughter; let me look down into thy eyes. I'm of a mind to think the sun has gotten into thy brain. It gets into every body's in this country." So saying, he turned her face toward his own. It was a bungling effort on his part to parry her thrusts with ridicule, the last weapon of the defeated.

She was a little indignant, but yet too earnest to be diverted, and so followed up her advantage.

"You were the stronger, every way, and fenced well against your other self. The woman erred, sometimes grievously, perhaps, and you had your sweet retaliations. How sweet you can tell. Each blow at her, fell on me, my brothers and yourself. Oh, it's the climax-revenge to lay open with giant thrusts, monstrous and keen, vein and nerve. One may mar a good purpose by pursuing it cruelly. Were not your efforts to set my mother right severe, sometimes?"

"Did the eloquent Hospitaler put these fine words together for thee, girl?" testily questioned Sir Charleroy.

"No matter who sent them, if they be true words. If you get angry, I'll be wounded. You need not try hard to hurt me. I will strive to be all filial, while all loyal; but not more so to father than to mother."

"Well, but she was a rheumatism to me."

"So be it; still she was part of you. Does one dismember a limb that aches, or give it tenderer care than all others?"

"'It is better,'" said Solomon, 'to dwell in the wilderness, than with a contentious and angry woman.' I got heartily weary of an ache that ached because it ached."

"I'll place Joseph by Solomon."

"Pray, how?"

"He espoused Mary and was with her, yet apart; thus showing God's idea of the needs of weary mothers in their trying hours, when giving their strength to another being. Joseph was kept as a lover only, until after Jesus was born, that his services might have a lover's tenderness. I have heard that the manhood of Jesus reflected the sweetness of Mary; Joseph kept his wife in those days sweet, so the kindness of that noble spouse lived after all, an immortal influence. Joseph, through Mary in part, determined the bodily traits of the child Jesus; the latter influences all time."

"Why, truly, thou hast found a beautiful flower, Miriamne, and I'm wondering that I never saw it before in Mary's life. But, finally, I tell thee I loved Rizpah as my soul at first."

"Oh, yes; you both loved with almost volcanic ardor. My mother told me so; but this very power and inclination of passionate loving gave you each for the other power of dreadfully hurting."

"Well, we'll speak further of this, perhaps, another time. The hyacinth lures me to Ichabod's tomb."

"The rose, emblem of Mary, flower of wedded love, is sweeter than the hyacinth. Go home to Bozrah, father, I beseech you, so you may prove yourself still a Knight of Saint Mary."

"Home? I've none! Bozrah is grim ruins within, without. There, as only fit and in fit dwellings, abide the cormorant and hyena. All hopes that ever centred in that place for me were but dancing satyrs at the last; all loves but eagles with hot-iron beaks, which devoured the hearts that fed them, then fled away! I hate Bozrah!"

"You have a wife and children there. I a mother. Where the brood is, there is home. Bozrah has no gloom for us, save such as we make for it. It may be a glad place yet. Remember that Kidron and Golgotha were made all beautiful by the fidelity of Mary and the cross-bearing of Jesus."

"Miriamne, this parley is useless. Once for all, hear me. Before I wed thy mother I took upon my soul an impious, almost desperate, vow, that I'd possess her though the possessing ruined me. The strong, hopeful Knight of the Cross was domineered over by his love. Before this I had some commendable principles and a little piety. What am I now, after long driftings about through wasted years of prime? I'm the wreck of a man; less! a part of a wreck, trying to get made over in a meaner pattern out of the fragments left. Thy mother unmade me!"

"Adam said something like that of Eve."

"Don't interrupt me, Miriamne. The Jewish maiden Zainab gave Mohammed, of Bozrah, the poisoned lamp which ruined his health; the Jewish Rizpah has such a lamp. See me, wrinkled, hair whitened, all too soon; chivalry, morality and piety dragged out of me bit by bit. I stand here the caricature of what I was or what I should be. I'm fit for neither war nor courtship. I'd make a pretty show attempting to court Rizpah! I've forgotten how such things are done, and, besides, I'm not the original Sir Charleroy she wed. Let her find him, or his counterfeit, and be happy. The original Sir Charleroy and Rizpah loved each other desperately, but these that I know hate each other as desperately. I tell thee it would be legalized adultery for these latter two to live under the same roof, pleading as justification the vows of the other two! Miriamne, I tell thee that thou mayst tell it on the house tops, or hill tops, as I'll cry it through eternity, if permitted, Sir Charleroy and Rizpah, of Gerash and Bozrah, died long ago! The devil stole their bodies, put an imp's spirit in each, and then parted them forever. If they ever meet it will be by the fiend's device, that he may revel over their warrings with each other! Ah, ha! What the Roman arena was to the blood-thirsty populace, such to the fiends the homes of the world when full of tumults!"

And Miriamne, alarmed by the outbreak, tried to calm her father:

"Oh, father, you will need mercy some day; merit it by bestowing it. You suffer an unforgiving spirit to inflame your passion!"

"Forgiving? What's the use? I've vainly tried mercy!"

"Try once more. The injured have resource so long as they have power to forgive. Remember Him who in the great extremity cried: '*They know not what they do!*' Trust Rizpah once more!"

"I do not see the shadow of a peg on which to hang a trust."

"You, a Teutonic Knight of St. Mary!"

"Thank God Mary was not a Rizpah!"

"Mary had the trust of Joseph in those dire days, when nothing but a miracle could prove her integrity. She presents not only woman's goodness but that which even the loftiest wife needs, the constancy beyond measure of her husband."

"Joseph was advised by an angel. I not."

"As you love your mother, honor the woman who mothers your children. They bear your image, yet she alone, with a sublime self-forgetting, struggles to have them grow up honorably, purely, and in the fear of God."

"She wants to make them Israelites."

"Perhaps so, and perhaps the Christian examples she has seen give her no reason to wish otherwise. But after all, her way is better than to have left them as their father left them, to become infidels or nothing. Oh, father, do not think me bold. I speak because I love you; as perhaps no other might care or presume to give utterance."

"Well, girl, I guess I'm a double man; for, determined to oppose, I feel a desire within to have thee win in this argument. I'm one compound of contradictions. I was a sworn bachelor, then a sworn husband, now I'm neither. I'm a widower, with a living wife; a parent of three children with only one. I bewail my homelessness, yet run from an offered home. I confess to being useless, yet see a mission most important at my own door. Swearing loyalty to Mary, I disregard all she exemplified—of late revealed to me; professing to be a Christian, I live a life that would shame a decent Jew. I have a daughter, said by all to be much like me in temper, feature, and mind, yet we are here utterly opposed in thought and purpose. I've heard the profoundest teachers in grandest temples unmoved to this duty, to-day presented; and, now, without the pale of any church, in the wilds of Jericho, a mere girl, my daughter, instructs me well! This all proves that I'm the caricature of Miriamne's father. If I be Sir Charleroy, then I'm beside myself!"

"A good half confession! Now for the atonement!"

"What, a bundle of contradictions making atonement? undoing the past! more contradictions?"

"Righteousness displaces all the contradictions of life!"

"I could make no atonement except by contradicting a score of years, and going to Bozrah! Now hear me finally; by the glory of God, alive, I'll never go to Rizpah's house!"

Miriamne felt that further persuasion would be futile. She made a last request, then.

"Will my father take me to the outskirts of that

city? I'll enter alone to comfort the woman who, notwithstanding her faults, I believe to be the noblest of mothers. She may not have a husband; she has a daughter."

As the father and daughter rested at noon, not far from the Giant City, some days after the foregoing events, they beheld a single horseman from toward Bozrah speeding along the great southern highway.

"I think he's a Jew and in peaceful pursuit. I'll hail him," said the knight, "in the language of Galilee."

The rider, hearing the call, halted. Glancing about him he discovered the source of the call, and promptly reined his steed toward where the pilgrims were sitting. Instantly he began in short, quick sentences:

"Wonder; the face of a Frank, the garb of a Turk, the voice of a Jew! An old man, a young woman! A Moslem in company with his slave? No, she sits by his side! A harem favorite? No! She is not veiled! Ye do not look cunning enough for magicians, too cunning to be pilgrims; not pious enough, old man, to be a priest, and too pious-looking to be a robber."

"True, Laconic," said the knight, "I'm at no loss as to thee."

"So it seems! But pray, Christian, Jewish, Druses, Turks, who are ye?"

"We're pilgrims, good runner."

"Ha, ha; these pilgrims are a mad-lot, with piebald customs!"

"What news, runner?"

"What news! A plague in Bozrah! De Griffin's twins are nigh to death—De Griffin? May be thou knowest him? Thou dost look like him: but he's dead

Now his twins have no nurses nor mourners, but Rizpah, and I'm racing to Gerash to see if I can find a soul to swell her wailings."

The rider turned his horse and with a word, "*Selamet*," —" peace," was gone.

Miriamne had heard enough, and now, with redoubled vehemence, reöpened her arguments and appeals to her father to go to her home.

" I'll not go into Rizpah's house. I tell thee thou art inviting me into hell ! "

Miriamne, in turn, replied: " There is good anywhere for those that earnestly seek it. Mohammed, they say, got his first inspiration in Bozrah, and he a Moslem, a crescent devotee ! ".

" Yes; he wed a rich wife there, too, and she was a saint. I may envy him in these things."

The young woman hastily entered the city and stopped for a little time at the mission house of Father Adolphus, briefly, hurriedly, to announce her return, inquire the latest report concerning the illness of her brothers, and to beseech the old priest to go out after her father ; if possible, to bring him into the city and to the desolate fireside.

" Well, well; there, now, I'd call thee bee or humming-bird, truly, darting from point to point, subject to subject, if I didn't know I was talking to an angel."

The sincere compliment was unheard by Miriamne, for she was gone ere it was sounded. The old man shaded his eyes, looked after her a few moments, then girding himself, hobbled down the street to seek at the city's outskirt the waiting knight.

And Miriamne, with heart beating high, sped on homeward. But as she approached it she slackened her pace, with questionings as to how she had best enter, so as to secure loving welcome and in no wise perturb by sudden surprise. She saw her mother through the doorway, bowed and swinging back and forth. The girl's heart divined all; "My brothers are dead!" The mother seemed oblivious to all about her, and Miriamne hesitated on the threshold. Just then the runner galloped up to the open door, reined his steed, and exclaimed: "Out of sight, out of mind! Death, like poverty, sifts our friends! Ye can hire mourners cheaper at Bozrah than at Gerash, and there are none to be had without coins! Gerash is distant. I had no coins, and was a fool to start, wise to return!" It was Laconic, and he was gone before any reply was given. Rizpah didn't even lift up her head to notice his coming or going.

Miriamne was glad of the circumstance, for the runner gave her words with which to enter: "A daughter never forsakes." She spoke thus, very softly.

Rizpah, perhaps not recognizing the voice, moaned on, swaying as she moaned:

"Mother, mother?"

Rizpah slowly lifted her eyes to the speaker; then, either by a masterful self-control or because sorrow dazed, she slowly and without emotion, addressed the maiden:

"Thou here? So, then, my three are safe together, before my eyes, in death. Thou wert buried years ago."

Without another word the daughter and sister quietly moved to the forms lying beside the mother, and knelt down, bowing, her one arm flung over the corses. Presently she reached out her hand and it met a warm clasp from her mother. The maiden knew full well that it meant welcome. It was death's victory; expressive, unspoken eloquence. There were four hearts; two still in death; two alive and breaking, but the dead hearts somehow drew the living ones together and then they beat as one, each all comforting to the other. Two dead hearts bridged the gulf between two living ones. There followed the embrace and kiss of peace, and then Rizpah questioned:

"Wilt stay with me a little while, my only—?" thereupon she sobbed and was relieved.

"Stay? Yes, always! But when, the burial?"

"At once! It's the plague and the law requires promptness. O Death, thou didst do thy bitterest for Rizpah!"

Rizpah soon rose up and began to busy herself about the bodies.

"Mother, tell me how to aid you."

"Yea, as I need. Thou and I wilt carry them to the cave of entombment."

"But will there be no funeral rites?"

"I'll perform such; keeping vigil as Rizpah of old. My children were crucified, as were hers. All mankind turned from us in our stress, and so they died in want."

"But, mother, the watching would kill you!"

"Thou dost comfort me, now. Oh, I'd be overjoyed, if I only knew for certainty that death would court me at my vigil."

Softly Miriamne spoke:

"Sir Charleroy is at Bozrah."

"Now thou makest Bozrah seem afar. Oh, the garments of people may brush together passing, but still to all things else the passers be eternities apart," replied quickly, and yet with cool self-possession, Rizpah.

"Death, that cools the pulses, also subdues the asperities. I could not hate an enemy if I met him amid his dead," persuasively responded the maiden.

"Imperious, fanatical, stubborn Charleroy! changeable in all but his determination to make conquest of the faith of others. Then, I can not ask his pardon for my serving God. Liberty came to Egypt because the mothers of captive Israel were faithful. So says our Talmud."

"Sir Charleroy respects at least, fidelity."

"Then 'tis well to have me die. He never did me justice to my face; let him embalm me in honey after I'm dead, as Herod did the wife he murdered. It's a way of some husbands. But we must be moving, daughter; I've prepared two biers. The plague is a stern messenger, nor leaves room for any dallying."

And Bozrah witnessed a strange, sad spectacle. Two roughly constructed burial couches; on each a body, and two women, the one aged, the other youthful, both bowed with grief, slowly bearing the biers away, down to the tomb-hill. The elder directed; and so they went; first a little way forward with one body, then returning to advance the other. There were no mourners following; the passers-by offered no help; the women of the city drew their doors shut, and the children playing in the streets, when they beheld this funeral procession, fled away with subdued exclamations.

The ancient Rizpah, watching her dead on their crosses, was standing that time in her valley of "dry bones;" her imitator, Rizpah de Griffin, was now walking through that same valley. Both made pitiable by desolation. Neither was able to hide her dead from her sight by looking for the hope of the blessed resurrection. Their loving had been fierce enough, but the soul-reviving Spirit of the prophet's vision was not yet seen to be in the valley for them. The two Rizpahs were "mothers of sorrow," but followed no cross that had on it besides "death," "victory." They went with tears, but not held by a love that triumphs in "leading captivity captive." These ancient Jewish mothers may be put in striking contrast with the Davidic Queen Mary, who wept from the Judgment Hall, past the cross, past the tomb, up to the chamber of Pentecost, from which she viewed the transports of the Ascension of her Son, her Saviour, her King."

CHAPTER XXX.

"THE KNIGHT OF ST. MARY" AND RIZPAH AT THE GRAVE OF THEIR SONS.

> "Courage, for life is hasting
> To endless life away;
> The inner fires unwaiting,
> Transfigure our dull clay."
>
> *   *   *   *
>
> Lost, lost are all our losses;
> Love set forever free;
> The full life heaves and tosses
> Like an eternal sea;
> One endless, living story;
> One poem spread abroad,
> And the sun of all our glory
> Is the countenance of God."
> —George McDonald.

"I am ascending unto my Father and your Father, and to my God and your God."—Jno. xx. 17.

HE Teutonic knight was standing in silent contemplation of a pile of ruins, from the center of which rose a number of stately columns like so many mourners about a grave. These were all left of a stately old temple. Art had done nobly here once; now desolation was master, even the name of the structure being forgotten. The priest approached, questioning within himself as to how he would address Sir Charleroy, when

they met. As he drew nearer, he thought here are two temples in decay. There came to his mind out of the distant past a vision of Sir Charleroy as he was when he stood erect, ruddy-cheeked and every wit a man by his bride's side, the time of the wedding at Damascus. The priest, contrasting the man before him, now aged and solemn faced, with what he was then, thought " of the two ruined temples, the man is the sadder one. A quarter of a century slipping over a life, though with noiseless feet, generally leaves its tracks; if pain and passion have been the companion of the years, havoc is wrought." Solemnly, and in measured tones, the priest's meditations having given him free utterance, he spoke, quoting the words long before sadly pronounced by the Savior concerning Jerusalem's holy place: "*Destroy this temple and in three days I will raise it up.*"

Sir Charleroy slowly, very slowly, turning his eyes upon the speaker, observed him from head to foot, but uttered not a word.

Again the priest spoke: "Time has so changed both knight and priest, that they forget themselves; nor is it therefore wonderful, they should not remember each other."

"Father Adolphus! Miriamne's work?"

"What matter whose act if we see God back of the actor. I've a message from on high!"

"Why, thou dost astound me!"

"Methinks no man more needs astounding. May righteousness enter the gates opened by wonder, and so move thee into Rizpah's home and thine; death is there!"

"Is there? has been! When love was slain, I shut

out its bleeding form with the mourning robes of a long forgetfulness.

"There are hopes that die to live no more; so there are homes which bereft of their household Penates are doomed to grim ruin forever. See these giant dwellings. They tell it all.

"Thou art a Christian, I believe; but like the disciples, Cleopas and Luke, with eyes holden; not discerning the Lord.

"Just as some, having embalmed the body, looked into the tomb at a napkin only, seeing merely the place where He lay. Though puzzled that the grave's seal was broken, they were still blind to the miracle of a new dawn, simultaneous with the unclasping of night's grim arms. They had heard of the resurrection to be, yet they reasoned that the Promiser was surely dead. Love alone, in the person of Mary Magdalene, most loving because most forgiven, overleaped all doubts, disappointments and fears, to hie away in the thinning darkness, in an utter abandonment to her trust in the words of Him, to whom her heart was given. That was love indeed."

"Oh, priest, 'tis so. A woman; a woman; leading in religion! I do not much bepraise her, for she, being a woman, easily could believe, where men doubted."

"It would have been cruel to have crossed her faith, would it not, Sir Charleroy?"

"Yes, on my soul, yes!"

"Then go to the bier of thy boys. Let love overleap all obstacles."

"But let me rest, priest. I've had the full draught of trouble's cup. I'm quit of further conflict."

"Thou believest? Listen:

"To whom also he shewed himself alive after His passion by many infallible proofs, being seen of them forty days, and speaking of the things pertaining to the kingdom of God——

"Christian Cross-bearing knight, hear me! The suffering Savior could never have revealed Himself, as the Almighty, Risen Christ, if there had been no cross. By what He suffered He had gain of power. Thy wrinkles, disciplines and all such like, fit thee now to minister in the chamber of death; even where now of all places on earth, thou art needed."

"But my case is so peculiar, my home so unnatural!"

"Is there no balm in Gilead, Sir Charleroy? If thou and she have been great sinners, He's a great Savior, and more, a patient one. Hast thou thought how He lingered near His followers in an overplus of love, lured from the triumphs of heaven, to personally deal, all comfortingly, all encouragingly, peculiarly with individuals? For thirty-three years in the flesh he wandered about, doing good, healing all those oppressed of the devil; but the finest hours of all His life lay in those forty days between the resurrection and the ascension. Well might He say to Mary: 'Touch me not,' when in love, she fain would have retarded Him by sentimental fondling. Listen now:

"I have not yet ascended: Go to my disciples, say to them: I ascend unto my Father and your Father, to my God and your God!' He was making a sublime ascent along golden steps, and the number of those steps were ten and two, even as the number of Israel's tribes."

"I do not comprehend this mysticism, though the word-frame is beautiful."

"Then know it. On the cross, Immanuel cried: 'It is finished!' Glorious salvation's work was finished; but then He lingered still to bless, especially His friends. Count the steps. He appeared first to Mary Magdalene, out of whom he had cast the seven devils and who doubtless clung to the Savior, her only hope, her only deliverance from the awful realities of the tragedy in her soul. Thy Rizpah was never so ill as Magdalene, yet surely she is worthy as much tenderness."

"Secondly. Jesus appeared to His mother; love's appearing. I see her now, in mind, by the record here unnamed—left in the sacred privacy of her grief; too stricken to minister, but close to the triumph, because all needful of its blessing. I see a third step—Jesus, by special appointment, meeting the backsliding fisherman of Tiberias, now gone away to his nets, persuading himself he had done and suffered enough, even as does Sir Charleroy to-day."

"I've been called Pilate. Go on. Call me Peter; I can bear it."

"Fourthly. The Christ joined Luke and Cleopas, the Greek proselytes, now doubters; but the chill of their misgivings was burned away in hearts inflamed, while they journeyed to Emmaus."

"Now call me Luke-Cleopas, priest. I've the chill of the doubts, I'm sure."

"Fifthly. He came to His own little church-of-the upper-room, to breathe on it peace and to display His all-convincing body; then He waited a week for a special unfoldment to Thomas, the all-doubter, leaving him filled with all faith."

"Oh, that He'd come to Sir Charleroy!" said the knight.

'He does, but the knight's eyes are holden, and he starves while toiling for fish in a dead sea. Listen to these words by the shore of Tiberias:

"'Then Jesus saith unto them, Children, have ye any meat? They answered him, No.

"'And he said unto them, Cast the net on the right side of the ship, and ye shall find. They cast therefore, and now they were not able to draw it for the multitude of fishes.

"'Jesus saith unto them, Come and dine. And none of the disciples durst ask him, Who art thou? knowing that it was the Lord.

"'Jesus then cometh, and taketh bread, and giveth them, and fish likewise.'

"Oh, Sir Charleroy, cast in the net on the right side, then come and dine."

"But I'm an odd man; not like others."

"He that is All Fullness later appeared to multitudes of every clime, the representatives of the Church universal, ever full of odd people; again to the apostle of good works, James, called the pillar of faith. The tenth appearing was at Bethany, as the blesser and promiser to all. After that he showed himself to Paul, proof that he was a returning Christ, and, last of all, to John on Patmos. This the John that was care-taker of Mary, the mother; John, the all-loving. I read each page of the glowing Apocalypse as a love-letter from heaven to a mother, from a Son who carries eternally within His glorious heart the image of the woman great chiefly for her great love of Him. She loyally followed Him to the grave; He lovingly followed her beyond it. When he set John to picturing heaven as a virgin-bride and His Church as a woman clothed with the sun, Christ had surely the choicest of women, Mary, in His heart."

"And the Heart of Heaven might well lovingly remember the mystical Rose," quoth the knight.

"As heaven loved Mary, so should noble men love 'bone of their bone, flesh of their flesh,' *as Christ loved the Church and gave Himself for it*."

"Thou wert never wed, good priest?"

"No; perhaps 'tis well so. I've had a work in helping those who were wed unhappily, to peace; forgetting, in serving their need, my own joy."

"Then thou hast no idea of what it is to deal with a Rizpah as a wife."

"I know she's a woman; a marvel in her fidelity to her children. She may have infirmities, but there was a woman, bowed grievously for eighteen years, fully restored by one kind touch of the man, Jesus, ever all-pitiful and tender toward women."

"But that one was willing to be healed."

"No; she was trying to hide, but the Savior called her out, just to heal her."

"Now, then, let me cross swords at close quarters, since thou dost press me. I ask thee, as a Christian priest, wouldst thou have me tolerate the sins of heresy in my own home? Remember, Jezebel, she beguiled Ahab, her daughter, Athaliah, and her husband, Jehoram, also, into gravest transgressions. So God's people were led, little by little, to the groves of Astarte. I think I've a good parallel: Jezebel was the daughter of a priest, so this Rizpah of Bozrah. With her hot temper, pride of exalted birth, and a mouthful of arguments; a man meets such a woman as a pigmy, to crouch, or as a knight, to resist."

"The name Jezebel means 'chaste.' Her pious namers must have respected chastity once. Her practices were all loyalty to Ahab and her children, though her theories may have been odious. All that is recorded of them, which engenders hate for her memory, is the hatefulness of the way she pressed her creeds upon others, the Jews. Which the more like Jezebel—Sir Charleroy or Rizpah?"

"But Rizpah was ardent to lay our love, and our children on her altar. Like the women who brought their jewels to Aaron to be transmuted into the golden calf! I could only protest, and I did."

"Did not the men of Egypt and Israel first proclaim the worship of Apis? Were not the women merely following their lords? There are many women who defile their jewels because, with contempts that turn their hearts to ashes, their lords do not, as they should, wear both the wives and the jewels on strong and loyal hearts."

"Oh, I perceive! Rizpah has been parading to thee her family troubles. A true woman would have rather given herself to nest-hiding."

"Thou hast not hidden thy nest, but, like a wandering bird, fled it."

"She never asked my aid; she left me in London."

The knight was charging blindly, and defeated.

"It was not for her to crave, but for thee to lavishly bestow. She left thee? What better could Abigail have done than turn her beautiful countenance and good understanding away from churlish Nabal, who lived chiefly to gloat about the cross on which he had placed her?"

"Does the sacrist advocate divorce?"

"No! No rupture of the tie sealed in heaven; but when by recriminations a home becomes a living burial, a hell, then two houses are better than one. I feel here keenly, knight. My mother had a monstrous man, my father, in wedlock. He left her to battle single-handed for her little ones. Her patient, sad face comes ever before me. Oh, how she eschewed all other men, though courted by worthier than he; how she strove to hide my father's faults and taught us, his children, to try to respect him! I was but a youth when he died, but I tell thee I dared not look upon his coffined face lest I should curse him, then and there!"

The knight cowered as if from a malediction.

"There, there! for heaven's sake pause, Sacrist! Abashed at home, lashed by the teacher of the faith I've suffered to defend, I'll be driven to flee to the wandering Bedouin, or to death!"

"They say Lucifer, unable to commit suicide, plunges headlong into the abyss when thwarted in any design.'

"Call me Lucifer; another epithet!"

"There are no black gulfs into which thou canst flee from the memories which conscience points to when duty is contemned."

"Is it the priest's purpose to harass my soul?"

"No; but rather to lead it back to its peace that thou didst leave long ago. There is only one way of return, that a very *Via Dolorosa*. Mary along it walked with her son, her God and Savior, to the cross and the resurrection! By the cross God gives, we go to our glory."

"I've tried my best to be a loyal, Christian knight. Give me, at least, that award."

"I can not praise justly; I dare not flatter; I must in all faithfulness say thou hast yet to learn the alphabet of loyalty, as interpreted by that glorious pair, Mary and the Christ—the triumphant Eve, the triumphant Adam. Thou hast been following afar off, nearer the flickering of Judas' illusive lantern than to Him who pleaded amid His griefs, all self-forgetting, with His Roman guards to let His little band of followers depart unharmed. The woman whom thou exaltest as the queen of hearts is, after all, not thy pattern. Judas and Mary are in lasting contrast; he all treason, she fidelity's choicest fruit. It is well to see to it to which one is the nearer. Oh, Gethsemane, garden of touching contrasts! There love was most grossly interpreted by the shrines of *Baaltis;* there most grandly interpreted by love's sublimest offering that night the Saviour agonized. There twice the enemy of man did his almost worst; once by the rites of the groves, once in the wracking temptations of the Man of Sorrows. The arch-fiend was baffled, and then the ingenuity of hell was taxed to one last, most terrific and dastardly assault. What thinkest thou was the climax? The last effort to blot out the hope of man was made through betrayal by a kiss; the finest sign of affection befouled by treason! When the wedded betray each other, alas, for the world!"

Sir Charleroy surrendered now, exclaiming:

"Oh, Father Adolphus; again I see there is a mist on my knightly cross! I'm unworthy to wear the sign. It has been an emblem of death; I see it now an emblem of life and love."

"Will the knight look on the dead faces of his sons?"

"Yes, yes! In the name of God, yes! Lead me as a child, for I'm nothing more."

The knight was in the throes of transformation. He and the priest walked side by side, mostly in silence, broken anon, only by questions of Sir Charleroy's, like these:

'Am I worth saving? Shall I ever become able to fully sound and truly express, in life, the depths of all thou hast told me? And Rizpah! what will Rizpah say or do?"

The old priest answered ever:

"'Awake, thou that sleepest, and arise from the dead, and Christ Himself shall give thee light!'"

The lone burial cave was reached. Nigh the two biers stood Rizpah and Miriamne and but a little way off Sir Charleroy and the priest. The maiden, with surprised joy, saw the two men, but Rizpah, busy with her thoughts, never lifted her eyes. The latter drew a slab away from the entrance of the tomb and then moaned: "Better I'd never been a mother."

Father Adolphus seized the opportunity to say in deep, entreating tones:

"'I will ransom them from the power of the grave: I will redeem them from death.'"

The mother supposing it was some kindly neighbor, still unnoticing any thing but the speaker's voice, moaned on, sitting nigh the tomb-door, between the dead, a hand on each.

Then the old shepherd drew nearer, saying:

"Sisters of Israel, only believe. Beyond this stony gate there is an eternal home fairer than any dream. There all broken homes shall rise in joy, their treasures reunited and happy."

Now Rizpah rose, and observing the speaker silently for a moment, she did not seem offended at the priest's presence. Misery had overcome, at least for the time, her prejudice. Presently she exclaimed:

"My family reunited in heaven? Ah! that can not be, and if it were so, what joy to ever repeat the bickering, blamings and wrongs of this poor miserable life?"

"Thou wilt know as thou art known there and see eye to eye," said the missioner.

"Oh, if it could be only so!"

"Wouldst like it so?"

"Yes, by the grave of my darlings, I swear it! I loved them with my life madly. All the love I had was concentrated in them. I knew when I began idolizing them that I had loved before full well my husband and daughter. I knew this, because the love I withdrew from them rushed forth to the boys. But my idols are dead, and now if my love do not dry up, it will hunger, feed on me myself, then turn to ferocity wolf-like."

"Perhaps a husband restored may fill and enlarge thy heart. There never was a great sorrow but there stood near it a great joy," spoke the priest.

"Ah, he is stubborn, I, perhaps, proud. Immensity is between me and Sir Charleroy."

"Hast thou not yet had enough of pride's dead sea apples?"

"Alas! why ask me?"

"If thou art ready for a better day, he may be."

"Ready? I've always been. What I did for conscience sake and these children is done. What he did to me he only can undo, as far as the past can be undone."

Then Miriamme waved her hand to her father, unseen by Rizpah, entreatingly, as if to say: "Come, but not too quickly, a little nearer."

Sir Charleroy complied and not as a laggard, for Rizpah seemed changed from what she was in London. He now saw her as in those golden early days at Gerash. But the truth was, the change was chiefly in himself.

"Rizpah!"

"Sir Charleroy de Griffin!" replied the woman addressed deliberately, and apparently emotionlessly, as she fixed her eyes upon the knight. Then her eyes turned toward the tomb, seemingly inviting his to follow there their course. She stepped back and glanced from man to tomb, by the glance saying more plainly than words:

"That is thy work. Thou didst open that grave in my pathway."

The knight stood by her side and put forth his hand to clasp hers, but with a respectfulness that betokened the cavalier and one not quite certain of his welcome.

Then spake Father Adolphus:

"Remember Damascus, both of you. Come, Miriamne," he continued, drawing the maiden aside, "I've a giant's grave to show thee."

The priest and the maiden moved to a turn in the road and passed behind the crumbled wall of a Roman palace.

"But, Father Adolphus, where now? What of the giant's grave?"

"Be content, girl. I mean the grave of mad love grown to mad hate. It will be made and deep enough by thy parents, but they can best make it alone."

And Miriamne fell upon her knees in silent, grateful prayer; a great burden that had borne her down for years seemed lifted from off her. The Miserere that had wailed through her life so long now changed to an Easter anthem.

Father Adolphus after a time recalled her by a single question:

"Dost see the fierce woman and the vultures fleeing away before the coming of our Christian Mother of Sorrows?"

CHAPTER XXXI.

THE ROSE, QUEEN OF HEARTS IN THE GIANT CITY

> " Around thy starry crown are wreathed
> So many names divine!
> Which is the dearest to my heart
> And the most worthy thine?
>
> * * * * * *
>
> '*Mother of sorrows,*' many a heart,
> Half broken by despair,
> Hath laid its burden by the cross,
> And found a mother there.
> '*Mary*,' the dearest name of all,
> The holiest and the best,
> The first low word that Jesus lisped
> Laid on His mother's breast."
>
> —A. A. PROCTOR.

HERE had come a great change to the home of the De Griffins at Bozrah, without and within. Shrubs and vines grew about the old stone house in profusion, birds sang contentedly at its casements, and kittens, undisturbed, played around its doors. These were tokens of the new inner life.

The queen of that domestic palace was happy; its king restored to his rights and duties; therefore there was abounding delight and peace within and without. Sir Charleroy and Rizpah, the two mature wed-lovers that abode there, had, out of all their estrangements and tribulations, come to understand at last that love grows out of law and is more than a sentiment, free to go when lured or flee from that which burdens. It was to them like a revelation from heaven to find that love is the vassal of the will and can be made to go where it ought, as well as be reined back from lawless rovings. They found there was great satisfaction in their efforts to be very agreeable to each other. Sir Charleroy constantly assured Rizpah of his belief that they were now more really lovers than they had been in those fervent days at Gerash. She believed this new creed with the avidity of a heart sore with long waitings for its proclaiming.

The knight bethought himself of a graceful advance, and introduced the matter with a sort of parable. "I've been thinking to-day that the only man whom I ever felt like kissing, the man who loved me to the full of his great heart, is present with us in spirit these days to joy over our reconciliation. I've felt a strange thrill at times which made me think I was touched by the glowing heart of Ichabod."

"Ichabod?"

"Yes; he that fell in our defense the day of that perilous battle with those Mamelukes, near Gerash. Ah, he had the heart of a mastiff, the soul of a martyr!"

"Thy love is constant. But what's in thy hand?"

The knight had hoped for the question.

"A token I took from his corpse. It was given him by a Copt priest, whose life he saved in Egypt. See."

"I see a stone in a gold setting; on the stone an image, I think of a woman? I've noticed it with thee before."

"I knew it! Once I thought thou didst observe it askance, as if a trifle jealous. Well, no more secrets, no more jealousies. What says Rizpah?"

"I say amen; and yet I say tell all, or none; either way I shall be content. Love's trust, when full, has few questions and no doubts."

"Nobly spoken, but yet I must tell all. The image is of *Neb-ta*, from the country of Hamites."

"What an odd figure! Her head-dress, a basket!"

"The basket on her head and the little house by her side betoken that she was the presiding spirit of domestic life. I love Neb-ta! She ever reminds me of woman at her best, as a mother brooding her chicks."

"Praise be the Patriarchs; they left us testimonies which makes it needless to go to Egypt for precepts concerning home-love!" responded the wife.

"But, Rizpah, thou dost divert me! Wait; I'm coming around with the patriarchs, by way of Jerusalem, to Bozrah."

"Now, that's a fine parade; I await it," the woman, with quick reply, answered.

"Tradition says this Neb-ta will stand before Osiris and Isis in the judgment 'hall of truth,' where another deity styled 'divine wisdom' opens the books of men's earthly deeds. As the great Anubis weighs them, Neb-ta stands by ready to cut away the failings of those weighed. When the scale of their merit is lacking, she herself leaps into it, to weigh it down in their behalf."

"A pretty myth for grim old Nile Land!"

"It proves man's belief that at last he'll need help."

"It is strange those women degraders should have allotted one of that sex so fine a part in the hereafter."

"It illustrates the constant conviction in men's hearts that woman's sympathy abides to the last."

"In some men's hearts, say. All are not equally just."

"I'll be direct, Rizpah, and sincere. I've felt an indescribable unworthiness of all I enjoy here in the house saved and brightened by my wife. I've been saying, 'Oh, that some one like Neb-ta would cut off my failings and enrich my merit.'"

Sir Charleroy, after this long journey around about, felt relieved. He had made his confession and waited his absolution.

Rizpah's eyes brightened up, and, though bedewed, shone with the luster of gleaming affection.

He knew full well how to interpret that look, and evinced the quality of the interpretation by quickly embracing her. There passed between them salutations having the purity of manna, the lusciousness of Escol's grapes.

"Will Sir Charleroy need to go to Egypt for a Neb-ta?"

"No, never, while I've an all-forgiving, all-blessing Rizpah!"

Encouraged by the success attending one simile, he attempted another later:

"I was thinking," tenderly replied the knight, "that I've sinned against God in the name of religion, and unconsciously offered 'the female lamb.'"

"Pardon my stupidity, but yet I do not gather what is thy meaning."

"My Rizpah has been sacrificed for years."

"The wife tried to reply, "I'm no lamb without blemish;" but her tears and his passionate embrace, checked her utterance. To those without, there is much incomprehensible in the estrangements and reconciliations of human pairs, made utterly one in wedlock. If, since the Incarnate died for love, and the Temple's veil was rent, there has been on earth an unrevealed Holiest of Holy places, it has been where wed lives, alienated, have been reunited. It is like a sacrilege to attempt its depicting to stranger eyes or ears. Many, for themselves, have been within that holy place; each twain meeting its own peculiar and varied experiences. But, having come forth with a natural and most meritorious reverence for the events of such supreme hours, they are wont to withdraw from human curiosity all that transpired, as completely as they hide from the world their souls' dealings with God. They who, have never been within that Holy Place, can not understand about what there transpires; those that have been there, defend their sacred right to keep from all the world that which they saw and felt, by refusing to give audience to the experiences of others.

Sir Charleroy and Rizpah, at the time of the foregoing conversation, entered serenely, lovingly that Holy Place. Then they took, as it were, wings of memory and shields of faith. The grim giant house was forgotten. Its walls seemed to thin away, until they had to themselves a broad, but secluded world. There was light, but not exposure; repentance, mutual, and forgiveness, not only free, but in every syllable seeming to have balm for healing. There followed an unutterable sense of getting nearer and nearer to each other. They felt as if they had but one will, and that guided by God; one mind, and that clear and heaven soaring. The only sense of being two, was in their beating hearts, and then two hearts seemed more blessed than one; for being two, there was the joy of their beatings for and against each other. Words fail; it would be sacrilege to go further. Let the curtain drop. Leave them with a thousand angels, winged and liveried in white, with wands of silence to keep watch and ward until morning!

On the morrow they knew that both had surrendered and both conquered. And by a paradox, to those uninitiated, each rejoiced as much in the surrender each had made, as in the victory which had been won by the one defeated. Defeat and victory was their common wealth. There was a full community between them, and that made both rich, whatever their possessions. Thenceforward, between them, there was perfect frankness and consideration; no sarcasms, no recriminations, and hence no need of foils nor masks. Christ had captured the Crusader's heart, and he was now, as never before, able to reveal the King of his soul to Rizpah. She moved unconsciously into a beauty of character like unto that of Mary, and her heart began singing a 'Magnificat.' The woman was transformed, if possible, more completely than the man. For years amid hurtings she had schooled herself to reticence, and had been an enigma to all who knew her; but now, under the rising of this new sun, she opened as the blossom of early spring. Sir Charleroy, indeed all who knew her, attested delight and surprise; but Rizpah was as much surprised at herself as any other could be at her.

"I didn't know I could," she exclaimed often with laughter and tears. She seemed to break away and run from her former self as one from some phantom, as a child from a reputed witch, or a freed bird from a prisoning cage. She saw herself growing in all these things every moment and exclaimed, in the rush of feeling; " I could fly, I'm sure!" Then tenderly, " I would not, my mate, for a thousand worlds, unless thou couldst fly with me. No, no, Charleroy, watch my wings; they are thine; cut them if they grow or flutter for rising. If they do, they'll do it themselves, without my willing." Again the sacredness of the holiest came over them.

"Oh, Rizpah, I know, I knew this wealth of love was in thee; I've wondered often why I could not find it."

"I did not know it, my lover king; I'm glad thou hast found it, for thy finding feeds me with light and glory! I'm carried back to Gerash and Damascus."

"I think not. There were flaming swords at Eden's Gate, after the fall. No going back; but the swords gave light for departure into broader places. I think that's the symbol of the sword and the flame, Rispah." Again he spoke: "Hadrian built a temple of Venus over the tomb of Christ, but Hadrian and Venus are no more in power and there has been a resurrection from that tomb."

" Ah, Sir Charleroy, I'm a child in thy creed, but I'm comforted by thy resurrection hopes, especially since conversing yesterday more freely than ever with our lovely child of God, Miriamne."

" Hers is an angel's visit, wife."

"And angel-like, with filial spirit, she comes, this time, with request for our consent to an act of great import to her."

"So; and what may it be? Though I know it can only be good."

"She came to tell us, that she desires publicly to profess the religion of the Naz—— of Jesus."

Sir Charleroy felt a twinge of an old pain, and for a moment queried within: "Will the old struggle over faiths again confront us?" But he dismissed it with an unexpressed "Impossible, we're all changed!" Then replied he quietly with a question. "Does the dear girl fully understand the seriousness of the act? If she do and then acts, I'll be glad to commit her to Christ as her Bridegroom and King."

"We cannot be with her always, and she seems determined to go through life unwed."

"A Neb-ta, an angel spinster, mothering other people's chicks! But what says my Rizpah of our daughter's purpose to profess her faith?"

"I? This: God being my Helper, I'll never again stand between Him and any soul, except it be to pray for that soul's health."

Just then the maiden entered bearing a lamp which suddenly lighted the room, now well nigh in darkness. She presented a most striking and suggestive figure. Her eyes were full of her heart's chief question, and, standing in the light of her own bearing, she seemed to fitly represent the part she had borne in that household.

Sir Charleroy, anticipating his daughter's question, greeted her with promptness thus: "Sunshine, thy purpose I know. It's all between God and thyself. Go gladden Father Adolphus and Cornelius with an early profession."

She was filled with surprise, and voiced its chief cause:

"Cornelius? He's at Jerusalem!"

"Well, if so, 'tis wonderful, since I met him here to-day."

"I wonder," she meditated, meanwhile speaking her thoughts as if unconscious of those about her, "What brought him here?"

"Oh," replied the father, "he says 'to see Father Adolphus about the church of Jerusalem;' but Father Adolphus says 'the young man came because he could not help it, to see his good angel.'"

"'His good angel!' Whom?"

"Now, Sunrise, guess! When thou dost so, to make short work, begin with the good angel of us all, Miriamne."

Miriamne lifted her hand reprovingly, but the telltale crimson hung confession on her cheeks, while her lips, wreathed in smiles, told her pleasure.

"Well, now, will my father go with me to good Adolphus about my profession?"

"As thou mayst like, but it will be easier to reduce three to two than four to two!"

Again the uplifted, reproving hand and the blush and Miriamne ran out.

* * * * * * * *

"Do not reöpen that question settled once; it can only pain us both to recur to it."

"'Reöpened!' 'Settled!'" exclaimed Cornelius. "Not with me. Nothing in silence can settle it; and it is always open to me, sleeping or waking."

"The consciousness of duty done comes like the breezes of Galilee, turning all moanings to a song within me."

"Oh, Miriamne, who is it decrees that we, belonging, all, each, to the other, should be torn asunder ruthlessly? Duty, conscience! Hard metallic words when they describe the links of a chain! Ah, our misconceptions often bind us to pain; this one I cannot bear!"

"And yet, Cornelius, you told me in that Adriatic storm you could as easily drown a passion rising against righteousness as you could drown the body then, by a plunge into the billows!"

"You held me back when I moved forward to show how easily I could make the plunge."

"But then you had no intention of leaping to death!"

"Not while held back by Miriamne!"

"I? Poor, weak I, hold you?"

"To me your touch has ever had persuasion and might! Oh, woman, you lead me captive to your will in chains riveted, unyielding, and yet of golden delights."

"Say not so. We have each a great mission, but apart.

"Apart! The decree that settles our courses that way is monstrous. It is not of God. He ordained that our race go in pairs. And when He set up the new kingdom of Jesus, its heralding disciples were sent forth two by two. As Moses needed his Hobab, Christ his confidants, so need I a yoke-fellow. I've no ambition to live, much less to work, unless I have my heart's idol with me."

"Illusion."

"Call it '*Maya*' if you like; but '*Maya*,' Brahm's wife, illusion, made the universe visible to him. So say those ancient mythologians. I can see nothing without my Miriamne!"

"Oh, man, hold; nor pain me further! I cannot help you. How can I, since my own chosen work seems too great for me! I'm like a mere shell, drifting with the tides, without sail or helm; the harbor unknown. I only know I carry a precious pearl, truth, and that there are those who need it. I must bear it to them."

"I'm a shell, without helm or sail, and have the same pearl. Let me voyage with you."

"And—what?"

"In all brevity—marry me!"

"That cannot be, I fear. I'd rather be the ——. Can't I be your ideal as Mary?" She blundered amid her efforts to express herself, and the tell-tale blush betokened defeat.

"Yes; be my Mary, and let me take the place as your Joseph. Mary was a wife and mother. The greatest of God's works in the old dispensation was to translate men; in the new dispensation, seeking to surpass the old, He presented a perfect woman, in her highest estate, as the queen of a home!"

The woman was silent for time. There then seemed to her to be two Miriamnes, and the debate was transferred from being between the young man and herself to these two which she seemed to be. One Miriamne said "Yield," one "Be firm." One said, "He has the better reasons," one said "Nay;" one said, "It is pleasant to be overcome," the other said "*Maya, Maya, Maya!*" Then recovering herself she exclaimed, "I wish the priest were here; he'd guide us by the Divine word."

"I have a holy text," and drawing a line at a venture, the youth repeated these words:

"'God said it is not good that man should be alone!'"

She smiled and stammered:

"Oh, Cornelius! I want to admire you and lean on you as my guide, teacher, pastor; but you meet all my approaches that way, transformed to a lover."

"*Maya! Maya!* Miriamne; let the illusion work; sleep the Leathen sleep; yield to love's dream; then comes the full noon to awaken to marriage joy. Thou wilt find, not above thee but at thy side, then, the teacher, guide; shepherd as well; but also the husband."

Miriamne had reached a point of hesitancy, which is, in all lives, just a step from surrender, and the lover, made alert by his ardor, perceived the advantage. Though a prey to hopes and fears, an incarnation of paradoxes, in which bashfulness contested with audacity for control of the will, he gathered all his powers into a grand charge. With a tender vehemence he stormed the citadel of the heart before him. First he imprisoned her hand in his; he had done so before. Now it fluttered strangely; presently it rested as a bird; at first as if frightened, then helpless, then content. All that followed may be easily imagined. Suffice to say that Cornelius Woelfkin just then believed life worth living and the universe made visible, though not by an illusion.

Just as many another of Eve's daughters placed as she in a tempest of delights, she confessed her capitulation by a series of retorts, which gave her relief from tears by affording apologies for laughter.

"No woman ever so loved as I now? You men all talk that way at betrothal!"

"'To death!' Miriamne, 'twill be true with me."

"Yes, at betrothal and when their wives are dead,

they say men are very affectionate. But, Cornelius, remember I'll expect sweets between times. Do not love me to death at first, vex me to death later, then go mad for love's sake after I'm gone!"

He vowed, protested and assured; she believed him without the shadow of a doubt. They were irrevocably committed to each other now. There was a rush of thoughts, plannings, questionings and hopes. Two lives apart converging, becoming mysteriously one. Over them arose that wondrous sun which illumines some betrothal days. They were both very happy, very proud, and also each to the other very beautiful. The harmless conceits of love possessed them and they persuaded themselves easily that they were at the center of all things, even of the infinite love of God. The glow of their own hearts brightened to them all things immediately about them, and they entered that arcana of delights where secret blessings may be experienced but can not be depicted. They ate of that hidden manna which is reserved alone for those who sincerely love and are loved. No being ever loved as they, who afterward despised or regretted the enchantment, although it brought some pain or at the last ended in disappointment. None ever having been for a season in that Beulah-Land but wishes himself there again. None who comprehends the thrillings of lover days can fail to envy more or less, if they are loveless, those who are in love as these twain were.

Much of the ridiculing of this grand passion, affected by some, is after all the result of envy, secretly longing for that beyond its reach. Sometimes the enraptured themselves attempt this deriding, but theirs is an hysterical laughter, a feeble effort to rest from the intensity of their rapture or to hide their secret from others. The laughter of all such as the foregoing is hollow and eventually turns the shame back upon the ridiculers who would cover others with it; for love, while it is an angel of sunshine, has also the power of carrying to every heart which shamefully entreats it remorse, humiliation and pains as numberless as nameless.

Cornelius and Miriamne, the young reformers, having embarked fully upon the full, glowing, exalting, triumphant tide of their love were themselves reformed and transformed. A while ago each was willing to die for the world, now each was willing to die, if need be, for the other and not for humanity's sake, unless some way the heart's idol was to be part of the reward of that sacrifice. This new tide carried them quickly to that place of paradoxical oscillations, the place where the lover is one moment utterly self-denying, the next utterly grasping; willing to be annihilated one instant in behalf of another, and then in an avariciousness without a parallel on earth, the next moment willing to annihilate the universe rather than be bereft of the one object deemed above all others.

The young lovers passed through the usual, often experienced, often depicted, old, old, ever new phases of this relation. The fire kindled in their hearts sped from center to center of their beings, the laughter of secret joy quivered along every nerve of each. Each was happier than it was possible to tell, even that other one that awakened the joy. Their gait, their blushing cheeks, their flashing eyes, and their words proclaimed unmistakable the complete coronation of love. They believed, and perhaps properly, that they were enjoying the seraphic, exuberant, mellow, yet exciting delights of an hundred ordinary lives merged into one. Each in turn, over and over, in repetitions that tired neither to utter nor to hear, said to the other: "I love you." A rain of impassioned kisses made reply. Time was not observed; they forgot their former hurry, that pushed them earnestly, ever toward duty, when they were committed to being reformers. They were only and completely lovers now, and lovers are beings whose existence is in a heaven where there are no clocks. The sun set over Bozrah while the twain communed, but there was so much light in their hearts they did not observe the lull of night around them. Existence seemed to them a living fullness, a soaring upward without friction or effort, and they incarnated that which at last makes heaven, perfect desire perfectly satisfied. They were presently recalled to the things outside of themselves by the sound of some one approaching.

"It's Father Adolphus. I know his step," remarked Miriamne.

Cornelius, remembering his recent, successful assault, was encouraged to attempt another. His heart whispered to him: "Why not make this matter final now?" His heart seemed to grow pale and trembled at its own whispering, until he himself grew pale and trembled throughout his whole being, at the audacity of the thought. But love's suggestions are ever very domineering; this one dominated the man instantly, and he acted on it.

"Miriamne, why not permit Father Adolphus now to seal our betrothal with his blessing?"

"He will bless us, I know," quoth the maiden, evasively; but she knew what her lover meant full well.

Not only so, her heart, against her judgment, was siding for the blessing.

The youth felt certain he had carried one line of defense, and now went charging onward, determined to carry all before him.

"Yes; he will bless us, I know, if we ask him. I'll ask him, and then, Miriamne, mine, I'll call thee no more sister, but wife."

"Oh, you are in such a hurry! This is all too sudden. I—only wanted to be engaged—not married, perhaps, for years. We could work for the Master—"

She was interrupted, as victorious lovers usually interrupt.

Just then the priest entered. Miriamne tried to greet him with a smile and a sentence, but she was under a spell. She seemed to herself to be a different woman than she was when he last met her guide. She spoke a few meaningless words, which were lost in the vigorous utterance of her companion, as he explained the betrothal and requested its ratification.

The aged man of God looked tenderly down on both, and then questioned:

"Miriamne, I know his heart toward thee; is thine resting on his?"

The maiden drooped her eye-lids, but the tell-tale blush on her cheek gave answer.

"Shall I commit you to each other before God, for ever!"

Her hand rose in an effort to restrain, but it fell back into her lap, as if unwilling to do so.

"Bless us quickly, good father, I pray you," spoke Cornelius.

"Clasp four hands crossed," said the priest.

The maiden's hands joined those of the young man, and yet one drew back a little, as if to say, Wait. The motion was slight; then she found voice.

"But, Father Adolphus, do you think God will condemn, if we do?"

"God made such as ye are to love each other. What says thy conscience? Speak frankly now, girl; thou art with those that care for thee with an eternal regard."

"My conscience does not condemn, and I commit all I am to the guidance of you two men. I feel quiet and safe in the committal."

And the solemn sealing words were soon spoken.

"Shall I pronounce you husband and wife?" questioned the priest.

Cornelius, like a knight in full charge desirous of taking all before him as trophy, exclaimed quickly, confidently: "Yes, yes, all!"

Then Miriamne recovered herself in the emergency, and with maidenly dignity and tenderness, yet with unalterable firmness, said: "Nay."

"But, Miriamne—"

The youth could proceed no further. He was defeated by the glance that met his, filled with pious, kindly, yet firm dissent. She spoke then freely.

"Before God we are affianced; the first step, as an Israelite, I've taken. We are now bound to each other forever. I am proud to wear the yoke of betrothal. We must wait before the final words are spoken, until we've seen my parents, and until God has given us further wisdom."

She prevailed. Shortly after the foregoing, Cornelius, taking a tender farewell, returned to his work at Jerusalem.

CHAPTER XXXII.

THE QUEEN AND THE GRAIL SEEKERS.

"My good blade carves the casques of men;
   My tough lance thrusteth sure,
My strength is as the strength of ten,
   Because my heart is pure.

"Sometimes on lonely mountain meres;
   I find a magic bark,
I leap on board, no helmsman steers,
   I float 'till all is dark.

A gentle sound, an awful light!
   Three angels bear the Holy Grail,
With folded feet, in stoles of white,
   On sleeping wings they sail.

So pass I hostel, hall and grange;
   By hedge, and fort, by park and pale,
All armed I ride, what e'er betide,
   Until I find the Holy Grail.
                        —TENNYSON.

"Moreover certain women of our company amazed us, having been early at the tomb."

ANOTHER Easter, to some the brightest yet, smiled in Bozrah, and Miriamne was at the Christian Chapel.

Father Adolphus, after serious, tender greeting, questioned:

"I wonder thy father came not to-day?"

"Oh, he's celebrating the resurrection of love, joy,

and peace, at home. You often told me these were the realities of Christ's rising."

"Thy joy in this must reach all fullness?"

"I don't know, I'm in a strange way—very happy, yet very restless."

"I have seen souls before at their noon; hast thou not observed how the air seems to tremble sometimes at midday? This is not fear but fullness."

"Oh, my shepherd, I'm not at noon yet, only dawn. I've only begun my work."

"Has our missionary Cupid other couples at odds to reunite?"

"Perhaps so; but whether God calls me to such work or not, this much I know, He has put a burden on me."

"Will Miriamne confide it to me—or has the lover dethroned the priest?"

"There now, never say that again! None on earth can dethrone in my heart my constant friend and guide; yea under God, my savior! Had there been no Father Adolphus there would have been no lover; at least no Christian Cornelius, as my heart's lord."

"I fear Miriamne in her generous desire to cheer a tired old man flatters."

"No; not flattery, but just award. As the ancient captives on their return to their own Israel gave their wealth to provide crowns for their priests, so do I to-day offer the finest gold of my heart to the man who piloted me with purity, patience, and wisdom, along and over perilous ways, to happiness beyond all words to express."

The old missionary's face expressed the wondrous comfort he felt in the words of his convert.

"And what is it that burdens thee, daughter?"

"I hope my pastor will not be offended, but I'm burdened by the slow dawning of religious day. Why does it take so long to convert the earth?"

"The zeal of the young convert fills thee!"

"Ah, but that trite answer, defense of the slow progress of true or false creed, after all does not answer. I feel those Easter services at times lifting me up, out of and beyond myself, out of all thought of my own final glory, and to anxiety for a lost Israel, a lost world! I think, at times, I comprehend what was meant by the descent to the grave, the captivity of death, the triumphal ascent, and then I wonder and doubt."

"Wonder and doubt?"

"Yes; I wonder at the grandeur of all that the resurrection implies, and seeing it unrealized I doubt whether my interpretation of it be the right one. Worse than that, I'm pained by darker doubts. Forgive me, but my poor soul sometimes questions whether or not God has grown weary or failed to keep His promises. Oh, these doubts pain me to my heart's core, but they will come! I see day by day on every hand such widespread gloom; not only that very few walk in the light, but how many shadows fall on those who profess to have entered the light of the Rising?"

"Alas, day drags wearily!" slowly responded the priest.

"Yes; the centuries since Calvary, filled with misery, ignorance, and sin, seem to me to have rebuke in them to all who saw, from time to time, the Gospel light, and imperious urgency for those who see it now."

"But the church is doing its best to get onward, Miriamne."

"That I doubt, though I'd fear to be heretical."

"Again, I do not comprehend thee, girl."

"That's it; I do not comprehend myself, or what it is that I'm stirred to be or do. I think that there's a reason for sadness at Easter time. It is the reminder of a great hope unfulfilled. Over twelve hundred years have passed away since Christ arose, typical of the rising of mankind by faith to all that was noble and blissful, and yet we are all in the dim twilight of the morning. Oh, my teacher, it seems to me as if a funeral chord went weeping through every Easter anthem."

The old priest sat silently for a time, then bowed his head and wearily sighed; " I have done my best any way!"

"Oh, do not think I doubt that! No, no; I'd not hint a rebuke of my noble guide; but I can't make you understand me! Nobody seems to grasp my meaning! Yet of this I'm certain, I want to do something differing from what has been; something great, revolutionary, for the world, for Christ."

"All reforms are revolutionary; all consecration to noble work, noble."

"I suppose I express myself as vaguely as other Christians, whose efforts are chiefly words. But why is it that there can not be a presentment of Divine truth in such a simple and attractive form as to make all hearing and seeing love it? Why is it that the followers of truth separate into armies, not only not sympathizing with, but opposing each other? Why do not all having a common Father and one Saviour, join as one loving family to bear aloft the banner of the Invincible?"

"That day will come in God's good time."

"Oh, again forgive me; but that trite apology for the delayed dawn seems to me to fling the blame on God in order to palliate man's indifference."

"Miriamne, thou art thoughtful beyond thy years, but what wouldst thou have?"

"Some one to show me how, and when, and where to proclaim a revolution! There is need that Israel believe; that one half the race, its women, be crowned with its full privileges and powers; that Christian humanity check war, banish poverty and bring in universal justice."

"Revolutionist, indeed; though a blessed one art thou!"

"So I'm often told; but who will show me how to work for such ends!"

"Hast thou among thy knightly companionships heard of the Grail knights?"

"I've heard of them; but not a great deal. Why ask?"

"Thou art like them."

"I'm glad to know whom I'm like; tell me of them that I may know myself."

"They, as their life work, and with charming enthusiasm, sought an object pure and noble, but which none but they themselves could see."

"Did they obtain their object and do much good?"

"They were a blessing to the world; but sometimes, like others seeking lofty ends, they failed. Eternity alone can estimate their work and worth."

"Where are they now?"

"Their successors are like thee. That grail guild of old is now no more."

"Tell me all about them and the Grail!"

"Listen. Joseph of Arimathæa, he that secretly followed the Lord in his lifetime, and openly, after he saw the glory of His crucifixion, is said to have caught the blood that flowed from the speared side in the paschal vessel or cup used at the last supper. There is a cathedral in Glastonbury, England, which once I saw, erected on the place where Joseph builded a little wicker oratory, when there as a missionary. At least they say he once was there. The aged Joseph died and the Grail or Passion cup passed into the custody of other holy men. Finally a custodian of it sinned, and thereupon it was caught away quickly to heaven. But there is a legend that it is brought, from time to time, to earth, only to be seen by those that are pure—virgin men and women. Then out of the yearnings for the cup's presence (for it is said it gave unutterable joy as well as miraculous healings to any that came nigh to it), an order of knights sprung up, to seek it, everywhere in earth. They were sworn not to disclose their mission, and bound, as their only hope of success, to keep their hearts noble and pure."

"But how am I like a 'grail knight?'"

"Miriamne pursues a heavenly cure for human ills, a something she cannot see nor quite explain."

"'Tis true and wonderful."

"The 'grail' story is almost as old as man, being shaped out of other most ancient pilgrim quests. All noble hearts yearn for a healer and ideal."

"Perhaps the time has come for a woman crusade, a new order of grail seekers?"

"Indeed, I think as much; and Miriamne, taking Mary as her model, may be the very one to proclaim it."

"But being a woman, and so young, I might be ridiculed as an enthusiast, as brazen, perhaps, or worse, if I attempted such things."

"If thou didst undertake any thing truly good, thou wouldst best know its goodness by the bitterness of its opposing. The cross is very bright on one side, on the other it casts shadows. Walking toward it we walk in those chastening shadows. But when we've passed the grave, which it ever guards, there is light, all light—not before."

"Sometimes I think I'm a very womanish woman and not the stuff of which the heroine can be made."

"To be a woman is to have within thee a wealth of power. To be queenly is to do in queenly spirit the work falling to thy lot. Behold the queenly women of the patriarchs! Rebecca watered the flocks, Rachel was a shepherdess. The daughter of Jethro, King of Midian, also kept the flocks; and Tamar baked bread. The Word of God records these things, methinks, to show in what a queenly way a queenly woman may perform a seemingly unimportant work. Doing humble works well, they had their honor in due time. Think of our Mary, Mother of Jesus, after her call, serving humbly as a good housewife to a carpenter."

"Oh, if I could only catch the flavor of her life more fully!"

"A worthy wish! Her life was a sermon on faith. Called of God to bring forth Immanuel, she accepted the trust with joyful humility, leaving the miraculous performance to the Promiser. For thirty years, from Bethlehem's cradle to Bethabara, where her Son was owned of God, she bore her pains and toils, facing persecutions, the leers and slanderous innuendoes of the rabble, all without faltering. Only wondrous faith kept her gentle young heart from breaking! I think she carried the cross all along the course of Christ's life—until He Himself took it. She wrought out her work as a satellite of her son, and yet as a poem most eloquent, voicing thoughts without which some of His wondrous, greater life would lack explanation."

"I fain would be like her, but then to be so seems beyond my capacities."

"If thou canst not be a satellite of the Sun as Mary, be a satellite of a satellite. Reflect her, and it will be well, since she reflected Him. 'Tis a simple lesson, but profitable; learn it; there is greatness in little things; regarding them we may at the same time lay hold of that that is great. I'd have all women heroines by teaching them what heroism is."

"Was Mary learned? She had to meet some grand company?"

"Wise, as thou mayst be in the solid culture of God's word."

"But I can never be a Mary," presently the maiden murmured.

"Thou canst be thyself, and what thou canst. A seraph could be no more. God needed for his lofty purpose but one like the Maiden of Nazareth, and for thy comfort remember Mary could not have been the mother of Jesus and Miriamne de Griffin of Bozrah also. She had her mission, thou thine; it is a judgment of God to attempt to say that each in her station was not and is not placed in the way most excellent." Their converse ended but to be renewed. At frequent intervals Miriamne advised with her guide upon the subject uppermost in her mind, and more and more became endued with the spirit of the missionary. To all questionings within herself, as to how she might compass her lofty and philanthropic designs, there came but one answer, "To Jerusalem!" It seemed to her that there, at the heart of Syrian life, she might obtain inspiration and wisdom, as well as the widest possible opportunity of applying these for others. To her to believe was to act, and so she soon had completed all her arrangements to join a band of pilgrims passing by way of Bozrah toward the great city. The parting was painful to mother and daughter, and unlike any they had experienced before. The daughter felt a misgiving. Her mother was aged. The tensions of trial and responsibility being removed so largely from the life of the latter by recent events, left her spiritless. Perhaps it would be more accurate to say that in the days of excitement and conflict she exerted herself beyond her ability; now, when the motive was gone, nature proclaimed its premature exhaustion. Miriamne was convinced that she would be motherless ere long, and was haunted by misgivings as to ever again seeing her if she left Bozrah. Rizpah herself, though she feared that the present separation and farewell were to be final, urged her child tenderly, earnestly, to go forward as conscience dictated. The parting between these two women was secret, they two being alone. It was affectionate and most tender, and yet cheered by the mutual hope both expressed of an eternal reunion after death. The eventful day and the supreme moment came to find Miriamne and her mother nerved for the parting. That was soon over, and the maiden moved out of the old stone home toward the white camel already caparisoned for her use. Father Adolphus and Sir Charleroy awaited her by its side, having repeated, over and over, to the maiden's chosen attendant a score of directions, and having in the fussiness of nervousness again and again examined bridle and girt and hamper. The maiden, glancing after the caravan of pilgrims which was to be her convoy, now slowly passing out of the city, turned toward her father to say the last words of parting. She began: "And now, dear father." Her voice, tremulous to begin with, broke down.

"There, Miriamne," interrupted the knight, "wait, we'll accompany thee a little distance." The three moved out of the city together, the attendant riding on before them. They were all too sorrowful to speak cheerfully, so each said nothing. On the crest of a hillock the old priest paused; simultaneously the father and daughter did likewise. "I'm too weary to go further," spoke the priest. Miriamne's eyes filled with tears, and Sir Charleroy, drawing close to the maiden, turned his eyes away. He stood in silence gazing afar, but at nothing. Each at the last seemed to dread to be the first to speak that one word so inexpressibly sad when believed to be about to be spoken as a last "farewell." The silence became oppressive, and then Father Adolphus murmured, "I suppose we must bid thee adieu, now." Sir Charleroy shuddered and drew his turban down over his eyes.

Just then all the child and all the woman in Miriamne's nature was awakened. Her feelings well nigh over-mastered her, and she exclaimed: "Oh, Bozrah, how can I leave thee and thy dear ones!" Bozrah to her meant home; for a moment her world seemed centred there. The old priest, ever adroit in ministering comfort, sought to divert the thoughts of those about him from needless pain, and so shading his eyes looked steadily eastward for a few moments. Then he questioned: "Daughter, canst thou see Salchad, at the Crater's Mouth. I can not see it for my sight faileth; but I know 'tis yonder." Miriamne followed the direction of the priest's pointing hand, though she knew full well without directing, where the grim fortress city lay. Habit had made it natural to follow the guidance of that old, trembling hand. Some way, it helped her; she seemed better to understand what she already partly knew, when it directed.

"Yes, I see it. It is there; changeless and dreary as ever. But why this question?"

"Dost thou observe how the prospect fades away south of it, until it reaches the spreading desert?"

"Yes, I perceive!"

"Turn to the north, what object is most striking?"

"Oh, Hermon! 'The old-man mountain;' the sun makes its snowy-top appear to-day very like the white on an old man's head and chin."

Sir Charleroy's attention was recalled from his contemplation of the pain of parting for an instant, and he questioned:

"Canst thou see aught of the ruins of the 'Temple of the Sun,' said to be at Hermon's crest?"

But before an answer could be given to the knight's question, Father Adolphus exclaimed: "Daughter, look back again to ruined Salchad! Beyond its 'war tower of giants,' there lies only the desert. Now turn thy back on it all forever, without repinings. Leave the desert and the war tower of the giants to the wandering Bedouin."

"And then what?"

"Turn thy face toward Jerusalem, thy back to the drear desert—"

The maiden almost involuntarily complied, and the priest continued:

"Go forward with Hermon on thy right. Remember that the temple of the Fire Worshipers is overturned, its altars cold; but more remember that on Hermon humanity was transfigured in answer to prayer."

"And so my shepherd and guide would promise me blessing and bid me God speed?" quoth the maiden.

"Thou read'st my heart, daughter."

"The same true heart; it never gets old or weary of cheering."

"I'm made grateful and happy, daughter, by thy words. He that saith, '*Let not your hearts be troubled!*' and '*comfort ye, comfort ye my people,*' is my leader. For cheering, I was called."

"How noble such a call seems to me, now."

"Yea; daughter, if one can not be as the stars that fought in their course for Sisera, he may be as a summer evening's breeze, in cooling pain's fevers, and in drying the tears from cheeks that blush through the rains of weeping times."

Gently, firmly she guided her camel from the hillock, on which it was feeding, toward the highway, along which the caravan was departing. "We must be going now."

At her words, Sir Charleroy and the old Sacrist each caught one of her hands.

"Oh, my fathers!" was her pitying but not pitiable exclamation. Sir Charleroy, standing on the hillock, by the camel, on which his daughter was mounted, drew the hand he held close to his heart, then his arm tenderly encircled its owner. The maiden's head rested upon the breast that had often borne her since babyhood, her lips met in unfeigned tenderness those of the man who not only loved her as a daughter, but as his good angel, almost savior. It was a scene for a painter ; the past and the present, sunset and morning; the one looking back in a confessed ineffectiveness of a life nearly spent, in contrast with a fresh, young, hopeful life, before which lay a world to be conquered. Miriamne, the called leader in a new crusade for women, for humanity, was bidding farewell to the ruins of giant land. and to a representative of the last of the sworded-crusaders.

Her staff fell on the side of the beast that bore her and it moved away quickly after the departing troop.

The parting was over, and yet the two old men silently lingered at the place of the farewell. Once or twice the maiden looked back to them, as she was borne forward, to wave an adieu. The lone watchers followed her with their eyes, until her white camel appeared but a speck moving along at the skirt of a column of dust. The eyes of the watchers dimmed by years, now supplemented by tears, presently could discern only dust. She was buried from their view forever. Then they silently returned to the city, each busy with his own thoughts. Thereafter there was a heavy loneliness on all hearts in that Bozrah circle. The priest moved about his chapel, and the parents about their home as though an angel of light had gone from their midst, or as if the angel of death had come among them.

"It seems strange like," said the Sacrist's sister, "to

let a girl go away to that far-off city, among strangers, and about such meaningless purposes."

"Never mind; never mind, sister, God's lambs are ever safe. Her mission is clear to her, at least, and she'll not be among strangers. The knights who secretly abide in the city of God have a charge concerning her in letters I've sent them. As well, Cornelius, her betrothed, is there. Pure love will be her wall of fire." Thus ended all arguments and misgivings.

CHAPTER XXXIII.

THE HOSPITALER'S ORATION.

"I do not say that a social cyclone is impending; but the signs of the times certainly admonish us that if Christianity is to avert a revolution of the most gigantic proportions, and the most ruinous results, we have not an hour to lose in assuring the restless masses that they have no better friends than are the professed disciples of Him whose glory it was to preach the gospel to the poor, and to lift up their crushing burdens."—REV. DR. A. J. F. BEHREND'S *Socialism and Christianity.*

"My soul doth magnify the Lord. * * * He hath put down princes from their thrones, and exalted them of low degree."—MARY.

HE daughter of Sir Charleroy found a home and a mother with Dorothea Woelfkin, the widowed parent of her affianced. What manner of woman the latter was may be readily inferred from the character of her beloved and only son, Cornelius. It sufficeth to say, mother and son were in all things wonderfully alike.

"Miriamne, I've called to ask, if we get the consent of my mother, that you attend a conclave of knights, to be secretly held, after Moslem prayers this evening."

"Where?"

"At the house of the Christian sister, aged Phebe; just by the second wall of the city."

"And why do they meet?"

"An eloquent Hospitaler, lately returned from a

long mission, is to address the companions and their friends."

"A Hospitaler; what's his name?"

"Ah, there it is; the question all ask, and none can answer! He has given full tokens of his right to confidence, but declines, for reasons which he says are most pious, to reveal himself further than that he is a Knight Hospitaler of Rhodes."

"Rhodes? Is he very tall, of piercing eyes, his hair long and jet, with streaks of gray?"

"Even so."

"My father knew such a man, whom he called 'silver-tongued.'"

"This man is as eloquent as Apollos."

"We met such an one, and were with him for a time. We left him here, on our journey from Acre to Bozrah."

"Did you penetrate his secret?"

"I did not, though my father once said to him 'Grail.' After that he kept aloof from us."

"A proof it must be as I've suspected; the Hospitaler is one of the new Grail-Knights!" exclaimed Cornelius.

"And he is here? I must hear him again. The words he spoke to me in Gethsemane have followed me night and day since. He made the journey of Mary and Christ, by way of Kedron, to the cross, seem like a present reality; a path typical of the one before every child of God. I saw it all then, but have been unable since to find it. Oh, I burn with desire to have the 'silver-tongued' guide me to that pathway again."

At the appointed time the twain sought the house of Christian Phebe, and found it wrapped in gloom; the only sign of life without being a man garbed as a camel driver, standing guard at the door. Cornelius whispered to Miriamne, " He's a knight—the warden." The young man gave the watchman a secret signal; the latter communicated through a little gated window, with those within, and quickly the door swung open, admitting Woelfkin and his companion. Within were light and cheerfulness contrasting with the gloom without. A goodly company was already assembled, chiefly made up of Crusaders, but now unharnessed. The faces of the pilgrim soldiers betokened a change within. They betokened spirits subdued, but not crushed; hearts having surrendered ambition for devastating conquest, to welcome a finer hope. There were few things about the place suggestive of war, and many suggestive of peace. At one end of the room stood a desk, in shape much like an altar. It was draped with a Templar banner, and to its side were fastened a sword, bent in the shape of a sickle, and two spears forming a cross, supporting a cup; the latter was in form the same as the cup of the Passion.

"There is something about this place that recalls the chapel of the Palestineans, in London, Cornelius."

"Well, you and I were there; now we are here. In that the two places have likeness," pleasantly responded the maiden's escort.

Miriamne's eyes wandered from object to object, as if seeking proof of her assertion, and her companion followed her gaze with a glance about the place, which finally rested, as his glances were wont, on the eyes of Miriamne.

"Oh, the devoutness, the peace, the fellowship!" she exclaimed.

Just then there was a movement: a number of the

men present arose; a hailing sign, significant to the initiated, was given by some, while simultaneously a slight applause passed around the room:

"Tis he," whispered Miriamne.

"Your Hospitaler?"

"Yes."

The knights all stood and sang in subdued voices, a psalm of hope. "The movement of the melody suggests pilgrims climbing a hill." At least, so the maiden said its movement seemed to her.

When the psalm was finished, the knights resumed their seats and the Hospitaler, without preliminary, at once addressed them:

"Knights of Christ, few and often in hiding, I would remind ye that no plan of God is futile, and that His cause has no backward movement.

"A dream of conquest, restoration and glory came over all followers of the cross. The dream had within it a hope of a holy land in Christian possession, and all the children of earth getting from it the story of the true faith. Then there was to come, we believed, the golden age, in which all mankind in sweet charity's glorious fellowship should go forward.

"Nature, man's mother, prays in a million mournful voices for that golden day; and God, man's eternal and loving Father, works by countless invincible agencies to cause its full dawning. We Crusaders gave our lives by thousands for our faith, but we seemed to have done little beside change the name of this land from Philistine to Palestine. One, to be sure, is softer to the ear than the other, but to the heart both names bring the same miserable thoughts. Yet there was more than this attained. Ye remember how our cavalier soldiers expressed their chivalric impulses in honoring that queen of women, Our Lady? Like the rising of sun at midnight, came the conviction to Christian Europe when at its worst, socially, that reform must begin by purifying the homes of the people, by exalting all home life. To do this, the mothers who bare and nurture the fruits of the home, as well as making them for weal or for woe what they are, must needs be exalted by right as well as by fitness to their queenship. Every knight's praise of Mary was an avowal of faith; his faith that woman could be, should be, what his imagination pictured Mary to have been.

"The knightly Christians were among the first to be moved by the belief that that was a monstrous blight, a heresy toward God and nature which regarded the finer sex as necessities or luxuries. Impressed by reverence for Mary, the banded soldiers of the cross began to feel their mission to be not only the recovery of the dead, but also of the living from infidel dominion; hence, each Crusade banner came as a sunburst to those, who, under the spell of gross passion, were enslaving their natural co-partners.

"Men, while the harem ideal stands, while woman is impotent because uncrowned, our lofty hopes can not bear fruit nor will our labors be ended!"

The speaker was interrupted by a murmur of applause that ran around the circle of auditors.

Miriamne glowed with delight, and raised her hand impressively and nodded toward Cornelius. He only saw the motion and easily interpreted it as meaning, "There, that's what I felt, but could not express."

The speaker continued: "God said it is not good that the man should be alone: time that resolves all mysteries, and experience which transmutes to gold all the rubbish of guess and experiment, has irrevocably declared that man cannot be to his fullness, in a state of solitary grandeur. He and the woman go up or down together; and, whether a seraph or a serpent leads her, the man by inclination or by force is sure to follow her footsteps.

"We Crusaders had a glimpse of the truth, but lost it to follow an *ignis fatuus*. Yet, in this land, we confronted the harem with the home ruled by one queenly wife and mother. The world, beholding the contrast begins to believe, as never before, in the supremacy, over all institutions, of that one where, under Eden's covenant charters, purity and mother-love mold the race in the name of sole and patient love. The Saracens paraded their houris, their concubines, and their slaves as the proofs of their prowess; but the Christians challenged the array by the quality of their possessions, commencing with their women of God's blood royal, and ascending to each revered personage, from love's companions, to Mary, to Jesus. He that nobly deals with the one by his side will find her putting on a glory that will brighten the luster of his kingliness, and bringing forth to him those having the power to grasp and mold the destinies of coming years. Listeners, mark me; there is a lesson profound in the record of the strugglings with each other of Rebecca's twins before their birth. Indeed, each being begins his career within the life that gives him life.

"Who will say, with assurance, that all of life lies within the reach of any man of himself? Nay, be it said, rather, that she who first carries, then leads, then inspires, as she only can, her sons and daughters, is the one who lays her gentle hands, with resistless power, upon the keys of all futures. It is the mother who impresses the prophecy of what is to be on the heart of the infant, before the event finds place upon the deathless page which records deeds done."

Again applause interrupted.

The Hospitaler continued, as attention was given anew:

"That profoundest of ancient teachers, Plato, enunciated at least a half-truth or truth's shadow, in his doctrine of the preëxistence of souls, though, as our church understands it, it pronounces the teaching heretical. Be that as it may, this much assuredly is true: if each man has not been on earth before, his present existence being the repetition of a prior one, his intuitions, vague recollections out of a past forgotten in a former death, surely there is none who is not the fruit of his parents. He is largely what they made him, and of the twain that beget, I affirm that the mother wields the ruling influence in the life and character of the begotten. I believe men perpetuate their worst traits through their posterity, easily and more persistently than do women theirs. In the giant of the human pair brawn and muscle predominate, and these, if depraved, feed every evil passion, giving each power to run with virulence from sire to son. The woman, formed by finer conceptions to be an angel, may fall to sinning and let weakness take the place of gentleness. So be it; yet even then her weaknesses and her sinnings, constantly repugnant to her nature as God framed it, antagonistic to the refinement that is native, ebb and die along the shores of her being's course. She more naturally and more forcefully transmits her good than she does her evil, as a general rule. They have in fable-lore a tradition that the mythical goddess of love, Venus, wore a resplendent girdle, the sight of which made every beholder love the wearer. Let me give present force to the legend by affirming that every true woman, girded with the virtues that it is her duty and her privilege to wear, is an object, among all earthly beings, superlatively, entrancingly beautiful—next after Christ, God's best gift to man."

Cornelius now plucked the corner of Miriamne's *pepulum*. It wàs a lover's restless, questioning act. Being a man, trained as men, he was naturally inclined to doubt the speaker and to join in secret ridicule, that substitute for gainsaying when arguments are utterly lacking; but being a lover, he was so far doubtful as to his old creeds concerning women, as to be ready to be led. Miriamne turned toward her lover with a smile lightened by eyes which glowed. Hers was not the smile of a girl flatly complacent in an effort to be very agreeable. She believed; the love she had for the man at her side was consecrated first to truth. Her will was that of a blade of steel—yielding, serviceable; but still elastic or firm, as need be and as its highest purposes required. She smiled, but the smile mounting to her brightening eyes, left her fine forehead, a very temple of thought, all placid. The smile and the glance routed all doubts from the young man's mind. She to him was a Venus, and more, a saint. She wore the invisible girdle of which the knight had spoken, and the youth felt its winning power. Another proof that the best advocate of a woman is a woman; and of her worth, the best argument an example.

The orator knight proceeded without pause:

"I know full well that some sneer and carp on woman's weakness, having recourse to Eden for argument. To these I reply: The enemy assailed not the weaker, but the stronger first, and exhibited masterly generalship in seeking to overcome the citadel that would insure the greatest loss, the most complete victory. And note how long and arduous his siege of Eve; then remember how quickly Adam fell. Crush the woman's heart, ruin her faith, degrade her body, and then, with this work completed, we are ready to ring down the curtain over the end of the tragedy of a wrecked world. When men hold women to their hearts, their manhood is enlarged and their queens become their angels, bearing a 'grail' that catches for both the choice things of heaven. But when a man turns his strength against a woman, she ceases to be his charming, alluring helpmate. He has brawn, and she, not having that, puts on that cunning which is the natural arm of the weaker. When the honey-suckle turns to poison-ivy, or the dove to a fox, then weep; but when woman lays aside the entrancings of her moral beauty to enter a desperate strife with armed cunning, let men go mad over their queens become witches. I tell you, hearers, when men become demons women will give themselves to sorcery. I speak not of spiritual possession, but of human deflowering. Shall our queens be uncrowned, disrobed, degraded? No, no, Satan alone could say 'yea.'"

When the burst of applause that had interrupted him subsided, the Hospitaler continued:

"We knights revere the sign of the cross because the world's Savior died thereon; it will be well for us to revere womankind because it was given to woman, not to man, to coöperate with God in bringing that Savior to the world. A woman bore him with crucial pains, as each of us was borne, before He bore the cross. And reverently I say it, companions, woman's cross is ever set, and all the earth is her Calvary. I can not but see, as must you who think, that all this pain to her has in God's great plan some vicarious element, some blessing for mankind. We Christians pray for the second coming of Jesus, the Jews wait and weep for the dawn of a day of salvation, the Mohammedans, like hosts of the Pagans, in every clime, are longing for some golden day; better than the present. This universal longing is a prophecy of good to come. I can not believe that the All-Father would suffer this universal and intuitive longing to end in disappointment and mockery. He is too good for that. By this longing I see standing out, less dimly, and yet dimly enough to be by many unseen, some sublime, prophetic hints. Read sacred Writ. Wherever therein you discern a prophetic character, emblem of Christ, forerunner of the golden age, you will find not far from him, as his partner and help, fittingly a woman!

"From the first it was so. Adam the first appeared, and a woman was his partner, helpmate and more. He fell. A way of recovery was provided for him, but it was the woman who was given to bring forth the One whose heel was to crush the head of the author of humanity's great catastrophe. Then came the second Adam—Immanuel. At his advent the chief figure, next after God the chief instrument in His bringing in, by His side along the years in all helpful ministries, a woman, Mary, the beautiful, the perfect, the ideal of women.

"Again and again we have puzzled over the records,

wondering why Matthew traced the genealogy of Jesus along the male line only, through David and Jacob to Abraham the father of the faithful, and that Luke traced that genealogy through Mary and her father, Heli. But there's method most wise in the records. Matthew wrote for the Jews, Luke for the Gentiles. The hint is herein given that when the Gentiles are fully gathered in, woman will be recognized in the ultimate religion, that knows neither race nor sex. As in the royal line which gave man a Savior, as in a queenly line having for man, society and home—the emblem of heaven expressed on earth—blessing and saving powers."

The knight closed with an appeal for the continuance of the revival of the chivalrous spirit toward woman, saying:

"It matters little what becomes of the dust of the pious dead; the past is secure, and Deity guards till the resurrection all tombs in His own unfrustrated way, but it matters much how we treat the living! That is a puerile piety which is ready to die to defend from foes that can not harm inanimate ashes that appeal for no favor, while suffering, willingly, living bodies encompassing bleeding hearts, to continue amid untold agonies, their whole existence one long appeal for succor! Christian knights, on with your new crusade, and may the golden age come grandly in, its fruits —love, joy, and peace in every clime, to every race, to every man, woman, and child!"

The speaker sat down; there was a moment of deep silence, followed by an outburst of approving acclamations.

Then ensued a hum of voices, the assembly breaking

up into little groups, one and another attempting each to prove his loyalty, his piety or his good sense to the man next to him, by certifying his belief in the knight's words.

Miriamne, half unconscious of her surroundings, exclaimed:

"Oh, will not some one tell me how to begin?"

"Can I aid my Miriamne?" asked her lover.

"I don't know; perhaps. But that Grail Knight with the silver tongue sees, in his soul, what I would reach. When he speaks my feet take wings. I can not tell you what or how it all is. He speaks and I see, as Moses in the mount, the outline of the tabernacle of God that is to be with men."

CHAPTER XXXIV.

MEMORIALS AT BOZRAH.

"I'm footsore and very weary,
  But I travel to meet a Friend;
The way is long and dreary,
  But I know it soon must end.
He is traveling swiftly as whirlwinds,
  And though I creep slowly on,
We are drawing nearer and nearer,
  And the journey is almost done.
I know He will not fail me,
  So I count every hour a chime,
Every throb of my heart's beating
  That tells of the flight of TIME.
I will not fear at His coming,
  Although I must meet Him alone,
He will look in my eyes so gently
  And take my hand in His own."

AN uneventful year passed over the missioners, but it was followed quickly by eventful times.

Two messages came, one after the other, and not far apart, to Jerusalem, which moved all the Christian colony at the latter place, but especially Cornelius and his consort. The first was from Father Adolphus and as follows:

"Your parents, Sir Charleroy and Rizpah, have departed Bozrah. They went out together, and their end was peace. They compensated themselves for the needless miseries they had wrought in their younger days by keeping out of all shadows during their journey after their reconciliation by the tomb of their children, even until sunset. I could not summon you, for they passed away quickly, only a few days coming between their goings."

Shortly after the foregoing, came the other message, and that accidentally, for the link between Jerusalem and Bozrah being broken by death, there was none left in the Giant City to send after or for comforting to the missioners. "Father Adolphus is dead." That was the report brought by chance to the Christians at Zion. Hundreds in Jerusalem had heard of him, and hearing of his death sighed mildly. The missioners were his mourners—really, solely.

Ere long Dorothea left Jerusalem of Syria for the New Jerusalem, and this event not only brought sorrow but also perplexity. Miriamne realized that she could not now continue in the house of her betrothed, simply as his betrothed, even if it were possible for the household to continue, the head being absent. Whither should she go, orphan and kinless as she was? Love protested mightily against any thought of going far from her affianced, and then she felt profound pity for the man who mourned and felt a mother's loss deeply, as did Cornelius. He entreated for a speedy wedding, and she, seeing then no alternative, consented thereto; but as she assumed love's yoke, she believed that the ambition of her life was frustrated. She was not disconsolate, neither was she tearless. She thought she discerned the leadings of God and submitted promptly, making it thenceforth her duty cheerfully to engage in the, to her, seemingly commonplace works of a missionary pastor's wife. Her husband was a "man of the people," and found acceptance with the lowly. He was wont to call himself "a priest forever after the order of Melchisedec." Said he anon to his flock: "Like that mysterious man who flits across your sacred histories am I! You of the Jews, self-elect, as God's elect, though disgrafted, would put me, intending to do so or not, by the unknown and unheralded Melchisedec. You think me, without father, without mother, beginning of days, or end of life, because you do not find my name in the chronologies of your high families nor myself in the covenants of the Hebrews. You Christians doubt my authority because no ghostly ordaining hands have been laid upon my head. But I'm the child of a King, and a towel, such as my Master wore as He ministered, is robing enough for me!" Old people, women and children, gave the young man unquestioning love, and thus was well indorsed the choiceness of his ministerings. Miriamne beheld these manifestations with secret joy, for she knew that through the one she loved she was, in part, expressing her own thoughts and sympathies. Once wed, she was too honest, too tender-hearted, too noble to be less than all that wifehood implied, and yet she felt at times as if the ambitions and hopes of her life, nursed through many years, had not been compassed. She tried to settle down and humbly do the work of a missionary's helpmate, and to overcome, through Divine grace, the ambition to do seemingly grander things than she was doing. Sometimes, smiling through tears, she would say to her husband as he sought to satisfy her heart's yearnings with mention of the good work they were doing:

"Well, a man has come between me and the 'grail.'

I'm following him, may he follow it, and God guide both."

After a time Cornelius and Miriamne made a pilgrimage to Bozrah, drawn thither by a desire common to both to honor their loved ones departed. They found the Giant City all pervaded by the spirit of the moribund past. Even the Christian church, once a light, a joy and a promise of a better day, had fallen into decline at Bozrah. The edifice had become dilapidated, the congregation was depleted.

In name, Father Adolphus had a successor, younger, more learned, more eloquent in his way, than the saintly man now sleeping. But the infidels, the very ones who were wont to confess that they could not, if they would, make headway against the old priest's godly life, now laughed to scorn the stately and scholarly arguments of the new leader. The converts under the new regime were few, the common people did not from him hear the word gladly; and the regular congregation was rent by schisms.

One chapel service sufficed both Miriamne and Cornelius. They found in it nothing but cold formality and the memory of what had been, but was now no more.

"Oh, Cornelius," Miriamne cried, "reverently I say it, but is it not strange that our faith edges its way over the world so slowly, with such heralds?"

"Leastwise, you may say, you do not see your 'Grail' here, Miriamne?"

"Oh, now, I realize the worth of Von Gombard as I never did before."

"Are you not sorrowed at his absence, Miriamne?"

"Sorrowed! Truly not; but unspeakably glad that

he walks with the sons of God; a very king, I know, amid the greatest. Oh, how sad I'd be to see the poor, dear, tired old man with his overfull heart and trembling limbs now going about in painful ministries here! God was twice good; in leaving him so long, then in taking him. Ah, if there were more like that old saint, those that there are would not need to tarry till their twilight."

"Shall we prolong our stay?"

"No! I've listened long enough to the lull of eternity here. Bozrah's past has taught me its all. I'm ready to go home."

"Home! When, to-morrow?" ardently questioned Cornelius, anxious himself to depart the Giant City.

"After to-morrow; the coming day, at my instance, the memorial of my parents is to be set up."

The following morning, just before sunrise, the husband and wife repaired to the tomb of their loved ones, to witness, by pre-arrangement, the unveiling of a memorial. It consisted of two figures carved from whitest marble; a woman's form with a face expressive of tenderness and beauty, marked with deepest grief, but not with hopelessness. Across her lap there lay the form of a young man, the rigors of death plainly marked on his face and limbs. There was no mistaking the representation, and Cornelius quickly exclaimed:

"I know the one that sits thus holding that crucified body! 'Tis real! Impressive! Awful!"

"It is fitting, think you?"

"I'm too much moved to judge, perhaps; though I do wonder that you have not had carved upon the pedestal the names of your dead, or some explanation."

"Names? What matter, to the stranger passing,

who lie beneath the stone? As for the meaning, let those who come and go question till it appear."

"I'm the first questioner, Miriamne. The application?"

"Remember that my mother, in her almost solitary grief, held her dead children for a time against her broken heart, but it was a heart filled with a mother-love which never faltered. There is nothing in love surpassing such on earth. Then at last, when her life work was done, her cup full, my mother, as her final consolation, held to her heart the Son whose death gives life, as yon Madonna holds the Christ."

"I bow to Miriamne's judgment; the creation is appropriate; Glorious Madonna!"

"I have a hope that it may stand here in the Hauran an enduring sermon to the varied races who pass. They who come and go here, reminded that the Nephalim with all their arrogant might left little but their crumbling tombs; that Astarte, once the potent, dangerous goddess of the groves, here faded from the love of her fevered hosts, who themselves in turn faded from the face of the earth, may pause to question what the meaning and power of this last, new, fresh presentment! Perhaps they will hear from those made wise, and in time learn to tell one another, that these two figures speak of the Deathless Kingdom, its white loves, its wondrous rewards and its Spirit of might expressed by all who are in it through the power of an endless life, and through the agency of immortal influence."

"Miriamne, I see thee a palpitating angel in the flesh! I can say no more!"

As the young missioner thus spoke he stretched out

his arms toward the woman he loved as if he would restrain her. The motion came from his heart, which was anxiously saying within: "She is growing upward and away from her consort." But he had neither courage nor words to voice the vague thought which brought admiration mixed with fears.

They turned toward their temporary home in the Giant City. As they went, the rising sun flooded the marble forms by the graves with a golden light, and the twain, beholding the glory of that morning benediction, felt an illumining in their hearts that some way made heaven seem very near.

"And now, darling, we'll return to Jerusalem, and quietly pursue our work until we join those loved ones gone on before," spoke the husband the day after the monument's unveiling.

"I trust we shall work in future with better plans and grander results than we have had before."

"Are you discontented with what we accomplish?"

"No, and yes," was her measured reply.

Cornelius turned his eyes full upon her, lifting inquiringly his eyebrows.

She continued: "I'm satisfied, if God so will, to blend my work into my husband's; I know this is my duty as a wife, but I long to echo nobler music. Can you make it?"

"Annata, the Assyrian goddess, was content to be the echo of her spouse the mighty Ammon. I'd be an Ammon if I could to be worthy being echoed by Miriamne. But, little wife, your words sound almost Delphic; and yet you are no such ambiguous oracle. Is there any wish unmet?"

"I've a misgiving."

"Why, wife of mine, see how strong you've been each year adding health! See the shadows over our people. We are sent to chase these away with Gospel truth. We've hitherto only learned how to work efficiently, and in the future will do braver, greater things than ever. We'll tarry, as Adolphus, ay, and by grace renew strength, turning back the dial pointer, as with prayer, did Hezekiah of old."

"I'll not go, I know, until my work is done. None go before such time."

"Oh, but we must go together everywhere, even to death."

"Ah, beloved, I know your meaning. It's the lover, not the consecrated missionary, who speaks now."

"I can't help it! I'll be useless without you. I'm useless now, except as you sustain me; as Abishag, the Shunnamite, the fairest young maiden of all Israel, brought heart to the bosom of David, old and shaken by years, so you put into me all the ambition I have. To my trembling heart you are what Deborah was to Barak's."

"God help you, Cornelius; I believe you, because I know your trusting nature and have joyed in the fullness of your lavish love, but let us bravely face this matter as it comes. For God, I know, I must quickly do my work and be gone."

"Oh, say not so, if I'm to be left alone! That must not be! By your love for me I entreat you to stay; a thousand ties bind my life to thine; it will kill me by inches to have them severed!——

"Miriamne, my own, nearer to God by far than am I; plead with Him to spare us this agony!"

"In spirit, my loyal spouse, we shall ever be near

each other, but I feel that in the body we shall not be together long. I shall finish my course and then——"

"No, not that," vehemently exclaimed the husband. "Say not that! I'll work for you, with you, for God. Help me to the end and let me so help you, beloved!"

"You may help me while I tarry."

"I'll joy to realize the prophet's vision, who saw the hands of a man under the wings of an angel. Here are the hands and Miriamne is the angel."

"But your imagination glows, kindled by the torch of a human heart almost idolatrous."

"Nay, not idolatrous; for the fire rises to things holy. I only plead that God let me walk with Miriamne; I know she will walk nigh Him. Go where you will my feet will bear me thither, undertake what you may, my heart and hand will help; point out any goal of darling desire and thither I'll carry you, if need be. For you I'll gladly die, if, at the dying, I have the comforting assurance that soon my other self will join me in the overshadowed land of life."

"How it would brighten the world, if all who take the holy vows of marriage on their souls were as truly wed in heart as we." As the twain stood by the white marble figures at sunrise the next morning, equipped for departure, they made a striking picture. The living and the dead; the exemplars of the purest, deepest wedded love committed to serving their fellow man; they rose grandly above the ruins of the place builded by those mighty self-seeking devotees of Astarte.

Bozrah sat in desolation, knowing no hope and having a bitter past only and forever to contemplate; the youthful gospel heralds had all life, rising to new life— hope beyond hope, joy beyond joy, and then life, hope and joy in endless unfoldments, stretching way through measureless eternities, all before them. Miriamne was pensive; Cornelius was chastened by the remembrance of the words she had spoken the day before, and both subdued by the presence of the majestic monument before them.

CHAPTER XXXV.

THE SISTERS OF BETHANY.

" Her eyes are homes of silent prayer,
  No thought her mind admits;
  But 'He was dead and there he sits!
  And He that brought him back is there!'

" All subtle thought, all curious fears,
  Borne down by gladness so complete;
  She bows, she bathes the Savior's feet
  With costly spikenard and with tears."
                              —ALFRED TENNYSON.

"In the day time He was teaching in the temple, and at night He went out and abode in the mount that is called the Mount of Olives."—LUKE xxi., 37.

"Gethsemane on one side, Bethany on the other . . . where He was wont to pray for His people and weep for a sinful world; where His feet stood on the eve of His ascension and where His wondering disciples received from white-robed angels the promise of His second advent. It will be admitted that above and beyond all places in Palestine Olivet witnessed 'God manifest in the flesh.'"
—*Porter's "Giants of Bashan."*

FTER Jesus had been driven from His native Nazareth, He found a home in the house of Lazarus, Martha and Mary, in the village of Bethany, on the eastern slope of Olivet. That was sweet, memorable Bethany of the Gospels; "the perfection of repose," amid the palm and oak-

covered slopes of Olivet; hidden by its quiet life, as well as its sequestering mountain, from Jerusalem, that great, throbbing heart of Palestine.

Thither, down the east steps of the Temple, through the "Golden Gate," along camel paths that wound past Gethsemane and across fitful Kedron, the Son of Man often went when worn out by His love ministries, or harassed by the gainsayings of the great city. So, preaching His new kingdom, He exalted its cornerstone, the godly home, by electing one such, that of Lazarus and his sisters, as a rest and a refuge for Himself. Beyond this He proved His own humanity by seeking earthly friendships, at the same time exhibiting Himself, though the favored of heaven, the object of constant angelic regard, as needing, because He was human, that which humanity ever needs—congenial human fellowships.

The history of that ancient Bethany family, gathered from various sources, but chiefly from the simple and touching narrative of the Evangelist John, is full of interest. The mother of that home, to us nameless, was dead. Yet she was not fameless; that circle of children in their several relationships witnessed full well of a finest mother-culture, that had been theirs. The father of that family was worse than dead; he was a leper, buried alive in the Lazar keeps of the plague-stricken, and the husband of Martha, the elder sister, early had left his bride widowed.

That was a circle cut through its center; but affliction had knit together in deepened affection the few left. The fatherly brother, Lazarus, well fulfilled his double obligation, and wins admiration, as do ever those sons and brothers who faithfully take the place of dead fathers. That he was such a brother, the grief of his sisters when he died fully proclaimed.

With a few fine sentences John depicts those sisters. Martha, widowed in life's morning, but surmounting all morbidness by giving herself to motherly ministries in her home; and then was Mary, a clinging, trusting, pious maiden; a poem of faith, a tear-bedewed rose-wreath. When Christ joined that circle there was presented the finest conceivable ideal of a home. They served and He blessed, and though their bereavements could never be forgotten, while His banner of love was over them, they were able to alleviate the poignancy of their griefs through the hope of a blessed resurrection and a final, eternal reunion.

The sacred associations gathering about the village of Olivet made it a place peculiarly attractive to Cornelius and Miriamne; for they, too, were bereaved; neither in all the world having a single living kinsman of whom they knew.

They determined, shortly after their final farewell to Bozrah, to take up their abode at the ' House of Dates," and were unmeasurably delighted in being able to secure for themselves a house reputed to have been the identical one occupied by Christ and His choice friends. If it were not the same, there seemed good reason to believe it was at least on the site of that ancient sacred domicile.

One day they conversed of their work, their hopes, and the needs of their field of labor.

"I'm led to think that we should establish a refuge for Magdalenes, Miriamne."

"If we did attempt the founding of an asylum for outcasts we would not belie the memory of a noble woman, who was never a harlot, by applying to it her name. But my 'grail' does not lead me that way. I'd go mad working for the utterly lost only! No; no, our work must be more radical, by beginning back of the falling so as to prevent it."

"Something must be done to educate the women of this country to better living and higher conceptions of womanhood. We need a school of some kind."

"A school? Good, if it be of the right kind; but there have been schools and schools for men, such as they were, and they have effectually proven that education alone is not a savior. Learning does not transform the soul, else God would have given Moses the pattern of a college instead of that of a tabernacle. My mother used often to tell me that the devil is superbly educated. The more he knows the prouder and more dangerous he becomes. I do not despise learning, but since it is impotent to transform men, why try it as the savior of woman? She who takes counsel less of the intellect than of the conscience and affections! We must seek for those we aim to help something surpassing in direct efficacy any thing yet attempted;" so saying, Miriamne paused.

"Shall we organize a church, 'fair as the moon, clear as the sun, and terrible as an army with banners?'"

There have been churches and churches. It would be vain for me to attempt to prove to you, a theologian and a churchman, that this you call the 'Bride of Christ' is imperfect or lacking in any energy of reform; but, though I heartily confess 'tis the choicest institution this side of the stars, yet I see it professing to have heavenly charity, abounding light, and measureless joys, leaving the needy without hospitals, the heathen in ignorance, and most of the world, including many churchmen, famishing for happiness. The trouble is, it infolds too many wolves and repels too many lambs. Your flocks are too much given to atoning for lean living by fat believing; memorizing huge creeds instead of incarnating them; putting their faith-confessions into themselves rather than themselves into their faith professions. You churchmen shut your ears to friendly criticism, sneer at those that censure, and in branding such heretics proclaim yourselves infallible. I'd not be a vaporing railler, but I hear within your ecclesiastical bodies of warring factions, of ambitious and multitudinous leaders, a proof that they are of the church militant; though theirs is an internecine militating. I doubt if there has existed Christ's ideal of a church since Pentecost. He gave a glimpse of its true outlines there, and it will yet come in its power and splendor; then, for the pæans!"

"You'd organize, perhaps, a *Vestal Band?*"

"Vestals?"

"Yes; an union of women of pure hearts, committed solely to such works as those performed in part by the holy sisters of our church fraternities."

"I revere such as are thus engaged with all my heart; but, churchman, you are narrow in your plan; even Pagan Rome, which honored Vesta, the fire goddess, by having an altar to her in every community, held that the State was a great family, and placed Vesta, the goddess of virginal purity, near the Penates, or gods of the household and family."

"I see nothing now in this juxtaposition."

"They saw that there was ruin to all society if their girls were impure; hence buried alive a Vestal, if she fell from her vow of chastity. You have heard, Cornelius, how good Romans were wont to invoke, often, as their family guardians, the manes of their departed kin; and this very naturally; they held to the belief that the family tie, the finest, strongest known among men, outlived, by virtue of its heavenliness, the shock of death. Imperial Rome trusted much its all-conquering swords, for this life, but for the life to come it appealed to Jupiter omnipotent or Minerva, the all-wise. No, no, a 'Vestal Society,' such as you imply, would not suffice. I've a broader clientage and vaster scheme in mind, good churchman husband—"

"Shall I venture another guess?"

"It would be needless. Let me explain myself fully. Good Father Adolphus, founder of Bozrah's *Balsam Band*,' which he sometimes called 'nursing preachers,' told me that in olden times there was in this country a fraternity of women, banded together to perform works of charity. They were remembered chiefly for their helpfulness to those that were in direst need and utterly friendless. They befriended criminals and social outcasts. He said that the women of Jerusalem who followed Christ weeping, were, probably, of that fraternity, since it was the custom of that pious company to offer their tears for those on the way to execution. More, these women were wont to furnish the pain-dulling herbs to victims dying condemned. You remember the Christ was offered such herbs? When I remember the spirit that actuated Martha and Mary, I readily believe they were members of that pious fraternity. More, when I remember how, for His own dear sake, they ministered to His human wants, there comes to my mind the possibility of a perpetual organization, for God's sake, ministering to human want, taking the home as its palace, and to be known to the world by the expressive, winning title, '*Sisters of Bethany.*'"

"Miriamne, if you were not Miriamne, I'd call you Gabriel. I'm dazzled by these words. In truth, thy '*grail*' is near, I believe."

"That I seek to build up I've explained, and here in Bethany I'll attempt it. We'll have a fraternity of women, Christ-guided, with burning hearts, and in methods simple, direct and catholic, reaching after women."

"Now for our pillow prayer, Miriamne. Then side by side, unto wondrous sleep land, side by side in heart and being at awakening.

"'The sun of the millennium will rise from behind the family altar,' Father Adolphus was wont to say. 'Twas well said; redeemed homes are the fruits of the restoration. Shall I read to-night?"

"Surely we need the Word to understand the throbbings of our own hearts when our prayers return, dove-like, with olive branches from heaven."

"What shall I read?"

"What came after Pentecost!"

Then the husband opened to the Gospel Story, and remarking the 'Ascension,' read:

"He was taken up, after that He through the Holy Ghost had given commandments unto the apostles whom he had chosen:

"To whom also He shewed himself alive after His passion by many infallible proofs, being seen of them forty days, and speaking of the things pertaining to the kingdom of God:

"When they therefore were come together, they asked of Him, saying, Lord, wilt Thou at this time restore again the kingdom of Israel?

"And He said unto them, It is not for you to know the times or the seasons, which the Father hath put into His own power.

"But ye shall receive power, after that the Holy Ghost is come upon you: and ye shall be witnesses unto Me both in Jerusalem, and in all Judea, and in Samaria, and unto the uttermost part of the earth.

"And when He had spoken these things, while they beheld, He was taken up; and a cloud received Him out of their sight.

"And while they looked steadfastly toward heaven as He went up, behold, two men stood by them in white apparel;

"Which also said, Ye men of Galilee, why stand ye gazing up into heaven? This same Jesus, which is taken up from you into heaven, shall so come in like manner as ye have seen Him go into heaven."

"And His farewell happened at Bethany? It makes our home seem still more like the gate of heaven, when I remember this; 'He'll come so as He went;' what if that meant His next advent is to be at this very place?"

"Or, what if it meant that He would appear the second time, in glory, at the homes of men; since He elected His home for the gateway of His earthly exit," replied the husband. Then they sat for a little while in a blessed silence; that kind that falls upon souls bowing to a benediction, or moved by thoughts that are holy beyond expression.

The wife broke in on their reverie: "I wonder how His departure affected the disciples?"

"I have it all here, darling;" then he took one of his parchments and read:

"And He led them out as far as to Bethany, and He lifted up His hands, and blessed them.

"And it came to pass, while He blessed them, He was parted from them, and carried up into heaven.

"And they worshiped Him, and returned to Jerusalem with great joy:

"And were continually in the temple, praising and blessing God.

"And they went forth, and preached everywhere, the Lord working with them, and confirming the word with signs following."

"I krew it was as I thought! If believers are as they say, enlisted soldiers, under the blood-stained banners, our Christ has not been true to His word, or there is universal treason in the camp! The world is not gospeled and the soldiers have not the miracle power. I tell you husband, there is need of a revolution, a revival of zeal, an improvement of methods! The Hospitaler was right. The Christian world needs to be led along the *Via Dolorosa* after Jesus and Mary, up to their measure of utter consecration, to their undying love, to their lofty, soul consuming zeal!"

And the young gospel herald was silent, for he could not gainsay her.

CHAPTER XXXVI.

THE QUEEN OF THE HOUSE OF DAVID.

"The harp the monarch minstrel swept,
The king of men, the loved of heaven.
    *   *   *   *

It softened men of iron mold;
No ear so dull, no soul so cold
That felt not, fired not to the tone,
Till David's lyre grew mightier than the throne;
Since then, though heard on earth no more,
Devotion, and her daughter, love,
Still bid the bursting spirit soar,
To sounds that seem as from above,
In dreams that day's broad light can not remove."
—BYRON.

"The king rose up to meet her, and bowed himself unto her, . . . and caused a seat to be set for the king-mother, and she sat at his right hand."—1 KINGS, 2, 19.

IRIAMNE, the heavenly host we imagined to be in bivouac about our Bethany home, methinks were really present, and gave color and form to my dreams. I was in a grail-quest all night."

"What a golden day is such a night! But tell me of the color and form of your visions, Cornelius."

"We fell asleep last night conversing of the Ascension; my dreams carried me on to Pentecost."

"And what have you brought from the the dream

land to help in the stern and pressing waking hours?"

"A panting heart, as one having climbed mountain above mountain. I burn to know and feel the whole significance of Pentecost!

"I've determined to seek holy companionship and wise guiding by attendance at the next 'Harvest Feast' at Jerusalem. I think I'll get peculiar help at the great city."

"The Israelites will not welcome a Christian to their feast."

"The one I aim to attend is that that will be observed by the Christian knights in an upper room, in the great city. They think they have possession of the identical apartment in which the disciples of our Lord met and witnessed the glories of Pentecost, after the Ascension."

"In Joseph of Arimathæa's house?"

"That is the accepted report. The Hospitaler, whom we believe to be a 'Grail Knight' of to-day, is quite earnest in so affirming."

"Wondrous white-souled Arimathæa! Jewish and a priest, yet secretly a disciple of Jesus! I dare to liken myself unto that holy man, in a measure. He left an old faith for a new one, and followed the cup of the Passion, as I, my ideal."

"*A good man and a just*," says the Testament.

* * * * * * *

We meet to-night in Arimathæa's house," said the Hospitaler to Cornelius, shortly after the arrival and welcome of the latter at Jerusalem.

"Can the uninitiated attend?" questioned Cornelius.

"Now, that's the joy of it, they can; and more; we

are to have a number of Jews present, among them some once priests; but now like that Joseph of blessed memory, seeing the true light."

"And the meeting?"

"The exalting of the Word, that's the need of the hour, world-wide. I tell thee, young man, set to teach; the needs are not more religions but more religion, not more revelators or prophets but surer interpreters. The world blooms with truth on every hand; who will pluck the blossoms?"

And the disciples were again, all with one accord, in the holy upper chamber.

The Hospitaler, with an abruptness of John the Baptist, merely throwing back his tunic and exposing the golden sign of knighthood for a moment to his companions, as he entered, at once began to address the assembly;

"Jews and Gentiles, all children by creation of a common Father—greeting! The fires of Pentecost are kindled everywhere in Jerusalem, but they are the old fires and cold enough; sacrifices smoke on the altars, but the day of such offerings is past.

"Methinks, the offered bulls, goats and lambs, if they could speak, would cry out against the priestly hands that shed their blood; 'How long, how long the blood of our flocks has pointed to the lamb of God, the All-Savior, who died to save men from sin and beasts from the altar; and yet we die as if our work were not finished!'

"The beasts join in the wailings of humanity.

"For centuries God's chosen people celebrated this feast of the harvest, the joy of Jewry: and now the world's harvest advenes. Yet, for the most part, the multitudes see not the ripening. For years the first fruits were offered, and as yet, the people do not understand that first fruits mean chosen, choice fruits, the elect of God.

"For centuries, Israel offered the shoulder and heart of the lamb, and yet Israel waits under the overshadowing smokes of its burnt offering, not discerning the Lamb Priest, whose heart of eternal love and shoulder of power, are given for the salvation of the people.

"Israelites, hear me; out of the altar's smoke emerges to view the kingdom of the house of David, refined, purified—the hope of the future. Ye have thought, hitherto, that David's kingdom, whatsoever it might have been, is, in these ages, to be reckoned with the dynasties and forces of an antiquity, whose influences long ago ebbed away along the shores of the all-entombing past.

"Yet such conclusion is as fallacious as it is evidently superficial. The God who works in unbroken time cycles, though men remit their tasks at the beck of sleep or death, pushes forth His forceful, faultless projects with a tireless consistency that knows no cross purposes. A real and present kingdom is that with which this Pentecost we have to do. We are not, *at that time* when *they shall bring out the bones of the kings of Judah and spread them before the sun.* David's throne is a verity, though long incrusted with neglects; it is a symbol of power in a dynasty that is ordained to overspread the earth. I'd summon my witnesses; first the weeping Jeremiah. 'Thus said the Lord: David shall never lack a man to sit on the throne of the house of Israel.' How bold! but amid the ruins about us, I cry never! never! Now call the God-nourished captive Daniel, who, sincere to the last, made all Babylon glow with his prayers and his visions. Saith Daniel:

"'The God of heaven shall set up a kingdom that shall never be destroyed.' The dream is certain; the interpretation sure. He was proof against the alluring blandishments of his royal captors, and as pure to the last as a knight of San Grail."

Cornelius saw a light on the Hospitaler's face, and knew it was that that comes from a conscience clear before God. The latter went on with a voice suddenly become tenderer than it was before.

"Let us hear the reply of the converted pagan king, Nebuchadnezzar: Whose *kingdom is from generation to generation!*'

"Hearken to Isaiah, to whom the scroll of human history through a thousand generations then yet to come was present and lucid: 'Unto us a child is born . . . his name shall be called Wonderful . . The Prince of Peace.' 'Of the *increase* of His government and peace there shall be no end upon the throne of David to *establish* it with judgment and with justice from henceforth and *forever*.' Surely he must be of dull comprehension who saith this is only the spiritual, heavenly kingdom of the glorified.

"Let us stand for a little under the light of the blazing tongues of Pentecost, enswathed in imagination by the mighty, rushing tide of Spirit manifestation, fresh from the Being of the Almighty. Now listen to Peter, transfigured and illuminated within and without. Error here, with him, was impossible! Untruth at such a time would be a madness like that of the attempted steadying of the ark. Saith Peter: '*David being a prophet knowing that God had sworn to him* that He would raise up Christ to sit on his throne.' Peter at last, a rock of God, I bless thee! Call that arch angel, who doth excel in strength, his name given him in heaven being Gabriel, the 'Champion of God.' He certified his mission to Mary in terms that can be made no finer: '*I am Gabriel, that* STAND IN THE PRESENCE OF GOD *and sent to show thee glad tidings. Thou shalt bring forth a son. And the Lord shall give unto Him the throne of His father David.*' Of His Kingdom there shall be no end. These are 'glad tidings,' indeed, sung as such to the joy and wonder of heaven, as well as proclaimed as the sovereign comfort of earth's inhabiters.

"The splendid, earthly Kingdom outlined so gloriously by the prophets has suffered no syncope, and David's royal line has not found its end in sepulchral palaces. That Kingdom and that line survives; their zenith not yet attained.

"In that zenith day, *Truth shall spring out of the earth, and righteousness shall look down from heaven.*

"So it was settled forever in heaven, for earth and to all eternity, that in the vocabulary of divine wisdom, 'first-born' means 'choice-born.' And he is choice-born no matter how ill his beginning, who is reborn by the all-uplifting, renewing Spirit of Grace! Jesus, in marked manner, even in this respect, parallels David in reäffirming in Himself this law of His refined, exalted kingdom. The line of the Christ from remotest generations is found to have deflected from the line of the first born. His descent must be traced through Seth, Shem, Abraham, Isaac, Jacob, Judah, David, Solomon and Nathan, and still others, none of whom were first in their advent into the families to which they belonged.

Again, the Christ and his progenitor, David, antagonized the barbarian tenet of all ages that a man was to be honored merely because of his gigantesque figure or prowess. In olden times men revered greatly the giantly. Among the primitives to be a weakling was to be pitiable, and to be huge to monstrosity was to be respected, if not actually worshiped. Indeed, paganism in its essence is but homage paid to the great, that is terrible. The princely David began his career in slaying wild beasts and monstrous giants, but we may cease admiring the prowess he had physically in greater admiration of the symbol that lies in his early exploits. He was to be the giant-slayer; evil giants and giant evils were to fall before him alike; and a shepherd's little sling, in pious hands, was shown to be invincible. In Solomon's time, there was more outward splendor, but less spirituality than in David's time. The latter witnessed the gilded decline in its beginnings. Decay followed swiftly. The world sighed for a restoration; the heathen manufactured gods; the Fire Worshipers followed stars; in the groves, virgins were, after a sort, worshiped, as in the forest night-services of the old England of some of you, the Druids prayed to a mystical 'virgin that was to bring forth.' There was a common yearning for the coming of a Champion to lead and defend the races of man. The yearning felt its way blindly toward the wonder to be, that of a woman of the children of men, mothering One all human, all divine, a Prince fit to link together the parts of David's kingdom, whether militant here or triumphant above. That full day has begun, but is only dimly seen by many. You Jews have been wont to keep a Pentecost of males only while Egypt deifies a woman as goddess of the harvest. One turns to brawn, the other to the bringer forth, and neither gets the truth, the royal truth, found in the faith that brings forth through all humanity!

"Would you see a real Pentecost? Now, look how the first was to the fathers. The holy ones, among Christ's followers, believing His promises, assembled at Joseph of Arimathæa's house, to await it. Hear the word:

"And in those days Peter stood up in the midst of the disciples, the number of names together were about a hundred and twenty.

"These all continued with one accord in prayer and supplication, with the women, and Mary the mother of Jesus, and with his brethren."

"Our holy Luke, said to have been an artist, artistically presents the scene. As we read his record, we behold the 'Queen of the House of David,' the representative woman; as she should be, in the company and honor of God's people. Not there as a beautiful creature to be admired; but there to pray with those who prayed for the dawn and the glory. With the genius of an artist, and the insight of a prophet, Luke displays his ideal thus. The Scripture record closes, leaving the typical woman amid God's people, on her knees, waiting in hopefulness for the full dawn; while for a little time over all falls the earnest of the promise in miraculous displays from above. There was a rushing of mighty sounds, the providences of God in motion, the movements of His spirits who minister, for a time made visible! The scene was one never to be forgotten, and the holy John, years after in the glowing visions of the Apocalypse, had brought to his mind its cent.al figure.

the woman clothed with the sun; the transfigured woman, and she as woman in her highest estate; that is mothering a child! He saw her rising above all perils, all evils; but as she rose, she bore aloft her child, a Man Child! Look at the picture, men and brethren, 'till it possesses your souls! BEHOLD THE WOMAN! Behold the interlaced symbols! As a mother holds above peril her child, so the peerless woman held aloft her Divine Babe; as the church holds aloft its offspring, so also in the apotheosis of the ideal mother, comes the uplifting of man's hopes, and the triumph of all that is best, all that is promised. We see to-day, but the smoke side of Pentecost, by and by we'll see, as do those in heaven, its fire side."

The speaker ceased his address, and all were filled with great and moving thoughts.

CHAPTER XXXVII.

THE CORONATION OF THE QUEEN.

> " My knowledge is so weak, oh, blissful queen,
> To tell abroad thy mighty worthiness,
> That I the weight of it may not sustain;
> But as a child of twelve months' old or less
> That laboreth his language to express,
> Even so fare I and therefore pray,
> Guide thou my song which I of thee may say."
> —WORDSWORTH.

F I could only carry to Bethany what I feel now!" ejaculated the young chaplain, as he hurried along from the knights' celebration of Pentecost, homeward, at the time that the Moslems were summoned to evening prayers by the minaret calls.

After his greeting, on arriving at his abode, his first words were: " I've seen the crowns of fire, and now comprehend the meaning of Pentecost, where men gathered from varied climes, heard each the spirit's message in his own tongue! The Spirit is the interpreter!"

" By what aid came this revelation?"

" God and the Hospitaler."

" We have the first here; let us call the other, that the temple on the hill be made to feel the glow. The time is opportune, for each day witnesses new triumphs of our cause."

When the knight arrived a feast was in progress. His air awed those to whom he was a stranger, and there were not a few who thought within themselves:

"Is he a prophet?"

Abruptly, as usual, he began:

"Friends: I would that all hearts here were moved by justice to enthrone the Queen whose praise your frank youths have been sincerely singing. I am here to-day to proclaim her rights, and in so doing I shall appeal to that sure word which survives when all else fails. She was of David's royal line; the noblest one of all the earth. To the proof? The Christian Scriptures, from the hands of Matthew and Luke, present her ancestral descent. These apostles wrote as God directed, and, after all, only reaffirmed that already set forth in the most carefully, religiously guarded records of all antiquity, the Jewish genealogical tables.

"You know that the ancient Jews held those tables in sacred regard, for on their integrity depended the proof of the things to them most dear, as they believed. By them every Jew could trace his Abrahamic descent, and to Abraham's seed were all the great promises of the covenant. By those tables they proved their title to the land of promise, Canaan. Every Jew, believing himself one of God's chosen people, and that his advancement and the advancement of his posterity in the Divine favor, depended on the purity of the blood of both, felt that he needed the guidance of those tables to preserve him from any admixture with alien or Gentile blood. The Aaronic priesthood was hereditary and the priesthood was initial in the religious system of the Hebrews. Its legitimacy was preserved chiefly by these hereditary charters. Then all true Israelites looked for the coming of a Savior, Priest and King to bring to the chosen transcendent glory, and to win an universal dominion, marked by love, joy and peace. Every Jew knew that Great One was to spring from the house of David, and all within that Judaic line hoping that he or his children might be near akin to the One to come, carefully, constantly, proudly guarded and studied these records of descent. Birth was the foundation upon which all Jewish institutions were founded. '*So all Israel was reckoned by genealogies.*' They lived in a reign of blood, and in blood to be Jewishly thoroughbred was, they thought, to be most highly favored. They had not yet discerned the law of the new dispensation, which declares all men akin; a dispensation seeking to build up a superior humanity by first of all transforming and exalting the inner life. By the revered records of these Jewish patriarchs, both holy and love-ladened, place the writings of Matthew and Luke, and with concurrent testimony, unimpeachable as well as conclusive, the legitimacy of Jesus the son of Mary is proven! He was beyond a cavil of David's kingly line. There were Christ-haters who contested at every point His claim of Messiahship. They forged lies freely; they hurled after Him slanders innumerable; they insinuated that He was born in fornication; they affected to flee from Him as one having a devil; they denounced Him to Jewish as well as Roman authorities as a liar, a seducer of men and a traitor. In a word, they howled Him down in every way they could, unabashed by the splendor of His baptismal indorsement, unsilenced by the awful warnings of His cross But in their desperation they never dared to challenge the records which proved Him '*the son of David.*' Now had His claims rested upon His relations to His earthly father, Joseph, they would have been disproven. All Jewry would have quickly, fiercely proclaimed Him a pretender and not in the family of promise. The Christ was heir of David's name and fame because His mother was, and so in exalting Him you crown the saintly woman who bore Him! He was the adopted son of Joseph, type of all His followers, adopted sons of a Royal Father. He was legitimate through his mother, type of all his followers, brought into the royal family of God by the power of a mystic new birth.

"But there is another line running backward, preserved through the centuries to connect the first Adam with this last one. This line runs from Christ through his mother to Eden. Behold the august truth suspended by that chain of names! Names; only names of the dead! names of the forgotten! Jesus by Mary is linked to the chain! It's an old, old chain, but yet it has gems in its links. Each named is the child of another living before, and the history of each is recorded in two words, 'begat,' 'died.' A chain of dust! One man precedes another. Each in turn vanishes until immortality is confronted in the last sentence: '*Adam, who was the son of God!*' The first mortal son of God uncrowned and led away from his kingdom, by a woman, to death! The twain go down together, each ruinous to the other, with nothing left them but a hope; and that hope rested upon a to them mysterious promise: '*The seed of the woman shall crush the head of the serpent!*' It would have staggered their faith had one told them that in God's revenges, all compensating, all healing, she that led down was of the sex that should lead upward. Out of their darkness there came a seeming dawn, and Eve cried ecstatically at the birth of Cain:

"'I have gotten a man from the Lord!'

"They thought he was a token of renewed favor and probably the redeemer from the curse. He turned out a murderer, and introduced them to the supreme horror of humanity—death. The conflict of light and darkness went on, and the first pair tasted death themselves, looking along the horizon of unrealized hopes to the last and waiting, as all their posterity through painful centuries waited, for the Man that was to save. The long years with leaden tread marched on, struggles amid suffering weighty and countless, accompanied the race; of them all woman bore the heavier part, but she kept somehow the larger hope. Each Jewish mother, with a pride of sex secretly cherished, watched and longed for the coming from herself of the ONE who was to lift her up and crown her queen, indeed.

"God at last gathered all woman's trustful hopings into one great answered prayer, and deigning, in sovereign love, His marvelous co-operation, brought forth another and a perfect Adam.

"We are informed that Joseph and Mary went, about the time of Jesus' birth, in compliance with Roman law, to Bethlehem to pay their personal taxes. The Roman tax lists were based upon the records of family descent so far as concerned the Jews.

"To make the collection certain beyond the possibility of any one's escape, the law required each taxable subject to pay his allotted tribute in the city of his nativity. The father and mother of Jesus were cited to the city of David. Thither they went. And so in the providence of God it happened that pagan Rome was summoned to the cradle of the infant Savior and made unwittingly an attester to all time that He was of a family by right recorded among those descended from great David.

"The son and the mother here stand or fall together. If Mary was not of David's line, then the Son she bore was not, and He is left without proof of being of the seed of David.

"Joseph was not the father of the Christ *after the flesh*. The lives of mother and son are eternally intertwined. If we honor one we must needs honor the other; abating the fame of one we degrade the other.

"Jesus' claims to being the Messiah depended upon the fact that His mother was of the tribe and family royal. The absolute requirements of prophecy can only be met in the Messiah by His being of the House of David. Jesus himself admitted and fairly met this necessity. So he questioned the Pharisees: 'What think ye of Christ? Whose son is he?' 'They say unto him, the Son of David.' Admitting this, the Savior propounded the question involving sonship and spiritual unity with God which His questioners could not answer:

"'If David then call him Lord, how is he son?'

"'*Neither durst any man from that day forth ask Him any more questions.*'

"Had He denied the necessity of Davidic origin they could have overwhelmed Him with Scriptures. Had he not been of that family the most ignorant Jew would have promptly rejected His claims to being the Hope of Israel.

"Peter the apostle, amid the soul-trying solemnities of Pentecost, speaking to the representatives of people from all parts of the earth and for all time, cried: 'Men and brethren, let me freely speak unto you concerning the Patriarch David: Being a prophet, and knowing God had sworn with an oath to him that of the fruit of his loins, *according to the flesh*, he would raise up Christ to sit on his throne.'

"This orator spoke then with the accuracy of one in the presence of the Holy Ghost, and not only made sincere, but illuminated, by the torch of God. This is conclusive, but the reiteratives of the inspired writers justify us in presenting their cumulative evidence.

"After Peter comes the learned Hebrew of the Hebrews, Paul; before his conversion to Christianity declaring himself to have been 'afte rthe most straightest sect a Pharisee;' after that conversion, rejoicing to the end of life, as of the true, new Israel by faith in Him that makest all new.

"Twice Paul met Mary's son mysteriously, face to face, within the very confines of Glory. Let Paul speak: 'Paul, a servant of Jesus Christ, separated unto the gospel of God, concerning His Son, our Lord, which was made of the seed of David according to the flesh!'

"Let us not longer make a mock of eternal, holy verities! Christ was of David's flesh through His mother, and born to be a real king of a real kingdom, not a phantom kingdom! That kingdom must come; yea, blessed be Jehovah! it is coming.

"Joseph, the putative father of Jesus, adopted Jesus as his son, but he could not, by that legal act, make his foster son, whose father was the Holy Spirit of the seed of David, *after the flesh!* Jesus received, then, His royal blood from Mary, and bore His Kingly title. after the flesh as '*the crown wherewith his mother crowned Him.*' Revelations harmonize; Luke and Matthew must therefore agree with Paul and Peter.

"The tables of Luke and Matthew agree down to David's time, but then they diverge, until they are converged in Jesus, through the undoubted legitimacy of Mary as a descendant of David and the adoption of Jesus by Joseph, a scion of another branch of the same great family. Luke gives a sentence, all luminous, but first puzzling: '*Jesus himself began to be about thirty years of age, being, as was supposed, the son of Joseph, which was the son of Heli.*' 'Ah, as was *supposed!*' sneers the infidel. 'As was *supposed!* SUPPOSED!!!' hatefully shouts some insinuating, ignorant Jews! But now let us fill out, naturally, Luke's statement, 'as was supposed, the son of Joseph, but in reality the son of Heli.' But here it may be asked, was Jesus the son of Heli? It is, I answer, not infrequently in the Scriptures that a grandson is called a son. Jesus was probably the grandson of Heli. It was a common custom of the Jews, except in cases of especial necessity, not to record the names of women in tracing lines of descent. Men kept the books, and it had become a habit with the lords of creation to thrust woman into the background. Mary was too insignificant a person, socially considered, in her time, to be registered in her own name in the hereditary charters. Joseph was put in her stead, as her representative. There was not any supposition about the descent of Mary, but these scribes, who had charge of the books, thought it were more creditable to the male sex to record Joseph as the father of Jesus, and, by a little fiction, suppose him to have descended through the former from Heli, than to say Mary descended from Heli and Jesus descended from Mary. The Romans encouraged this, and also the politicians. Men were the only ones to fight or pay taxes, and, as political factors, were strictly watched by those in authority. Luke, in reality, gives Mary's line. He was scholarly and accurate, besides that a physician, and we judge by all experience that there is that in the profession of medicine which makes its followers tender toward all suffering, consequently especially tender to women, the largest inheritors of the pains that beset our race. Doctor Luke, like those of his fraternity, by an act of graceful justice, in the spirit of Christianity which is essentially humane, just, and courtly, accorded gladly the woman her place. But the '*doomsday books*' of the Jews, containing their family trees or genealogies, perished with the perishing of the Jewish nation. Those records had done their work; it was time for them to go. They had become by misuse agencies of evil. They stood long enough to demonstrate that God works through cycles vastly wide, and that His definite promise made to Adam, Abraham and many of their successors, had finally been fulfilled, at the end of thousands of years, with a miraculous explicitness. The records disappeared after Christ came, and herein was a providence saying to the watchers: 'He is come. No need further of the patents of His ancestry to aid your watching.' More than that, they being gone, no other could arise claiming to be Shiloh, with hope of convincing any by appeal to proof from the records of ancestry.

"Shiloh and his white kingdom have come. It is

ruling the earth; not in memories of its mighty dead, but by its regal, potent virtues and charities. The battering rams of Titus destroyed wall and Holy Temple, but thus was let in new dawn. Above the storm of that awful conflict the spiritual may discern in living letters the mightly words of God which dispelled disordering darkness from the universe at the beginning: '*Let there be light*,' and, indeed, 'light was.' The obliterated records of Jewish ancestral lines, on which alone many a worthless child of Abraham based his claims to superiority, his right to despise and neglect his fellow men, his justification to tyrannize, and finally his hope of favor with God, ceased to present their sturdy barriers to the entering in of a better hope. Then came in the beginning of this new era ; now the patent of nobility is noble character; this is the time to be marked by an universal recognition of universal brotherhood in a kingdom where there is neither Jew nor Gentile, bond nor free, male nor female. A kingdom where righteousness, impartial justice, liberty, equality, purity and humanity are to be the regnant potencies. In this kingdom, how fittingly, Christ stands as the king and ideal of man, and how fittingly his mother supplements his sway by being presented herself to all womankind as a queenly ideal. Let him or her dispute her title, who can surely say the earth, in this redemption period, needs no such sublime epitome of womanly virtue and worthfulness.

" My words are ended for to-day, assembled men and women. Some of these things spoken may seem like deep sayings, but I leave them to find their lodgment in your hearts and minds. I trust them, knowing that Truth has a sword which cuts her way, each sweep of that sword making light."

CHAPTER XXXVIII.

THE "LIGHT OF THE HAREM" IN "THE TEMPLE OF ALLEGORY."

" Would I had fallen upon those happier days,
And those Arcadian scenes . . .
Vain wish! Those days were never! airy dreams
Sat for the picture, and the poet's hand
Imposed a gay delirium for a truth.
Grant it; I still must envy them an age
That favored such a dream; in days like these
Impossible when virtue is so scarce,
That to suppose a scene where she presides
Is tramontane, and stumbles all belief."
—YOUNG.

"The glory of the Lord came from the way of the east, . .
and the earth shined with His glory. Thou son of man show the
house to the house of Israel, that they may be ashamed of their in-
iquities, and let them measure the pattern."—EZEKIEL, xliii.

"MY Cornelius once said I might expend the fortune coming from my grandfather, Harrimai, as I chose."

"Why, that's so without my saying. I did not court your grandfather, nor his ownings, and have gotten affluence beyond the wildest dreams of a lover in Miriamne's self."

" I think the old church on the hill is smiling day by day, more and more."

"I've noted the improvement, and it assures me our

hearers are growing. A meanly kept sanctuary, witnesses of starved worshipers. Some churches might be called stables for all-devouring, nothing-giving, lean kine."

"I'd like to be brought to confession; question me!"

"Question? I can not doubt either Miriamne or her doings; to question, one must doubt."

"Sir Courtly! But I'll flank your courtesy; I've purchased and furbished up the old ecclesiastical pile."

"I might have guessed it was Miriamne's work! Now, good Bishop of Bethany, appoint me Rector."

"Churchman forever! We'll have no Rector."

"No Rector? No sermons? No congregation?"

"We'll have a multitude, if we can get into the place the God-shine; that brightens and draws ever."

"Allurement by light! A new device. Are we to have a tryst where lotus-dreamers may take sun-baths?"

"Curiosity, too proud to question directly, travels around with banterings."

"Incisive Miriamne, my ægis, thin as paper, is shredded: I confess!"

"Confession compels pardon and counsel. I'll give both. The restored sanctuary is to be the capitol of our fraternity, the '*Sisters of Bethany.*'"

"Capitol? Are you inviting the Sultan to take your homes and your heads? A capitol sounds like politics, revolution and things governmental."

"There is to be war and a revolution; our munitions are to be solely moral agencies; our aim, to revolve the world around toward Paradisiacal days. I'd have parting streams flow out from Bethany to water the earth, and sing anew the jubilant strains of Pison, Gihon, Hiddekel and Euphrates."

"Arcadia! Alas, how sad such dreams, because so impossible to realize. The Arcadians, so charming in the poet's pictures, were, in fact, very warlike, very loutish, very human."

"Say not that what has been must always be. Moses, at a time when Israel was at its lowest dip, received of God a pattern of the Tabernacle. The God of Moses is unchangeable. I've gotten from Him a pattern, also."

"And now I question, as you wish!"

"The old sanctuary is to be a '*Temple of Allegory.*' We shall attempt therein to picture the finest truths by symbols that shall make them tangible and irresistible."

"A splendid ambition! Possess me of your intricacies of canon and catechism. I'd accept them."

"You overlook our simplicity by expecting complexity. We shall not walk like ghosts, hampered by the grave-clothes of the dead, though august forms. Seven words, enough for each day of the round week, are our whole profession; '*Humanity toward humanity, with godliness toward God.*'"

As they conversed, they walked toward the old sanctuary at the suburbs of Bethany, and now were drawing near it.

"Behold, Miriamne, the Hospitaler; yonder."

"Yes, I've called the knights hither; the Hospitaler will dedicate our temple to-day."

"But has he ecclesiastical authority so to do?"

"The same authority that these growing shrubs and vines have to make the place beautiful. See, I've pierced the walls of the grim pile, wherever I could, to make a window. The Hospitaler is to take them for a theme."

"Windows for themes?"

"He is able; and understands by them that we'd have let into musty beliefs floods of sweet light."

"The knights are singing!"

"Yes, the Grail song, '*Faint though pursuing*;' the dedication has commenced."

The words sung recited the grail quest; but its chorus, a simple one, was much the same as that sung at the May-day festivities on a former occasion. The people gathered, heartily joined in the chorus. When the singing ceased, the Knight, in his usual abrupt manner, began addressing the assembly:

"The beloved young missioners have undertaken, by means of their handiwork here, to strikingly present the noblest truths, and they have taken a step in the right direction. Love for the pictorial, manifest especially in children, grows with growth; those adult needing and seeking, as they grow, finer, grander symbols. Our Divine Lord, who '*knew men*' and '*knew* what was in man,' did not rebuke, but rather utilized this taste of man, by teaching the profoundest things of His Kingdom by means of it. He came as close as close could be to the very core of human life, as it was or to all time will be. While He might have navigated Galilee in a palatial barge, borne over be-flowered waves by perfumed breezes and golden wings, with the aureoled spirits, '*who do excel in strength*,' by thousands, to escort Him, He chose rather to journey in an all-winning humility, borrowing, as He had need, the old boat of some poor Tiberian fisherman. He might have entered Jerusalem, that last time, in an Elijah-like chariot, dazzling the city with splendors surpassing those that the rapt John beheld on Patmos ; but the King of Glory, seeking to be the King of all men, elected in that supreme moment to get near to men by approaching the august courts of Herod and Caiphas, and the commons as well, on an ass—an humble beast, and borrowed at that. All this allegorized the condescension and sympathy of Jehovah. The universe is full of patterns! The books of Nature, Revelation, and Providence, having a common authority, are constant in the use of pictured truth. Nature gives us the dawning of light and the mar-

shaling of order out of darkness and chaos. There is the
low earth, the high firmament, ripe summer going down into
the winding sheets of winter and up to the resurrections
of spring. Twig, flower, seed, forest; insect that creeps,
and bird that flies; the speck-life moved, and the behemoth; the atom and the planet-system — waning and
growing, dying and living, from formlessness to beauty, from
time to eternity! Then take the inspired picture-history:
Eden's fall, Egyptian captivity, the Red Sea passage, the
wilderness, the manna by the way, the rest by the Mount of
the Law, the entrance to the Promised Land. Lastly, the
Incarnate One, an eternal symbol, the realization and fulfillment of all preceding. 'Which things are an allegory,' exclaimed Paul, with a sweeping back-look. The three books
present to the thoughtful pictured banners innumerable, to
wave him onward. This temple is dedicated to the purpose
of pointing to these pictures. Fitly the 'angels of the
mount' have determined to make prominent the beautiful,
patient, modest Mary, Mother of Jesus. And to study her
intelligently or profitably, it is necessary to know her not only
as an historical personage, but as one in the cavalcade of
symbolism unfolded by Sacred Writ and by Nature. She
passes by, herself every way unique, the exemplar of God to
those aspiring after gentle, devout girlhood, pure and wise
maiden-life, constant wifehood, and patient, consecrated,
and influential motherhood. Turn again to the Divine
Word, the beacon of the ages, the history of Providence, the solver of life's problems. It is made up of
an entrancing array of symbols, types, prophetic dramas,
and gorgeously constructed visions, constantly representing
or dextrously pointing, by countless trophies and allegories, to its Ideal and Darling, Mary's Son, *who 'spoke as
man never spake, yet who without a parable spake nothing.'*
Though the literary ages are strewn with long winrows of
dead books, no work of man long surviving the mutations
of time, God's picturesque handiwork, the inspired volume,
as potently molds the thoughts, charms the affections and
quickens the hopes of our race with its tokens, types, idyls
and illustration as it did when the earth was younger by far
than it is now. It is a living fountain, not only giving, but
retaining its immortality! It abides because it masterfully
deals with the things that pertain to the wonderland of the

soul. How necessary its methods is at once apparent to any one who considers, discerningly, man as a complex union of spirit and matter; wonderful forever, but '*very good*,' since the All Holy, Great High Priest performed the nuptial ceremony of that union. If there could be found a being able to reason, as a man, who had not within himself this unity, and who had never experienced its phenomena, such would at once combat the possibility of its existence. Even those so organized, and momentarily realizing the jointure of the God-like spirit with the earthly body, the higher condescending to and communing with the inferior, the inferior at times over-persuading, dominating and utterly shipwrecking its great spiritual co-partner, are compelled to admit the whole as being a fact without parallel, alike inscrutable and bewildering. A life-time of profoundest introspection can carry the greatest mind, herein, only to the confines of new wonders. But the interest in the study of the unwritten, unvoiced language of symbolisms by which the wonderfully united twain, soul and body, confer and commune with each other deepens with the study. What a fine, expressive, rapid, exact, exalted language that must be! To each well understood; without their arcana unknown, unheard, incomprehensible. And it is of necessity all symbol, natural, intuitive, without a single arbitrary sign! This sign-language acts by *symbol* in the royal temple of memory and imagination. And so again we perceive the representative, picturesque or typical is the medium of the fine, the deep and the lofty in expressing truth. This is the soul's language, by which it communes with whatever else there is in man, through which it receives the songs of Heaven, and the august or tender messages of the Spirit, out of the deathless land.

"When this sphere of ours was rolling swiftly onward through the shadows of night, as well as swiftly downward through darker shadows of sin, Divine love said 'Let there be light.' Then the hosts of heaven saw at Bethlehem a mother and babe marking the place of world-dawn, unfolding the design of Deity to effect redemption by touching the race of man at infancy; the most effective because the most plastic point; through motherhood the most influential because the tenderest instrumentality. The never-to-be-forgotten spectacle thrilled, with a new ecstasy, the beings of glory whose every throb of life is joy. They tracked the heavens about with light as they sped out to keep abreast the fleeing earth and shout over Bethlehem, 'Glad tidings! Glad tidings!' They saw Eden restored through the advent of a new, pure home; they saw a mystic covenant between God and man typified in the child begotten of a human mother in conjunction with the Eternal Father. By this there seemed to be an attesting that humanity was to be raised to Divine favor; there also was a symbol showing the value of law; for through the incarnation, Deity, in the form of a babe, became submissive to law administered by a mortal mother.

"He is blind who can not see in all these things God's purpose to elect some of His creatures to be His co-laborers in the choicest co-operations, and also to be exemplars of what He does and would do. These things being so, we do well to learn the alphabet of His goodness from His elect heroes, heroines and saints; and I proclaim to-day my innermost belief in Christ as the argument, logic and fruit of God's love; but, at the same time, I praise, as one enravished, the character of her who was God's poem, God's peroration! We now proclaim this temple dedicated to the purposes of showing forth the things I have spoken."

The Hospitaler abruptly ceased his address, as he began it. There were other services consisting of psalm-singing and prayers, and the service was ended.

As the congregation dispersed, the young missioner, Cornelius, exclaimed: "Miriamne, the Hospitaler has awakened me as from sleep by God's truth. Oh, the heavens are not as full of shining stars as God's truth is full of beauty' It seems strange that men like myself, and wiser, are so long in bringing these things to their minds. You, my dear little mystic, are my interpreter.

"It's just as I told you, wife. We must go in pairs. In the Egyptian mythologies, Osiris had his Isis, Amen-Ra his Maut, and Kneph his Sate. Thank God I have my adolescent other self!"

"I, a woman, help you? My sex is honored by the praise. Are they worthy of all they need? Is it madness to seek to gather all women having gifts and needs into a helped and helping fraternity whose creed is a fine example? If I help Cornelius, can not a peerless one like Mary help all?"

"Pardon the thought, but one word haunts me—idolatry!"

"Impossible! We all need soul company, and have room within for such. We must have an inner population of real heroines and heroes or be filled with ghosts and myths. The empty soul, eaten up with self-worship, goes mad; the myth-possessed becomes an idolater. If we harbor the God-like, keeping the highest place for Deity, our inner selves will be no hideous chambers of imagery, but a counterpart of heaven."

"But some have fallen into putting Mary before Jesus, and so we've seen the advent of Mariolatry."

"But this only, and surely, here I know, no friend of the Divine Son can dethrone Him by honoring her, aright; indeed, as He, Himself, did. It was of Him she spoke when exclaiming: '*My soul doth rejoice in God my Savior!*' Can one truly honor Him and despise and ignore the woman who gave Him human birth? Can one have His mind and forget her for whom love was uppermost to Him in His supreme last hours? Can one honor her aright, and yet dethrone the Son whom she enthroned? She bore Him, then lived for Him. She honored herself in bearing Him, and was His mother, His teacher and His disciple. He revered her, she worshiped Him. Awed by His augustness, she was yet conscious of an ownership of

His greatness; believing in His divinity, she yet enjoyed the nearness to Him of a mother.

"I can not but believe that she is a queen, indeed, high among the glorified who reign with God! I question again: Who ever did, or could, become heretic or carnal by sincerely revering the peerless woman whom Christ enthroned on His heart?"

"I know at least that the fathers at imperial and pagan Rome placed a representation of Mary in their Pantheon when public policy made it an imperative necessity to overthrow the influence of the lewd, fanciful and ungodly ideals that had been set up therein," responded Cornelius.

"The world is a Pantheon full of corrupt ideas. Let us raise high the choice ones God has sent us—But see, yonder is the wife of a poor old Druse camel-driver. She was once a sinner in the streets of Jerusalem. Now she is a Sister of Bethany, allured to goodness by our Temple's allegories!"

"A woman that was a sinner, a scarlet woman?"

"Only such. No; all of that! One woman; a lost one? How little to man; how much to God! Had nothing else been done, heaven would have been set singing, as ever, over a sinner's return. That's reward enough for all we've attempted."

"Now I'm interested, indeed!"

"Well you may be, when you hear all. We've here one once a harem beauty, who, having lost her power to fascinate, was committing her life to that hag-cunning belonging to old women who supplement their decaying power by wickedness, fox-like and serpentine."

"The old, old story; yet I thank God if her life be sweetened."

"Hers is a strange story."

"May I know it?"

"Yes; it is, as I've gathered it in scraps, a sad romance. She was born of Georgian parents, among the mountains of Armenia, and gifted, in her youth, as are most of those of her sex in that country, with unusual personal beauty. She early attracted the attention of the monsters who dealt in human flesh, and a Georgian noble unrighteously claiming her family as his serfs, bartered away Nourahmal to merchants seeking recruits for Mameluke harems. She became, in time, part of the retinue of a sheik by the name of Azrael, a desperate adventurer, who, on account of his blood-deeds, was called by his followers the 'Angel of Death.' His luxurious and desperate way of living justified his claim to Turkish extraction; his adroitness and avidity for intrigue stamped him as a Mameluke."

"Nourahmal? Azrael? Why, these must be the same of whom I've heard Sir Charleroy speak?' queried Cornelius.

"The same!"

"She comes out of the past as one from the dead!"

"And her story is a series of strange events. It is as follows: Azrael suspected her of having abetted the escape of my father and Ichabod, therefore determined to kill her. She gained a temporary respite through having saved her master's life from an assassin plotting to supplant him; though she periled her own in so doing.

"As Azrael awaited her recovery from the wounds she had suffered in his behalf, he devised another scheme which he hoped would compass his favorite's destruction and his own elevation. He was ambitious to be Sherif of Mecca. To attain that honor he saw he must needs do something to enhance his popularity greatly with his Mohammedan followers, and so conceived the plan of getting into his power, Harrimai of the Jews and Adolphus of the Christians. His purpose was to rack those two leaders into apostasy and the betrayal of their followers. Had he succeeded, the event would have been crushing to Jews and Christians east of Jordan. He promised Nourahmal her freedom and restoration to her Georgian home if she aided him in his design; though he did not disclose his purpose to her beyond that of securing the presence of Von Gombard and Harrimai in his camp. She felt that there was some malign, hidden purpose in her master's breast, but deemed it expedient, at the outset, to seem to co-operate in his plan."

"But how was the sheik using his strategy against Nourahmal?"

"As a fiend! He, having no conception of a friendship between a man and a woman that was pure and free from intrigue, suspected the relations between his favorite and Ichabod. He thought the two only needed the opportunity to precipitate into perfidy. He laid his plan darkly, and, leaving a trusty follower to carry it out, hastened forward to Mecca."

"But surely, Nourahmal was not what he thought her!"

"No; though training her as a plastic child, he judged she was what he had tried to make her; at her worst she was. But let me continue. The assault on my parents and Ichabod, on the road between Gerash and Bozrah, was the opening of the drama. The plan then was to seize Rizpah, and under pretense of negotiating for her ransom, inveigle Harrimai into the hands of Azrael's followers. Nourahmal was to aid in this by affecting tears, pleading for pity and suggesting the sending for the girl's father."

"What besetments perilous we pass through, all unknown to us! Harrimai and your parents, to their death, never suspected the devices worked against them!"

"Nor dreamed that a harem favorite, a mere girl, and an utter stranger to them, was their good angel!"

"Good angel! How?"

"She witnessed the assault from behind a sequestering wall, in company with a follower of the sheik, commissioned to kill her instantly if she faltered in the part appointed her. This infernal guard was also charged to insinuate into her mind the feasibility of elopement with Ichabod. If she could be compromised, Azrael knew he could justify her death to those who remembered her heroic defense of himself. That was to follow as soon as she had done her part in inveigling Harrimai to Azrael's camp."

"A demonstration of a personal devil, Miriamne."

"I'd say rather of an overruling God."

"How fared Nourahmal after Azrael's chagrin?"

"Cornelius anticipates me. When she saw Ichabod fall, a sudden desire for liberty for herself and to help the imperiled Rizpah, prompted her to drive a dagger into the heart of her guard and cry, 'Rescuers come!' That cry drove the remnants of the assailers of Sir Charleroy to sudden flight. She asserted to the fugitives that Laconic, the new runner, just passing, had slain her guard, and so allayed suspicion until opportunity of escape came. She soon made her way to Bozrah, where she found among the Christians a temporary home. From thence she drifted into Jerusalem."

"'Twas strange she did not turn toward Gerash."

"I said as much to her, but desire to get as far as possible from Azrael, and as near as possible to the Holy City, of which Ichabod had so glowingly spoken to her, determined her course; besides that, Ichabod being dead, Gerash was a strange place to her—Jerusalem seemed to her, she said, near heaven."

"Had she only known it, she was near heaven in Bozrah, being near Von Gombard."

"Her story weaves a chaplet for his tomb to-day; for now it appears that from Nourahmal the old priest foreknew the intention of those Saracens, who assailed the city that day I was with him. Though they designed capturing him to put him on the rack, he rushed into the conflict, crying, 'Kill the foe with kindness!' The assault would have been fatal to Bozrah, too, had not the leader of one of the invading bands ordered a retreat, just at the point of victory. This was indirectly Nourahmal's work; for that leader had been won by her to esteem Christians far enough to be unwilling to murder them, though not adverse to plundering them. That was a great improvement in a Mohammedan."

"And Nourahmal knows from you that you are Sir Charleroy's daughter?"

"Yes, by that I won her confidence. Indeed, she began this confidence at first, by saying, 'I love you, because you so remind me, angel of the mount, of a Christian knight, who was the dear friend of the only pure and unselfish man I knew in all my youth! Such words led to questions and explanations. The rest you know."

"And you have allured, comforted and enlightened her?"

"By God's help, I have. I have told her of the universal sisterhood of all women, who take as their exemplar the worthy mother of the One who proclaimed the universal brotherhood of man. This knowledge is her joy and inspiration. When I am with her, she never tires of hearing of the 'Queen of David's House,' the mother of mothers."

"But how have you allured her hither, Miriamne?"

"You have questioned curiously with your eyes, at least, concerning those gated alcoves and curtained balconies in our Temple of Allegory. They helped her!"

"Since you say they are not 'Confessionals,' as I call them, tell me what they are?"

"'Rock clefts' our sisterhood calls them; some are doors to little adjacent chapels; some are quiet resting places, where, in impressive solitude, souls in prayer may find the mountain manna, for which the Savior sought in many a lone night-watching; and some are places where are presented, under entrancing symbols, exalting truths."

"Words have failed to turn the world to faith; may signs do better."

"I've put truth into visible form, that they who get it here may learn that truth thus is only up to its full might. I'd have my followers believe in visible, not phantom, truth; so believing, truth will not be a ghostly proclamation, the toy of the mind, but a force moving hands and hearts!"

"And you have met Nourahmal's case?"

"Yes; fully in what we call the 'Lover's Bower,' yonder. Remember she has been the victim of mock love, from first to last."

"The 'Lover's Bower'?"

"Behold the trophy and the bower! There is Nourahmal, now rapturously contemplating the picture of Joseph putting the ring of espousal on the hand of the Virgin Mary."

"Nourahmal? That gray-haired, hard-faced woman, holding the hand of a charming girl?"

"That is Nourahmal; the younger woman is Beulah, her grand-daughter; they two are almost inseparable now."

"An oleander by a limestone cliff! And so she takes her station by a scene of betrothal, forgetting that hymen's altars can be fired by youth alone!"

"The world says so; but yet a disappointed life may sometimes learn why it has been a failure, by studying the ashes of time gone in the light of quickened memories."

"What finds Nourahmal there?"

"Golden lessons. First for her grand-daughter, her idol. She never tires of saying before yon picture to that maiden now her charge: 'My flower, my lamb, be always as pure as the espoused of Joseph, and you will be a jewel which your husband, if he be a true man, will ever proudly wear on as his heart, My flower, my lamb, no woman should leave all for any man, unless she is certain of finding in him father, mother, brother, sister, companion, as Mary found in Joseph!'"

"But how did these things bless Nourahmal herself?"

"Love counterfeited, blasted her life. She believed that it was only gross passion masquerading in attractive, delusive colors. So believing, it was difficult to tell her of the Love of God so she could realize its wealth. Love was only great selfishness, excited and persistent, to her mind. It was something to teach her that the genuine affection was utterly otherwise; in fact the foundation and crown of all the noblest sentiments implanted by God in His choicest creations.

"I have sought to allegorize here, true affection in all its perfection. It seems to be fitting to do so, for my ideal queen was ruled by it. She never could have loved to the depths she did, as a mother, if she had not had within her being all the possibilities of woman's love. And in a rightly balanced woman love is all-impressive, all-controlling; with her worship is loving and loving is worship. Here I shall seek to refine that sentiment in the hearts of my sisters until each becomes an evangel in its behalf. Then mankind will understand the wealth a woman bestows on the man that wins her. There is nothing in her career that surpasses it, except that sovereign act wherein she lays herself a convert on God's altar. I am seeking to exalt this sacred act, the loving of the gentler sex, until all men, brought to revere it as they ought, shall become true knights; until society shall be of one mind in crying traitor to every man that contemns it in wedlock, and ready to lash naked around the world every betrayer who awakens it in innocency to lead it astray."

"I can only again exclaim, oh! how full of flowers and honey is my Miriamne's creed and gospel!"

"And the churchman so exclaims because I've put love where God put it, at the front of religion's cohorts!

Can there be a religion worth the name that does not masterfully meet the requirements of the relations most sacred between human beings?"

As she spoke she led her husband under the splendid painting of Joseph espousing Mary, toward the entrance of the bower, remarking: "This vestibule, from the Roman word Vesta, Goddess of Purity, is suggestive. Rome placed Vesta among the household gods, and was wont to have an altar at every outer door. If Purity guard the door, Light and Love will dwell within. See the laurel, emblem of victory, as the ancients put it by Purity's altar; so do I. Love, when pure, is all-victorious!"

"Miriamne, these old truths seem to me very charming as you now present them; but can Nourahmal and others like her enter into their meaning?"

"A pious saint of our church says that the star which guided to Bethlehem finally sank into a spring, where it may be yet seen by women if they be pure."

As they thus communed he passed through an arched doorway, and was admitted to a grand court, three sides of which were inclosed by the temple and two of its wings, the fourth side hedged by palms, vine-interlaced. The sky was the roof, the carpet the floor of that country. Just in front of the palm-hedge, on a grassy hillock, conspicuous beyond all else, was a colossal stone face. It seemed as if it had emerged from the earth, bald of all life—desolation expressed in mute stone.

"Astarte here!" exclaimed Cornelius.

"Yes; that's part of my Bashan inheritance, from Kunawat, the land of Job."

"A woman and a devil beset him; (the two are in this

face, methinks). Its hideousness, as its import, seems inappropriate in Love's Bower."

"Yes, 'tis hideous now, though once the face had beauty. It is not futile for young-love to remember that time gouges deformity into beautifulness, nor for all to remember how the Kings of the East in Moses' time overthrew the Rephaim, the fallen giant followers of the goddess. The East is the home of light, and light is fateful to evil lives. Where are the Astarte-devotees now?"

As the man listened his eyes wandered to the place where the palm grove came up against the temple wing, and there he observed a purling ribband of water.

"Cornelius sees my poem of silver. It comes from a grove of cedars and sharon roses, out of a spring in the bosom of a hill. Look the other way. It passes under the alcove, under the temple wall; a short, dark passage brings it to liberty, ending in the Virgin's Pool of Kidron. The sun allures it up to the clouds at last. But listen; it sings as it runs!"

"I hear many blending melodies."

"Do you see that canopied dais? There the instructor, or preacher if you will, stands. The stream passes near it, getting impulse by a fall; true love is speeded when it runs by truth. That's my lesson. Then there are Æolian harps this side and that of the dark alcove, the latter the type of the tomb."

"But why?"

"True love has music both sides of the grave."

"Mystic!"

"Interpreter, say."

"But I hear the songs of birds?"

"There they are, this side the dark exit; but in a

cage, supported above the current by an hour-glass and sickle."

"Grim emblems."

"Yes; but it's a grim truth that love's joy notes here are caged, hampered and transitory. The hour-glass and sickle are, when those notes are sung, ever.

"Look to the West."

"I look, and see nothing but the picture of a sunset."

"Yes, and that curtains the 'Rest of the Aged' in our temple."

"But whither am I led by these words?"

"Led to look toward sunset, for morning, by faith. You remember the Christ was never old; neither are they who draw their life from Him. The 'Ancient of Days' not only has, but gives, eternal youht. Oh, there were young men at His sepulcher; yet those angels could count their years by centuries! Let the hour glass make record and the sickle reap; the passion flower recalls a vernal life, where the oldest saints are the youngest, where all existence is growth, refreshment, glory, exultation! There, love is law and law is love, and to love is to live and to live is to love. We get a breath of this life here as we enter the vicinage of the immortal pair, Jesus and Mary; and we get a distant view of the whole from the mountains of the gospel."

"I believe, and yet sometimes start back at the question, 'What if, after all, at the end almost of eternities there come monotony, decadence, satiety— death?' Next after hell, and nigh as horrible, is annihilation; and worst of all, eternal existence with nothing for which to strive—a living death!"

They say, that in Egypt, a palm bowed to give shade to the mother, Mary; while the aspen refused to her any comfort. Then Christ blessed the palm and it became the fruitful evergreen, while the aspen leaf is fated to the end of time by constant tremblings to betoken the agues of a cursed life. But, under the sun in submission, our aspen lives are turned to palms! We, having His life, need never tremble at death, for we shall ever throb with a loving like His."

"But there are many conditions and needs to womankind. Let us speak of these, since the present is hers, the future God's."

"The knights vainly tried swords; my King promised to draw all men to Himself. You told me how Sir Galahad, the pure knight, had made, about the Holy Grail, when he found it, a chest of precious stones and gold. Now, I've found the virgin pattern of perfection, representative of the human-like beating heart of God. Here I've set her, exalted her. This shall be her golden precious palace. Though dead, here shall be presented in the grandeur of her character, the sweetness of her power. By and by, it may come about that all mankind akin, shall make it the chief duty of Church and State, to care, with a loyal tenderness, for all women, all children, from first and last; that not one such shall be left miserable. That will be the world obeying the Crucified's, 'Behold thy mother.'"

CHAPTER XXXIX.

CROWN JEWELS.

"The VIRGIN MARY unquestionably holds forever a peculiar position among all women in the history of redemption. Perfectly natural, yea, essential to a sound religious feeling, it is to associate with Mary, the fairest traits of maidenly and maternal character, and to revere her as the highest model of female love and power."
—PROF. PHILIP SCHAFF'S *Church History.*

"THERE'S a footman at the door; the good man that talks, I think; he would speak with Cornelius."

With such words, at sunrise one morning a few weeks after the May-day service, the missioners of Bethany were aroused by an attendant. Quickly robing himself, the young chaplain went forth, and, sure enough, the Hospitaler stood before him.

"Selamet; but what haste brings our ever-welcome friend so early?"

"To relieve your minds! I've purchased immunity! The Mameluke sheik, at Jerusalem, has secured the Sultan's revocation of the order of razing and banishment," answered the knight. Cornelius gazed at the Hospitaler with anxiety, questioning within himself as to whether the knight had taken leave of his reason or not.

The abrupt soldier-priest perceiving the perplexity of his hearer broke forth: "Why the edict that the

Temple on the hill be despoiled, and the 'Angels of the Mount' be summarily driven out of Syria, has been rescinded; the 'Faithful,' as those infidels style themselves, have been converted; seen a great light which came by mighty gold."

"All Saints defend us! I did not hear of this. Tell me all!" exclaimed Cornelius.

"Not now; the peril is past. I knew it was impending sometime, and supposed ye did. I promised a reward, if time were given. I got money help from foreign knights. The vandals took it with a mighty thirst, and then with a great show of piety promised toleration."

"I see, as usual with them, great gain with godliness is contentment; but what are we on the mount to do?"

"Go on; the Sultan isn't God, nor his sheik the Devil."

"The Hospitaler comforts. Now let us enter and breakfast together, that we may get wisdom by conferring."

"I may not tarry longer; I staid all night without the city's wall so as not to be delayed by awaiting the gate-opening. I must be with my companions by the time the Moslems have ended their first prayers, or my comrades will be alarmed. I'll return to-morrow."

Another dawn, another noon, and another sunset, came and went; but the knight did not reappear at Bethany. The chaplain vainly tried to suppress his anxiety. He feared some treachery on the sheik's part. Again and again the former went to the housetop to look along the Jerusalem road. It was a hot June day; the watchings flushed the young man's face but fears' rigors in the heart paled it. He was a picture of misery. Darkness followed sunset; then came tidings:

"There's a company with garlands and torches coming around the bend!"

The news was brought by a company of Sisters of Bethany. The missioner was excited, yet reasoned:

"Garlands and torches! Their bearers can not have baleful report nor evil designs."

The visitants quickly arrived, and singing a roundelay, encircled the house of Cornelius and Miriamne. With delight the latter recognized the Hospitaler and his companion knights. With them were a number of the friends of the new movement at Bethany. They also observed, standing by his camel, a little aloof, a tall, gaunt man, garbed as a Druse; by him, an elderly woman, and also a maiden.

"'Tis Nourahmal and her grand-child!" whispered Miriamne, following her husband's questioning eyes.

"The maiden wears the flower crown of a bride, and see, there is a young man by her side!"

The Hospitaler interrupted their converse:

"I've kept my promise to the 'Angels of the Mount' and to God. I'm here, and to celebrate a proper thanksgiving!"

"Welcome! Now command us," exclaimed Miriamne. "Yea, welcome, though coming in mystery!"

"Another surprise, good chaplain? Well, 'tis fitting, since this one is cheering. There was need of offset to thy painful astonishment of yesterday. I've trapped a wolf for our festivities."

"A wolf!" exclaimed Miriamne.

"Yes, even the shiek. He swore that he'd make

all Bethany bald by fire and sword if it were attempted here to establish a Christian church. To him I explained that the work on the hill was festal. Praise God, it is to be such, to all eternity! And Miriamne's disavowal of the title church, the use of the appellations 'Pool of Bethesda,' 'House of Mercy,' 'Temple of Allegory,' and the like, by your followers in the city, concerning your place of gathering, helped the righteous diversion. I finished the argument by parading with my cortege, as you see us now. Indeed I even asked the sheik to come to the wedding!"

"A wedding?"

"The cruel sheik invited?"

"Two questions and two questioners to be answered with more surprises. Nourahmal's grand-daughter, Beulah, is to be joined to a Jewish convert! I asked the sheik to attend with us as one of her next akin; for I believe him to be a son of Azrael, though he denies that parentage, as well he may, since the 'Angel of Death' was strangled at Bagdad for treason. Be assured, Miriamne, the young Mohammedan will not be present at our ceremonies to-night!"

"Will wonders never cease?" spoke Cornelius, at a loss to know what to say.

"No. Let us be going now," abruptly spoke the Hospitaler.

"Do you return to the city so soon?" queried Miriamne.

The question was answered indirectly:

"Let's to the temple, or 'House of Bethesda.' I've taken the liberty to order its illumination. Come, we'll see how its jasmines climb on its sturdy walls by the light of the torches kindled for hymen!"

So saying, the Hospitaler turned in the direction mentioned, and all, including the missioners, followed him. The scene was fairy-like. There were lights and flowers and songs. The feasters from Jerusalem were in holiday attire, and those of the villagers that joined in the concourse were hearty participants in the festivities.

Arriving at the temple, the Hospitaler led Beulah toward the speaker's dais.

"Will not the camel-driver enter?" questioned the knight of a companion.

"No; he's half way back to the city by this time."

"Stand by thy other self," said the knight to the Jewish groom.

The latter obeyed with alacrity; his zeal and his bashfulness precluding grace of action.

"Four hands clasped; crossed," said the Hospitaler.

The twain did as commanded, the youth with avidity, the maid with a timorous, modest reserve. The touch of each, electric to the other, was recorded in their faces, over which passed rapidly a poem of emotion. The audience became silent, hushed by admiration akin to adoration. The old, old, yet ever new, ever-entrancing spectacle of love's full crowning, brought to all minds the splendor and holiness of that royal gift which finds in earth its completest unfoldment in wedlock. Each of the auditors, conscious of admiration of the presentment, was also conscious of self-approving. There is a cleansing of conscience like that which follows prayer in the act of heartily approbating the thing which is good and beautiful. With the espoused for his inspiration and his background of light, the Hospitaler, with his usual abruptness, began addressing the assembly:

"You of the East hear best when your eyes are treated together with your ears, hence I speak at this time, most propitious, of themes pertinent. You have heard how the ancient Romans named this month, deemed by them favorable to marriage, Junonius, in honor of their chaste and prudent goddess of conjugal life. She was the *Hera* of the Greeks, the only lawfully wedded goddess of all their mythologies. The myths prove that those pagans discerned the potency and beauty of holy wedlock. They polished jewels and wove girdles for its personifications, and to-night, in this temple dedicated to womanhood at her best, I'd take the girdle and crown and place them upon the Queen of Women, the peerless Virgin. For such a real woman the ancients were seeking when they had their dream of the myths. She was what they yearned for, and her exaltation as the representative of all that she truly did represent, will be found of lasting profit to all. Behold her, an orphan girl, yet by faith having an Eternal Father. As a girl, abhorring waywardness; as a woman, therefore, free from wantonness. Mark me, ye maidens, the wayward becomes the wanton. Coquetry brushes the down from the cheek of the peach, and she that frivolously plays with passion in the morning will be likely to seek the groves of Astarte at noon. Our ideal woman reached maidenhood's roses all portionless, as world-help is counted, but with the inestimable affluence of prudence, constancy and purity. Thus she set the finest youths of all Jewry to striving for her heart and hand. What Juno was to Rome, Mary was to Israel. The Romans proclaimed their faith in the good wife as the producer and conserver of wealth by putting their mint in their temple of '*Juno-Moneta.*' The carpenter of Nazareth, building up a clean, honest, though humble home, by the aid of his consort, built more enduringly, and presents a finer historical figure, than that once mighty, once wise Solomon; though the latter erected the wondrous Temple. The home and love of Joseph and Mary will be praised by the ages that abhor the ivory houses of pleasure of the great and fallen king. The story of that home life at Nazareth has not been written, and we must gather it from fragments and eloquent silence. Mary's jewels as a wife were unostentatiously treasured within the four walls of her domicile. The devastating tornado leaves enduring, though hateful history; but the constant, man-blessing tides of the ocean come and go without having their recurring blessings recorded. So the constant, loyal, patient woman of Nazareth passed noiselessly by in her day. Her exclamation to the Angel of the Annunciation, '*Behold the handmaid of the Lord, be it unto me according to thy word*,' was the keynote of that life ever enhanced by the beauty of duty. There was submission to right because it was righteous. And this was not mere passiveness. You remember how she challenged her Son in His early youth, that time He was absent for a season from His parents, at first without explanation? The words Mary spoke that day burn like polished gems when considered aright: '*Why hast thou dealt thus with us? Behold, thy father and I have sought thee, sorrowing.*' She did not forget her Son's divine origin, but exalted the rights of motherhood and fatherhood, confident that even Deity could not ignore them. She challenged the right of a son to cause parental sorrow without instant strong reason for so doing. She put her husband's cause before her own, and made his honor her sacred wifely trust. There are in this history some very fine things expressed by implication. We know the woman was beautiful and much younger than her husband; the disparity of years did not hinder full affinity. She did not fall into the weakness of feeling self-sufficient and all-complacent because feeling pretty. All she was and all she had was centred in her consort as a commonwealth between him and her. That the sycophant and flatterer crossed her path there can be no doubt; but she who was not intoxicated by Bethlehem's *gloria in excelsis* could not be dazzled by the honeyed words of mortals. Wearing such a wife on his heart, Joseph was rich indeed. Silence is once more eloquent. We know that the mother of Jesus, having been widowed, never wed again. Her first love suffered no eclipse. That she was courted, after her spouse's death, we must believe. The mother of a Son so famous as was hers, and the possessor of personal charms enshrining a soul that knew how to utilize sorrows until they became refinements, doubtless had many suitors in her widowhood days. And there was no law forbidding her a second marriage, except the unwritten law of fine sentiment; but to the Queen of the House of David the law of fine sentiment was all-controlling. All her heart was filled with love for her husband, her Son and her Savior. When her consort died, the niche in her heart that he occupied, the only part with room for conjugal love, became a shrine. Its door was sealed then until the final resurrection. Where such constancy exists there is certainty of pure homes. Sanctity, chastity and faithfulness were the lights of the temple, dedicated to the mythical Juno, within whose precincts no impure woman was suffered to enter. To-day I claim for the True Ideal all that was accorded the mythical one."

When the speaker paused, some of the men present broke forth, as was the custom in the synagogue service, with an "Amen," and some exclaimed "Rabbi, thine are good words for our women to hear!"

The Hospitaler's black eyes flashed; a hint of retort of lightning-like directness to come. And it came, instantly:

"I shall fail of my duty if I give all to one-half. I shall fail of my intent if my words seem like railings at the sex most tender, most burdened. Since we are treating of the weeds of the mourners, let us question why it is that widowers more frequently seek remarriage than do widows. The bereaved man easily says: 'Get me another wife.' The bereaved woman more frequently says: 'Let me hurry on heavenward after my only and ever beloved.'

"With the true woman marriage is a committal so utter that it is difficult for her, generally, to make it more than once. Again me thinks that marriage brings the graver, heavier loads to women. Once experienced, there is need of a mighty love to allure her to a second trial. The man rises by self-assertion, and wedlock does not hinder him. With the woman wedlock means self-denial; her name changes, her career is merged into that of her consort; her body is given, literally, to the new beings she bears. To woman marriage has no parallel, except death. Her only possible compensation is love, and that she should receive with measures knowing no stint. Oh, men, all fair to other men, all merciful to the beasts that toil, all prudent in keeping in motion, by day and by night, the water-wheels in your orange and mulberry groves, be fair and merciful to your consorts. Yea, and evermore water with love's most grateful refreshments the bearing vines whose tendrils intwine your hearts, whose fruits enrich your homes. This is religion ; what is less is heresy, and he who deals unkindly, cruelly or niggardly with his other self, can not face God. The prayers of such are hindered and like unto a tree whose leaves are storm-stripped. You know the race, by birth, comes forth in two sexes, of equal numbers, a hint of God's plan to have mankind live as pairs ; but the men are a constant majority. Why ? I answer that, notwithstanding the perils falling upon the sterner sex, by exposure, by war, and all such things, the trials fal'ing to woman's lot work the greater havoc, keeping her sex in huge majority in the places of the dead. Now you praise me, because I've told your women to be like the glorious Mary? Praise me again for telling them, as I do this instant, to be like her in choice of consorts. If they can not find Josephs to begin with, God grant to make the men they have like the choice spouse who fell to Mary's lot !"

The Hospitaler paused for a moment; there was a wave of excitement, very near to applause, running over the audience. The bride and the groom, together with all the women present, by their faces expressed their delight. The men who had exclaimed at the first, looked blank and kept silent now.

Abruptly, as before, again the knight spoke:

" I'll touch now another pertinent theme—*Mary under the shadows of scandal!* I'd exalt her as one having sounded the depths of woman's misery, and yet preserving her integrity. I know that some here will think themselves offended, since it's the fashion so to think when listening to discourse such as I now intend. Society, more prudish than sincere or wise, has demanded that the burning, scarlet, social wrong be spoken of only by scrupulous hint, half words and reserves, at least among decent and happy folks. For once, as God's accredited ambassador, I'll change all this, and by Purity's earthly throne, the marriage altar, denounce the crime of crimes, the blasting curse of all mankind. Let him that's conscious of his own impurity mince words. I'll not ! Jehovah might have brought forth the Christ without subjecting Nazareth's Virgin to the painful necessity of being doubted. It was as He decreed and wisely ordered. The happening was not because Deity was frustrated, but because He knew that she whose example was to be woman's inspiration, could be so more surely, if her career took her along all lines of woman's needs. There was a time when almost all who knew Mary doubted her integrity; a time when her name was banded about by the roués of her native place; a time when even her betrothed was resolving to renounce, if not to denounce her. First I'd speak of how impurity is abhorred of God, and then of His wondrous effort to allure those lost by it, as evinced in sending out after them the two lambs—the Eternal Lamb and the lamb-like woman.

To say that they whose trend is toward things unclean are abhorred of God is to re-echo the edicts of nature and history. They say whenever a sin is committed a devil is created to avenge it. What legions avenge this sin which, most of all, brutalizes man and turns all social relations into anarchy! Ask your men of science. They will tell you that all the evils flesh is heir to seem to get their seeds herein. Immortal revenge haunts it! You know, how in the Christian's holy book, it is affirmed that many sicken and die because partaking of the cup of the holy communion unworthily. Presumptuous hypocrisy thus meets the wrath which paralyzed Uzzah and Jeroboam. But the cup of the passion was love's highest gift, and the offense is not against the cup but against love in its sublimest display. Therefore forever death is the penalty that overhangs those who outrage this finest gem of angels and mortals. Treason to love is suicidal as well as murderous! They say that there is a demon whose touch causes hideous, coiling, stinging serpents to grow from the bodies of those he touches. I'll tell you his name—Lasciviousness, and he works fatefully wherever man abides. But the pure home is an invincible bulwark against him, and hymen's torch his blinding horror."

There were some of the knight's auditors, both men and women, who felt it their duty, because of custom, to affect disapproval of the free speaking they heard. Of these dissenters the women uttered no word, but their eyes glared, and the color went and came in their cheeks. The disapproving men exhibited faces as hard as marble, while their lips mumbled incoherently.

The knight was not slow to perceive the rising storm, but he was undaunted. He waxed more earnest and more eloquent; his words and theme inflamed him.

One favorable to his faithfulness remarked to a comrade:

"The Hospitaler seems to grow taller, as if filled and enlarged by an inspiration."

His face shone as that of Moses when bearing the law, and some cowered as if they heard coming toward them, from afar, the rumblings of Sinai. Some white souls present wept, moved more by the truth in its beauty and power than they could have been by any play on their emotions. It was an hour of true oratory's triumph; logic set on fire; a consecrated herald grappling awful sin with the power of omnipotence.

Presently, after the thunder and lightning, came "the still, small voice." The man of God spoke with loving persuasiveness; he healed with words, the woundings truth had made. Then he carried his audience with him. Many bowed their heads to weep, as trees beaten by winds that carried rain!

"We can all entreat fallen men as to most sins, why not as to the chief sins? We speak to the fathers, brothers and sons faithfully, pleadingly; why not to the women who are elect to companion creation's lords? Alas, the women have the greater need of helpful admonition, when they fall, for revilings and black despair fill up the cup of their remorse! You have heard of the Feast of Lanterns among the Chinese? Those pagans, once a year, go out with many-colored lights to symbolize Mercy seeking lost daughters. Shall God's choicest people fall behind the pagan? Never, if true to the noble, tender, pure spirit that emanates from

God's own ideal of womanhood. No, no ! let us vow with unwonted zeal, amid the lights, lessons and joys of this hour, to be knights of new order ; knights of the white cross ; sworn to denounce all impure practices on our own part, and on the other hand to strive to allure the fallen to that that is clean and white as the souls of the angels which do excel ! Let us go to those whom sin has made drunk, in their despairing. Let us tell them that doubt castles are stormed ! Let us proclaim the seed of the woman the serpent's destroyer ! Go, women to women, in woman's name, remembering that pity in the soul makes him or her that hath it successful suppliant for all mercies at the throne on which forever the Interceding Son of the Virgin reigns ! Go, fathers, making your fatherhood godlike in its just tenderness ! Go, brothers, sons of women, as pure, strong brothers indeed ! There is many a scarlet woman to-day with scalded eyes and ashen heart who is so because she believed men brothers and fathers and found some wolves and vultures. Go to those who have all days as nights, all joys as apples of Sodom. They were not always so, and need not so continue. Do not belittle their sin, yet seek to allure them by a noble presentment of purity and by all encouragement to attempt to win back their lost crowns. Tell them of the woman that stood serenely amid bitterest scorns, and say as did her Son to one like them : '*Go, and sin no more.*' Then teach those who have no such blot upon them to be kind and helpful. We can never judge any soul's guilt until we at last know the measure of the temptation ! God alone knows that.

"I could speak on this theme for hours ; but this is enough ! The story of Mary has somehow ever had peculiar efficacy with the blighted of her sex. They easily are led, when all men fail them, to dare to trust the One who had a mother so tender. Many a motherless outcast has found Christ in trying to find mother-love in Mary. After the phantasmagoria of illusive pleasure it is healing, through faith in God's exemplified love, to dream of how it seems to have a real mother's arms enfolding one. I hold that it is profitable to the impure man, sometimes looking within the Pantheon of memory, to find therein conceptions he treasured in his purer days ; but with more determined assertion I find that it lifts up the soiled woman to come in contact with the girdle of power and crown jewels of that maiden and mother of Nazareth and Bethlehem It was she that stood against imperial Rome, in the person of Herod; a chaste young Jewess against corseted animality; a country maiden, heaven-endowed, against an old fox; the loyal mother-eagle against the python! But she that was simply good evaded, outran, soared above, and finally confounded the evil at its lowest dip, its highest power!"

Then the orator-knight, waving his hand to Cornelius to signify to him that the missioner was to conclude the ceremonial, abruptly closed his address and retired to one of the little alcove-chapels.

A simple espousal service followed, and then the company gathered dispersed, going to join in hastily-arranged festivities in the park by the temple. The Hospitaler and the missioners were auditors.

"Nourahmal, I can well believe, was a rare beauty; her grand-child has her features, and she's a vision."

"What time my friend here, the Hospitaler, did not engage me I was admiring the groom," Miriamne responded to her husband.

"He hails from the Jabbock country," remarked the knight.

"Jabbock? Faithful Ichabod's native place?" exclaimed Miriamne.

"He was the groom's uncle," quoth the knight.

Then the trio were silent, the thoughts of each following back over the past years and along God's providences. The way life's lines were crossed, interwoven and entangled seemed to each very wonderful.

CHAPTER XL.

THE QUEEN'S VISION OF THE "AGE OF GOLD AND FIRE."

> "Oh, moist eyes,
> And hurrying lips and heaving heart!
> The world we've come to late is swollen hard
> With perishing generations and their sins;
> The civilizer's spade grinds horribly
> On dead men's bones, and can not turn up soil,
> That's otherwise than fetid. All successes
> Prove partial failure * * * * * *
> * * * * All governments, some wrong;
> The rich men make the poor who curse the rich,
> Who agonize together, rich and poor,
> Under and over in the social spasm.
> * * * * * * *
> Who being man and human, can stand calmly by
> And view these things, and never tease his soul
> For some great cure.
> —MRS. E. B. BROWNING: "*Aurora Leigh.*"

> "They went up into an upper room,
> With the woman and Mary the mother of Jesus."
> "Many signs and wonders were done.
> All that believed had all things common."
> —ACTS.

I'M anxious for the coming of the people to-day; Beulah said, a week ago, at her wedding, that she'd have the old Druse camel-driver at this service; though he ran away from her marriage feast."

"I've heard that she and her grandmother had a convert to our faith, nearly ripe," replied Cornelius to his wife.

At this instant one of the "Bethany Sisters" timidly approached the speakers, evidently anxious to deliver some communication.

"'Tis 'Brightness' by name and by nature," remarked Miriamne.

"Well, sister Ziha, what is it?" questioned the chaplain.

"Pardon me; but there is waiting without, a grave and taciturn man who says he would speak with the 'Prophetess.' He means our Miriamne."

"Of what flavor is he, Ziha?"

"Surely, I can not imagine, sister Miriamne! His countenance is that of a Persian Jew; his turban is Turkish; his tunic Christian. But his bearing is that of a prince, though all his belongings, except his gorgeously dressed camel, are those of a beggar!"

"I'll see him, Ziha; bid him enter," exclaimed Miriamne.

"That I did; but he says his haste is too great and his limbs too stiff for dismounting. In truth, his brow, bleached to the bone, tells of weighty years."

"Let's go to him," said the chaplain.

The missioners going forth, at the easterly side of their temple, were confronted by a majestic figure, mounted on a splendidly caparisoned white camel, evidently a borrowed one.

"*Ullah makum,*" "God be with you," said the man on the camel with great courtliness and dignity, at the same time extending to the chaplain a parchment roll.

"This for me?" questioned the latter.

"For thee," replied the rider, bowing as before, but looking past the question with fixed, though reverent, gaze at Miriamne.

"But who are you?" again questions the chaplain.

"God knows," was the sententious reply of the rider, his eyes still turning, not with curiosity, but with a deferential and affectionate interest, toward the chaplain's wife.

"What message here, my father?" questioned again Cornelius, in the language of Galilee.

The aged man's dark face lightened at the words, and turning his reverent gaze from Miriamne toward the questioner, he slowly responded:

"The 'Angels of the Mount' are not too proud to call a poor camel driver 'my father?' Age has respect here! I might have known this: Nourahmal is full of the odors of this new Bethany!"

"And do you come from Nourahmal?" quickly interrogated Miriamne.

"Nourahmal and I are one, by the voice of God spoken through the holy Hospitaler, who is alluring me daily from the secret faiths of my fathers to learn the prayers that Nourahmal learns here."

"I see," continued Miriamne; "I speak with Nourahmal's consort. Pray dismount for refreshment. We bid you every welcome, Mahmood."

"Mahmood! called by such fine people by my proper name; not 'dog' or 'here you,' or 'old camel goad!' Wonderful!"

"Will Nourahmal's spouse dismount?"

"Blessed woman, I've had great refreshment in being thus permitted to see thee face to face, and thank thee and thine for what thou hast done for me and mine; but I can not tarry; old age and poverty have bargained to make constant toil my master. I must keep moving or the swifter youths will take away my master and leave me to hire out to starvation;" so saying, the speaker smote his camel and the beast moved away, slowly, along the road toward Jerusalem.

Cornelius, recovering himself from his meditations, called after the departing Druse.

"What of this parchment?"

"The Hospitaler sent it! He said it would talk with 'the Angels of the Mount.'"

The camel driver had stopped his beast to say this much. For a moment he looked at the missioners, then at their temple and its surroundings. There was a world of questioning, and wonder, and yearning in the old man's countenance. Again his goad fell on the beast he rode and the latter bore him along.

"Shall we meet again, father?" Cornelius called after him.

"Stay master work! Go master want! 'Till good shade Death takes to the cool rest-land the holy Hospitaler, the Angels of the Mount, my Nourahmal, and may be me; even me the poor, old, camel-driver, Mahmood!" was the slow reply as the Druse departed. A turn in the road soon shut him from view.

"Well, my spouse, Miriamne, our new Bethany sees strange visitants these days," remarked her husband.

"The mystic Druse is finding something that is finer than the creeds of his mountain clans," rejoined Miriamne.

"Be not too certain; those Highlanders of Palestine are ever politic; they'll quote the Koran to one of

Islam, kiss the Bible in the company of Christians; but once alone are Druse to the last."

"That is their character; but we've a transforming gospel; no man as old as he and companion of such advocates of the White Kingdom as the Hospitaler and Nourahmal, could talk as did that old man to kill time or conventionally.—But you do not study your parchment." Cornelius, recalled by Miriamne's words, unfolded the document given him by the camel-driver, and read aloud:

"My son and my daughter: Greeting; the streams of gospel blessing rising in the springs of your mountain temple reach refreshingly even unto Jerusalem, as I daily perceive. Therefore, for your consolation and for the enkindling of your pious zeal, I herewith send these lines. Work onward, beloved, believing, hoping you have arrived at the dawn of a new revelation and well commenced a true work for God. To-day, as I sought to interpret His prophecies, it came to me that that you are attempting to do is nigh to being a fulfillment of His word as recorded in the manner following by Ezekiel:

"Then the glory of the Lord departed from off the threshold of the house, and stood over the cherubim.

"And the cherubim lifted up their wings, and mounted up from the earth in my sight: when they went out, the wheels also were beside them, and every one stood at the door of the east gate of the Lord's house; and the glory of the God of Israel was over them above.

"The word of the Lord came unto me, saying:

"Thus saith the Lord God: I will assemble you out of the countries where ye have been scattered, and I will give you the land of Israel.

"And they shall come thither, and they shall take

away all the detestable things thereof and all the abominations.

"And I will give them one heart, and I will put a new spirit within, and I will take the stony heart.

"That they may walk in my statutes, and keep mine ordinances, and they shall be my people, and I will be their God.

"Then did the cherubim lift up their wings, and the glory of the God of Israel was over them above.

"And the glory of the Lord went up from the midst of the city, and stood upon the mountain which *is* on the east side of the city.

"These solemn words tell how the glory and favor of God was driven from the people of old by their sinning; how slowly, yearningly, God departed; how in every land He provide *little sanctuaries* for the faithful few. And more than all this, the Holy Word describes God in Spirit as pausing on the mount to the east of Jerusalem. That pausing place was your Olivet. The Jewish Rabbins in their sacred histories affirm that for three years God, in manifest form, tarried, near where your Temple of Allegory stands, repeating over and over the solemn call, '*Return unto me, and I will return unto you!*' Beloved, since then the eternal voice, through Jesus Christ, has spoken through three ministering years from these mountains to the world. You are now re echoing the cry. God be with you, as He is, and give you faith to call and call until the ascended Christ come into all hearts."

"No name to his letter, as usual?" remarked the chaplain.

"He seems to loathe names almost; but recently, when I made bold to ask him his, he sententiously observed, 'God knows; 'tis in a white stone, I'm to get; for this life I'm only remembered by what I've done.' But what engages my husband's attention now?"

"I'm trying to interpret the picture yonder, over the door, to the retreat you call the '*Mother's Pillow.*'"

"What think you of it? You perceive it's the legend of the mother pelican feeding her famishing young with blood drawn from her own bosom, which she has wounded for their food."

"I think the picture likely to depress nervous mothers!"

"That's a picture of one side of mother life; look beyond it."

At that the light from a distant window was let fall, by some unseen attendant, all about the entrance to the "*Mother's Pillow!*"

"I see a splendid 'Gabriel' above the pelican; the angel's hand points upward."

"Glorious Gabriel! Angel of mothers and victories, by interpretation, 'God's champion!' You've heard his titles, Cornelius?"

"I know that he bore victory to Gideon and lightened the way for Daniel's conquest of all Babylon; nor do I forget that he was the angel which comforted giant Samson's mother before her child was born."

"Yea, he that made the sign of the cross, doing wondrously, above the smoke of Monoah's altar, was after commissioned to greet and guide Mary, the mother of the Giant King of the new dispensation."

"You've fine insights, Miriamne, but there's incompleteness in your symbolism here."

"True, I feel that; all interpretation of motherhood is inadequate; but look further."

"I see the 'Queen of Mothers!' Why have you left her and the babe in such deep shadows?"

"That's this life's reality; but look higher."

The chaplain complied; a vine trellis was swung aside, and he beheld, above the shadowed picture, in an arch reaching nearly to the roof of the temple, another, the latter a marvel of light and color.

"Glorified Mary, uplifted by the babe, now grown and Kingly!" exclaimed the chaplain.

"And so is taught for mothers' comfort, that the Son of God honored her who bore Him, because she was to Him a true mother. May we not believe that this love for Mary, in thé God heart, is widened into peculiar tenderness toward all who give the earth its lords and paradise its elect through the crucifixions of maternity?"

"Oh, Miriamne, I've learned in the past to stand, as it were, with bared head, all reverential in the presence of true motherhood; when I see it strengthened by faith, enriched by suffering; the most entrancing example of self-abnegation on earth! To-day I feel, if possible, in these surroundings, a deeper reverence than ever, for that estate of woman. Say on."

"Paganism worshiped the sun, the earth, woman; whatever brought forth; it was its best attempt at expressing a vaguely realized yet noble sentiment. The religions that repudiated paganism, in their efforts to extirpate all idolatry, went to the extreme of denying merited honor to some most worthy. Then came the Christian revolution, and God turned all eyes toward a pure woman. He proclaimed forever the honors of motherhood by presenting through it to the world His Unspeakable Gift."

"So heaven's last appeal to our race, after Sinai's thunders and the rapt visions of the prophets became ineffective, was made by the eloquence of the life of the silent Mary."

"Well said! Now filled with that belief, herald the White Kingdom!"

"I'll help Miriamne, encouraging, upholding her; for the rest I've learned to lean and follow."

"I'm a column of dust, not a pillar of fire; and dust, alas, to dust returns. There is much to do here, more than I shall be able to compass. I've hitherto but vaguely taught the meaning, power and blessings of motherhood."

"I think more than vaguely."

"The sun rises in the east. I think we've sunrise, but the depth, height and breadth have not been sounded nor measured yet. Shall we go toward the west wing?"

"Yea, lead, though I'm charmed in this presence."

"I'd lead to the '*Rest of the Aged.*'"

"To the retreat with door like a castle? What are those amazon forms in armor?"

"The Peri?"

"I bid them welcome in Miriamne's name, having learned that she is serious as well as cunning in weaving the manna-bearing garlands of every myth about her ideals. Say on."

"They say there is beneath the Caucasian mountains a wondrous city builded of pearls and precious stones, in which dwells a race of surpassing beauty of person. I've utilized the tradition."

"Oh, the fabled Peri; but I'm mystified."

"They also say," continued Miriamne, "that Dives, a wicked genus, wages constant war against the Peri, hoping to possess the treasures of the Peri capital, but that they successfully repel him and make their happiness secure. I have a similitude of the Peri city."

"In truth, I wonder now. What fitness for such an allegory here?"

"I think I have come near to a profound truth. Listen; here at the west, I have planned to show what makes approaching age a terror."

"There are many evils which fall upon man's declining years."

"Judge me if my philosophy is faulty. I see ever that the fear of being left poor and also old here haunts most lives. This fear is the parent of avarice, and avarice is a serpent of glowing head and deadly sting. It robs society and individuals of the two choicest jewels, plenteous benevolence and serene hopefulness. You will find that most of the wrongs from man to man arise from hearts made cruel by the rigors of avariciousness. If we could stay that master passion, all streams of benevolence would rise to their flood, and hoarding, now a seeming necessity, most frequently a curse, become the occupation solely of a few monomaniacs."

"Miriamne's philosophy is as invulnerable as a knight's hauberk, but how can you make it a general practice?"

"Oh, very easily. I've planned to endow our Temple of Allegory so that it may not only teach but also do beautiful things. I'd have it a Pool of Bethesda, stirred continuously to meet every human need."

"Miriamne will have a vast following; the masses believe in loaves and fishes!"

"True, avarice prompts some to a mean faith, but

I seek to slay avarice and blast the love of money, that root of all evil."

"'Enthusiast!' a gainsaying world will cry."

"And the cry of the world will be then, as often before, a burning lie! So be it. I'm holding up the truth, the royal truth of Christianity. I'll hold it up while I have breath, and leave that truth, if God gives me grace, as the beacon light on our hill to glow until all Christendom puts on a charity as multiform and broad as the needs of humanity."

"But there is a large and needy world."

"I have a rich Father; the earth is His and the fullness thereof. The only difficulty is in securing from His stewards an accounting and a beginning of payment."

"This, Miriamne, sounds like the dream of a poet. I'll not waken you from your beautiful trance, but still the rough fates of life as it is, and the very common commonplace confront us."

"What a world this would be if all mankind was as one family, realizing universal brotherhood!"

"This, too, is the dream of the poet, Socialism; Astarte's devotees practiced it in the past."

"Now, I'll say silence! You speak of heathen socialism. Whatever its form, lust was its corner stone, and a barbarous selfishness, which limited it to those of each tribe or clan, its best expression! I speak of a vastly finer, grander creed! I look out and forward to a day when all shall know the Lord; a day when law shall be love and love shall be law. Then earth shall be an Eden, with plenty for all, such plenty as Divine bounty bestows. Christianity means the bringing in of that day; the 'Precious Gift' was an earnest of all needed gifts from on high. When that day comes we shall understand why the Pentecostal fire came to all hearts in the time when all worshipers were thanking the All-Giver for the bounties of the harvest. Then avarice shall cease from the earth, and men, no more harassed by it, learn to practice all bountifulness in youth and mid-life, and also serene restfulness when their powers of bread-winning are paralyzed by the burdens of years. All will be noble, therefore none indolent. There will be no beggars, for charity will run before want, ever glad to serve those that can not serve themselves. Then those who wear the glory-crowns of gray will be nourished reverently and gladly, not as if they were useless paupers; not with a niggardly service which seems to be constantly saying, 'How long are you going to live!' There will be no more worriment, no more crowdings of each other, no more dishonesty among men! It is, I say, the constant fear of coming, in the day when the heart is beating the last strokes of its own funeral march, to doled charity or to nothing, that makes men pile up gain in dishonor and hoard it with miserly grasping. Do you remember that Mary returned from ministering to Elizabeth to sing her 'Magnificat' with these prophetic strains:

"' His mercy is on them that fear Him from generation to generation. He hath filled the hungry with good things. He hath holpen His servant Israel.'

"From the song she went to humble, painful ministries in behalf of all the world. Mary supplemented the wondrous work of her Son and King, all the way bearing as best she could her part of His cross; all the way her quivering heart pierced by the sword that finally slew Him. She saw His bloody tears turning to crown jewels as He ascended from Olivet, and with unfaltering faith knelt among His earthly followers that she with them might receive her crown of flame. That room was the highest point of outlook on earth. It was the place of supreme beneficence; the place where God gave Himself up freely for His followers and established the memorial-superlative of the ages. Thither they hasted that they might learn how all-receiving comes from all-giving, that they might realize the measure and splendor of perfect charity, which is perfect love."

"Miriamne, whence do you get such wondrous insights?"

Then the young wife turned aside to her "own little mountain," as she called a secret praying place in the chapel. She quickly returned, and handing a manuscript to Cornelius, said:

"Read, please, of Pentecost."

He complied:

"Then they that gladly received His word were baptized; and the same day there were added unto them about three thousand souls.

"And they continued steadfastly in the apostles' doctrine and fellowship, and in breaking of bread and in prayers.

"And fear came upon every soul, and many wonders and signs were done by the apostles.

"And all that believed were together, and had all things common;

"And sold their possessions and goods and parted them to all men, as every man had need.

"And they, continuing daily with one accord in the

temple, and breaking bread from house to house, did eat their meat with gladness and singleness of heart,

"Praising God, and having favor with all the people. And the Lord added to the church daily such as should be saved."

CHAPTER XLI.

A CHIME AND A DIRGE AT CHRISTMAS TIME.

"Oh, not alone, because his name is Christ;
  Oh, not alone, because Judea waits
This man-child for her King—the star stands still!
  Its glory reinstates,
Beyond humiliation's utmost ill,
  On peerless throne which she alone can fill,
Each earthly woman! Motherhood is priced
  Of God, at price no man may dare
To lessen or misunderstand.

* * * * * *

The crown of purest purity revealed
Virginity eternal, signed and sealed
Upon all motherhood."
—Helen Hunt.

"In sorrow thou shalt bring forth."—Gen. iii. 16.
"Thou shalt be saved in child-bearing."—Tim. ii. 15.

UNDREDS of willing hands, directed by Miriamne, were engaged in preparations for fitly celebrating the feast of the Nativity at Bethany. There was cheerful expectation everywhere in the village, and the Temple of Allegory was smiling and glowing by day and by night with flowers and lights.

"Miriamne, look forth! There approaches our domicile a company of singing maidens, wearing holly wreaths and bearing a kline! What can it mean?"

An instant of wonderment ready to echo the chaplain's question possessed Miriamne, then with a glow of satisfaction on her pale face, she cried:

"I know it all! The maidens of our fraternity have been declaring for a month past they'd have me this Christmas at our Temple on the Hill, if they must needs carry me thither!"

"And they knew you were drooping? Who told them? Not I."

"Love has quick eyes, and my sisters love indeed!"

"But, Miriamne, you surely will not risk your life, so precious to all, by going forth to-day?"

"The holly, over-canopying the couch they bear, says to me: 'Yea, go.' I told them the secret of the holly, and how those ancient Romans, thinking their deities largely sylvan, cherished this shrub, so persistently evergreen, in the belief that it afforded a safe and certain abiding place for their gods in bitter, biting days of winter. The maidens remember their lesson."

And shortly after, all went forth toward the temple, the physically weak but spiritually strong woman borne by her followers in a sort of triumph, and Cornelius leading; the latter, that day was one of the happiest, proudest men in all Syria. He rejoiced and exulted in being companion of a woman such as Miriamne was.

Miriamne entered the temple to find a vast congregation awaiting her. There was a ripple of excitement, a deep murmuring of satisfied voices almost reaching the proportion of a masculine outbreak of applause, as she appeared. Contentment was depicted on all faces, on many real happiness. Neither was it transitory; there was a throbbing of gladness running back and forth, rising higher and higher, until it finally broke out into an impromptu "*Gloria in excelsis!*" Then followed a scripture lesson:

"And Ezra the priest brought the law before the congregation both of men and women, and all that could hear with understanding, upon the first day of the seventh month.

"And he read therein before the street that was before the water-gate from the morning until midday, before the men and the women, and those that could understand; and the ears of the people were attentive unto the book of the law."

And now the attention of all was drawn to the sound of footsteps in the throbbings of a march, keeping time to the tones of the organ and the flourishings of cymbals. Nigh an hundred Syrian maidens, wearing girdles and crowns of evergreen, moved with graceful evolutions from the temple's east entrance and quickly formed in a crescent nigh to Cornelius and Miriamne. They paused in their progress but still kept time with their feet and swinging cymbals. Then the crescent was broken; those in the center standing in lines that made a cross; those at either end grouping as stars.

"Sisters, we'd hear the fitting song of this day," said Miriamne. Forthwith the gathered company of garlanded maidens began to retire, but in perfect order, the two star groups passing along as the company making the cross went, so preserving the form of the tableau, until the exits were reached. As the procession went forth the temple bell tolled solemnly, and the maidens sang, accompanied by organ-notes which died away finally like the sigh of tired waves on a beaten strand. Cornelius was silent, though his eyes were like the eyes of a child awakened from a dream of wonderland.

Miriamne penetrating his thoughts remarked:

"Is Cornelius weary of questioning?"

"I listen as to autumn winds in a scared flight through weeping forests, instead of to Christmas exultations!"

"The singers are of my 'Miriamne Band,' as they call themselves, in honor of the sister of Moses, Israel's greatest law giver."

"Methinks all here are mystics in thought and poets in expression!"

"Then so was God. We are but reproducing His lessons! Remember now how the Egyptian Pharoah once commanded that all the male children of his Israelitish captives be put to death, to the intent that eventually all the females should become the prey of his people."

"Miriamne journeys far from Bethlehem."

"The mother and the sister watched the ark in which the infant Moses was given to the cruel mercies of the Nile."

"I remember, but there come no carols from the bullrushes."

"Yea, finer than from the reeds of Pan. Listen; the ark, emblem of God's covenant, carried the law. The mother and sisters, by the ministries of a love which never faltered, frustrated wily Egypt, saved themselves, their male companions, and finally their whole race. When God embalms a history it is well to look into it for germs of mighty portent."

"But thinking of this distant and bitter history, we are kept from Bethlehem, Miriamne."

"So the Red Sea and the wilderness preceded the Promised Land. You remember there were fears and tears before Miriam and her mother saw their babe safely adopted at the palace; so there were pains and toils to Mary along the way from Bethlehem's manger to Bethany's mount of Ascension."

The words of Miriamne were broken off by a strain of the organ that was very like a moan of the distressed.

"Look yonder!"

The chaplain did as bidden, following a motion of his wife's hand, and saw the folds of a huge black curtain slowly rising from in front of one of the temple alcoves.

"Woman's sorrow is tardily lifted!" exclaimed his wife; then there came to his ears words of human voices, which were joining in the almost human-like moanings of the organ;

> "In Rama was there a voice heard;
> Lamentation and weeping and great mourning;
> Rachel weeping for her children,
> And would not be comforted,
> Because they are not."

"Rachel and funeral dirges seem still distant from the songs of the angels in Judea!"

"Rachel is here likened to Mary by the Apostle Matthew."

"I liken Rachel to Miriamne: for the former Jacob served fourteen years which, for the love he bore her, seemed but a few days. Cornelius could have done as much for Miriamne."

"My knightly spouse goes from Bethlehem himself toward Bethany. Go back now."

"I listen; lead me."

"At Rama, the site of the tomb of Mary's son, the converted publican, St. Matthew, told how death began its cruel hunt of the Virgin's loved Child at His very cradle. Sorrow envies joy; death battles life, and ever more woman's love, the choicest rose of life, has been crossed by the destroyer of human happiness; that is human hatings."

"But how is Rachel so like Mary?"

"A common agony and common needs make all women akin."

"I accord great homage to the woman who taught one so selfish. gnarled and rugged of soul as Jacob was to love so deeply, as he was taught to love by her, and yet almost infinitely I separate her from our Rose and Queen."

"Rachel died a martyr in maternity and therefore is worthy of place among the regal women of earth. She was one of that line of women who gave their lives for others. The line survives, and suffers through the years; all-worthy, but not fully honored. Saint Matthew touched an all-responsive chord when he voiced the Divine pity for all motherhood, by placing the sorrows of Rachel and of Mary side by side. The plain man unconsciously soars to the plane of the prophets and poets when he is moved by human need or Divine justice."

"The lesson is irresistible, but still I'm waiting for the celestial melodies that awakened the shepherd the night of the Nativity!"

"My partner shall get by giving. Here is a parchment given me years ago to read for my mother's consolation after the death of my brothers. Read it, thou, to the matrons and maidens when the chantings cease."

After a time there was silence! the hush of expectation, for that gathering was wont at ti.nes to wait for words of blessing from the missioners, as the hart for the rivulet at the beginnings of the rain.

"Read!" whispered Miriamne, "but not as the tragedian! Read as a father and lover, both in one." The young man complied, and these were the words of the parchment:

"There was a man named Jehoikim who, impressed of God thereto, offered a lamb in sacrifice. As he slew it his heart was touched with tenderness, and he would have staid his hand, but God gave him strength to perform the command. After this a daughter, called Mary, was born to him. Whenever he looked upon her gentle face he remembered the bleating lamb, and was certain that some way his child was to be a sacrifice to God. And it was so; for she bore a Son to whom she gave all the wealth of a mother's love, but at last He was offered for man's sin upon a felon's cross, the agony He felt reaching the heart of his mother. As the Son gave Himself up for the world, so she gave herself up for her Son. She was sustained through it all by a conscience void of offense, and by the ministry of angels. Alone to the world, she had no solitude, for though her espousal to God had no human witness, even as Eve's to Adam had none, and both were inexperienced, God was at her nuptials, as He is ever with those who purely give themselves to Him."

Then the wife wept and was silent.

"My darling, what so moves you? I've never experienced such a Christmas. You make the feast as solemn as the holy supper."

There came no answer; but ere the husband could turn to seek a reason it came in a cry from the audience, and a thronging from all directions toward where the missioners were.

"Miriamne has fallen!"

"'Tis a swoon?"

"No, 'tis death!" There were surgings back and forth, voices suggesting helps, voices filled with stifled sobs, and voices of fright in the trebles of hysteria.

The sick woman was borne by strong men to her domicile, and then began the tension of waiting. The young chaplain was entering the valley of poignant pains by sympathy's pathway, bound by that mystic chain whose links are in the words: "These twain shall be one flesh." Herein is a mystery often repeated; the man's grief was supplemented by a consciousness of vague pains passing along unseen lines from the woman to himself. Slowly Miriamne recovered consciousness; but still she hovered on the confines of woman's supreme hour, the hour when great fear haunts great hopes, great weakness yields to miraculous influxes of power, and great joy, in company with unutterable yearnings, moves along under the shadows and by the gulfs of greatest perils. About her gathered a group of matrons of her sisterhood, pressing to serve their beloved.

One whispered to another: "Her face is unearthly, like Mary's as we saw it in the 'Assumption' to-day."

The one that heard the words answered with a sob. The voice of pain called the drooping woman quickly from her semi-stupor to ministry, and opening her eyes she tenderly murmured to the woman that sobbed, "Remember what he said: 'Women of Jerusalem, weep not for me; but weep for yourselves and children.' If I go 'twill be all well; yes, by His grace, all well with me. Let all your pity follow the pilgrims of our sex who tarry to painfully journey through years of trial, unrequited."

A little later Cornelius was hastily summoned by one that sought him, from the shadows of an arch of the roof, whither he had gone for a few moments' solitude, in which to plead, as only can a man who writhes in the fear of having his life torn in two.

"Miriamne asks for her husband." He heard the words and was by his consort's side instantly. Her eyes were closed, but taking her pale hand tenderly in his he impressed a kiss on her brow. She opened her eyes full upon him, with a gaze of undying love.

"You kissed my brow, the first kiss as a lover. Then you said it was given in the spirit of reverential admiration. Has marriage ever changed the thought?"

"Never!"

"If I should leave you, do you think you could tell others how to love so?"

"Oh, I can, surely; if I can do any thing, alone!" And then came to him the silence of a dumb grief. She saw his agony and pitied him, yet serenely she spoke:

"Go onward, beloved, in the way of the prophet's vision; the power of Christ be with you; the life of Mary is an open book; speak to, work for those most needing, then will you have your constant Pentecost with the ever present 'Grail.'"

Cornelius pressed the hand he held tenderly; he could not speak.

"Repeat to me the beautiful words concerning the Harvest Feast which you heard out of Moses at the service that so blessed you at Jerusalem," she continued again. Then, mastering his voice, he complied:

"And thou shalt keep the feast of weeks unto the Lord thy God with a tribute of a freewill-offering of thine hand, which thou shalt give *unto the Lord thy God*, according as the Lord thy God hath blessed thee:

"And thou shalt rejoice before the Lord thy God, thou, and thy son, and thy daughter, and thy manservant, and thy maidservant, and the Levite that is within thy gates, and the stranger, and the fatherless, and the widow, that are among you, in the place which the Lord thy God hath chosen to place His name there."

When he finished the words he hid his face in his hands.

"Thou art weary, my good master," spoke a Jewish mother present. "Go now and rest. I'll watch."

Quickly, gently, firmly he waved her away, as one unwittingly trying to draw him from the gates of heaven.

"It is not usual," she persisted, "for a man to serve this way; then thou hast other and more important duties, our holy missioner!"

He found voice to speak, and needed to restrain himself from indignant tone. It seemed as if it were impiety now, so great his love, to speak of any duty as higher than that he had toward this one woman, more to him than all the world beside. "No; if I were on the cross she would be there, another Mary; if I am now in torture I'd be no Christian if I did not emulate Him who, amid crucial agonies, between two worlds, cried as inmost thought of His heart, '*Behold thy Mother!*'"

He felt Miriamne's hand pressing his, and drawing him closer to herself.

"Cornelius, I'm leaning now as never before upon my husband's loyal heart!"

It seemed to the man as if she were nigh to crying: "My God, my God, why hast thou forsaken me!" and as if to answer his own thought he exclaimed:

"He will be Father, I as a mother, Miriamne, my Miriamne!"

Grief had made him an interpreter. It was as he thought, the heart of the young woman, woman-like, had been groping about for mother-love. Memory had been busy, but had sent the heart of the woman back from groping amid the graves of Bozrah all weary, to nestle and rest on the breast of him that gave mother-love, and promised all else that loyal heart ere gave.

But all was not gloomful; the clouds were shot through and tinted by some light-rays.

"What if our forebodings prove untrue?"

Hope's question was as a north wind to a desert noon.

Once the man bashfully questioned his spouse, with broken sentence that was half signs.

"Does Miriamne feel aught of reproach toward the great love, seemingly not far from utter selfishness, which enchanted to this peril?"

"Could Madonna reproach God when she felt the heart-piercing sword? To Him she submitted, no less do I in doing and suffering as He wills!"

It has been said a woman's heart is complex, but this one's was not now. It lay open, as a book, before her lover-husband. He saw no idol there but himself. Had there ever been hidden remembrance of some girlish love, some secret scar left by a romance, both burning and brief, it would have been opened or effaced now.

As she beheld her consort, this time more loved, if possible, than ever before, knightly, courtly and tender, alert and strong to help, lavish in caressing, she not only felt conquered, but filled with desire to surrender to the uttermost; for she joyed to place this man on the throne of her being next after God, supremely lord over all. So together they moved amid the flowers of Beulah-land, under the glorious lights of married love. She all compensated for the pangs the trying hour brought; he thrilled, as he ascended higher and higher from lover love to husband love, to that holy delight that comes to a man beginning to feel fatherhood, the gift of the woman his heart has enthroned. For a little time both were too happy to speak, so they let their thoughts wing their way upward to the eternities where hopes eternally blossom. She presently signaled him to draw close to her, then his clasped hands lay on her heart, and their lips met. She said nothing, yet by a sign-language well understood by each, plainly entreated him to tell her over and over, more and more, his inmost thought, that her heart knew full well already.

She heard his heart's beatings, then she whispered: "Don't be anxious; all is well, for all is as He that loves us wills."

"Oh, Miriamne, I loved you never as now; God bless you! bless you! bless you!"

She interrupted him again. "The crisis is coming, and I thought perhaps I might not survive, Cornelius, but if I do not—"

Her words were silenced by an impassioned kiss.

She continued, "I dreamed, last night, that I saw the shadow of a cross, but on it a woman's form."

"Oh, beloved, do not think of it!"

"I do. I must! I understand it all."

Pity now silenced her.

"Oh, Miriamne!" he cried anon, as he saw her descending into the vale of agony, from which he could not hold her back. He dare say no more. He feared to voice his thoughts, lest his fears become ponderous and huge, once they found escape in the garb of words.

Just past midnight the dispatched courier arrived, bringing twain of the most skilled physicians of Jerusalem.

Cornelius watched them with an interest beyond words. His heart sank down and down again, as he saw them in serious consultation. Unable to restrain himself, he seized the elder, and drawing him hastily aside, demanded an opinion. The grave old man only shook his head, saying: "We may save one."

"One? One! Which? What?"

"Young man, be quiet; do not let thy emotions disturb the patient or the nurses. Prepare for the worst."

The husband seized the wrinkled hand of the aged practitioner, and then flung it from him, crying: "It must not be! It shall not be!" Instantly he rushed toward the couch, but the two men of healing intercepted him. Then the elder one said: "We must be obeyed, or else we will give no commands! Shall we go or stay?"

What a revulsion came! It seemed to Cornelius as if these two men of skill were angels, and flinging his arms about them, he hoarsely whispered: "Save,

save! Stay and save! All I have I give you, only save her!"

Quietly they led him to the adjoining apartment; then charged him, as he hoped for any good to his wife, not to re-enter her chamber until sent for. Reluctantly he consented, not daring to do otherwise and yet believing in his very soul that in this hour of peril the bestowment of love's caresses on the invalid would be better than any skill of the stranger. He withdrew to the arch on the roof, where unmolested he could pray. But his meditations were full of miserable sights. He thought of the Egyptians in their feats of Osiris, leading to sacrifice the heifer draped in black; then of Rizpah defending her relatives; then of the monument in Bozrah, with the mother holding her dead Son. He thought, amid the latter meditations, of himself creeping about that monument, in the night, until he came to another, on which he deciphered the name, "*Miriamne.*" The imagination gave him a shock, and he gave way to it exhausted. An hour or so after he was awakened from a sort of stupor by the younger of the physicians, who, standing by his side, addressed him:

"Sir Priest, thou mayst come now; but as thy profession teaches, nerve thyself to confront any fate, good or ill."

"How's my wife?" exclaimed the stricken man, leaping from his couch and approaching the speaker, that he might devour with his eyes the thought of the one he questioned.

The emotionless features of the man accustomed to confront human suffering softened a little to pity. The quick eye of the missioner discerned the change, then he cried:

"What, dead!"

"No; if thou wilt but control thyself, thou mayst see her for a little while; there'll be a change soon."

The man of healing had done and said his best, but that was bad enough. He had tried to comfort, but the exigencies were beyond human powers. "A change soon!"

Hard, mocking words. Apology for bad news! Stepping-stone to saying the worst is at hand; words so often used by the man of healing when his art is defeated! How like a funeral knell breaking the heart has come, again and again, to tingling ears those terrible sounds: "In—a—little—while—there'll—be—a—change!" Cornelius felt all their stunning force, and was instantly by the side of Miriamne. What a change met his hungry eyes! The fever had died away; fever, that blast from the shores of Death's ocean, had passed, because there was nothing longer for it to attack. The tide was ebbing. She lay silent, pale and haggard; motionless, except as to a feeble breathing. The husband would have encircled her with his arms. It was love's impulse, but science, the men of healing, restrained him. There was a little wail just then, and he glanced around with a look of joy. The nurse had brought the babe close to him, turning away her own face to hide her tears, but holding the little one out as if trying to say: "This shall compensate." Then again the grief-stricken man turned to the physicians and whispered, in a half-fierce, half-terrified way: "She'll live—she'll be better now."

The aged man, slowly adjusting the paraphernalia of his profession preparatory to departure, replied: "Few survive the Cæsarean section. It was a dire necessity."

"Lord, behold whom Thou lovest is sick," moaned the young chaplain, as he knelt by the couch and buried his face in its disordered covering. So the tide of life ebbed at midnight, leaving a stranded wreck at Bethany, and the Christmas chimes turned to dirges.

CHAPTER XLII.

THE MOTHER OF SORROWS TRIUMPHANT AT LAST

> Are we not kings? Both night and day,
> From early unto late,
> About our bed, about our way,
> A guard of angels wait!
> And so we watch and work and pray
> In more than royal state.
> Are we not more? Our life shall be
> Immortal and divine;
> The nature MARY gave to THEE,
> Dear JESUS, still is THINE;
> Adoring, in THY heart I see
> Such blood as beats in mine.
> —A. A. PROCTOR.

HUNDREDS were assembled within the "*Temple of Allegory*," and other hundreds, unable to effect an entrance, tarried around about it. The knell of Miriamne, the Angel of the Mount, had called the vast congregation together from Bethany, from the country round about and from the City of Jerusalem.

There were many signs of subdued sorrow, but the intensive expression of grief common in the East was absent; neither was there any of the paganish blackness, which sometimes characterizes Christians' funerals, manifest. Though Miriamne was dead, her sweet, trustful, cheerful spirit still survived and still ruled.

The knights of Jerusalem, led by the Hospitaler, were present, the latter to direct the services, by request generally extended.

After a "grail" song by his companions, and at its last words, "*I shall be satisfied when I awake in His likeness*," the Hospitaler began discoursing.

"Men and women, death, the leveler, makes us all akin; therefore all of us feel impoverished by the departure of the angel who shone upon us here from the form that lies yonder. Miriamne Woelfkin, daughter of a knight, consort of a Gospel herald, devoted friend of womankind, disciple of Jesus, was gifted with almost prophetic insight and power of alluring unsurpassed in our day. Hers was the power of a burning heart entranced of a superb ideal, and therefore was it the power of immortal influence. She will live not more truly in the life she died to give than in the lives she lived to save. She was an unique woman, but only so because of her superior womanliness. Being dead, she reaches the reward generally denied the living, full appreciation. Her career was in part a parallel of her choice exemplar's. You have heard how the Mother of our Lord sung her '*Magnificat*' out of a heart as free as a girl's, yet as proud as that of a woman's glowing in the prospect of honoring maternity. But the last note of her rapture died on her lips full soon, and she never after in this life rose to such measure of joy. God permitted her life to pass through a series of suppressions and griefs, doubtless that she might exemplify the sad side of woman's career. The histories of women, mostly written by men, are marred by the conceits of their writers, and are at best but obscure pictures. The man with the pen lacks insight as to the being, whose life is so largely an expression of heart and soul. The lordly writer clothes his heroes in the light of his fevered imagination, depicting with bold stroke the mighty deeds of stalwartness; but he sees few heroines in his horizon. Those he does see are beyond his power of analysis. He falls to actual worship of his masculine demi-gods, perhaps as a partial atonement for his failings toward the fine and noble characters whose traits are too spiritual for his thought-limits or vocabularies. The generality of those who discourse concerning women, do it in a patronizing way, and feel to praise themselves as paragons in doing justice in this, even by halves. The queenship of Mary is constantly disputed, and so her lot is more closely linked with that of her sex. As she received the royal gifts of the Magi, holding them as a sacred trust for Him to whom her life was utterly devoted, so woman, the bearer and nurse of the race, gives all that she has without stint to others. Her life is a suppression; all bestowing; her reward the joy she has in the lavishness of her bestowals. Hers is the joy of the fountain that sings because it flows.

"But recently ye saw the Jewish priests deposit on this mount, after a custom constant since Moses, the ashes of the red heifer. They burned their sacrifice with red wood. Red pointed to the blood that can only atone for sin. But underneath all lies a deep lesson. 'Twas the female instead of the male thus offered, and her ashes gave potency to the waters of purification. I read this hidden truth: the sacrifices of the gentler sex work out the purification of the race. As the moss in the heart of the stone, I see this truth lying in the heart of the ceremonial! As Christ's cross precedes the cleansing of regeneration, so woman's cross is the means by which the decays of life are offset by new created beings. By the bier of the wondrous comforter of others, I may surely appeal to those who hear me and loved her to seek with quickened ardor to offer the pain-assuaging myrrhs to those grand souls who go along the way to life's crucial glories. I'd have such justice done as would cause all women to cease pitying themselves because they are such, and go about rejoicing that God gave them the superlative privileges of womanhood."

There came forth a loud cry, with moanings, from the part of the temple, called the "Mother's Pillow," where the honored dead lay.

"Miriamne, oh, Miriamne, you brought me through Gethsemane to your Calvary!"

A silence almost oppressive fell on the assembly. It was the silence of a pity too deep for words.

Then spake the Hospitaler, in words as invigorating as a herald of God's should be, and yet as soothing as a mother's to her child in pain:

"Christ, who loved the young man who was very good and yet not perfect, loves thee, for He is unchanging in His mercy. Hear me, an old man, stricken with the years that have schooled, and one who has experienced the bitterness of widowerhood after loyal, full loving. God's hand is on thee. He is schooling thee to carry on the work begun by thy wondrous consort now asleep."

"Oh, Miriamne, Miriamne! alone in the dark, I move through Gethsemane toward thy Calvary!"

Again the silence of pity was broken by the voice of the knight.

"Remember how David of the White Kingdom was called and furnished for his kingship. 'He chose David, also, His servant, and took him from the sheep folds, from following the ewes great with young. He brought him to feed Jacob, His people, and Israel, His inheritance.'

"Missioner-shepherd, God calls thee to a ministry of love, for those whose trials thou hast now been taught, in part, to measure. You have heard how Hadadrimmon, the fabled god of the harvest, ever comes, bearing sheaves, with tears.

"Thus speaks the prophet:

"'In that day shall there be a great mourning in Jerusalem, as the mourning of Hadadrimmon.

"'And the land shall mourn, every family apart; the family of the house of David apart, and their wives apart.'

"Young man, God is giving thee a crown in David's royal line.

"Once more I turn to her who was thy Miriamne's exemplar and queen. Let me tell you all of the last hours of Mary, that you may find instructive parallels. I'll read from my treasured book of traditions:

"After the ascension of Jesus, our Mary dwelt in the house of John upon Mount of Olives, and she spent her last days in visiting places which had been hallowed by her Divine Son; not as seeking the living among the dead, but for consolation and for remembrance and that she might perform works of charity.

"In the twenty-second year after the ascension of the Lord, she was filled with an inexpressible longing to be with her Son; and, lo, an angel appearing with the salutation, 'Hail, Mary, I bring thee a palm-branch, gathered in paradise; command that it be carried before thy bier, for thou shalt enter where thy son awaits thee.' And Mary prayed that it be permitted that the apostles, now widely scattered under their great commission to gospel the world, be gathered about her dying couch ; also that her soul be not affrighted in the passage through the pale realm of death. The angel departed ; the palm-branch beside her shed light like stars from every leaf ; the house was filled with splendor, and angel voices chanted the celestial canticles. The Holy Spirit caught up John as he was preaching at Ephesus, and Peter, offering sacrifice at Rome, and Paul, from his place of labor, Thomas, from India, while Matthew and James were summoned from afar. After these were called, Philip, Andrew, Luke, Simon, Mark and Bartholemew were awakened from their sleep of death. These holy ones were carried to the Virgin's home on clouds bright as the morning, and angels and powers gathered round about in multitudes. There were Gabriel and Michael close beside her, fanning her with their wings, which never cease their loving motions. That night a supernal perfume of ravishing delightsomeness filled the house, and immediately Jesus, with an innumerable company of patriarchs and holy ones, the elect of God, approached the dying mother. And Jesus stretched out His hand in benediction as He did when ascending from the world, long before at Bethany. Then Mary tenderly took the hand and kissed it, saying: ' I bow before the hand that made heaven and earth. Oh, Lord, take me to Thyself !' Thereupon Christ said, ' Arise, my beloved ; come unto me.' ' My heart is ready,' she replied ; a few moments after : ' Lord, unto thy hands I commend my spirit.' Then having gently closed her eyes, the holy Virgin expired without a malady ; simply of consuming love, permitted now by the loving Creator to melt the golden cord binding spirit to body. And triumphantly amid mourners who rejoiced exceedingly in spirit, the body of this Queen of the House of David was entombed amid the solemn cedars and olive trees of Gethsemane. Now, this happened upon the day that the true Ark of the Covenant was placed in the eternal temple of the new heavenly Jerusalem, as they say ; and the saying is good, for surely, in her heart, this saintly woman kept the law; the divine manna as well. Even more, she was the fulfillment of God's covenant that a woman should bear the masterers of sin."

The speaker then knelt ; all heads were bowed ; he

spread out his hands as in benediction, but spoke not. Yet all in the silence were blessed, for the manifestation of Christ was there. After the benediction the companion knights chanted an old grail psalm, repeating again and again the stately words:
"*I am the resurrection and the life.*"
As they sang their eyes were turned upward in a rapture as of men who saw a glorious appearing; and indeed they had a vision of splendor; but they saw it within, not without.

"There are angels hovering round," reverently whispered Mahmood to his camel. He was too full to keep silent; too distrustful of his wisdom to confide his thoughts to a human being. But the thought of the old Druse was as exalted as that of the Hospitaler, for the latter exclaimed, as the congregation slowly moved out to the strains of the organ:

"Methinks I hear the beatings of mighty wings! Not far away is Gabriel, the 'angel of mothers' and of victories! Yea, verily, I believe that the spirits of Adolphus, Rizpah, Sir Charleroy and Ichabod are ministering nigh us!"

Many looked up through their tears fixedly, as if they felt what the knight had said in their souls.

Then they laid the body of Miriamne in a new-made tomb nigh the Garden of Olives, not far from the burial-place of Mary the mother of Jesus.

CHAPTER XLIII.

A COFFIN FULL OF FLOWERS AND A GIRDLE WITH WINGS.

"Behold thy mother!"—JESUS TO JOHN.

TWO travelers journeyed slowly along Mount Olivet, pausing anon to observe the flower-dells between them and Mount Zion, or to contemplate the wilder prospects where the wilderness of Judea edged close up to the hills they traversed. As the travelers passed, the natives looked after them with curiosity; for the garments of the former, though dust-covered, were those of personages above the ranks of the common people; also of a fashion that betokened them strangers in that vicinity.

One of these men was a youth, stalwart and comely; the other was gray-haired and bent as if by the weight of years, though a closer view suggested premature blasting, rather than senile decline.

"Winfred, before entering Bethany, we'll to the 'Hill of Solomon,' the site of Chemosh, the black image of the Roman Saturn."

Thereupon the twain turned away from the village and soon came upon a company of revelers, each wearing a crown of autumn fruits, and all gathered about a platform crowded with hilarious dancers

"Saturnalia!" exclaimed the elder.

"The worship of Saturn ceased ages ago, did it not?"

"Of the image, yes; but the folly, little changed, continues."

"This is strange enough; and yet it's a relief to meet a few happy people in this land of solemn faces; even if those happy ones do joy like fools."

"They celebrate the passing of summer-heat and the coming of the rains of autumn. Say not fools; they are trying to be glad about something good, somehow coming from some one somewhere above them. Perhaps God can resolve scraps of thanksgiving out of it all."

"Theirs is the laughter of wine! the laughter of the goat-god, Pan, whose face scared his mother and whose voice scared the gods!"

"We've a persistent custom here, son; and men do not play the fool for generations after one manner, at least, without cause.

"These attempt to press into the court of Pleasure to cajole her; all men do that; these have chosen merely an old way. They cling to the myth of Saturn, the subduer of the Titan of fiction. They say that deity, dethroned in the god-world, fled to Italy, where he gave happiness and plenty through life, and the freedom of air and earth after death, which latter he made to be only a little sleep."

"That was not more than a mock golden-age; it never came, I think."

"But very alluring to those that long for it; they dance half-naked, typifying the primitive times when men had fewer cares, because fewer wants."

"Can one laugh hard fates out of countenance, and make his troubles run with a guffaw?"

"The devotees of Saturn were wont to offer their children in his altar-fires, and so ever more it happens; he that bends to the materialistic solely, kindles altar-fires for his posterity."

"After to-day what comes to these, peace?"

"Nay, a year all dark and colorless; then another spasm called a feast—a brief lightning-flash revealing the darkness."

"And so the years come and go; one generation of madmen, then another; death the only variety?"

"Nay! I'd have you look upon pleasure of sense deified, taking its pleasures under the shadows of Chemosh, for a purpose. You remember we read together, under the palms at Babylon, how the holy Daniel saw in vision the four winds of heaven striving on the sea?"

"I remember the prophet's reverie or revel."

"The four winds and the sea! the meaning, opened, is conflict on every hand on earth! Out of the follies and turmoils David's White Kingdom will emerge at last. Listen to the words of the inspired seer:

"'Behold one like the Son of Man! There was given Him a dominion and a glory that all people should serve Him; an everlasting dominion!'

"It is coming; my poor faith, amid the conflicts and revels of man, hears the voice of God crying through the night, as in Eden's dark hour: '*Where art thou?*' My last lesson to my son awaits us at Bethany; let's be going."

Ere long Cornelius Woelfkin and his son Winfred stood silently, and with uncovered heads, before, but a little apart from, a stately marble shaft that rose up amid the olive trees of Gethsemane. It was night, and they were alone. The father motioned the son back, and alone glided under the shadowing trees, toward the pillar. There the elder one threw himself down on the earth, close beside the monument; the youth, deeply moved, but unwilling to intrude upon the scene of sacred, silent grief, stood aloof. In a small way, there was a repetition of the grief of the Man of Sorrows, who there, ages before, yearned in His humanity over a lost world, over those from whom His heart was soon to part for life. To be sure, the cross of Cornelius Woelfkin was infinitely less galling, less heavy than that borne by his Master; and yet it was as heavy as he could bear, and hence the pitifulness of his grief.

Who can lift the curtain from his thoughts? The years roll back and memory's pictures pass through his brain, at first in joyful train. The lovers in London; the betrothal at sea; the wedding at Jerusalem; the ecstatic consummation in years of marriage. Then the painful, almost awful separation by death, that never to be forgotten Christmas time. And then, twenty years with leaden feet carrying the lone-hearted man so painfully slow toward death's portals, for which he longed with unutterable yearning. "Oh, Miriamne, Miriamne, let me come," he cried. The youth, hearing the agonized utterings, was instantly by his father's side. But the old man, still oblivious to all but his sorrow and his memories, moaned on with deepening fervor.

"Father," called out the son. The father rose to his feet and calmly said: "My boy, pity me. I'm weak.

But oh, you never knew what it is to have your life sawn in twain and be compelled then to drag your half and lacerated being along the over-clouded vales of an undesired existence!"

"My mother's tomb?"

"Yes. I promised, as my last service to you, to bring you to it. Its study shall be the finish of your schooling."

Just then the clouds broke away and the moonlight fell full upon the monument. It was a shaft, terminating in a crucifix; by its side were two forms, one that of St. John, with face turned toward the figure of the dying Savior; the other that of a woman kneeling, her face buried in her hands. On the base of the cross was the brief sentence: "Behold thy mother." As the youth gazed on the farewell charge of Jesus to John, when He commended to the care of that beloved disciple His sorrowing mother, he started. It seemed as if the words had grown out of the marble suddenly while he was gazing, and for himself only. He felt as if he could almost embrace the stone.

The two men were silent and heart full. After a long time, they simultaneously turned away toward Bethany. They came to a turn in the road that would shut out all view of the garden of sorrow, and the elder paused, loath to leave the place where his heart was buried.

Presently he spoke again, as if unconscious of any other being with him: "Oh, Miriamne, I failed to carry out the work thou left'st me! How could I, alone? I was but half a man without thee, my other self! Miriamne, Miriamne, I can be only nothing when I can not be with thee." Then the old man lifted his hands as in benediction or embrace, and continued: "Farewell, a last farewell, sweet, white soul, until upon the tearless, healing shores of light I say good morning!"

There was a mighty pathos in the display of this old, ripe, strong grief, which lived on a love that could not die. The man was a study. He was of fine fibre, almost effeminate, never firm, except in his affection for that one woman. That was the one strong trend, the one anchorage of his life. He need not study the man far, who strove to know him, to discover that this tenacity was not natural to him always. It had been a growth under the influence of the peerless wife.

"Shall we go on?" after a little asked the son. With a shudder and a suppressed sob the elder moved on, but with laggard step, which soon paused. Just now, the moon being beclouded, it was very dark about them, and the father reached out his hand and drew the youth to his embrace. He whispered: "Winfred, son of Miriamne, you bear her image in your face, bear it ever in heart, as well. I'm glad you're not so like me." The son tried to speak, but the elder interrupted:

"You'll ere long be fatherless as well as motherless, but take your mother for your guiding-star. You know what your birth cost her. By her death you obtained life, as by the Christ's, immortality. She saved others, she could not save herself; but if you're true to her memory she'll have a mother's immortality, that life that lives in the life of her child."

* * * * * * *

Let us gather up the *last* threads of our story. After the death of Miriamne, the "Sisters of Bethany" soon ceased to congregate at the "House of Bethesda," in the city on Olivet. Cornelius Woelfkin attempted for a time to carry forward the work of the mission, but, utterly miserable himself, he did not know how to bestow comfort on others; a man, without the intimate companionship of the woman who had been his inspirer, he had no discernment of the needs of woman, nor power to interpret the truths that were in the Book or in nature, those garners of manna.

The Hospitaler was sent for as an aid. He came but once, and then spoke as kindly as he could to the women of Bethany and Jerusalem, and took his farewell of them all, in closing words like these:

"The blessed Miriamne, child of Jesus, and emulator of Mary, has passed away, but Christ her Comforter and Savior may be such to each of you, that will. Mary's example, as the inspiration of all women, can never die. The world has been a battle-ground, and each of you can here see over the whole field of conflict. Shall all pleasures be found under the leadership of Bacchus and Venus, or in Him that is the God of Joy? Shall woman echo the passions of man or the '*Magnificat*' of Mary? Shall the strength that man seeks be that of the giants, brute force; the strength of woman be, in her youth the bewitchings of personal beauty, in old age the cunning of the witch-hag? Shall it not rather be in the girdle of her moral worth?

"The world needs to seek and find love, beauty and light. Some go after it, vainly, as did the Egyptian devotees of Phallic Khem; to whom, with pitiful incongruity, were offered rampant goats and bulls, decorated with most delicate flowers. They called Khem the 'God of births,' the 'beautiful God,' but we know to put mothers on the throne as the beautiful; their flowers, their jewels, their glories being their offspring!

"Women of Jerusalem, never forget the Savior's own words to the women that envied His mother, crying that the one that bore Him and nursed Him was therefore peculiarly blessed! His reply was: 'YEA, RATHER BLESSED ARE THEY THAT HEAR THE WORD OF GOD AND KEEP IT.'"

Then the Hospitaler, bending his eyes upon the pale-faced, widowed missioner, continued: "I'll tell thee a tradition of our Lord's mother. Doubting Thomas, laggard because doubting, came late to the burial-place of Mary. He begged to have her coffin opened, that once more he might gaze on the face of his Savior's mother. It was done. But there seemed to be nothing in that coffin except lilies and roses, luxuriously blooming. Then, looking up, he saw the spirit of the woman 'soaring heavenward in a glory of light.' But as she soared, she threw down to him her girdle. Here is a beautiful parable. The graves of the holy are to memory full of the ever-blooming roses of love and the lilies of purity. If we may not have them we loved with us always, we may have the virtues with which they engirdled themselves, for our conflicts."

The Hospitaler paused, cast a glance of yearning tenderness upon the assembled women and the heart-stricken Cornelius; then exclaimed:

"Long partings are painful. Farewell!" He glided away ere any could clasp his hand. Not long after this event the Sheik of Jerusalem, Azrael's putative son, raided Bethany, razing the "Temple of Allegory" to the earth. He was maddened because, after the disappearance of the Hospitaler, there came to him no stipend to buy immunity for the "Bethesda House" of the "Sisters of Bethany." He despoiled it, hoping to find a treasure therein, but though there was in and about the place a great wealth, it was all beyond his grasp or ken, for he knew naught of the worth or power of precious truths and precious memories. Cornelius, after this, taking his infant son, soon departed from Syria. His dream of evangelizing the world and the great designs of Miriamne faded from his hopes, as the vision of universal empire has faded often from the hopes of dying conquerors. For years he devoted himself to being father and mother to his child. At last we behold him, as in the foregoing pages, looking toward sunset. He stands finally in Bethany, his dismantled home and Miriamne's ruined temple not far away, her tomb close at hand, himself like the fragment of a wreck; altogether presenting a sad, dramatic tableau. He stands there as the last of the new "Grail Knights," the last of those who in his time were devoted to the new grai' quest. It was Saturnalia-time, and it was night.

"VIRGIN AND MOTHER OF OUR DEAR REDEEMER!
 *   *   *   *   *   *
" IF OUR FAITH HAD GIVEN US NOTHING MORJ
" THAN THIS EXAMPLE OF ALL WOMANHOOD,
" SO MILD, SO STRONG, SO GOOD,
" SO PATIENT, PEACEFUL, LOYAL, LOVING, PURE,
" THIS WERE ENOUGH TO PROVE IT HIGHER ANT
    TRUER
" THAN ALL THE CREEDS THE WORLD HAD KNOWN
    BEFORE."
                    HENRY W. LONGFELLOW.

www.ingramcontent.com/pod-product-compliance
Lightning Source LLC
Chambersburg PA
CBHW021223300426
44111CB00007B/408